Land of Savagery
Land of Promise

Land of Savagery
Land of Promise

The European Image of the American Frontier
in the Nineteenth Century

by Ray Allen Billington

University of Oklahoma Press : Norman

ISBN: 0-8061-1929-2

Published by arrangement with W. W. Norton & Company. Copyright © 1981 by Ray Allen Billington. Manufactured in the U.S.A. All rights reserved. First printing of the University of Oklahoma Press paperback edition, 1985.

This book is gratefully dedicated
to those Ph.D.s of mine at Clark and Northwestern Universities
of whom I am so proud:

Howard W. Bell, Jack Blicksilver, Thomas Bonner,
William Catton, Edwin B. Coddington, John A. Davis,
Daniel Gahl, Herschel Heath, Charles A. Johnson,
Angus J. Johnston II, Clifton C. Jones, Helen Knuth,
Daniel Levine, Robert Levine, Edward Lurie,
Edward Muzik, Richard Oglesby, Martin Ridge,
Alfred Rockefeller, Jr., Joel A. Tarr, Edgar A. Toppin,
Lawrence W. Towner, Henry Warnock, Alfred Young.

CONTENTS

Contents

Contents

[*ix*]

Contents

PREFACE

THE ORIGINS OF THIS BOOK can be traced to a warmish winter day late in 1973 when Dr. Paul L. Ward, then Executive Secretary of the American Historical Association, visited the Huntington Library. Would I, he asked, listen to a request? Of course I would. When we were comfortably seated on the small porch adjoining the readers' entrance he told me his story. The International Congress of Historical Sciences was to meet in San Francisco in the summer of 1975, its first meeting in the United States. These assemblies were held every five years; the last had been in Moscow in 1970 and had been highly successful save for the opening address—a paean of praise for Lenin—which disturbed some of the delegates. Hence the planning committee sought an opening plenary address free of political overtones, yet revealing a unique facet of the host country's past. They felt that a subject dealing with the American frontier would be most suitable. Would I deliver such an address?

Would I? Those of us who believed in the frontier's importance in the shaping of our nation had been dwindling in the years since the death of our patron saint, Frederick Jackson Turner, in 1932. We had witnessed a devastating attack on his theories by younger scholars during the 1930s and 1940s, and a revived respect for his frontier hypothesis and sectional concepts that began to emerge during the 1950s and 1960s. But professional opposition still ran high. An address before such a prestigious assemblage might win a few new converts to the cause and help restore courses on the nation's expansion to college curricula. Of course I would deliver that address, and gladly.

But what should I talk about? No rehashing of the Turner theories, no sensational tales of cowboys and Indians, would do for such a diverse group. As I grappled with that question, I pestered my friends for advice, with happy results. Why not, asked Professor Andrew F. Rolle of Occidental College's history department, discuss "The World Image of the American Frontier"? People everywhere were familiar with the legendary Wild West of fiction, films, and television. Why not explore the origins of that vogue, and investigate its influence on the attitude of the world toward the United States of today?

That decision launched me into the half-dozen years of reading and writing that produced this volume. My procedures were obvious: I would read as widely as possible in the books and articles about the American frontier that people of other nations might have read, and that would have shaped their image of the West. That meant immersion in travelers' accounts, guidebooks, "America Letters," promotional literature of land and railroad companies, propaganda circulated by territorial and state immigration agencies, emigration newspapers, and fiction published abroad. The fiction proved particularly enlightening, for I soon found that the popularity of James Fenimore Cooper's *Leatherstocking Tales* had spawned hundreds of imitators in Europe, most of them ill informed, and all of them flamboyant sensationalists who pictured a Wild West ruled by violence and personal justice. I discovered too, that many writers of Westerns had enjoyed remarkable popularity; Germany's Karl May had written some seventy books during the late nineteenth century that had sold thirty million copies in twenty languages and been read by as many as three hundred million people. Here was an image-maker who deserved a niche in history.

But how to sample that mass of information? Like most Americanists I am a linguistic illiterate, capable of stumbling through a page or two of French, but lacking even such fragmentary German as I crammed into my head to qualify for the doctoral degree. Clearly some aid was required, and obviously this meant foundation support. By this time I had decided to restrict my investigations to nineteenth-century Europe, for preliminary correspondence with friends on other continents showed me that South Americans, Australians, Asians, and Africans were too little interested in frontier America at that time to form significant impressions. Hence I would confine my study to the frontier image as it took shape in Europe.

This decision made, I was bold enough to apply to the National Endowment for the Humanities for sufficient financial aid to employ research assistants in key European countries, and translators who could make their discoveries understandable to me. My first effort was unsuccessful; the Endowment, I was politely informed, could not support research for public addresses, even to international societies. There was a strong hint in the correspondence, however, that if I reapplied with a book in mind the reception might be more cordial. I did, and it was. That generous grant alone made this volume possible.

The addresses came first, much to my benefit, for their composition and reception were of vast help in shaping the ideas now contained in this book. Their initial appearance was in three lectures sponsored by the Norman Waite Harris Lectureship of Northwestern University in the spring of 1975, then in still more condensed form as the opening address of the International Congress of the Historical Sciences on a sparkling August afternoon later that year in San Francisco. The latter has since been published as "Cowboys, Indians and the Land of Promise: The World Image of the American Frontier," in the *Proceedings: XIV International Congress of the Historical Sciences* (New York, 1976), and reprinted in such diverse media as the *Congressional Record, Representative American Speeches, 1975–1976,* and the *English Westerners Tally Sheet.*

With the lectures behind me, and with assurance of financial support, I asked the American Council of Learned Societies for a list of Americanists in Europe who might be able to recommend students for the tasks I had in mind, or whose own suggestions would be helpful. The result was a revealing correspondence with a group of scholars who proved to be not only thoroughly well informed but utterly generous with their time and knowledge. Some advised me that research assistants in their countries would find too little to be of use, but went on to provide me with essential information themselves. Among these I am particularly grateful to Professor N. N. Bolkhovitinov of the Institute of General History, the Moscow Academy of Sciences; Dr. Alexander A. Foursenko, Institute of History, the Academy of Sciences of the USSR at Leningrad; and Professor Jerzy Jedlicki, Institute of History, Polish Academy of Sciences at Warsaw. All supplied me with useful information and shared with me their own research findings on the subject.

Others were not only of help themselves but generously recommended students to serve as research assistants under their direction. Without the help of the following this book could never have been written: Professor Claude Fohlen of the Center for North American Historical Research of the University of Paris, and his hard-working student Alain Piatte; Professor Harry S. Allen of the School of English and American Studies, University of East Anglia and his student Andrew Hirschhorn; Professor Ingrid Semmingsen of the Historical Institute, University of Oslo, and two brilliant students under her supervision, Karin Elizabeth Jensen and

Nina Oppedal, whose reports, one on Scandinavian travelers, the other on
fiction writers, made an important contribution; Professor Günter Molt-
mann of the Historical Seminar, University of Hamburg, and Michael
Kuckhoff whose reports were remarkable in quantity and quality; and
Professor J. W. Schulte-Nordholt of the Faculty of Letters, State University of Leiden and Marian Schouten whose extended essay on the frontier
image in the Netherlands was a genuine accomplishment.

Particular thanks are due also to Dr. Charlotte Kretzoi of Budapest
whose investigations into Hungarian travelers opened fresh vistas and
whose ingenuity led to the discovery of hitherto unknown Hungarian
writers of western fiction. Dr. Kretzoi was good enough to suggest that
other Hungarian Americanists share their knowledge with me; two who
sent me essential information were Elizabeth Mészáros and Anna Katona.
My debt to all is great.

I also owe thanks to a number of translators who rendered the findings
of these researchers into excellent English. This task was performed by
three of the researchers themselves with excellent results: Karin Elizabeth
Jensen and Nina Oppedal of Norway, and Dr. Charlotte Kretzoi of Hungary. Within the United States the Dutch materials were expertly translated by Dortée Farrar, the Polish by Dr. Maria J. E. Copson-Niećko, the
German by Dr. Geoffrey Cocks, the French by Dr. Edric Cane, and the
Russian by Gilbert Rappaport and William M. Mandell. To all I am grateful.

Essential to my needs as were the investigations of European scholars
and translators, I also leaned heavily on American students who generously allowed me to use their unpublished findings pertinent to my problem. Foremost among these was Dr. D. L. Ashliman who offered me free
access to his doctoral dissertation and other writings, both in and out of
print, on German authors who dealt with the American West. Others
whose unpublished doctoral dissertations I have used to my vast advantage were David H. Miller, Gary Carl Stein, Alfred Kolb, Bjorne E.
Landa, and John D. Steele. Larry McDonald was kind enough to allow
me to use his studies of the frontier in Victorian literature even before
they were submitted at Arizona State University as his doctoral thesis. I
am also greatly indebted to Richard H. Cracroft who supplied me with a
copy of his excellent master's thesis on Karl May that I have used to provide most of my information of that important image-maker.

With the help of these many colleagues and assistants this book has
been written; without their aid it could not have been. The structure of
the book, and such interpretations as have emerged are entirely my own. I
recognize that both are far from perfect. Any proper study of the European image of the American frontier would require far more years than are
left to me and far greater skills than I possess. My hope is that this pilot

study will encourage other investigators, particularly in Europe, to dig more deeply into the sources and substantiate their findings by a broader use of local evidence. If they do, and if their findings help illuminate a dark corner of the past, the years that have gone into the writing of this volume will have been well spent.

Ray Allen Billington
The Huntington Library

I

Prologue: Early Visions
of the New World

FOR HALF A CENTURY after Christopher Columbus's landfall the New
World remained a *terra incognita*, a mystery-shrouded land little known
even to the navigators and explorers who probed its secrets. Yet an image
of that distant frontier was already shaping in the minds of Europeans,
based not on what they knew but on what they hoped to be there. They
saw America as a slightly improved version of the Garden of Eden, overflowing with Nature's bounties, and peopled by a race of superior beings
who lived in a perfect state of equality, without want and without masters—a model that would lead decadent Europe into a better future of
which philosophers dreamed. Then, as colonists brought back word of the
realities of pioneer life, that image changed, to picture first a land of savagery where barbarous Indians tortured and murdered, then once more an
idyllic wonderland where Noble Savages sported in forest bowers—a
wonderland rooted not in actuality but in the spirit of romanticism that
swept Europe in the eighteenth century.

That these images bore little relationship to reality was to be expected, for images have always mirrored the tastes, temperament, training, and background of their transmitters. These tastes, in turn, have been
governed by the physical and intellectual environment in which they have
lived, and have changed with the changing environment. A Londoner accustomed to the squalor and bustle of a seventeenth-century city would

see Virginia's dense forests through different eyes than a Swedish wood-chopper reared amidst the trees that provided him a livelihood. A philosopher nurtured on the cold rationalism of the seventeenth century would view Nature through different eyes than a poet wedded to the soulful romanticism of the eighteenth century. Each would be mirroring prejudices that had been conditioned by prevailing habits and tastes. Each was seeing what he had been taught to see and approving what he had learned to approve, not what was actually there. Knowing this, we can understand why not one but a kaleidoscopic succession of images shaped Europe's attitude toward the New World during the ages of discovery and colonization.

Nature Glorified: The Golden Age

For centuries before the discovery of the Americas, medieval Europeans had believed that somewhere to the west, far beyond the Pillars of Hercules, lay a terrestrial paradise where all lived in plenty, and happiness and liberty were men's natural rights. Plato and Homer agreed that in that mythical Eden "the earth gave men an abundance of fruits which grew on trees and shrubs unbidden," in such plentitude that private property was unknown and all enjoyed perpetual happiness. Medieval philosophers added details; typical was Roman d'Alexandre who described a western paradise where a nation of Brahmins lived in a state of Nature beside a great river, so free of avarice and envy that law courts were unnecessary.[1] This vision was substantiated by tales of imaginary voyages where navigators, blown from their courses, happened on islands that they called Groenland or Antillia or Cibola where lived godlike men and women without guile or servitude.[2] These were not substanceless shadowlands, but real islands where mankind's dream of prosperity and freedom could be realized.

As news of Columbus's discovery filtered through Europe, scholars leaped to the conclusion that he had happened upon this mythical paradise. The Great Navigator himself gave substance to their hopes by insisting that his landfall was in the vicinity of the Garden of Eden, where the soil "was fertile to a limitless degree," and the people gentle and loving, "free of avarice because they claimed no property but held all things in

[1]   An excellent account of Europe's dream of the Golden Age is Loren Baritz, "The Idea of the West," *American Historical Review* 66 (April 1961): 618–40. One chapter in Arthur O. Lovejoy and George Boas, *Primitivism and Related Ideas in Antiquity* (Baltimore, 1935), deals with "The Noble Savage in Antiquity," pp. 287–367. Robert Berkhofer, Jr., *The White Man's Indian* (New York, 1978), expertly summarized the changing attitude of Europeans and Americans since classical days.
[2]   These themes are skillfully explored in Howard Mumford Jones, *O Strange New World. American Culture: The Formative Years* (New York, 1964), pp. 2–7.

common." So did the Spaniards who followed in his wake, many of them kindly priests such as the Franciscan Bartolomé de Las Casas who were concerned with the welfare and salvation of the Indians. To these men of faith the Native Americans were simple and good, lacking only a knowledge of God to be the happiest people on earth.[3] Living comfortably in a state of Nature, they were worth imitating.

Here was opportunity for humanitarians dissatisfied with the economic and political absolutism that burdened Europe's peasantry. They would describe the New World not as it was, but as Europe should be. They would picture a people living in a Golden Age such as philosophers believed Europeans had known in the past and could know again. They would create a model that would serve to hurry the return of that Golden Age to Europe by demonstrating that greed and envy could be banished from men's natures. Their image would be a land of abundance and liberty too tempting to resist.

What an ideal land they invented! There Nature's bounties were so abundant that none need labor: partridges so heavy they could not fly, turkeys the size of sheep, fish in such plenty that six hundred could be caught with a single cast of a net. There a perfect society had been achieved, unmarred by want or evil. Humanists such as Pietro Martire d'Anghiera in his *Decades of the New World or West India* (1550) described the Indians as "living in that golden world of which old writers speak so much, . . . without quarreling judges, and libels . . . without further vexation for knowledge of things to come." They were the "most happy of all men," simply because "Myne and Thyne (the seeds of all Mischeefe) have no place with them."[4]

His words were echoed by a succession of writers through the sixteenth century: Amerigo Vespucci wrote glowingly of a land without crime where "neither king nor lord" existed and all lived in harmony; the poet Pierre de Ronsard lauded the Native Americans as now "in their golden age," knowing not "the names of Senate or King" but living without care or troubles; his countryman Loys Le Roy described them as "living yet as the first men," "not governed by discipline, nor cojoined in habitations, neither do they sowe or plant."[5] For nearly a hundred years after

---

[3]   This material, including the quotations that I have used, is drawn from Jones, *O Strange New World*, pp. 15–17, Hoxie N. Fairchild, *The Noble Savage: A Study in Romantic Naturalism* (New York, 1928), pp. 6–10, and Edmundo O'Gorman, *The Invention of America* (Bloomington, 1961), p. 101. A parallel concept, also rooted in medieval tradition, pictured the West as a land of sunset, of darkness, of death. This is briefly described in the helpful work by Richard Slotkin, *Regeneration through Violence: The Mythology of the American Frontier, 1600–1800* (Middletown, Conn. 1973), pp. 27–28.
[4]   Pietro Martire d'Anghiera, *The Decades of the New World* (1555), in Edward Arber, ed., *The First Three English Books on America* (Birmingham, 1885), p. 71.
[5]   Clements R. Markham, ed., *Letters of Amerigo Vespucci and Other Documents Illustrative of His Career* (London, 1894), p. 7.

Columbus, Europeans believed that the distant frontier attracting their venturers was the reincarnated Golden Land of their hopes.

The capstone of this glorified image was placed by Michel, seigneur de Montaigne whose essay *Of the Caniballes* appeared in 1580. Seeking to define "civil" and "uncivil" governments, he concluded that the people of the latter were immature, innocent, lacking in culture—and gloriously happy. One by one he ticked off the virtues that defined them as "barbarians": "no knowledge of letters, no intelligence of numbers, no name of magistrate, nor of politike superiorite; no use of service, of riches or of povertie; no contracts, no successions, no partitions, no occupation but idle; no respect of kindred but common, no apparel but naturall, no manuring of lands, no use of wine, corn, or mettle."[6] Living in a state of natural goodness where all were equal, all were well fed and happy, strangers to oppression and conflict.

That this image was firmly implanted on the European mind was shown when Shakespeare borrowed not only the thoughts but the words of Montaigne when he described the "simple ways" of the Indians in *The Tempest* (1611):

> No name of magistrate;
> Letters should not be known; riches, poverty,
> And use of service, none; contract, succession,
> Bourn, bound of land, tilth, vineyard, none;
> No use of metal, corn, or wine, or oil;
> No occupation—all men idle, all;
> And women too, but innocent and pure;
> No sovereignty—

Here was a perfect social order where men lived free. This was the image of the first American frontier conjured from Europe's hopes—an Elysian paradise matching the Golden Age of the past described by medieval dreamers.[7]

In this unrealistic dreamworld the Indian was not a real person, but a symbol of Europe's longings, not a true child of Nature but a model of what Europeans would like to be. Artists pictured the Indians as men and women of unbelievable grace and beauty, better suited save for their nudity to illustrate a commentary on the Book of Genesis than a treatise

---

[6]   An excellent summary of concepts of barbarism from classical times to the Renaissance is in Margaret T. Hodgen, "Montaigne and Shakespeare Again," *Huntington Library Quarterly* 16 (November 1952): 25–27. The subject is also briefly explored in Fairchild, *Noble Savage*, pp. 15–21.

[7]   Thomas More's *Utopia*, published in Latin in 1516 and "Englished" in 1551, was supposedly based on descriptions òf the New World although his ideal state relied more on European tradition than on the American experience. George Woodcock, "The Lure of the Primitive," *American Scholar*, Summer 1976, pp. 388–89.

on the New World. Seeing was not believing to those under this tradition; Jacques Lemoyne de Morgues, who accompanied a French expedition to the Floridas in 1564 and whose paintings were widely popularized by the talented engraver Théodore de Bry for a generation thereafter, depicted Spartan men and full-bodied Renaissance women, tastefully unclothed, who would clearly be more at home in a Roman forum than in the wilds of America.[8] The picture of America and its occupants that gained credence in the sixteenth century tells us far more about Europeans than it does about Indians or that first frontier.

Nature Degraded: The View from America

By the end of the sixteenth century colony planting was beginning on the North American coast, and with it a gradual change in the European image. The landscape must be viewed now not as a resurrected Garden of Eden but for its commercial potential, the Indians not as Nature's noblemen but as savage barbarians barring the advance of God's chosen people. When Shakespeare pictured his mythical isle in *The Tempest* he described not only the inhabitants of Montaigne's paradise but the Indians seen by the first colonists. Caliban was no reincarnation of Arcadian innocence but a slightly subhuman individual at an evolutionary stage where he lacked any moral sense, intellectual perception, and social culture. He could show Prospero and Trinculo how to live in the island forest, just as Indians were showing colonists how to live in the American wilderness, but his stunted body mirrored his stunted mind and soul.[9]

This did not mean that Europe's image-makers abruptly transformed all American Indians into Calibans. Instead they began picturing two types of Indians, the "good" modeled on the friendly Arawaks found by Columbus on Hispaniola, the "bad" on the cannabalistic Caribs found by later explorers on other Caribbean islands. The "good" were worthy descendants of the Golden Age—upright, moral, and staunch friends of the white men; the "bad" were the Wild Men of medieval legend, symbolizing the evil sure to beset all who rejected social organization as a way of life. The New World could be made habitable only if Europeans aided the Good Indians in their perpetual warfare against the Bad Indians, just as

[8] Phillip D. Thomas, "Artists among the Indians, 1492–1850," *Kansas Quarterly* 3 (Fall 1971): 3–7 is a useful brief account. More extended is Benjamin Bissell, *The American Indian in English Literature of the Eighteenth Century* (New Haven, 1925), pp. 5–6. Most sixteenth- and seventeenth-century accounts of Indians contain woodcuts showing them as naked, brown-skinned Apollos. Typical is Hernández de Oviedo y Valdés, *Historia de las Indias* (1535).
[9] I have based this account on Sidney Lee, "The American Indian in Elizabethan England," in *Elizabethan and Other Essays by Sidney Lee*, ed. Frederick S. Boas (Oxford, 1929), pp. 282–301.

had the handful of Spaniards who relied on native assistants to conquer the evil Montezuma and the Incas.[10]

The "good" Indian as a symbol of Nature's virtues persisted in European imagery well into the seventeenth century, for he was a necessary ally of promoters seeking to convince colonists that Virginia or New England were rural paradises. Their message was understandable; the land of the New World was so rich that it "bringeth foorth all things in aboundance, as in the first creation, without toile or labour"; the Indians "loving and faithfull, voide of all guile and treason, and such as lived in the manner of the Golden Age."[11] Settle in America and know eternal peace and prosperity!

This image of docile, amiable Native Americans was heightened by the captives brought back to Europe by early colonists, for most were of the gentle agricultural stock who lived along the coast and all knew that only good behavior would return them to their homelands. Typical was Pocahontas, bride of Virginia pioneer John Rolfe, who reached London in 1616. Sweet and comely, she won the hearts of commoners and noblemen alike. Such was her popularity that James I worried lest the heirs of this daughter of Chief Powhatan, who "carried herselfe as the Daughter of a King, and was accordingly respected," lay claim to Virginia in conflict with Britain's own claims.[12] The image of the Indian as Nature's nobleman died hard.

Its demise was hastened by word that drifted across the Atlantic from explorers with good cause to question the nobleness of the red men. The tales that they told were shudderingly realistic: of natives who were often drunk and "given to much beastlinesse," committed sodomy, and "with their mothers and daughters they have their pleasures and pastimes"; of warring barbarians "whose food is men's flesh, and have teeth like dogges, and doo pursue them with ravenous myndes to eate theyr flesh"; of near-animals who lived in caves or huts "and hunt for their dinners or praye, even as the bears and other wild beastes do."[13] These were not godlike creations of the Deity, but clearly disciples of the Devil.

This harsh image was sharpened by word from the early settlers at Jamestown and Massachusetts Bay. Even the most friendly Virginia Indians would steal anything left unguarded, ambush stray settlers, and

[10] Edward Dudley and M. E. Novak, eds., *The Wild Man Within: An Image in Western Thought from the Renaissance to Romanticism* (Pittsburgh, 1972), pp. 28ff., admirably develops this theme.
[11] Arthur Barlowe, an agent for Walter Raleigh's ill-fated Roanoke colony, quoted in David B. Quinn, *The Roanoke Voyages, 1584–1590* (London, 1955), pp. 106–8.
[12] Carolyn T. Foreman, *Indians Abroad, 1493–1938* (Norman, 1943), pp. 22–28.
[13] Stefan Lorant, *The New World: The First Pictures of America* (New York, 1946), p. 65; Richard Hakluyt, *Principal Navigations, Voyages, Traffiques and Discoveries* (Glasgow, 1904), 7: 224, 386–97.

were incurably treacherous—"perfidious Savages," Captain John Smith called them.[14] Their much-lauded freedom was really animalistic primitivism; they lived "like heards of Deare in a Forrest: they have no law but nature, their apparrell skinnes of beasts."[15] With the Massacre of 1622 the last lingering belief that the Indians were Nature's simple children vanished, and with it the hope that they might be civilized. They must be exterminated, and as rapidly as possible. "Our hands which before were tied with gentleness and faire usage," wrote a Virginian, "are now set at liberty by the treacherous villance of the Sauvages."[16] From this day on frontiersmen saw the only good Indian as a dead Indian; "perpetual enmity" was the rule.

This hostile picture was darkened as the Pilgrims and Puritans of Massachusetts made known their views. These dissenters were lofted by an unquenchable sense of mission. They were God's agents entrusted to create in America a spiritual Eden whence true believers, freed from the taints of Popery and Anglicanism, would go forth to create in the New World a Celestial City, warmed by the sun of God's approval, and blessed by the fertility and beauty that all the world had known when it was youthful and vigorous. There all men would be purified and rejuvenated—God's chosen saints girded to repeople the earth with His disciples.

There was no place in this transplanted Eden for the Indian; to Pilgrim and Puritan alike he was an agent of Satan, sent by his evil master to frustrate the divine will. To the Pilgrim William Bradford they were "savage and brutish men who range up and downe, little otherwise than the wild beasts"; to the Puritan Samuel Purchas, they were "more brutish than the beasts they hunt, more wild and unmanly than that unmanned wild Countrey, which they range rather than inhabite."[17] To kill these disciples of the Devil was the clear duty of every Christian; they must be driven from the Garden as the snake was from Eden. "The whole earth is the Lord's garden," pronounced Governor John Winthrop of Massachusetts Bay, "and He hath given it to the sons of Adam to be tilled and improved by them."[18] The Promised Land must be snatched from Satan's clutches by eliminating his agents.

[14] Smith's hostile appraisal is in *The General Historie of Virginia* (London, 1624 ed.), 29–39.
[15] Richard Johnson, *Nova Britannia* (1609), in Peter Force, *Tracts and Other Papers* (Washington, 1836), vol. 1, no. 6: 11. An excellent summary is in Gary B. Nash, "The Image of the Indian in the Southern Colonial Mind," *William and Mary Quarterly* 29 (April 1972): 197–230.
[16] *Virginia Company Records*, 3: 557–58, quoted in Nash, "The Image of the Indian in the Southern Colonial Mind," p. 218.
[17] William Bradford, *History of Plimoth Plantation* (Boston, 1898), p. 33.
[18] Alexander Young, *Chronicles of the First Planters of the Colony of Massachusetts Bay* (Boston, 1846), p. 272. This argument is well developed in Roy H. Pearce, *The Savages of America: A Study of the Indian and the Idea of Civilization* (Baltimore, 1953), pp. 7–8, which relies on th

This hostile image of the Indian was to spread and intensify as new settlements pushed ever deeper into the interior. Each advance stirred conflict between red men determined to retain lands that had been theirs from time immemorial and white who saw those lands as theirs through God's decree. News of this border warfare, transmitted in exaggerated form, solidified the growing image of the red men as ruthless savages who killed women and children indiscriminately, scalped and tortured their victims, and denied honest yeomen the right to serve God through industry. Each new encounter piled evidence on evidence: of Susquehannocks who seared captives with "pieces of Iron, and barrels of old Guns, which they made red-hot"; of tribes who ate their enemies even though human flesh was not a part of their "common diet"; of others who each four years sacrificed a young child to the Devil.[19] These hate-ridden dispatches made clear that the red men were unreformable savages, forever committed to barbarism and the Devil's work.

This image was most firmly planted in England where land hunger was strongest and conflict most frequent. The French were more kindly disposed, partly because their colonists saw the Indian as a necessary tool in the fur trade that sustained the economy, partly because they gained their impressions through the reports of Jesuit missionaries whose faith in the goodness of men was too deep to be shaken. Their reports—the yearly *Jesuit Relations* published regularly after 1611—painted the Indians as innately noble, thoroughly honest, and blessed with lives that were free of conflict or greed. "The most content, the happiest, the least addicted to vice of all the peoples of the world," one Jesuit labeled them.[20] Eastern Europeans too, and particularly the Poles, also continued to laud primitive societies, largely as proof that despotism was not needed to sustain orderly governments.[21]

These rose-tinted views were far from typical; increasingly in the seventeenth century most Europeans, and nearly all Englishmen, saw the Indians as Satan-guided idolators standing in the way of industrious yeoman seeking to carry out God's will by making the deserts bloom. They were the enemy of God and man, and deserved only extermination.

---

reasoning of Samuel Purchas, *Purchas his Pilgrimes* (1625, reprint ed., Glasgow, 1906), 19: 218–67.

[19] George Alsop, "A Character of the Province of Maryland (1666)," in *Narratives of Early Maryland, 1633–1684*, ed. Clayton C. Hall (New York, 1910), pp. 368–69.

[20] Reuben G. Thwaites, ed., *The Jesuit Relations and Allied Documents, 1610–1791* (Cleveland, 1896–1901), 75 vols., contain these reports. They are summarized in Dudley and Novak, *Wild Man Within*, pp. 224–26.

[21] Jerzy Jedlĭcki, "Images of America," *Polish Perspectives* 18 (November 1975): 28.

Nature in Eclipse: Seventeenth-Century Rationalism

Mounting evidence that the New World was somthing less than the Garden of Eden and that its inhabitants lacked the orderly governments, religion, and moral standards essential to civilized societies posed a serious problem for Europe's men of learning. Were the Indians simple children of Nature, culturally retarded but still capable of adopting European ways and Christianity? Or were they truly the "Wild Men" of legend, too subhuman to accept the benefits of civilization? If the former, Europe's duty was to mould them into replicas of its own advanced peoples. This could be done either by allowing them to occupy the land and "enjoy equall priviledges with us" (as a Virginia humanitarian suggested in 1609),[22] or by exchanging their lands for the benefits of civilization and conversion—"to buy of them the pearles of earth, and sell to them the pearles of heaven" (as a Virginia Company brochure proposed).[23]

The second alternative—to judge the red men incapable of civilization and hence fit only for extermination—also posed problems. Should "good" and "bad" Indians alike be eliminated? Fortunately for expansionists, every dispatch from America piled evidence on evidence to prove that not a single Indian was worthy of salvation. Even those allied with the colonists were so treacherous and cruel that they must be constantly watched and feared. Why permit such "brutish savages" who "by reason of their godless ignorance, and blasphemous Idolatrie, are worse than those beasts which are of most wilde and savage nature" to occupy lands that good Christians could use to benefit mankind?[24] A holy crusade of extermination was justified.

This solution intensified a conflict among scientists that had raged virtually since the days of Columbus: whence came the Indian? Everyone knew that all humans were descended from Noah's three sons: all Asians from Shem, all Africans from Ham, and all Europeans from Japheth. Where did the Native Americans fit into this triangle? Learned men squandered pages of manuscript on this question, arguing heatedly that Noah's ark must have touched on the American continent, or advancing implausible theories to explain how Noah's offspring reached the New World. Not until the publication of José de Acosta's *De Nature Novi Orbus Libri Duo* (1589) was a sensible explanation suggested: that in the remote past men and animals had crossed to America from Asia over a yet-undiscovered land bridge. This theory was given substance a few years later

---

[22] Quoted in Edmund S. Morgan, *American Slavery—American Freedom: The Ordeal of Virginia* (New York, 1975), p. 47.
[23] Quoted in Nash, "Image of the Indian in the Southern Colonial Mind," p. 210.
[24] Robert Gray, *A Good Speed to Virginia (1609)*, ed. W. F. Craven, New York, 1937), unpaged.

when Gregorio García's *Origen de las Indias del Nuevo Mondo* (1607) described eleven logical ways of peopling the New World, but favored
Acosta's suggestion of an Asian advance over the Straits of Anian.[25] The
debate continued for years, but by the middle of the seventeenth century
most scholars agreed that the Indians were descendents of the Tartars,
and hence were the true children of Noah. As God's wards, human rather
than animal, they deserved the respect due all His creations.

But doubts remained. Were they a species new to man's knowledge,
subhuman rather than human, degraded by the passage of time and the
debilitating effect of the American environment, and hence unworthy of
treatment as a civilized race? The philosophical basis for this conjecture
was laid by Thomas Hobbes whose *Leviathan* (1651) struck a fatal blow at
the longheld belief in Nature's rejuvenative powers. Civilization's restraints, Hobbes argued, were essential if men were to live together in harmony; a State of Nature would inevitably lead to constant wars as each individual plundered and killed to satisfy his own needs. This was proved
by the American Indians, who lived in a constant state of conflict. In such
a society there could be no place for industry, no opportunity for culture—"no account of Time; no Letters; no Society; and which is worst of
all, continual fear, and danger of violent death; and the life of man solitary, poor, nasty, brutish, and short."[26]

Hobbes's thesis struck a chord among men of learning because it coincided with the scientific revolution that ushered in the Age of Rationalism.
The mysteries of the universe, scientists preached, could be explained not
by faith in traditional authorities but by doubt, experiment, and reason.
Spurred on by this new challenge, men of science peered far into the
vastness of space to reveal that the earth was but a tiny speck in the infinity of the universe, probed the planet's own secrets to explain the
changes in its surface since the Creation, and began the monumental task
of arranging and classifying plant and animal species into logical patterns.
Their findings, often incorrect, were less important than their techniques.
Encouraged by the Royal Society of London after its formation in 1622,
they substituted doubt for faith, empirical methodology for classical and
biblical authorities, and experimentation for blind acceptance of tradition.
One of their numbers summed up their creed when he wrote: "Let us our-

[25] These developments are expertly explained in Lee E. Huddleston, *Origins of the American
Indians: European Concepts, 1492–1729* (Austin, 1967), pp. 48–54, 60–128. Travelers and nov-
elists continued to argue the subject well into the nineteenth century. See, for example, J. C.
Beltrami, *Pilgrimage in Europe and America* (London, 1828), 2: 259–61; Frederick L. G. von
Rajmer, *America and the American People* (New York, 1846), p. 137; and Frances Brooke, *The
History of Emily Montague* (London, 1769), 1: 72.
[26] Thomas Hobbes, *Leviathan*, ed. Michael Oakshott (Oxford, 1947), p. 82. Hobbes's
views and influences are discussed in Dudley and Novak, *Wild Man Within*, p. 155, and
Fairchild, *Noble Savage*, pp. 23–25.

From Gustave Aimard, *The Tiger Slayer* (London, n.d.).
(From the collections of the Library of Congress.)

selves examine things as we have opportunity, and converse with Nature as well as with Books."[27]

Unfortunately those who "conversed with Nature" lacked both the learning and the skills to interpret their findings correctly. Instead they were tempted into translating a few random observations into sweeping "Natural Laws" that were always dubious and often flagrantly incorrect. The most tragic victims of their faulty reasoning were the American Indians who in a single generation were degraded from idyllic children of Nature into a race of despicable subhumans, ranked far below Europeans in the Great Chain of Being.

The prophet of those who preached this false doctrine was George-Louis Leclerc, comte de Buffon, who summed up the findings of a generation of humanistic investigators in his *Natural History of Animals* in 1761. Basing his theories on the observations of scientists and colonists who reported on the flora and fauna of the New World, Buffon reasoned that the newness and coldness of the American continent stunted all growth there, forcing the natives to feed on such inadequate meat and vegetables that they themselves were dwarfed and rendered sexually impotent. "In the savage," he wrote, "the organs of generation are small and feeble. He has no hair, no beard, no ardour for the female. . . . His sensations are less acute; and yet he is more cowardly and timid."[28] Too weak and too impotent to perpetuate their race, the Indians were doomed to early extinction.

Buffon's theories correctly mirrored the European mind of his day. Swayed by the spirit of rationalism that was then on the ascent, men of learning were convinced that Nature was man's enemy unless tamed by man's intelligence—that a civilized society was vastly superior to a primitive society. Buffon's purpose was not to degrade Indians, but to demonstrate that Europeans were better equipped to occupy the Americas than the red men. Nurtured in a healthier environment, and hence stronger and more energetic, they were able to cut down trees, drain swamps, and improve the soils. The Indian had surrendered his birthright by overlong dependence on Nature; Nature was a ruthless destroyer unless man directed its aimless forces into productive use.[29]

These fantasies were popularized by a Dutch scientist, Cornelius de Pauw, whose *Recherches philosophiques sur les Américains* (1768–69) was trans-

[27] Quoted in E. D. H. Johnson, ed., *The Poetry of the Earth: A Collection of English Nature Writings* (New York, 1966), pp. vii–xi. A brilliant discussion of the rise of scientific thought is in Marjorie H. Nicolson, *Mountain Gloom and Mountain Glory: The Development of the Aesthetics of the Infinite* (Ithaca, 1959), pp. 251–70.
[28] Quoted in Gilbert Chinard, "Eighteenth Century Theories of America As a Human Habitat," *Proceedings of the American Philosophical Society* 91 (1947): 30–31.
[29] These points are made in Bernard W. Sheehan, *Seeds of Extinction: Jeffersonian Philanthropy and the American Indian* (Chapel Hill, 1973), pp. 68–69, 86–87.

lated into most European languages and won its author invitations to lecture before the continent's leading universities and scientific societies. His message was uncompromising: the American environment stunted the growth of all natural objects—plants, animals, and men—and even weakened iron until it was useless for nails. It also doomed the Indians to a Hobbesian state of perpetual chaos, so weakened physically that "in a fight the weakest European could crush them with ease."[30] Even Europeans who made the mistake of migrating to the New World would eventually be degraded to a state of perpetual childhood.

Absurd though the theories of Buffon and de Pauw were, they attracted almost universal support among Europe's intellectuals. In France, Guillaume-Thomas, abbé de Raynal, whose *Histoire philosophique et politique* (1772) went through no less than thirty-seven editions, described Indians as hairless incompetents, living forever in "a sort of childhood similar to that of people on our continent who have not yet reached the age of puberty."[31] In Britain a whole school of Scottish philosophers, led by William Robertson whose *History of the Americas* appeared in 1777, agreed that the red men were more animal than human, destined always to remain "the enemy of other animals, not their superiors."[32] The message was clear: man's rationalism was essential to a proper social order; a State of Nature doomed him to decay and eventual oblivion.

Such was the revolt against the glorification of Nature that even the landscape was transformed to glorify man and reason. Designers of seventeenth- and early-eighteenth-century gardens had one purpose: to impose order by hiding imperfections of Nature behind man-made features. Their creations were distinguished by elaborate formalism and geometric design, all deliberately fashioned to hide natural features of the countryside behind terraces, stone walls, grottoes, fountains, urns, and groups of statuary. Hills were leveled, water encased in square basins, hedges shaped, trees clipped into artificial shapes, ruler-straight lines substituted for curves, even flowers planted in symmetric patterns. Wrote one de-

---

[30] De Pauw's theories are examined in ibid., pp. 69–71; Chinard, "Eighteenth Century Theories of America," pp. 35–36; Durand Echeverria, *Mirage in the West: A History of the French Image of American Society to 1815* (Princeton, 1957), pp. 3–11, and particularly in Antonello Gerbi, *The Dispute of the New World: The History of a Polemic, 1750–1900* (Pittsburgh, 1973), pp. 55–65.

[31] Quoted in Chinard, "Eighteenth Century Theories of America," pp. 36–37. Raynal's views are summarized in Gerbi, *Dispute of the New World*, pp. 46–47, and Echeverria, *Mirage in the West*, pp. 11–22.

[32] William Robertson, *History of America* (reprint ed., London, 1808), 2: 61–76, sums up his views on the American Indian. They are analyzed in Gerbi, *Dispute of the New World*, pp. 157–69, Sheehan, *Seeds of Extinction*, pp. 33–38, and Pearce, *Savages of America*, pp. 82–88. The theories of Hegel, Voltaire, and other philosophers who preached this doctrine are well summarized in Gerbi, *Dispute of the New World*, pp. 43–45, 157–65, 389–433.

signer: "So far from making gardens appear natural, every expedient was used to display the costly efforts of Art, by which Nature was subdued."[33]

In the end the revolt against Naturalism went too far. Scientists who judged Indians to be impotent simply because they lived in harmony with their forest environment, or garden designers who saw in the leaping cataract or the tint of a rose evidence of Nature's disordered ugliness were inviting rebuttal by their own absurdities. Scholars, too, were altering their perspectives; as they mastered the techniques of investigation and classification they began to realize that Nature offered lessons in orderly arrangement and aesthetic splendor that dwarfed man's own feeble creations. In the monumental record of the Chain of Being was proof that man could be elevated by Nature's healing graces, not degraded by its disorders. The time was ripe in the early eighteenth century for a revolution in popular taste that would alter the European image of America, and bring Nature worship into style once more.

Nature Glorified: The Age of Romanticism

Underlying this revolution was the rediscovery of the beauties of untamed Nature by scientists, poets, artists, and landscape designers. This viewpoint emerged slowly during the dawn-years of the eighteenth century, nurtured by the popularity of a little book by one John Ray, *The Wisdom of God Manifested in the Works of Creation*, first published in 1691 and circulated widely in a dozen editions over the next generations. Ray's modest purpose was to demonstrate that mountains, long viewed as "wens and unnatural Protuberances" on the perfect sphere created by God, were practically and aesthetically useful to mankind, creating harbors, directing the course of the winds, diversifying the landscape. He saw the earth with its hills and promontories, "so rude and deformed as they appear," as a beautiful and pleasant object, far more attractive than "a level country without protuberancy to terminate the sight."[34] Mountains were of God's creation, and men should venerate their rugged beauty as another example of His beneficence.

These were far from bold judgments, but the time was ripe for a completely fresh view of the Nature that Ray venerated. Over the years, as the eighteenth century progressed, poets and painters discovered in the grandeur of the Alps, the lonely sweep of the sea, the endless infinity of the

---

[33]   Humphrey Repton, *An Enquiry into the Changes of Taste in Landscape Gardening* (London, 1806), p. 35. These changes are expertly summarized in Derek Clifford, *A History of Garden Design* (London, 1957), pp. 64–124.
[34]   Quoted in Johnson, ed., *The Poetry of the Earth*, p. x, and discussed in Nicolson, *Mountain Gloom and Mountain Glory*, pp. 251–71.

open plain, an awesome beauty that was more than beautiful, and that they called "sublime." To glorify Nature was their purpose in life. Poets soared to the vastness of the heavens, to the grandeur of the wilderness, to the dizzying mountain heights as they quested for examples of natural wonder to extol. Sang James Thomson in his famed *The Seasons:*

> O Nature! All Sufficient! Over all
> Enrich me with the knowledge of thy works.

Painters discovered a new inspiration in the landscape and invaded every nook and cranny of Europe in search of natural beauty; "may not landscape painting," wrote one, "be considered as a branch of natural philosophy, of which pictures are but the experiments."[35] By the mid-eighteenth century all the arts were paying tribute to Nature; the Age of Romanticism had arrived.

Its impact was nowhere better illustrated than in changing garden design.[36] For more than a century architects had sought to hide Nature's imperfections beneath orderly geometric forms, substituting artificial patterns for anything that remotely resembled a natural creation. Voices began to be raised against this practice early in the century; "for my part," wrote Joseph Addison in *The Spectator* in 1712, "I would rather look upon a tree with all its Luxuriancy and Diffusion of Boughs and Branches, than when it is cut and trimmed into a Mathematical figure." His was an early protest, but as others fell in line the face of Europe was changed once more. All artificiality must be banished to give way to sweeping curves and boundless natural vistas; "Nature abhors a straight line," one planner wrote. Gardens designed for England's great houses emphasized meadow-like lawns broken occasionally by clumps of trees; even fences needed to restrain cattle were replaced with "Ha Has" (hidden ditches so-called because one came upon them by surprise). One artful designer even proposed that "the children of some poor but worthy cottager, prettily disguised as shepherds, might be employed to keep the sheep from straying."[37] Nature must reign unchecked. "The perfection of Landscape Gardening," decreed one prominent designer, "depends on the concealment of those operations of *art*, by which *nature* is embellished."[38]

This transformation of the British countryside—duplicated in Europe where a Rousseauian veneration of Nature inspired a similar revolution—altered the perspective of Europeans as they viewed the American wilds. In Nature run riot there, they found beauty sublime, not terror.

[35] Quoted in Johnson, ed., *The Poetry of the Earth*, p. ix.
[36] Two essential works·on this subject are Henry V. S. Ogden and Margaret S. Ogden, *English Taste in Landscape in the Seventeenth Century* (Ann Arbor, 1955), and Elizabeth W. Manwaring, *Italian Landscape in Eighteenth Century England* (New York, 1955).
[37] Clifford, *History of Garden Design*, pp. 129, 136–40, 147.
[38] Repton, *Enquiry into the Changes of Taste*, p. 70.

British navigators wending their way along the Oregon coast could remark that the countryside was "almost as enchantingly beautiful as the most elegantly finished pleasure grounds in Europe," or that it was blessed with a "beauty of prospect equal to that of the most admired Parks in England."[39] British novelists could describe the American forests with a passionate enthusiasm; "I love the country," remarked a character in one novel, "the taste for rural scenes is the taste born with us."[40] Lofted by the spirit of Romanticism, Europeans who sought beauty in the "lovely simplicity of Nature" found in the American frontier an attraction unrecognized by prior generations.

They found also that the Indian, long berated as an inferior subspecies, was worthy of respect and imitation. Responsible for this about-face were the findings of American scientists who were beginning to observe and understand the red men as they really were, not as they were conceived to be. Two of their works, both widely reprinted abroad, were particularly effective. Cadwallader Colden, of Irish birth but New York residence, in his *History of the Five Indian Nations of Canada*, which appeared in London in 1747, painted a sympathetic sketch of Iroquois life and customs, picturing them as having "such absolute Notions of Liberty, that they allow no kind of Superiority of one over another."[41] A generation later James Adair in his *History of the American Indians*, which was reprinted in London in 1775 and Germany in 1782, found the Native Americans living amidst abundance and liberty. "Their whole constitution," he reported, "breathes nothing but liberty"; even their chiefs must persuade, rather than command, their followers to obey.[42] These were no sub-human savages, but a gentle people whose example was worth following.

This favorable image was sharpened by travelers who began invading frontier America in force during the late eighteenth century. To a surprising extent they agreed that the Indians were abundantly provided with "the spontaneous productions of Nature," and enjoyed a life-style that Europeans might envy. English visitors were still inclined to raise their eyebrows at the refusal of males to labor (how could anyone bred in the belief that the hunt was the sport of kings picture hunting and warfare as arduous occupations?), but their disapproval scarcely hid a hint of envy; "Who would seek to live by labour," wrote one, "who can live by amusement?

[39] These comments are by George Vancouver and others who accompanied him on his voyages of exploration along the Pacific Coast. Their significance is discussed in Douglas Cole and Maria Tippett, "Pleasing Diversity and Sublime Desolation: The 18th-Century British Perception of the Northwest Coast," *Pacific Northwest Quarterly* 65 (January 1974): 2–4.
[40] Brooke, *History of Emily Montague*, 4: 12.
[41] Cadwallader Colden, *The History of the Five Indian Nations of Canada* (London, 1747), pp. xiv–xvii, describes the "Form of Government" in glowing terms.
[42] James Adair, *The History of the American Indians* (London, 1775), pp. 379–80, pictures the liberty of the Cherokee Indians.

. . . Want is said to be the mother of industry, and their wants are supplied at an easier rate."[43] The Indian braves were fortunate, not indolent; they were also wonderously brave in battle, rivaling the German warriors described by Tacitus in their courage and skill.[44]

Best of all, the Indians enjoyed a degree of freedom and equality unknown to less favored people. This rested on their wilderness lives, for only a state of Nature offered such abundance that there need be no squabble over "mine" and "thine" to stir disputes. Freedom from restraint was possible only where there was freedom from want. "The love of liberty is innate in the savage," wrote a popular author in the 1760s, "and seems the ruling passion of the state of nature."[45] Those living amidst such idyllic conditions could not understand obedience, either to kings or to fellowmen. "They cannot reconcile the idea of submission with the dignity of man," another visitor observed. "Each individual is a sovereign in his own mind."[46] Free of greed, disdainful of groveling subservience, the Indians were "possessed of virtues which do honor to human nature."[47]

Nor were these untutored children of Nature inferior to Europeans in their spiritual beliefs and social practices. They might not worship the God of Christianity, but their faith in their own deities was unshakable; they sought daily support from their Master of Life and followed His injunctions with touching humility.[48] They might not elect parliaments, but in their councils they showed the same willingness to listen to views hostile to their own and to abide by the will of the majority. Travelers described these conferences as dignified assemblages, not unlike those of European heads of state. They were also universally impressed with the oratorical skills of the red men whose simple language couched in metaphor charmed Europeans as pure poetry.[49]

The image of the Native American implanted on the European mind by the closing years of the eighteenth century was as opposite from that of a century before as day from night. Living amidst abundance and freedom, they were the most blessed of all humans. "They appear as blithe

[43] Henry Timberlake, *Memoirs of Henry Timberlake, 1756–1764* (1765; reprint ed., Marietta, Ohio, 1948), p. 99.
[44] Julian U. Niemcewicz, *Podróze po Ameryce 1797–1807* (Wrocław, 1959), p. 265.
[45] William Smith, *Historical Account of Bouquet's Expedition against the Ohio Indians, in 1764* (1765), reprinted in *Ohio Historical Series*, no. 1 (Cincinnati, 1868), p. 95. This book was reprinted in London, Dublin, Paris, and Amsterdam within four years of its publication.
[46] John Long, *Voyages and Travels of an Indian Interpreter and Trader* (London, 1791), p. 30.
[47] Jonathan Carver, *Travels through the Interior Parts of North America, in the Years 1766, 1767, and 1768* (3d ed., London, 1781), pp. 99–100.
[48] Timberlake, *Memoirs of Henry Timberlake*, pp. 87–89, gives a sympathetic account of the Indians' religious views, as does Long, *Voyages and Travels*, p. 139.
[49] Louis Milfort, *Memoirs, or a Quick Glance at My Travels and My Sojourn in the Creek Nation* (Keenesaw, Georgia, 1959), pp. 124–35. This is the first English translation of this volume, published in Paris in 1802.

and free as the birds of the air," wrote one observer; added another, "Care and anxiety, ambition and the love of gold, and every uneasy passion, seem banished from this happy region."[50] These children of Nature were worthy of comparison with the dwellers in Europe's Golden Age of legend.

The Noble Savage

Belief in a Golden Age in the sixteenth century was rooted in mankind's longing for a better world; belief in Nature's rejuvenating powers in the late eighteenth century stemmed from the social upheaval that accompanied industrialization and urbanization. As the social structure underwent sweeping changes, and as the archaic political and economic systems then in use proved incapable of solving the problems these changes created, thinking men realized that only a major catastrophe could restore equilibrium in Europe—the upheaval soon to explode in the French Revolution.

This might be avoided if a sufficiently persuasive alternative could demonstrate that a better way of life was possible. When sixteenth-century philosophers sought such an example, they invented a reincarnated Golden Age that they located in the mystery-shrouded New World; when men of learning in the late eighteenth century required a similar model they created a primitivistic paradise that they placed along the little-known American frontier. That distant land and its inhabitants could serve as commentators on Europe's decadence, and through their example prove the need for reform. By glorifying primitivism and agrarianism the reformers could modernize and democratize a Europe sadly in need of both. In doing so, they elevated the yeoman farmer and the Noble Savage as ideals worthy of imitation by all Europeans.

The torchbearer for this cult was Jean-Jacques Rousseau. Deeply concerned with the sickness of Europe, and thoroughly familiar with the travelers and missionaries then discovering virtues in the Indian way of life, Rousseau convinced himself that Europeans would know peace only when they ceased to pay the excessive cost of progress. They might be persuaded to abandon their headlong quest for worldly goods if they learned of more primitive societies where all were well-fed and contented. The American Indian was the nearest approximation to this happy ideal, and would serve as the example. Through him Europeans must be taught that a utopia did exist, and was within their reach.

Rousseau voiced his views in his *Discourse on the Origin of Inequality*

[50] William Bartram, *Travels through North and South Carolina, Georgia, East and West Florida, the Cherokee Country* (Philadelphia, 1791), pp. 211–12; Robert Rogers, *A Concise Account of North America and the British Colonies* (London, 1765), p. 210.

among Men (1755), a dynamite-packed plea that sent tremors across the Continent. The Indians, he wrote, could be compassionate because they were not tempted by wealth, kind because they did not covet other men's possession, generous because their simple wants were abundantly supplied by Nature. Jealousy and violence were the product of an unequal division of the world's goods. "Before those frightful words thine and mine were invented," he wrote, "there were none of those cruel and brutal men we call Masters, and none of other lying and indecent men we call slaves."[51] Indians enjoyed equality and plenty; Europeans were in chains.

Their companions on the American frontier were the pioneer farmers, elevated to glory by Michel-Guillaume St. John de Crèvecoeur whose experiences in backwoods New York were the theme of his *Letters from an American Farmer*, published in London in 1782 and Paris two years later. His message was inescapable: the nearer men returned to Nature, the more abundant their lives and the greater their happiness. The yeoman farmer enjoyed blessings beyond the reach of city dwellers, but the ultimate in good living was the lot of the Indians. "Without temples, without priests, without kings and without laws, they are in many instances superior to us."[52] They alone of all men could live without care, sleep without inquietude, and die without apprehension. They alone could live in liberty, each his own master. Europeans could approximate, but never equal, this bliss by fleeing civilization and establishing their own pastoral paradise in the American West.

Crèvecoeur's tempting picture of life in the wilds stirred envy in a dozen lands, but the ultimate benefactor of Europe's cult of primitivism was the American Indian. For the next half century he was to be glorified by novelists, poets, and essayists as a symbol of the freedom that blessed Nature's own children—a true "Noble Savage" and the most fortunate of all men. What matter that his title had been borrowed from an earlier century when John Dryden wrote in his *The Conquest of Granada* (1682) of Alamanzor:

> I am as free as Nature first made man,
> 'Ere the base laws of servitude began,
> When wild in woods the Noble Savage ran.[53]

[51] Rousseau's views are discussed in Fairchild, *The Noble Savage*, pp. 42–44, and Bissell, *American Indian in English Literature*, pp. 120–23. The spread of his ideas through such philosophers as Johann Gottfried Herder in Germany and James Burnett in Britain is described in Paul C. Weber, *America in Imaginative German Literature in the First Half of the Nineteenth Century* (New York, 1926), pp. 20–21, and Bissell, *American Indian in English Literature*, pp. 45–46.
[52] Michel-Guillaume St. John de Crèvecoeur, *Letters from an American Farmer* (London, 1782), pp. 320–21. The origins of the agrarian myth are discussed in Echeverria, *Mirage in the West*, pp. 33–34.
[53] John Dryden, *The Conquest of Granada by the Spaniards* (London, 1672), p. 7.

What matter that Alamanzor was a Caribbean native rather than an American Indian, or that in his next incarnation he was a Negro in Mrs. Aphara Behn's *Oroonoke; or, The Royal Slave* (1688).[54] His transition into a Noble Red Man was easily accomplished when Europe's intellectuals demanded such a hero.

Fortunately the "Noble Savage" appeared on the scene just as a new literary form was emerging. The romantic novel, which was far better suited to the popular taste than the essays of Rousseau or Crèvecoeur, was ideally designed to glorify frontier life, depending as it did on fast-paced action and rampaging adventure. For the next century novels were to serve as the principal avenues for the armchair adventurers of Europe to learn of the American Wests.

First to appear was *Lydia; or, Filial Piety*, written by John Shebbeare and published in four fat volumes in 1755. Its hero was the Iroquois Cannassatego, who stood tall and strong, his comely visage all that a Greek sculptor might desire, clad in beaver skins and the hide of a shaggy wolf, his shining locks ornamented with "the tufted Plumage of the Eagle's Tail which his fatal Arrows had brought headlong from the Clouds."[55] His beloved was Yarico, the fairest maiden of all the Five Nations, her eyes "vivid as a Diamond's Rays and black as Ebony," her soul as compassionate as her body was beautiful.[56] Lovely though she was, Cannassatego must leave her, for his noble instincts compelled him to visit England to plead with the "Sachems" there to cease oppressing his people. His adventures in Britain revealed the contrast between the purity of life in the wilderness and the corrupt foppery of England's society; he found the people living in dismal huts, the women as eager for dalliance as were their husbands for gain, the leaders immoral, and all so bent on the quest for wealth that deception and dishonesty reigned. Cannassatego fled back to the forest and the "simple and incorrupted Manners of his people," convinced that true nobility could be found in savagery rather than civilization.[57]

Another dimension was added to the emerging picture of the "Noble Savage" with the London publication in 1766 of Robert Roger's play, *Ponteach*. Its heroes were Pontiac and his Indian allies who were models of compassion, constantly sought peace, and always freed the women and children when they were captured inadvertently; its villains were French and British traders who plied the red men with rum, cheated them of their furs, and goaded them into warfare. An old trader set the tone when he told his young partner:

[54] This book is described in Fairchild, *The Noble Savage*, pp. 29–41, as are others dealing with the Noble Savage in the West Indies and South America.
[55] John Shebbeare, *Lydia; or, Filial Piety* (London, 1755), 1: 4–5.
[56] Ibid., 1: 17.
[57] Ibid., 1: 46.

From Gustave Aimard, *The Prairie Flower: A Tale of the Indian Border* (London, 1878). (From the collections of the Library of Congress.)

> Curse on the Law, I say, that makes it Death
> To kill an Indian, more than to kill a Snake.
> What if 'tis Peace? These dogs deserve no Mercy;
> Cursed, revengeful, cruel, faithless Devils.[58]

Sympathy was a powerful emotion, and could be stirred readily by the Indian's sad plight. Novelists had discovered a new device that would popularize their works in that era of romanticism.

These entwined themes—the purity of the "Noble Savage" and the cruelty of his European oppressors—provided grist for dozens of novelists during the late eighteenth century. Their plots were routinely unimaginative—usually involving life about frontier posts or the rescue of maidens by kindly Indians—but all made known that the red men shared virtues scarcely known among whites; they were universally kindly, generous, hospitable, honest, compassionate, and reverent. If they occasionally took to the warpath they were driven to such an extreme by mistreatment, and took up the tomahawk reluctantly. "If those passions were attach'd by good treatment," readers were assured, "they would be the most affectionate, steady, and careful friends."[59]

They were also infinitely thoughtful and always lofted by the highest sense of morality. Female captives universally testified that they had been treated kindly and their virtue respected; some even were so overwhelmed with tenderness and attention by their captors that "they have from gratitude become their wives."[60] Even heroes were reminded of the knights of old by the chivalrous respect paid them, and felt that they could not have been better served at King Arthur's Round Table. "I see you are in distress," quoth one Noble Savage to an injured white man. "That is reason enough for an Indian to pour the balm of consolation into the wounds of adversity."[61] "These untutored savages," one novelist concluded, "have in their minds those natural principles of humanity, which is the foundation of true politeness."[62]

Compassion and respect for others came naturally to a people sheltered from oppression. Europe's novelists saw the red men as living proof that authority was unneeded among men who viewed each other as equals and who enjoyed such freedom from want that the terms "mine" and "thine" lost their meaning. Their society was no anarchy; they chose leaders

[58] Robert Rogers, *Ponteach; or, The Savages of America* (London, 1766), p. 10. The background of this play is discussed in Slotkin, *Regeneration through Violence*, pp. 234–39.
[59] Charles Johnstone, *Chrysal; or, The Adventure of a Guinea* (London, 1765–66), 3: 142–43. This and similar novels are described in Fairchild, *The Noble Savage*, pp. 158–59, and Lois Whitney, *Primitivism and the Idea of Progress in English Popular Literature of the Eighteenth Century* (Baltimore, 1934), pp. 78–83.
[60] Gilbert Imlay, *The Emigrants* (Dublin, 1794), p. 258.
[61] *The School for Fathers; or, The Victim of a Curse* (London, 1788), pp. 226–27.
[62] Charlotte Lennox, *Euphemia* (London, 1790), 4: 70.

known for their superior courage and skills, but these ruled only so long as the majority "found it just and advantageous to them." [63] A "perfect freedom," one author called their society, "where greatness cannot use oppression, nor wealth excite envy." [64] Here was an example worth following. Proclaimed one novelist hopefully:

> The Indian loves liberty, and all will be free
> And so have Britons been, and still will be. [65]

The life-style of the fictional Noble Savages was as laudable as their idealism. They dressed sensibly in the skins of animals or blankets of brilliant hue that contrasted with the foppish ornamentation of European dandies, and if they occasionally adorned themselves with brass rings or daubed colors on their faces, this was no worse than fashionable ladies who sported gold rings and painted their cheeks white or red. Their days were spent in fun and frolic—"they dance, they play; weary of this they bask in the sun and sing." Or when weary of dancing they enjoyed happy games, "chucking shells or pebbles from the brook, into holes dug in the sand, for prizes of bits of tin or brass." [66] Idyllic pleasures, these, when contrasted with the dull routine of existence in Europe.

Such characters as these were made to order for the romantic poets. Their favorite Noble Savage was the dying warrior who tearfully lamented the wrongs done his people in an interminable death song, thus symbolizing the cruelty of all whites to all Indians. This was the theme of Johann Gottfried Seume in his *Der Wilde* and of Johann von Schiller in *Nadowessiers Totenlied;* [67] this was formula used by many a justly unsung British rhymester for verses on *The Death-Song of the Cherokee Indian* or *An Indian's Speech to His Countrymen:*

> Death comes like a friend: he relieves me from pain,
> And thy son, O Alkanomock, has scorn't to complain. [68]

Even better poets were not immune, as witness the lines in William Wordsworth's *The Excursion:*

> Free as the sun and lonely as the sun
> Pouring above his head its radiance down
> Upon a loving and rejoicing world.

All the literary world, from the lowest hack to the most exalted versifier, was paying tribute to the Noble Savage by the end of the eighteenth century.

---

[63] Johnstone, *Chrysal*, 3: 147.
[64] Henry Mackenzie, *The Man of the World* (London, 1773), 2: 182–83.
[65] William Richardson, *The Indians: A Tragedy* (London, 1750), p. 83.
[66] Johnstone, *Chrysal*, 3: 154.
[67] D. L. Ashliman, "The American West in Nineteenth Century German Literature," (Ph.D. diss., Rutgers University, 1969), pp. 122–24.
[68] "The Death-Song of the Cherokee Indians," *The Bee, or, Literary Weekly Intelligencer* (Edinburgh, March 1791): 109–10.

The ultimate glorification was reserved for France's François-René, vicomte de Chateaubriand, a moderate disciple of Rousseau who in 1791 was driven by the exesses of the French Revolution to spend six months in the United States. He absorbed enough in that brief visit to devote the next years to a massive novel based on the revolt of the Natchez Indians against their white oppressors. The first two portions, published in 1801 and 1802 as *Atala* and *René*, were immensely popular, with German and English translations appearing almost at once, and edition after edition required to meet the demand.[69]

Atala's tragic hero was the Natchez chief Chactas who, captured by a band of Muskogee and Seminole, managed to escape with the aid of the chief's lovely daughter, Atala. Together they fled northward to find haven in a Catholic mission. Chactas slept well that night, knowing that on the morrow he would be accepted into the church and thus eligible to marry the Christian Atala, and awoke to the songs of mocking birds and cardinals nesting in the acacias: "I went and plucked a blossom from the magnolia, and deposited it, all bedewed with the tears of the morning, upon Atala's head as she lay sleeping."[70] Alas for such hopes. Atala had made a vow of celibacy to her mother and, fearful that she might not be able to resist Chactas's charms, swallowed the traditional deadly potion, dying in her beloved's arms as she sang her death song: "I do but go before thee this day; and go to await thee in the celestial world."[71] Chactas, "shedding a flood of tears," rejoined his people to live in appropriate misery and tell the story of his lost love.

There was nothing of realism in Chateaubriand's Noble Savages. His heroines were borrowed straight from European romanticism, fainting delicately at the slightest excuse, blushing or turning pale alternately (Chateaubriand explained that "the blush of young Indians is perceptible"), and dissolving into Niagaras of tears at predictable intervals. They quaffed "the water of the apple" or "the cream of nuts" from bamboo cups, dined daintily on fruits and persimmons, and were "as sweet as the plants on which they were nourished."[72] All were radiantly beautiful with cheeks as white as dazzling ivory, hair of "veils of gold," and garments fashioned from the inner bark of the mulberry tree that were lifted as they walked by their rosy heels.[73]

This was carrying a good thing too far. Not even the most gullible

---

[69] Chateaubriand's American experiences are described in Emma K. Armstrong, "Chateaubriand's America: Arrival and First Impressions," *Modern Language Association of America Publications* 22 (June 1907): 347–69.
[70] François-René, vicomte de Chateaubriand, *Atala; or, The Love and Constancy of Two Savages in the Desert* (reprint ed., Stanford, Conn., 1930), pp. 60–61.
[71] Ibid., p. 83.
[72] Chateaubriand's *Les Natchez*, quoted in Armstrong, "Chateaubriand's America," p. 368.
[73] Chateaubriand, *Atala*, p. 43.

could believe in Chateaubriand's Indians when contrasted with portraits etched by the travelers. The irascible Samuel Johnson, listening impatiently to the effusions of an advocate of Noble Savagery, spoke for a good many of his countrymen when he burst forth with: "It is sad stuff; it is brutish. If a bull could speak, he might well exclaim,—'Here I am with this cow and this grass; what being could enjoy greater felicity?' "[74] Even novelists guilty of overglorification themselves had second thoughts; wrote one of Rousseau: "I have all due respect for this philosopher, of whose writings I am an enthusiastic admirer; but I still have greater respect for the truth, which I believe in this instance is not on his side."[75] These seeds of doubt were to mature in the early nineteenth century, as a new mood of realism and materialism gained credence in both Europe and the United States.

The Changing Image: The Captivity Narratives

Long before that time Europeans were enjoying another variety of reading matter that painted the Indians as savage barbarians so unlike the Noble Savages that they seemingly belonged to a different species. The "Captivity Narratives" that skyrocketed to popularity during the late eighteenth century were inevitable by-products of the series of wars that raged along the American backcountry as France, Spain, and England sought to hold or extend their empires. In all, captives were taken by the Indians; a surprising number of these unfortunates survived to pen accounts of their adventures. The success of these hair-raising narratives inspired novelists to exploit the same theme in their works. The result was a body of writing that painted the Indian as impossibly "bad," competing with a literary school that pictured him as unbelievably "good."

For the red men of the "Captivity Narratives" were as unsavory a lot of barbarians as ever were created by fevered imaginations. They were slovenly, slothful, degenerate, and mercilessly cruel, degraded by their contact with whites and instinctively animalistic in their savagery. All were "remarkably dirty and lousy," their dark skins encrusted with grease, their bodies smeared with mud, their tattered clothing crawling with vermin. All were so lazy that they lived on decaying fish and spoiled scraps rather than hunt.[76] Above all, they were monsters of sadism, fiendishly torturing and mutilating their victims for no purpose other than their own pleasure.

Such were the villains described in one of the most popular of the nar-

---

[74] Quoted in C. B. Tinker, *Nature's Simple Plan* (Princeton, 1922), pp. 24–25.
[75] Brooke, *The History of Emily Montague*, 3: 107.
[76] Jonathan Dickenson, *God's Protecting Providence, Man's Surest Help and Defence, in Times of the Greatest Difficulty, and Most Eminent Danger* (London, 1770), pp. 24, 38.

ratives, Peter Williamson's *French and Indian Cruelty, Exemplified in the Life and Various Vicissitudes of Fortune, of Peter Williamson,* published in Glasgow in 1758 and in numerous editions thereafter. Williamson's baptism into Indian ways began soon after his capture in backwoods Pennsylvania in 1754: he saw a frontier family hacked to death and their bodies fed to swine; a trader roasted alive and "then, like *Canibals,* for want of other food, they eat his whole body, and of his head, made what they called an *Indian* pudding"; three prisoners slowly roasted before a slow fire until the impatient red men "ript open their bellies, took out their entrails, and burnt them before their eyes"; a captive buried to the neck and a fire lighted about him "until his eyes gushed out of their sockets."[77] Even their fellow Indians did not escape these monsters; Williamson witnessed the death of a warrior who had outlived his usefulness and was beaten to death by a boy so small that he had to be lifted by a tall brave. "Thus are they from their youth inured to barbarity," he wrote.[78]

The lesson in this narrative, and in dozens like it, was clear: Indians were sadistic barbarians, trained from childhood in the fine art of torture and "taught hardiness of heart, which deprives them of the common feelings of humanity."[79] They must be wiped from the earth, or driven so deeply into the wilderness that settlers would be safe. The Noble Savage was a myth; the true red man was more beast then man, unfit to associate with Civilized Christians.

The lesson—and popularity—of the "Captivity Narratives" did not escape the attention of novelists. Sadistic tortures were as appealing to readers as the romantic musings of Noble Savages. That they learned this lesson well was amply demonstrated in the dozens of books circulated in the late eighteenth century. The red men who ravaged the frontiers in these lurid accounts were reincarnations of the Wild Men of medievalism: their faces hideously painted, their greasy hair flecked with red dust, their ears barbarously decorated with bits of tin or shell, their appetites gluttonous, their taste for drink insatiable.[80] All were masters of the most sophisticated techniques for torturing their victims. These were described with obvious delight: the Indian woman who cut off a captive's arm and gave her children the streaming blood to drink;[81] the victim whose body was seared with a hundred charges of gunshot then made to walk on live coals until he collapsed, the captive whose open wounds were filled with

[77] Peter Williamson, *French and Indian Cruelty, Exemplified in the Life and Various Vicissitudes of Fortune, of Peter Williamson* (Glasgow, 1758), pp. 17–19.
[78] Ibid., p. 23.
[79] William Walton, *A Narrative of the Captivity and Suffering of Benjamin Gilbert and His Family* (London, 1790), pp. 3–4.
[80] Lennox, *Euphemia,* 3: 19, 25–26.
[81] Brooke, *History of Emily Montague,* 1: 22–23.

gunpowder which was then exploded, blowing him to bits.[82] The savages guilty of such tortures was far from noble.

Yet they were typical of the "bad" Indians paraded in volume after volume as models of sadistic ferocity. One of the most popular, Ann Eliza Bleecker's *The History of Maria Kittle* (1797), told of a pioneer housewife whose cabin was attacked while her husband was away. Little Billy, who opened the door, was shot at once, and his corpse mangled and scalped. A young woman who had taken refuge in the cabin was killed with a tomahawk blow, her body split open, and an unborn infant dashed to pieces against the wall. Maria, knowing that her own infant son would be next, screamed her protest: "O God, O Christ! can you bear to see this? O mercy! mercy! mercy! let a little spark of compassion save this unoffending, little angel." As well ask mercy of Satan himself. The brutes "dashed his little forehead against the stones" as she heaped curses upon them: "O barbarians . . . surpassing devils in wickedness! So may a tenfold night of misery enwrap your black souls as you have deprived the babe of my bosom, the comfort of my cares, my blessed cherub, of light and life."[83] Maria was eventually to be rescued by her husband in an emotion-charged climax, but the point was made. Indians were cruel monsters worthy of extermination.

That same point was made even more strongly in another of the best-read novels of the day, Tobias G. Smollett's *The Expedition of Humphrey Clinker* (1771), a tale of the woes of a young Englishman who fell prey to the Miami Indians during the colonial wars. His tortures began with a bang:

The joint of one finger was cut off, or rather sawed off with a rusty knife; one of his great toes was crushed into a mash betwixt two stones; some of his teeth were drawn out, or dug out with a crooked nail. Splintered reeds had been thrust up his nostrils and other tender parts; and the calves of his legs had been blown up with mines of gunpowder dug into the flesh with the sharp point of a tomahawk.

The torturers paused now to refresh themselves by eating flesh stripped from his body, then resumed their sadistic orgy. An old lady scooped out one of his eyes with a sharp knife, then jammed a glowing coal into the socket. "The pain of this operation was so exquisite that he could not help bellowing, upon which the audience raised a shout of exultation, and one of the warriors, stealing behind him, gave him the *coup de grace* with his hatchet."[84]

[82] Mackenzie, *The Man of the World*, 2: 179–80.
[83] Ann Eliza Bleeker, *The History of Maria Kittle* (Hartford, Conn., 1797), pp. 9, 19–22.
[84] Tobias G. Smollett, *The Expedition of Humphrey Clinker* (London, 1771), 2: 167–68.

Scenes such as these helped draw the lines that were to shape the image of the Indian during the coming nineteenth century. Some red men were of saintly goodness, noble in deed and purpose, and good friends of the white men. Others were a Devil's crew so steeped in cruelty and so lacking in conscience that their slaughter was essential to civilization's advance. The image of both the "bad" Indian and the "good" Indian was to be altered by the next generation of writers, but the outlines had been drawn. That generation was to add refinements shaped by the changing intellectual atmosphere in Europe and America, and by the course of history as settlement advanced toward the western horizons.

II

The Image-Makers:
Land of Savagery

UNTIL THE CLOSING YEARS of the eighteenth century, Europeans saw all
America as a vast, uncharted frontier where savagery and civilization
mingled and where East and West were one. When settlers began occupy-
ing the trans-Appalachian hinterland, as they did in the 1780s and 1790s,
this attitude changed as realization spread that a fresh society was forming
beyond the mountains, differing from the older coastal settlements. Travelers noted a cultural fault as apparent as a geological one as they crossed
into the Mississippi Valley. "We seemed," wrote one early in the nineteenth century, "as if we were entering into a wholly new country; as if
the mountain barrier which we had just crossed forced a complete separation between us and all that we had left behind."[1] That cultural fault
shifted westward with settlement—to the Mississippi, the Missouri, the
Pecos, the Rockies, the Sierras—but until the continent was occupied it
separated a "frontier" from the occupied portions of the United States.

Those successive "Wests" offered European image-makers—travelers,
promoters, and novelists—a challenging opportunity. Each differed from
the other, and could be described in imaginative detail; each spawned its
own larger-than-life heroes—from Daniel Boone to Buffalo Bill Cody—
whose colorful exploits were made to order to thrill readers. Of these who

[1]   E. Stanley, *Journal of a Tour in America, 1824–1825* (n.p., 1930), pp. 181–82.

[29]

capitalized on this chance, the novelists were the most important and the least restrained by actuality. Their soaring imaginations created a school of writing that played a larger role in misinforming Europeans about the frontier than any other. European Westerns won few of their authors a niche in the literary pantheons of their homelands, but they did create a lasting image of the frontier as a land of lawlessness and savagery.

Europe's Coopermania

In the beginning was James Fenimore Cooper. The first of his *Leatherstock-ing Tales, The Pioneers; or, The Source of the Susquehanna*, was published in England and France in 1823, almost simultaneously with its appearance in the United States; it was translated into two German editions within a year, into Swedish and Spanish in 1827, Danish in 1828, and a variety of additional languages during the next decade.[2] All the ingredients of a lusty adventure story were there: the grizzled old trapper Natty Bumppo, chases along forest trails in moccasined feet, wilderness feats of incredible daring, a dainty maiden awaiting rescue from a deadly panther. Natty spoke the untutored vernacular expected of woodsmen, befriended good Indians, was the implacable foe of bad, and was humane to wild animals save when food was necessary. What European with an ounce of adventure in his being could resist?

Few did, as the editions of Cooper's works that rolled from the presses testified: *The Last of the Mohicans* (1826), *The Prairie* (1827), *The Pathfinder* (1840), *The Deerslayer* (1841). No less than thirty German publishers vied to make his works available; one promised his "Complete Works" in thirty-eight volumes, four more than allotted any other American or British author.[3] French buyers had their choice between eighteen of his novels. In Russia thirty-two of his collected works appeared before 1917, and two more after the Revolution.[4] Translations appeared regularly in Italy, France, Spain, and eventually every European nation as well as in Turkey, the Middle East, and North Africa.[5] Reported a traveler: "In the little kingdom of Holland, with its three million inhabitants, I looked into four different translations of Cooper in the language of the country";

---

[2]   Willard Thorp, "Cooper beyond America," *New York History* 35 (October 1954): 522–39 describes Cooper's reception in Europe. The popularity of his works in Germany is the theme of Preston A. Barba, *Cooper in Germany* (Bloomington, 1914), pp. 73–78.

[3]   Paul Haertl, "Cooper in Germany," *German-American Review* 3 (June 1937): 18–19.

[4]   Clarence L. F. Gohdes, "The Reception of Some Nineteenth Century American Authors in Europe," in *The American Writer and the European Tradition*, eds. Margaret Denny and W. H. Gilman (Minneapolis, 1950), pp. 113–14; Robert Magidoff, "American Literature in Russia," *Saturday Review of Literature* 29 (2 November 1946): 9–10.

[5]   John D. L. Ferguson, *American Literature in Spain* (New York, 1916), pp. 3–4, 34–35, 41–42; Emilio Goggio, "Cooper's 'Bravo' in Italy," *Romantic Review* 20 (July–September 1929): 222–30.

another found copies in the languages of Turkey, Persia, and Egypt, as well as at Jerusalem and Isfahan.[6] All over Europe children learned to "play Indian," walk in "Indian file," wear feathers in their hair, and greet each other with "Hoogg," their equivalent of Uncas' "Ugh." Even today German blades salute the final bottle of the evening as *"Der letzte Mohikaner."*[7]

With popularity went literary acclaim. English journals were not quite willing to concede that Cooper outshone their own Walter Scott, but other critics felt no such restraint. To the French he was "le Walter Scott des sauvages" but far more competent in his wilderness descriptions;[8] Spaniards acclaimed him "The American Scott" and ranked *The Last of the Mohicans* as a "classic in every language of Europe";[9] Russians compared him to Shakespeare and reveled in tales of "the boundless steppes, where herds of bison roam, where the redskinned children of the Great Spirit hide."[10] To the Germans the *Lederstrumpf-Erzählungen* were marvelous examples of their own medieval legends of Teutonic knights as chivalrous as they were bold.[11]

Remarkably, Europeans saw Cooper as a realist who accurately portrayed the frontiersmen and Indians—a judgment that would astound modern readers. "Never," wrote a German reviewer, "has an author presented the natural scene with such . . . fidelity. Everything is action, character, poetry. He is incomparable when he describes the speech of the Indians and life in the wilderness."[12] Here was Nature's gospel literally presented. And here, too, was a lesson for Europe's authors. Their audience was eager for reasonably accurate descriptions of the pioneers and the red men, not for the Noble Savages of Rousseau and Chateaubriand. A major market waited works that exploited the towering grandeur of the American forests, the brooding silence of the prairies, the horizonless sweep of the Great Plains; works that pitted leather-clad hunters in spine-tingling battles with painted Indians or savage beasts. Here was a challenge to European novelists, and they met it with such success that Westerns became the standard literary fare of Britishers, Germans, Scan-

[6]   Quoted in Barba, *Cooper in Germany*, p. 53.
[7]   Ibid., p. 93; Halvdan Koht, *The American Spirit in Europe: A Survey of Transatlantic Influences* (Philadelphia, 1949), p. 111.
[8]   Eric Partridge, "Fenimore Cooper's Influence on the French Romantics," *Modern Language Review* 20 (April, 1925): 175–76; Henry Blumenthal, *American and French Culture, 1800–1900* (Baton Rouge, 1975), pp. 202–3.
[9]   Ferguson, *American Literature in Spain*, pp. 39–40, 53.
[10] I. I. Uspenskij, *Russian Writers in America* (Moscow, 1952), p. 21.
[11] Morton Nirenburg, *The Reception of American Literature in German Periodicals, 1820–1850* (Heidelberg, 1970), pp. 61–62.
[12] Quoted in Harvey W. Hewett-Thayer, *American Literature As Viewed in Germany, 1818–1861* (Chapel Hill, 1958), p. 24. A number of German reviews of Cooper's works are printed in translation in this volume, pp. 54–74, and in Barba, *Cooper in Germany*, pp. 79ff.

dinavians, Frenchmen, Spaniards, even Hungarians and Poles, for a century to come. Carrying realism well beyond Cooper, these authors became the principal image-makers for Europe's literate and semiliterate masses. ·

The Cult of the Western

To explain the popularity of James Fenimore Cooper and his imitators is to probe the art of storytelling, human psychology, and the subtleties of popular taste, but it is also to ask another basic question: why the unique appeal of the American frontier, then and now, to Europeans? What in the social and intellectual climate of the Old World accounted for the astounding popularity of Westerns and of all information about the frontier? In answering these questions, modern scholars have proposed a number of explanations, most of them significant.

One recognizes their role as logical successors to the symbolic dramas that have fed the romantic dreams of Europeans from the dawn-days of their history. They had been bred on tales of mythological folk-heroes—Gilgamesh, Odysseus, Siegfried, Thor, dozens more—who battled the forces of evil until righteousness emerged triumphant. Now the American West provided an ideal backdrop for stories told in the same tradition; Leatherstocking and his successors satisfied a strong psychological need as they carried the torch against Indians and beasts and reptiles that symbolized the Devil's agents.[13]

This association was made easier by the novelists who cast their characters as their own countrymen. English heroes in the best middle-class, public-school, imperial-servant tradition clung to the habits and language of their homelands, besting their enemies through pluck and hard-business judgment, never omitting afternoon tea, and occasionally bursting into a "By jove," or an "Egad" when plagued by the villain. German heroes never abandoned their mother tongue, were adept at locating Indians skilled in their language, clung doggedly to a rigid code of Teutonic morals, and dreamed always of returning to the Fatherland. French heroes succumbed more completely to primitivism than others, but never forgot that France was Europe's most cultured nation. Europeans could empathize more readily with such heroes than they could with "foreigners"—even Americans.

Novels about the frontier were prized as emotional safety valves for the millions caught in the dull routine of tasks demanded by industrialization. For a moment as they read they were transported from fac-

---

[13] John G. Cawelti, "God's Country, Las Vegas, and the Gunfighter; Differing Visions of the West," *Western American Literature* 9 (Winter 1975): 273–74 is excellent on these points.

From Gustave Aimard, *The Prairie Flower: A Tale of the Indian Border* (London, 1878). (From the collections of the Library of Congress.)

tory or harvest field to wilderness depths hard on the trail of the villain who had abducted the golden-haired heroine, or galloping pell-mell across the plain with six-shooters blazing. Every Western was an open portal into a land of spine-tingling adventure for legions of armchair Walter Mittys. A minister to Great Britain from the Republic of Texas revealed one reason for their popularity when he reported a conversation with a group of intellectuals: "They listened with much deference to all that I said . . . , but evidently with delight to the accounts of our Indian fights—prairie life—buffalo hunting, etc."[14] Men of all times and all places yearn for vicarious indulgence in acts of aggression, and this the frontier stories gave them.

They appealed also to Europeans who for generations had glorified primitivism. Westerns offered Germans and Frenchmen and Scandinavians a mirror image of themselves—a glimpse into a social order where strength and chivalry were virtues as they no longer were in decadent Europe. The frontier was a virgin land, bursting with the exuberance of youth, where primitive values transcended sophistication and hope triumphed over despair. It also was a land where the qualities of civilization and primitivism—personified by Natty Bumppo and Uncas—could unite against the forces of evil. The American Wests offered storytellers brave new themes and made-to-order heroes guaranteed to captivate the hearts—if not the minds—of their readers.

These were elements that endowed Westerns with enduring popularity, but their immediate success during the 1830s and 1840s was linked to the political climate of the Old World. There the Old Order, struggling for rebirth after the French Revolution, was locked in bitter philosophical conflict with liberals bent on perpetuating and expanding the social gains resulting from that cataclysm. To men of this ilk the restrictions on thought and action that resurfaced during the Age of Metternich were intolerable. The voices of reform were particularly strident in Germany, stung by the humiliation of Napoleon's victories, strengthened by dislike of control by Prussian and Austrian despots, and frustrated by the feuding Hohenzollern and Hapsburg families whose quarrels dimmed hopes of unification. German intellectuals saw aging Europe as a victim of unreversible weariness—a *Europamüdigkeit*, they called it—while in America new societies were aborning and the winds of change blew strong. They were eager for every crumb of information about this rebirth, and particularly of the frontiers where virgin communities were forming and men shaped their own destinies. The land of the future could teach much to the land of the past, and they were eager to learn.

---

[14] George W. Terrell to W. D. Miller, 20 January 1845, quoted in Mark E. Nackman, *A Nation within a Nation: The Rise of Texas Nationalism* (Port Washington, N.Y., 1975), p. 8.

To readers of lesser intellectual bent, novels about the American West held a more personal appeal. As social and economic discontent in Europe started the immigrant tide rolling, information about the United States, and particularly the western United States that was the target of most migrants, was eagerly sought. By 1850 one in every ten Germans had departed for America, and scarcely a family but boasted a friend or relative living there.[15] Novels might not be the most accurate purveyors of information, but they were better than nothing. What more pleasant way to conjure up an image of a loved one than to read of the land that he had adopted, even in the distorted imagery of the storyteller.

Beginnings of Realism: The Early Novelists

Swept along by the mounting tide of interest in America, European authors began turning to the frontier as a setting for their stories early in the nineteenth century; even Johann Wolfgang von Goethe, Germany's brightest-shining literary light, planned a novel about the West in 1827 and urged others to try their hand. From the beginning they divided sharply in their views. Better writers with upper-class backgrounds, some of them disillusioned by their own experiences, were inclined to be harshly critical of frontier crudities and materialism; typical was Heinrich Zschokke's *Ein Bückliger* (1839), which painted the frontiersmen as uncultured illiterates totally unaware of the beauty of God's creations unless they could be used for profit.[16] Better the *Überkultur* of Europe, this school was saying, than the *Unkultur* of western America.

At the opposite extreme stood writers who saw Westerns solely as tools for their own propaganda. Some of this breed were scattered through western Europe, but most were in Poland and Hungary, where they could equate the plight of the Indian with that of their own despot-ridden people. To Poland's Sygurd Wiśniowski the red men were "survivors of a great race defending the inheritance of their fathers" from greedy Americans, a pattern repeated in such powerful tales as *Orso* and *Sachem* by Henryk Sienkiewicz.[17] There was little of reality in these stories; one of Hungary's most popular novels—*Vadonban* by Ferenc Belányi—described

[15]   Nelson Van de Luyster, "Gerstäcker's Novels about Emigrants to America," *American-German Review* 20 (June–July 1954): 22.
[16]   These writers are discussed in two works by Lawrence M. Price, "English Literature in Germany," *University of California Publications in Modern Philology* 37 (1953): 364–65, and *The Reception of United States Literature in Germany* (Chapel Hill, 1966), pp. 96–97, and in George R. Brooks, "The American Frontier in German Fiction," in *The Frontier Re-examined*, ed. John McDermott (Urbana, 1967), pp. 156–57.
[17]   This novel is described in the introduction by Marion M. Coleman to Henry Sienkiewicz, *Western Septet: Seven Stories of the American West* (Cheshire, Conn., 1973), pp. v–viii.

the hair-raising adventures of an Hungarian farmer who became so popular among the Indians by teaching them industrious ways that they made him mayor of "Payuta City."[18] Their purpose was to propagandize, not to elevate their authors to literary fame.

More moderate, but still in the reform tradition, was Charles Sealsfield, born Karl Postl in Austria, who in 1822 fled his native land for the Louisiana frontier. The admitted purpose of his six novels was, in the words of an early biographer, "to transfer the freshly pulsating blood of the Transatlantic Republic into the senile veins of the Old World, to acquaint his countrymen with the spirit of true liberty."[19] His objective was clear in his first novel, published in Germany in 1833: *Der Legitime und die Republikaner*—a moving tale of the struggle of the Cherokee chief Tokeah to preserve his peoples' tribal lands from the grasping whites under Andrew Jackson. In the end they failed, sending Tokeah to his death beyond the Mississippi—a symbol of the impossibility of reconciling Nature with the greedy materialism of the American pioneers.[20]

Sealsfield's stories moved Europe's impression of the frontier far toward realism. His Indians might be maudlin victims of the white men's greed but they were far from Noble Savages; he once castigated Chateaubriand for "the extraordinary exaggerations of which he makes himself guilty at the expense of veracity."[21] His frontiersmen—American backwoodsmen, Creole planters, Acadian huntsmen, villainous Yankee peddlers—were "dregs repelled by civilized society" who indulged in brawls, fights with bowie knives, and eye-gouging matches as would no civilized man.[22] Sealsfield's lusty works formed a bridge between the romantic imaginings of Cooper and Chateaubriand and a robust new school of European writers who were to produce the first true Westerns during the 1830s and 1840s.

Their models were the increasingly realistic works of American authors in rebellion against the genteel tradition that had long burdened writing in the United States: James K. Paulding's *Westward Ho*, William Gilmore Simms *The Wigwam and the Cabin*, Charles F. Hoffman's *Greyslayer: A Romance of the Mohawk* and *Wild Scenes in Forest and Prairie*, and others

[18] Ferenc Belányi, *Vadonban: Regények az Észak Amerikai Államokból* (Pest, 1865), pp. 101–222.
[19] Bernard A. Uhlendorf, *Charles Sealsfield: Ethnic Elements and National Problems in His Works* (Chicago, 1922), p. 30, quotes this passage.
[20] Charles Sealsfield, *Tokeah; or, The White Rose* (Philadelphia, 1828), passim. *Tokeah* was republished in Germany as *Der Legitime und die Republikaner: Eine Geschichte aus dem lezten amerikanisch-englischen Kriege* (Zurich, 1833). It is discussed in Price, *Reception of United States Literature in Germany*, pp. 202–4.
[21] Uhlendorf, *Charles Sealsfield*, pp. 13–14.
[22] Quoted in ibid., p. 123.

like them. All were widely translated in Europe and favorably reviewed. Two were particularly influential.[23]

One was Robert Montgomery Bird's *Nick of the Woods: A Story of Kentucky* that was published in no less than nine English editions after its appearance in 1837, and under the title *Nathan der Quaker, oder der Satan des Urwaldes*, in three editions in Germany, one in Denmark, one in Holland, and one in Poland.[24] Its hero, Nathan Slaughter, roamed the forest killing Indians in a life-long quest to avenge the massacre of his wife and children, marking each with a cross carved in the mutilated flesh. His Indians were far from Noble Savages; all were sneaking renegades so cruel and worthless that they deserved their fate at the hands of the Jibbenainosay, or "the Spirit that Walks," as the red men called him.[25] Here was a new formula for European storytellers to imitate, one in which the villains were red and the heroes white.

Scarcely less influential was Charles W. Webber whose frontier thrillers—*Old Hicks the Guide, The Prairie Scout, The Gold Mines of the Gila*, and a half-dozen more—were reprinted widely in Europe during the 1840s. All broke with tradition by moving their scenes of action from eastern forests to the desert Southwest, and all allowed no nonsense about Noble Savages to slow their helter-skelter plots. Webber's frontiersmen were cold-blooded adventures who would as soon shoot a redskin as a rattlesnake; his Indians blood-thirsty barbarians fully deserving of their fate. His blood-and-thunder tales were immensely popular on both sides of the Atlantic; he himself boasted that one had been read by more than a million people.[26]

These American authors stirred a whole school of European imitators into action, partly by demonstrating the demand for thrillers about the Wild West, partly because their realism opened the door to greater sensationalism than had been socially acceptable in the past. Each major country produced its share: Norway, Rudolf Muus whose several thousand titles won him a place among the "Big Five" of his country's authors; France, Gabriel Ferry, Paul Duplessis, and Gustave Aimard; England, Percy St. John and Mayne Reid; Germany, Otto Ruppius, Balduin Möllhausen, Friedrich Armand Strubberg, and Friedrich Gerstäcker; Italy, Elilio Salfari—to name only the most prominent. Their purpose was not to preach liberty or shed tears over the plight of Indians; their concern was

---

[23] The popularity of these books in Europe is discussed in Nirenberg, *Reception of American Literature in German Periodicals*, pp. 76–89.
[24] Curtis Dahl, *Robert Montgomery Bird* (New York, 1963), pp. 132–33.
[25] Robert Montgomery Bird, *Nick of the Woods: A Story of Kentucky* (London, 1837), 1: 65–66.
[26] Charles W. Webber, *Tales of the Southern Border* (Philadelphia, 1853), introduction.

to attract readers with rousing tales plentifully spiced with bloodshed and violence.[27] Little known to historians of literature, these best-sellers played a larger role than any other writings in shaping the European image of the American frontier.

To call the roll of their works is to make this clear. Among the German novelists, Otto Ruppius was least typical. Like most of his contemporaries he had lived in the United States between 1848 and 1861; unlike them he had never seen the Far West. Hence the bulk of his stories glorified the German settlers of the Midwest for their saintly ideals and Teutonic morality. Only his best known, *Der Präirieteufel* (1861), followed a young German trapper across the Mississippi where his iron fist downed a succession of sniveling Yankee speculators and scoundrelly Indians variously called "red devils," "wild animals," and "red scamps."[28] Ruppius's tales won him no niche among Germany's literary greats, but they did demonstrate that Europeans would buy adventure stories in profit-assuring quantities.

Far more prolific than Ruppius was Friedrich Armand Strubberg whose sixty-odd novels capitalized on the knowledge of Texas gained during his years there as an agent of German colonizers.[29] He was particularly at home with two themes, one exemplified in his *Bis in die Wildnis* (1858) where a band of honest German immigrants were bilked of their belongings by land sharks but survived by using their Teutonic talents to become skilled frontiersmen, the other his five-volume *Ralph Norwood* describing the incredibly bloody battles between American troops and Seminole Indians that drove the red men westward toward extermination.[30] Strubberg's scenes were surprisingly realistic but his Indians were either Cooperesque noblemen or degraded wretches fleeing westward before the white advance; *lumpen* he called them, with as much pity as contempt.

[27] In addition to these major authors, many others wrote two or three books about the West, including in Germany, August Schrader, Andrä Heinrich Fogowitz, Adolf Bourset, Rudolf Scipio, and Sophie Wörishöffer. Their works, and those of the major authors are listed in Preston A. Barba, "The American Indian in German Fiction, *German-American Annals* 15 (May–August 1913): 167–68, and expertly discussed in D. L. Ashliman, "The American West in Nineteenth Century German Literature" (Ph.D. diss., Rutgers University, 1969), pp. 28–39.
[28] Frederick F. Schrader, "Otto Ruppius, A Career in America," *America-German Review* 9 (February 1943): 28–33, contains a brief account of his life and excerpts in translation from one of his stories. A thorough discussion of his work is in Theodor Graewert, *Otto Ruppius und der Amerikaroman im 19. Jahrhundert* (Jena, 1935).
[29] Strubberg spent most of the time between 1826 and 1854 in the American West. His experiences are described in Preston A. Barba, "Friedrich Armand Strubberg," *German-American Annals* 14 (September–December 1912): 175–225 and 15 (January–April 1913), 3–63, and 15 (May–August 1913): 115–42.
[30] Strubberg's western novels are summarized in ibid., 15: 3–63, and 15: 115–42; those dealing with emigration in Preston A. Barba, "Emigration to America Reflected in German Fiction," *German-American Annals* 16 (November–December 1914): 202–12.

Both Strubberg and Ruppius were overshadowed by a more widely acclaimed German novelist: Friedrich Gerstäcker, a compulsive wanderer who spent six years after 1837 drifting about the West, living as a hunter, traveling with Indian bands, and on one occasion joining with a vigilante committee pursuing a group of outlaws.[31] His first novel, *Die Regulatoren in Arkansas*, appeared in three stout volumes in 1846, to be followed by a host more before his death in 1872. Like Strubberg he exploited two themes, one the experiences of German immigrants carried on the wings of hope to the West only to be cheated by immigration agents, loan sharks, and land speculators;[32] the other—developed in such works as *Mississippi-Bilder* (1847–48) and *Die Flusspiraten des Mississippi* (1848)—glorified vigilantism and lynch law as the only means of keeping order in the thinly settled West.[33] This was a shocking message for Europeans reared in the belief that laws were sacred, but an important one if they were to understand the true frontier.

Balduin Möllhausen needed no such preaching to be hailed as the "Cooper of Germany." His credentials were impeccable; born in Bonn in 1825, he reached America in 1849 and after a year of seasoning began his far-western adventures; visiting the Rocky Mountain country with the famed expedition of Duke Paul Wilhelm of Württemberg, joining with a surveying party plotting the route of a Pacific railroad in 1852, returning again with an expedition exploring the route of the Colorado River.[34] The one hundred and fifty books that he wrote after his return to Germany were unquestionably accurate in the minds of their readers; Möllhausen had seen the elephant and was to be believed down to the last scalp-lifting. "I relate what I have seen and observed," he wrote in one novel, "and even if I have not personally experienced that which I narrate, I have heard it . . . from old hunting companions around a secret campfire in an inhospi-

[31] Gerstäcker's American experiences are in George H. R. O'Donnell, "Gerstäcker in America, 1837–1843," *Publications of the Modern Language Association of America* 42 (December 1927): 1036–43. Harrison R. Steeves, "The First of the Westerns," *Southwest Review* 52 (Winter 1968): 74–84, argues that during a period in 1837 when he apparently disappeared he was riding with a band of Regulators in Texas.
[32] Notable among his immigration novels was *Der Deutschen Auswanderer Fährten und Schicksale* (1847), describing the experiences of a party of Germans on their way to lands purchased on the Tennessee frontier. This and others are discussed in Barba, "Emigration to America Reflected in German Fiction," pp. 68–70.
[33] These and other novels of this genre are described in Alfred Kolb, "Friedrich Gerstäcker and the American Frontier" (Ph.D. diss., Syracuse University, 1966), and more briefly in Paul C. Weber, *America in Imaginative German Literature in the First Half of the Nineteenth Century* (New York, 1926), pp. 152–56.
[34] The fullest account of Möllhausen's life in English is Preston A. Barba, "Balduin Möllhausen, the German Cooper," *Americana-Germanica Monograph Series* 17 (1914): 1–144, but his American experiences are better described in two articles by David H. Miller, "The Ives Expedition Revisited: A Prussian's Impressions," *Journal of Arizona History* 13 (Spring 1972): 1–25, and (Autumn 1972): 177–96, and "A Prussian on the Plains: Balduin Möllhausen's Impressions," *Great Plains Journal* 12 (Spring 1973): 175–93.

table wilderness."[35] To doubt such a witness was heresy. So Germans believed as they made him their best-read writer during the 1860s and 1870s.

His first novel, published in 1861 as *Der Halbindianer*, set the pattern; it described the adventures of the half-breed son of a Louisiana planter as his efforts to prove himself his father's heir led him to the upper Missouri Valley and a series of cliff-hanging episodes with Indians, gamblers, horse-thieves, trappers, and of course German immigrants. Here was a no-nonsense adventure story, unblemished by any social message, and first-rate reading for the armchair adventurer. Möllhausen's sole concern was a fast-paced plot, and while his books were crammed with information about the West (more or less accurate as the situation dictated) the story always came first. Yet there was much to be learned from his realistic sketches: Indians loitering about a frontier trading post; the thoughts of a solitary trapper as he mused about the advantages of life in the wilderness; the sufferings of a fur-trading party caught in a mountain blizzard; the plight of Indians driven westward by the white men's greed. Here was the stuff of the true Western rich in color and action, and it was to prove irresistible to Europeans.

Nor did Germany monopolize the trade. In France a triumvirate of writers contributed significantly to muddying the true image of the American frontier. Two of these were of a kind: Gabriel Ferry and Paul Duplessis; both laid their scenes largely in the Southwest, both glorified French-American frontiersmen as their heroes while picturing Americans as uncultured barbarians, and both were immensely popular, not only in their homeland but throughout much of Europe in translation.[36] Ferry's best-known books—*Le Coureur des bois* (1850) and *Les Squatters* (1858)—and Duplessis's *Le Batteur d'estrade* (1856), *Les Mormons* (1859), and *Les Peaux-Rouges* (1864) were jam-packed with wild chases across the deserts, lynchings, and vividly described scalpings that bore the stamp of authenticity while teaching their readers a good many untruths about the Far West. Typical of Duplessis's distortions was *Les Mormons*, a fanciful tale of two Parisian sisters seduced by the president of the Latter-day Saints to join his harem, and of their rescue by their brother, Georges de Médouville, who followed their abductor's wagon train westward.[37] Thousands of Eu-

---

[35] Quoted in D. L. Ashliman, "The Novel of Western Adventure in Nineteenth Century Germany," *Western American Literature* 3 (Summer 1968): 142–43. Summaries of his novels are in Barba, "Balduin Möllhausen," pp. 88–91.

[36] Ferry wrote under the pen name of Baron Louis de Bellemere. A brief biographical sketch is in Carl Wittke, "The American Theme in Continental European Literature," *Mississippi Valley Historical Review* 28 (June 1941): 7–8.

[37] Paul Duplessis, *Les Mormons* (Paris, 1859), passim.

ropean readers were treated to grossly false accounts of Mormonism, and persuaded that in western America personal vengeance took precedence over the orderly working of the law.

Dwarfing these novelists was another whose popularity, if not his literary skills, was unrivaled in his day. Gustave Aimard, born Olivier Gloux in Paris in 1818, spent many of his youthful years in the American Southwest, living for almost a decade with Indians along the Mexican-American border, and joining in the 1854 expedition of the comte de Raousset-Boulbon in a vain effort to establish a monarchy in Mexico. His readers were never allowed to forget his frontiering days. "It is his life that he is relating," one of his books promised, "his disappointed hope, his adventurous courses. . . . In a word *he has seen*, he has lived among, he has suffered with, the personages of his recitals."[38] Here was the unvarnished truth; let the scoffer beware.

And here was the passport to Aimard's unbelievable popularity. His first two novels, *Les Trappeurs de l'Arkansas* and *Le Grand Chef des Aucas*, appeared in 1858; during the next years he wrote furiously, often at the rate of a book a month, to satisfy the demand. Nor were the French his only patrons; his books were automatically translated into a number of languages, to be hailed always as masterpieces.[39] Such was his appeal in England that no less than three publishers vied in showering his works on the public, using such devices as altered titles; *Loyal Heart; or, The Trappers* listed by G. Routledge & Company became *The Trappers of Arkansas; or, The Loyal Heart* in the catalogue of Ward & Lock Company of Fleet Street.[40] Collectors were offered more enduring examples of Aimard's genius than the cheap paperbacks usually circulated; one publisher promised a hardbound edition magnificently illustrated with engravings guaranteed to picture "the peculiarities of the country in which the scene is laid."[41]

No one could have been less worthy of such adulation. Aimard's writing was atrocious, his language stilted and cliché-laden, and his plots so awkwardly structured that he was repeatedly forced into such explanations as: "The preceding explanations given, we will resume our story at

[38] Gustave Aimard, *Loyal Heart; or, The Trappers* (London, 1858), preface. A brief biography of Aimard is in the *Dictionnaire de biographie français* (Paris, 1933), 1: 975–76.
[39] A laudatory appraisal of his works is in "Gustave Aimard," *Bentley's Miscellany* 49 (1861): 100–104. Among his many German titles were *Die Trapper in Arkansas* (1859), *Die Prairie-Piraten* (1860), *Das Goldfieber* (1861), and *Lynch-Gesetz* (1861).
[40] In addition to these publishers, John and Robert Maxwell, Inc., brought out no less than eight series of his novels; these are listed on the endpapers of his *The Missouri Outlaws* (London, n.d.). His principal English translator was Percy St. John, a well-known author of Westerns. Despite his own extensive experience in the West, St. John endorsed without comment Aimard's many distortions.
[41] Gustave Aimard, *The White Scalper: A Story of the Texan War* (London, 1861), pp. iv–v. The three series published by Ward & Lock are listed, pp. iii–iv.

the point where we left it at the end of Chapter Seven."[42] His heroines were pale shadows of unreality; his villains (such as "White Scalper the Pitiless") unrealistically unreal, and his heroes caricatures of the plains-men they were supposed to represent. Two appeared most often: "Loyal Heart" who pursued Indians and bad men with two giant bloodhounds always at his side, and Valentine Guillois, Aimard's own alter ego, a pro-fessional damsel rescuer who shed blood only when necessary, lived a life of exemplary morality, and never uttered a word "which would prove of-fense to the most delicate mind."[43] Literary grace was certainly not the magnet that attracted his readers.

They were lured instead by Aimard's remarkable ability to develop his plots at such lightning pace that the reader was left intellectually breath-less. Things happened in his novels, and it little mattered that they taxed logic and truth. His art can be revealed best by summarizing the final pages of one of his most successful books, *The Pirates of the Prairies*.

We take up the story as Valentine and his friendly Comanches are hard on the trail of the white renegade, Red Cedar and his Apache com-panions, in the Gila River valley. As they burst into Red Cedar's camp, guns blazing, that arch-villain shouts: "Malediction! Those wolves again. To arms, lads; here are the red-skins," then plunges into the deep forest. Before he can be captured a sudden earthquake sends the Gila roaring over its banks and scattering the camp fires, setting fire to the prairie grass. Amidst the confusion the renegade escapes, carrying with him his captive, the lovely Dona Clara, but forsaking the Apaches. Caught between the fire and the raging river, they appeal to Valentine for aid. They should, he tells them, kill some of the buffalo that are running madly about, make boats of their hides, and take to the river. Moments later, "the red-skins, after making, with their peculiar quickness and skill, some twenty canoes, were already beginning to launch them." Red Cedar also took to the water on a raft he had constructed in record time, taking Dona Clara with him.

This was Valentine's supreme challenge. Knife in teeth, he plunged into the foaming stream, shouting "Courage! Courage!" (no mean feat when clenching a knife between his teeth). Before he could reach the beau-tiful damsel Nature again played him false. "A formidable sound, resem-bling the discharge of a park of artillery, burst from the entrails of the earth, a terrible shock agitated the ground, and the river was forced back into the ground by an irresistible force." This second earthquake cast Red Cedar on the bank, where he plunged his knife into Dona Clara's heart. Shouting with demonical triumph, he leaped on a horse that was conve-niently at hand and galloped away. Valentine made no effort to pursue

[42] Gustave Aimard, *The Trapper's Daughter: A Story of the Rocky Mountains* (Philadelphia, n.d.), p. 51.
[43] Gustave Aimard, *The Adventurers* (New York, n.d.), p. iv.

him, explaining that he must "pay his last duties to his victim." Dona
Clara is laid to rest in a desert grave and the reader is assured that the pursuit of Red Cedar will be resumed in a sequel, *The Trapper's Daughter*,
which "will speedily appear."[44]

England's contributors to this emerging "literary" school were many,
but all were dwarfed by the "Giant of the Westerns," "Captain" Mayne
Reid. His seventy-odd novels, his innumerable stories in boys' magazines,
and his carefully nurtured reputation as an authority on the Far West won
Reid a role in English letters not unlike that of Balduin Möllhausen in
Germany and Gustave Aimard in France. No Britisher of his day enjoyed
a greater reputation as a master of escape literature or spinner of adventure
tales; "We enjoy," wrote a leading critic, "the impossible carpet which
goes where it likes, and the impossible rifleman, who kills when he
likes."[45]

Reid based his stories on less extended American experience than he
would have liked. Born in Ireland in 1818, he was in New Orleans in 1840
in time to join a trading caravan to Santa Fe and Chihuahua, then spent
some years in the East before enlisting with American troops in the Mexican War. After being wounded at Chapultepec and adopting the title of
"Captain" he returned to England in 1849, where his first book, *The Rifle
Rangers*, was published a year later. Its success turned him toward a career
as a prolific writer of novels, boys' books, travel accounts, short stories,
and enough miscellaneous scribblings to fill a modest library.[46]

Reid's western tales pictured the frontier as a land of opportunity
where the humble could achieve affluence, but as a land also of strife, cruelty, and constant violence. Typical of his novels was The *Scalp Hunters;
or, Romantic Adventures in Northern Mexico*, published in 1851 in three volumes, a sensational account of a young Englishman who journeyed westward with the Santa Fe traders and lived for a time amidst the dangers of
the borderlands. There he met a handsome Creole who had been hired by
settlers to rid the countryside of Navajos and Apaches. Together the two
followed a life of harrowing adventure that reached a climax with the rescue of the Scalp Hunter's daughter from the red men. Simply to count the
number of scalps lifted in those three volumes would test the capacity of a
computer.

Mayne Reid's principal offense against humanity was not his cluttered

---

[44] Gustave Aimard, *The Pirates of the Prairies: Adventures in the American Desert* (London,
1862), pp. 146–52.
[45] *The Spectator*, 27 October 1883, quoted in Joan D. Steele, "The Image of America in the
Novels of Mayne Reid: A Study of a Romantic Expatriate" (Ph.D. diss., University of California at Los Angeles, 1970).
[46] By far the best study of Reid's life is in Steele, "The Image of America in the Novels of
Mayne Reid," passim. Briefer but useful is Roy W. Meyer, "The Western American Fiction
of Mayne Reid," *Western American Literature* 3 (Summer 1968): 115–32.

plots, his contrived climaxes (in one tale he introduced a new character on the last page to allow all the cast to be married), his artificial language (his grizzled trappers when annoyed exploded with "Jeehosphet an' Pigeon Pie"), or his infliction of Victorian prudery on the frontiersmen ("I have endeavoured to Christianize *my* trappers as much as lay in my power").[47] Instead his cardinal sin was to parade as such an unquestioned authority that his wildest misstatements would be believed. Who could doubt an author who urged his readers to follow the southward course of the Pecos River on a map of North America, then cautioned: "Your map is not correct, as for several miles the Pecos runs within degrees of the east."[48] There was little of the truth in Mayne Reid's works, but rare was the reader who could challenge his misstatements.

The Impact of the Western

Despite their faults—or perhaps because of them—the works of Reid and Aimard and Möllhausen, and dozens like them, found a ready market in Europe. French books were translated into English, German into Norwegian, English into Hungarian. Friedrich Gerstäcker was a best-seller in Hungary; Poles and Norwegians ranked Möllhausen among their most popular writers. Three of Mayne Reid's novels were published in Norwegian translation in a single year; Gustave Aimard's works were so sought-after in the Netherlands that thirty-two of his novels were available there at one time, with nine of Gerstäcker's and five of Gabriel Ferry's.[49] Such prominent Dutch journals as *De Hollandsche Illustratie* and *De Nederlandsche Spectator* deemed them worthy of praise, although wondering a bit at their popularity.[50] The Western had found its true niche in the reading patterns of Europeans by the beginning of the 1870s, and was to grow in popularity for generations to come.

It was also to play a role unplanned by the authors in revealing the basic attitudes of those who wrote them far more accurately than of those they wrote about. All displayed the ethnocentrism natural in that day of flag-waving nationalism and incipient imperialism. To a German author all Germans were good and all other nationals bad. In British novels Ger-

[47] Quoted in "The Western American Fiction of Mayne Reid," p. 118; Mayne Reid, *The Wild Huntress* (London, 1861), 3: 75 Mayne Reid, *The Scalp Hunters; or, Romantic Adventures in Northern Mexico* (London, 1851), 1: ix–x.
[48] Mayne Reid, *The White Chief: A Legend of Northern Mexico* (London, 1855), pp. 125–26.
[49] Marcus L. Hansen, *The Immigrant in American History* (Cambridge, 1940), p. 19. Portions of a Norwegian play by P. M. Petersen, *The Frontiersman's Daughter: A Play in Three Acts* has been edited by Ray A. Billington from a translation by Nina Oppedal, and published as "The Wild West in Norway, 1877," in *Western Historical Quarterly* 7 (July 1976): 271–78.
[50] *De Nederlandsche Spectator* 3 (1864): 257; 11 (1872): 202. One of Gerstäcker's stories was published in ibid. 7 (1870): nos. 27–31.

From Karl May, *Das Waldröschen oder die Verfolgung rund um die Erde*
(Dresden, 1902?). (From the collections of the Library of Congress.)

man characters were usually comic blunderers or impractical professors
with odd accents, French lard-eating servants, Irish dim-witted buffoons,
Scandinavians stupid dolts. Americans, or Yankees as they were universally called, were seen as lanky cadavers, gaunt and bony, mouths stuffed
with tobacco, and shifty grey eyes alert for financial gain. They were also
heartless, ready to kill Indians at the slightest excuse. "Yankees, like Mexicans, are evil-doing animals," quoth a French hero disdainfully, "which I
kill if the opportunity arises, without any scruples."[51] Ethnic understanding was hardly the purpose of the Westerns.

They also told a great deal about the countrymen of their authors.
French heroes were inclined to dwell on past glories, talking much of
France's role in the exploration of North America and speaking wistfully
of what might-have-been had the colonial wars been decided differently.
"You French," an Indian reminded them in one, ". . . are the lost children
of history and humanity."[52] German authors looked more to the future
than to the past, as befitting a nation on the verge of unification and greatness. Insufferably disdainful of other peoples, certain of Germany's destined mastery of the world, their heroes exemplified Germanic virtue and
strength in their every word and deed. In their blatant assertion of national superiority they unwittingly displayed the doubts and insecurity
natural in a young nation yet to prove its greatness.[53]

No such insecurity haunted Britain's writers. Their nation stood atop
the world in those days; there was no need for any stout English lad to
apologize for anything he thought or did. Nor was there need to look
backward to a golden past; British concern was for the future and her own
expanding empire. Her writers saw the frontier not as a nostalgic re-
minder of Nature's glories or as a sanctuary for the Noble Red Man, but
as a garden of resources waiting exploitation by an advancing Anglo-
American civilization. They shed no tears for the vanishing Indian or the
ravaged wilderness; both must give way to material progress.

Their purpose was to hurry this advance. England's authors, knowing
that their books were read largely by boys from upper-middle-class families, deliberately larded their adventure stories with information useful to
future governors of their country's trading network. To teach these lads
botany and geography and the American way of life would be to assure
greater profits for themselves and their country. So they crammed their
books with encyclopedic information on the flora and fauna of the West.
"Would it not be interesting, Basil," says one of Mayne Reid's youthful
characters, "if Lucian would give us a botanical description of all these

51 Paul Duplessis, *Le Batteur d'estrade* (Paris, 1862), 1: 19.
52 Pierre Paël, *Les Derniers Hommes rouges* (Paris, 1896), p. 8.
53 Ashliman, "The Novel of Western Adventure in Nineteenth Century Germany," pp.
140–41, develops this point well.

trees and tell us of their uses?" Lucian responded, of course, with a deadly chapter on the life cycle of the mulberry tree.[54] Dull stuff it must have been for the young readers, but they did learn more than they probably cared to know about the frontier.

The ethnic traits mirrored in Westerns of mid-century cast light on the national traits of the day, but they contributed little to an accurate image of the far western frontier. Yet that image was to be distorted still more by another group of writers who emerged during the last decades of the nineteenth century.

The Sensationalists

Their appearance was made possible by a remarkable spread of literacy among Europe's middle and lower classes after mid-century, and by technological innovations in printing that lowered the cost of the books to their financial level. For the first time in history a mass audience existed for stories geared to the unsophisticated tastes of the newly educated—stories that were fast-moving, uncluttered by complex plots or characterizations, and packed with the violence and primitive emotionalism that appealed to the uncultured. Here was a market for cheap thrillers that no hack writer could resist.

Basic to this revolution was the spread of common schooling as industrialization provided a tax base for a public educational system. In England the Elementary Education Act of 1870 required free compulsory schooling for all children between the ages of five and ten; six years later a second measure decreed penalties for parents who did not assure their offspring adequate instruction in reading, writing, and arithmetic.[55] Sweden's Riksdag as early as 1842 passed a measure requiring each parish to maintain a school, and gradually this goal was achieved. Germany's educational reforms were so effective that by the 1890s some seventy percent of the people could read and write. The story was much the same for all western Europe.

At the same time the costs of books and magazines was drastically reduced by technological innovation and mass-marketing techniques. Particularly important was the "colporteur system" that was devised in Germany and soon spread elsewhere. Responsible were a number of young publishers who began hiring door-to-door salesmen—known as colporteurs—to peddle their books on the installment plan, with the first chapter

[54] Mayne Reid, *The Boy Hunters; or, Adventures in Search of a White Buffalo* (London, 1853), p. 84.
[55] Mercy Muir, *English Children's Books, 1600–1900* (London, 1954), pp. 148–49; Dorothy B. Skårdal, *The Divided Heart: Scandinavian Immigrant Experience through Literary Sources* (Bloomington, 1974), p. 139.

given away or sold at a pittance, and those following at ten pfennigs. Few could refuse such a bargain, for the tiny weekly payment was within the reach of all. By the end of the century some ninety percent of the German people were buying books under this plan; they were also purchasing lurid paperbacks at the bargain prices made possible by mass production—"three-penny-bit books" they were called.[56]

If the educational and publishing revolution dictated the size of the market for sensational Westerns, two imports from the United States helped shape their plots and characters. One was the flood of dime novels that inundated England—and to a lesser extent all western Europe—during the 1870s and 1880s. Publishing reprints of these lurid American paperbacks was a profitable business, for until the International Copyright Law of 1891 they could be "pirated" without the expense of royalties to their authors.[57] Rare was the British publisher who could resist.

The first to be imported set the tone, a hair-raising adventure story of the New York frontier by a popular author, Edward Ellis: *Seth Jones; or, The Captives of the Frontier*, published in London in 1861 as Number 1 of "Beadle's American Library." During the next five years Beadle's American Library added sixty more titles to its list, then, after transfer to the respectable firm of George Routledge & Sons, eighty-four more. It was soon challenged by a second series, "Beadle's Sixpenny Tales," with such authors as the famed Ned Buntline, and such titles as *Thayendenega the Scourge; or, The War Eagle of the Mohawks*.[58] This was only the beginning; over the next years dime novels and their "penny-dreadful" imitators flooded England with trashy adventure stories about the American West, each outdoing the last in violence and bloodshed. Most important; they followed their American counterparts in gradually shifting their scenes of adventure from the forested frontiers of the East to the Great Plains and deserts of the Far West.

This trend was hastened by another import from the United States: Buffalo Bill Cody's "Wild West Show." William F. Cody, a minor scout and plainsman, had won unjustified fame as the hero of some two hundred dime novels, and as an actor of less-than-questionable histrionic ability when he decided to capitalize on his popularity with a brand-new form of entertainment. His "Wild West Show" opened in St. Louis in 1883, complete with a stagecoach robbery, riding and shooting contests, gunfights galore, and enough howling Indians to terrify any audience. Such was its

[56] Ronald A. Fullerton, "Creating a Mass Market in Germany: The Story of the 'Colporteur Novel,' 1870–1890," *Journal of Social History* 10 (March 1977): 265–68.
[57] Clarence Gohdes, *American Literature in Nineteenth Century England* (New York, 1944), pp. 14–25, 106–7.
[58] Albert Johannsen, *The House of Beadle and Adams and Its Dime and Nickle Novels* (Norman, 1950), 1: 38–39, 113–20; 2: 48.

success that after a few years of touring the United States a wider audience seemed feasible. In the spring of 1887 the whole troupe—240 performers, and a menagerie of buffalo, long-horned steers, and bucking horses—landed in England to a fanfare of publicity that was any showman's dream. Here was the real West brought to Britain's doorstep, and the press joined in a chorus of greeting. "An event of first-class international importance," the *London Illustrated News* called it, and there was no dissent.[59]

A series of well-publicized command rehearsals before Prime Minister William E. Gladstone, the Prince of Wales, and Queen Victoria herself heightened anticipation for the grand opening on 9 May 1887. Earl's Court, a sporting arena holding forty thousand persons, had been transformed with an artificial hill, trees to hide lurking Indians, and a background of Wild West scenery. There an entranced audience at a shilling a head watched enraptured as William Sweeney's Cowboy Band blared its opening fanfare and the show went on; Pony Express riders sweeping across the prairie, the Deadwood stage attacked by Indians, a raid on a settler's cabin with real fire and smoke, bucking horses, feats of skill by trick riders, expert marksmanship by Buffalo Bill and Annie Oakley, all climaxed by the refighting of "Custer's Last Stand."

Londoners loved it; "the most thoroughly howling success that America ever sent abroad," one critic opinioned.[60] By autumn, however, the flood of shillings was slowing and the troupe moved on to play in Britain's major cities before returning home in the spring of 1888. A year later they were back again with an expanded company, to stage their grand premier at the Exposition Universale in Paris before fifteen thousand of the "most notable persons in Europe"—according to one exuberant observer.[61] By autumn the show was on the road once more, this time to perform in the principal cities of southern France before journeying on to Spain, Italy, Germany, and Belgium. By the fall of 1892 most of the Continent had seen "Guillaume Le Buffle" and thrilled to "Le Dernier Combat de General Custer."

More was to come. Buffalo Bill's first imitator was Dr. W. F. Carver, a celebrated marksman, who toured Europe in 1889 with twenty-five per-

[59] Quoted in Carolyn T. Foreman, *Indians Abroad, 1493–1938* (Norman, 1943), p. 202. This account of Wild West shows abroad relies heavily on the excellent book by Don Russell, *The Lives and Legends of Buffalo Bill* (Norman, 1960). I have also used to my advantage Clifford P. Westermeier, "Buffalo Bill's Cowboys Abroad," *Colorado Magazine* 52 (Fall 1975): 277–98, and the reminiscences of the show's general manager: Nate Salsbury, "The Origins of the Wild West Show, Wild West at Windsor, At the Vatican," *Colorado Magazine* 32 (July 1955): 204–14.
[60] Quoted in Russell, *Life and Legends of Buffalo Bill*, pp. 334–35.
[61] *New York Herald*, 19 May 1889, quoted in Westermeier, "Buffalo Bill's Cowboys Abroad," p. 289.

forming Indians hired from reservations. Others followed regularly, the most famous headed by a showman called "Pawnee Bill," until in all, some forty companies crisscrossed the European countryside. Buffalo Bill's own show, splendidly renamed "Buffalo Bill's Wild West and Congress of Rough Riders," returned in 1903 for another triumphant tour that was repeated yearly thereafter.[62] The American cowboy was better known in Europe at century's end than the president of the United States.

His fame was heightened by the flood of Buffalo Bill novels that began appearing in 1887 to capitalize on his first tour, all bound in pink paper bearing such titles as *The Life and Adventures of Buffalo Bill; or, Cowboy Life in the West.* These soon gave way to sturdier fare as publishers leaped to the challenge. One printed over seven hundred titles as the "Original Buffalo Bill Library," with such names as: *Buffalo Bill's Red Rescuer, Buffalo Bill and the Mormons,* and *Buffalo Bill's Boy Pards;* a rival series known as the "New Redskin Library" featured Cody as a gun-toting hero.[63] The craze spread to Germany where publishers in Leipzig and Dresden hurried dozens of *groschenromane* into the bookstalls as *Der Kampf im Sakramenti-Fluss* and *Buffalo Bill die Sioux-Schlacht am Grabstein.*[64] Everywhere in Europe youthful enthusiasts donned western garb, fashioned imitation six-shooters, and dreamed of the day when they could ride hell-for-leather across the plains with Buffalo Bill.

The Buffalo Bill fad, coinciding as it did with the vogue of the dime novel in America and Europe, basically altered Europe's image of the West. Until this time the frontiersman-heroes of novels written there were frozen into the Fenimore Cooper mold; all were transplanted Natty Bumppos adventuring in forest depths and matching skills with woodland Indians. This tradition continued strong on the Continent until into the twentieth century, but in England where the American influence was strongest, the setting gradually shifted to Buffalo Bill's Great Plains and deserts, with the plainsman and the cowboy replacing the hunter in the hero's role. The plainsman had been exploited in the past, but the cowboy made his first appearance in 1887 in a novel by Prentiss Ingraham, a professional writer of dime novels, and sprang into instant popularity. Well he might, for he admirably fitted the stereotype American as Europeans pictured him: rugged, somewhat brutal, fiercely independent, self-made, democratic save to Indians and Mexicans, and the personification of bravery.[65] Here was a hero worthy of the role.

[62]   Westermeier, "Buffalo Bill's Cowboys Abroad," pp. 290–95.
[63]   Russell, *Life and Legends of Buffalo Bill,* pp. 278–79, 401–2.
[64]   Ashliman, "American West in Nineteenth Century German Literature," pp. 225–26.
[65]   Marshall W. Fishwick, "The Cowboy: America's Contribution to the World's Mythology," *Western Folklore* 11 (April 1952): 85–86; Jules Zanger, "The Frontiersman in Popular Fiction, 1820–1860," in *The Frontier Re-examined,* ed. McDermott, pp. 141–42.

The authors who catapulted plainsmen and cowboys into the limelight were many, most of them now mercifully forgotten. Their books were hurriedly written, couched in language guaranteed not to tax the abilities of the semiliterate, free of all complexities in characterization, and so cheaply printed that they were sure to self-destruct within a few years. Not many have survived, and even these are virtually unknown to literary scholarship. Yet they played a major role in creating an image of the frontier that persisted in the European mind. Three deserve attention for their influence, if not for their literary merits.

Robert M. Ballantyne lived for six years in the Canadian West as a clerk for the Hudson's Bay Company before returning to England to write seventy-one books on such themes as *The Wild Man of the West: A Tale of the Rocky Mountains* and *The Red Man's Revenge: A Tale of the Red River Flood*—all of them fast-paced adventure tales of questionable stylistic excellence.[66] Of even lesser storytelling skill was Bracebridge Hemyng, whose "Jack Harkaway" tales usually appeared first in boys' magazines—*Up To Date Boys*, or *Jack Harkaway's Journal for Boys*—then were reprinted as *Jack Harkaway on the Prairie*, *Jack Harkaway Out West amongst the Indians*, and *Jack Harkaway in Search of the Mountain of Gold*. The last and best of this trio, George A. Henty, was a respectable literary stylist whose historical novels won him acclaim among the youth of England and America. Most of his seventy-seven books dealt with the empire but he was unable to resist the western adventure as testified by such hair-raisers as *Captain Bayley's Heir: A Tale of the Gold Fields of California*, *The Golden Canyon*, *Redskin and Cow-Boy: A Tale of the Western Plains*, and *In the Heart of the Rockies: A Story of Adventure in Colorado*.[67]

In all the boy-heroes were unabashedly British lads who never forsook the King's English or their country's ways, peppering their speeches with "By jove, I thought my last hour had come," or assuring grizzled trappers that there was "nothing like a good cup of tea out in the wilds to put life in one."[68] Each was supremely confident, fully aware (as one of them put it) that in his blood ran "a large share of the restless spirit of enterprise that has been the main factor in making the Anglo-Saxons the dominant race of the world."[69] No crisis was too great to disturb their faith in themselves and their homeland. Even death was faced with British determination; one who had been captured and heard the redskins discussing tortures they

---

[66]   Eric Quayle, *Ballantyne the Brave: A Victorian Writer and His Family* (London, 1967), is a useful biography.
[67]   Henry's books on the West are listed in Louis Coffin, "George Alfred Henry: A Bibliographical Study," *Bulletin of Bibliography* 19 (May–August 1849): 241–43.
[68]   Bracebridge Hemyng, *Jack Harkaway Out West amongst the Indians* (London, n.d.), p. 21; G. Manville Fenn, *To the West* (London, 1891), pp. 199–200.
[69]   George A. Henry, *In the Heart of the Rockies: A Story of Adventure in Colorado* (London, 1895), p. 16.

would inflict on him told himself: "I will be brave and dignified. Everybody respects bravery, and I will die like a Briton."[70] No parcel of Indians could subdue the free spirit of an Englishman. All, too, were determined to return home after they had made their fortunes; one, isolated in Oregon, consoled himself with the thought that if all went well, he would "return in two or three years with ample means to live once more in dear old England."[71] The frontier was a nice place to visit, but no self-respecting Briton would want to live there.

This was a far cry from the days a century earlier when romanticism ruled and Europeans dreamed of the revitalizing impact of the virgin forests of America on them and their decaying Continent. Frontiers now existed only to be conquered; Nature must give way to civilization no matter the tools used in its conquest. When a British schoolboy tried to start a fire by rubbing sticks together as had Natty Bumppo he "voted Fenimore Cooper a fraud."[72] Even the weaponry used by British heroes was designed to eliminate the largest number of enemies in the shortest amount of time, whatever its effect on traditional English sportsmanship. Jack Harkaway, besieged with his friends by a band of Sioux, filled a trench with nitroglycerine and blew them to bits as they approached; on another occasion his companions used a balloon to drop hand grenades on the Indian camp where Jack was held captive.[73] Utilitarianism overbalanced tradition and romance by the century's end. Success was measured in pounds-sterling, not by notches on a rifle stock.

Episodes such as these underlined the gap between British image-makers and those picturing the Far West to Europeans. In Germany traditionalism still reigned, even though novelists shifted their adventure stories to the plains and mountains and employed plainsmen rather than forest-hunters as their heroes. Those who made this transition were many, but three won special prominence.

Two of these have been forgotten today. Friedrich Pajeken, a merchant seaman who lived for a brief period in the United States, began writing in the late 1880s and was guilty of such thrillers as *Bob der Fallensteller* (1889), *Bob der Städtegründer* (1891) and *Jim der Trapper* (1892)—all picturing the frontier as a land of terror and lawlessness.[74] Even better known in his day—and unknown today—was Wilhelm Frey, or Fricks, whose production-line techniques produced fifty-nine books between

[70]   F. M. Holmes, *Raff's Ranche: A Story of Adventure among Cow-Boys and Indians* (London, 1901), p. 97.
[71]   E. R. Shuffling, *The Fur Traders of the Far West*, quoted in James K. Folsom, "English Westerns," *Western American Literature* 2 (Spring 1967): 11–12.
[72]   C. Phillipps-Wolley, *Snap: A Legend of the Lone Mountain* (London, 1899), p. 95.
[73]   Hemyng, *Jack Harkaway Out West amongst the Indians*, pp. 63–64, 69.
[74]   These writers are discussed in Barba, "The American Indian in German Fiction," pp. 171–72.

1887 and 1890, another seventeen between 1891 and 1894, fifty-five more between 1895 and 1898, and another forty-six between 1899 and 1902, nearly all set in the West, exactly sixty-four pages long, and aimed at a juvenile audience capable of reading about *Die Apachen am Rio Grande, Das Blockhaus*, and *In Indianerhänden*. [75]

The last of this trio was by far the best and belongs in a different category as an image-maker. Karl May never saw the American West, but his seventy books, about half on the American frontier, shaped the views of millions of Europeans and are still influential today. Born near Dresden in 1842 and only sketchily educated, he wasted much of his youth behind prison bars before writing his first Western in 1875. [76] In it he introduced his alter ego and favorite hero, also named Karl, who appeared in St. Louis as a brönzed, blue-eyed German demigod with a Tarzanesque physique and unimpeachable Teutonic standards. His potential as a *Westmann* was immediately recognized by a famous gunmaker, Mr. Henry (a German, of course), who found him a job on a railroad-surveying party. Not far from St. Louis the surveyors were captured by a band of Kiowa. When their chief challenged Karl, the strongest of the lot, to a duel he suggested that they battle with their fists to avoid the bloodshed that he abhorred, and knocked the Indian out in one blow. "We really should call you 'Old Shatterhand,' " suggested one of the surveyors. "Thus, entirely without my consent," Karl adds, "I was outfitted with a war name that I have borne ever since. That is the custom in the West." [77] (May's novels overflowed with western "customs".)

Karl and his companions were freed by the Kiowas, but were captured almost immediately by a party of Apaches (distances shrank miraculously

---

[75] Christian G. Kayser, *Deutsche Bücher-Lexikon, oder Vollständiges Alphabetisches Verzeichnis der von 1700 bis zu Ende 1910* 26 (1887–90): 665; 27 (1891–94): 845; 30 (1895–98): 919; 32 (1899–1902): 943. I have edited one of Frey's stories in a translation by Brita Mack, as Wilhelm Frey, *The Apaches of the Rio Grande: A Story of Indian Life* (Glendale, Calif., 1978).

[76] By far the best study of May in English is Richard H. Cracroft, "The American West of Karl May," (M.A. thesis, University of Utah, 1963); the author has been kind enough to loan me a copy and allow me the free use of his findings. He has summarized some of his research in "The American West of Karl May," *American Quarterly* 19 (Summer 1967): 249–58. Extracts from several of May's novels with appropriate commentary are in Ernst A. Stadler, "Karl May: The Wild West under the German Umlaut," *Missouri Historical Society Bulletin* 21 (July 1965), while additional information is in Ralph S. Walker, "The Wonderful West of Karl May," *American West* 10 (November 1973): 28–33. The reactions of a German who read May's novels as a boy are in Joseph Wechsberg, "Winnetou der Wild West," *Saturday Review* 45 (20 October 1962): 52–53, 60–61, reprinted with useful notes by Richard H. Cracroft in the *American West* 1 (Summer 1964): 32–39. Klaus Mann, "Karl May, Hitler's Literary Mentor," *Kenyon Review* 2 (Autumn 1940): 391–400, reprinted in *Living Age* 352 (November 1940), as "Cowboy Mentor of the Führer," places the blame on May for many of Hitler's ideas and actions.

[77] Karl May, *Winnetou I: Ungekürzte Ausgabe* (Vienna, 1953), pp. 92–93. All of my footnotes to May's works are to this and similar reprint editions used by my research assistant in Germany, Michael Kuckhoff, and translated by Geoffrey Cocks.

for Karl May) who took them to their "pueblo" where he met the chief, Itschu-tschuna and his son Winnetou.[78] Winnetou wore a light linen robe and carried a book "on whose spine in large gold letters was emblazoned the word 'Hiawatha.' " Shatterhand was amazed. "Longfellow's famous poem in the hands of an Apache Indian! I would never have dreamed of such a thing."[79] His amazement grew when he found that Winnetou spoke fluent German and ended his lengthy speeches with "Howgh, Ich habe gesprochen," to which his tribesmen answered "Uff Uff."[80]

This remarkable Indian's literary tastes did not save the captives from the usual Apache tortures, allowing Shatterhand to prove himself so brave that he was adopted into the tribe as the chief's son in a ritualistic ceremony in which he and Winnetou drank each other's blood. "You are now exactly the same as Winnetou," the old chief told him, "the son of my body, a warrior of our people."[81] Thus began a friendship that lasted through several thousand pages and fourteen years of wandering together, hunting down outlaws, saving homesteaders from attacks by gangs of tramps, outwitting Yankee villains, rescuing damsels from the hands of evil Comanches, and blazing a path of virtue across the plains and mountains of the West. Their adventuring only ended when Winnetou threw himself in front of a bullet intended for Old Shatterhand and died in his blood-brother's arms as Karl sang the Ave Maria and administered the *Nottaufe*, or private baptism that would assure a place in the "eternal hunting ground of the Christians." As the last words of the song faded Winnetou whispered: "*Scharlih*, I believe in the Savior. Winnetou is a Christian. Farewell."[82]

Winnetou and Old Shatterhand were Karl May's favorite characters but there were many more, each more improbable than the last, but all models of Teutonic virtue: Old Firehand, Old Surehand, Old Death, Old Wabble. All were mountaineers or plainsmen (May despised cowboys and miners, those greedy grubbers after the "deadly dust"); all were glamorously clad in fringed leather jackets and leggings ornamented with the paws and ears of grizzly bears or, in Old Shatterhand's case, with "hummingbird skins in which Indian symbols were carefully cut."[83] All were animated arsenals, weighted down with revolvers, bowie knives, lassos, and rifles such as Shatterhand's two-barreled *Bärentöter* and twenty-five-shot *Henrystutzen*. All were reincarnated Germanic Galahads, bent on

[78] May apparently realized that Apaches did not normally live in pueblos, for Shatterhand is told that "only the Mescaleros are an exception and even among them only the chief's family and some subordinates." Ibid., p. 155.
[79] Ibid., p. 151.
[80] Cracroft, "American West of Karl May," pp. 255–56.
[81] May, *Winnetou I*, p. 208.
[82] Karl May, *Winnetou III* (Vienna 1951), p. 241.
[83] Karl May, *Der schwarze Mustang* (1896; reprint ed., Vienna, 1952), p. 19.

From Karl May, *Das Waldröschen oder die Verfolgung rund um die Erde* (Dresden, 1902?). (From the collections of the Library of Congress.)

clearing the West of desperados and bad Indians, and glorying in their missions of mercy. They bore slight resemblance to the rough-and-ready plainsmen of actuality, but they won the hearts of Germans as did the creations of no other author.

For Karl May's books were purchased over the next years by over thirty million people, translated into twenty languages, and read by an estimated three hundred million persons. Karl May was Adolph Hitler's favorite author—and Albert Einstein's. To generations of Europeans he was Germany's James Fenimore Cooper—"the greatest writer since Homer."[84] Even in the soberer judgment of a leading journal, *Der Spiegel*, May's influence was "greater than that of any other author between Johann Wolfgang von Goethe and Thomas Mann."[85] His image of the American West was cast wide indeed.

May's popularity far surpassed that of any other European writer of Westerns, but the sale of any book laid in that glamorously romantic land was surprisingly large. Circulation figures are nonexistent, of course, but occasional bits of evidence reveal the demand. A respectable British library reported that the call for books by Fenimore Cooper, Mayne Reid, and Robert M. Ballantyne exceeded that for the works of Walter Scott and Charles Dickens.[86] The tawdry paperbacks of Wilhelm Frey sold more widely in Norway during the 1880s than those of any author, foreign or native. So great was the demand for books about the West in Scandinavia that publishers deliberately falsified titles to capture readers: one called *Among the Redskins* was actually a love story set in a local village; another, *Gold Prospectors of California*, was not about California at all,[87] but Australia. Books about the American frontier were in vogue, and few others could rival them.

And why not? Asked a capable Norwegian novelist as he surveyed bookstalls laded with "blood-reeking adventure stories," what red-blooded youngster could resist such titles as *The Blood Drinker of Tonqua Taba*, or *A Fight With the Indians; or, Life and Death?* "Who," he went on, "was Hannibal, or Scipio, or Alexander, or Napoleon, or Gustav Adolphus compared to 'Falcon-eye' or 'Rattlesnake,' or any of the other heroes who fought their summer battles in the heart of the forest primeval?"[88] What respectable novelist could grip his readers with such lines as: "Suddenly in the darkness he felt a lithe, sinewy hand grip his shoulders from behind,

---

[84] Wechsberg, "Winnetou of der Wild West," p. 52.
[85] "Karl der Deutsche," *Der Spiegel* 16 (12 September 1962): 73.
[86] Sara Keith, *Mudie's Select Library. Principal Works of Fiction in Circulation in 1848, 1858, and 1868* (Ann Arbor, 1955), quoted in Steele, "Image of America in the Novels of Mayne Reid," p. 289.
[87] Unpublished essay, "Colportage and Related Problems," by my research assistant in Norway, Nina Oppedal, currently in my possession.
[88] Bernt Lie, *Sorte Ørn og andre Guttefortellinger* (Oslo, 1894), p. 7.

and then dart at his throat. He whipped out his knife in a moment and dashed its sharp point into the aggressive hand."[89] Here was the stuff of adventure, and few readers could resist.

The overwhelming appeal of the Westerns to Europeans underlined their significance as image-makers. The land that they pictured was far from attractive to sober folk: there plainsmen and Indians, settlers and outlaws, vigilantes and homesteaders were in constant conflict. There each man enforced the law with bowie knife or revolver or the lyncher's rope. There robbery was a daily event and neither life nor property safe. The West of the novelists, in other words, was suited only to the fool-hardy and the brutal, and was entirely unfit for men and women who wanted to live in peace as they tilled the soil.

This hostile image posed a problem for the millions of Europeans who were tempted by the freedom of opportunity promised them if they mi-grated to the Land of Liberty. Were the riches and independence prom-ised there worth the risk of the venture? Should they gamble their lives against the hope of freedom, wealth, and equality? That millions during the nineteenth century decided to emigrate to the West testified to the ef-fectiveness of another group of image-makers whose picture of frontier America was so tempting that it was worth the venture.

[89]   Holmes, *Raff's Ranche*, p. 27.

III

The Image-Makers:
Land of Promise

HOW, ONE MIGHT ASK, could Europeans who read the lurid Westerns of the nineteenth century possibly decide to emigrate to the American frontier? Why should they abandon the comforts and security of their homelands to risk their lives amidst violence and mayhem? Why forsake civilization for a wilderness where danger lurked at every crossroads, where orderly legal processes were forsaken, and where existence was of uncertain and brief duration? That thousands upon thousands did migrate is indisputable, for during the century nearly twenty million immigrants reached the United States, with perhaps a majority (until the 1880s) bound for the cheap lands of the West.

They came, obviously, not because their appetite for adventure had been whetted, but because they believed that western America offered a better opportunity for economic and social escalation than the Old World. They had been taught this lesson by a second group of image-makers who trumpeted the frontier as a Land of Promise, where fortunes waited the industrious and equality the oppressed. They came with hope in their hearts, not fear, and they came because the propaganda of this group proved more believable, and more acceptable, than that of the novelists.

Some among these image-makers were out-and-out promoters, bent on fattening their own incomes whatever the cost in human dignity. Included in their ranks were agents of steamship and immigration companies, hirelings of land-grant railroads seeking occupants for the excess acres granted them by a generous government, speculators who had invested heavily in western real estate, and employees of state and territorial immigration agencies paid by the head for settlers lured westward. Others were guide-book authors and editors of "Emigrant Newspapers" who capitalized on curiosity about frontier America. Some were reformers seeking to rid their countries of excess population by picturing the United States and Canada and Australia as modern Edens. Still others were travelers who described their own experiences in the backwoods, or successful im-migrants whose letters home glowed with exciting tales of their own pros-perity and happiness. Most, save the travelers, stood to profit if they could convince Europeans that the West was a land of milk and honey where riches and social prestige awaited all.

Their message found a receptive audience in a Europe where the polit-ical tensions unleashed by the Napoleonic Wars were still unresolved, and where an emerging industrialism disrupted the economic and social life of millions of laborers and peasant farmers. Instability, and a sense of im-pending doom were the facts of life for the common people, and with them a belief that aging Europe had passed its prime and that the star of empire was shifting westward. When Goethe in 1831 sang "Amerika, du hast es besser," he was voicing a growing belief that the wave of the future was sweeping across the Atlantic.

Just at this time the educational revolution opened the vision of a bet-ter world beyond the seas to the economically deprived most likely to respond. School children told their parents of an unsettled paradise where farms were plentiful and rent low, and where tyrannical landlords and meddlesome tax collectors were unknown. Many an immigrant later tes-tified that his ambition to reach the American West was first stirred as he sat in an European schoolroom with a map of the world before him, dreaming of the fortune that waited him in the Land of Gold.[1]

Parents, curious to learn more, and unable to afford or read books and newspapers, began gathering in "Reading Clubs" to hear of American op-portunity. Such groups were most common in Germany and Scandinavia, but played their role everywhere. In most the guiding hand was the local pastor, so eager to aid his parishioners that he would even allow pipe-smoking and an occasional glass of beer to lure them to his sessions. Once there, members reported in succession on books or magazines they had purchased, reading passages now and then that they had painfully mas-tered at home, and leading the others in spirited discussion. More often than not the topic was that Land of Promise that lay to the West, and the

[1] Marcus L. Hansen, *The Atlantic Migration, 1607–1860* (Cambridge, 1940), pp. 150–51, 164.

riches that awaited there.[2] Europe's peasantry, unhappy at home and eager to be on the move, was ready to listen to the siren call of the image-makers.

The Promoters

Of all they heard the most persuasive—and least reliable—were the dollar-hungry promoters who stood to gain personally by luring emigrants to the West: self-seeking agents of railroads, states, and land and immigration companies. The methods used by these "unofficial ambassadors" were of a kind. All distributed glittering brochures and pamphlets, lectured whenever an audience could be assembled, exhibited gargantuan fruits and vegetables "grown in America" at local fairs, advertised widely in newspapers and plastered the countryside with gaudy posters glorifying this Eldorado or that, all conveniently "within three weeks" of Berlin, or Gothenburg, or Copenhagen, or London. Many haunted the embarkation ports, button-holing emigrants at dockside to convince them that their true Valhalla lay in Wisconsin—or Nebraska—or Oregon. The measure of their success was the number of settlers they attracted, for there was a discernable relation between their activities and the destination of the newcomers. When in the 1880s California sought to determine why it was attracting fewer Europeans than Oregon, it was told: "You keep your state entirely in the dark. If you have lands that can be secured by immigrants we do not know it."[3] Blow your own horn, and loudly, if you want to sell your lands. So the states, and land companies, and speculators, and railroads learned.

And blow they did. Speculating companies set the tone when they began selling vast tracts of western land in the 1840s, just as mass migration was beginning. Texas, then much in the public eye as it fought its revolution and joined the Republic, was the scene of their first campaigns. In Germany the *Mainser Adelsverein* and in England a whole galaxy of Texan land companies—one affluent enough to hire the famed painter, George Catlin, as its agent—began peddling property that they might or might not own. Such was their success that by 1850 the British emigration commissioner was compelled to warn would-be buyers that statements "recently circulated respecting the salubrity of climate, the fertility of soil, and the richness of the mineral productions of Texas, are reported by authority to be greatly exaggerated."[4]

Success spawned imitators, and throughout western Europe selling American land blossomed into a major industry as speculating companies

---

[2] *American Settler*, 27 November 1880.
[3] Quoted in James B. Hedges, "Promotion of Immigration to the Pacific Northwest by the Railroads," *Mississippi Valley Historical Review* 15 (September 1928): 200.
[4] William and Robert Chambers, *The Emigrant's Manual: British American and the United States* (Edinburgh, 1851), p. 113. The Texas settlements are described in Carl of Solms-Braunfels, *Texas, 1844–1845* (Houston, 1936), passim.

multiplied; in Sweden alone the Louisiana Emigration Company, the Western Migration Agency, the Chicago Emigrant Agency, the Columbia Emigration Company, the American Emigrant Company, and a half-dozen more were operating shortly after mid-century. The story was the same in Norway, Denmark, Germany, France, and Great Britain. Most pointed the emigrant stream toward the cheap lands of the West, even warning prospective settlers to "avoid the Atlantic cities, and to distribute themselves throughout the land."[5] Most, too, were careful not to over-exaggerate frontier opportunity lest reality disappoint anticipation; "The company," read one circular, "does not picture an eldorado for the emigrant. The healthy, industrious, and temperate can attain economic prosperity in America, but the lazy and intemperate will fall into greater poverty there than here."[6] Believe our advertising, the companies were saying, and you will not be misled.

Working hard-in-glove with the land and immigration companies were the hundreds of guidebook authors who hurried to capitalize on the sudden demand for information about the United States. In Germany at least one hundred were published between 1827 and 1865; in Sweden more than one hundred fifty.[7] Some were based on actual experience—a fact that their authors never allowed their readers to forget: "I have witnessed the great work of civilization in all its various stages, from the lone cabin to the frontier settler."[8] Others had a lesser claim for their inaccuracies; Moritz Beyer whose *Book for Emigrants* was a best-seller in Holland, and Johan Bolin whose *Description of North America's United States* captured much of Sweden's ma·ket, had never visited the United States. All guidebooks were of a pattern: descriptions of the western states and territories, specific instructions on how to obtain land, suggestions on farming techniques suitable to a converted wilderness, advice on transportation, and page after page extolling the rich soils and bracing climate of the author's favored spot. Most stressed the ease of obtaining a farm in a land where high wages and low land prices allowed "even the poorest to acquire eighty acres of their own after two years."[9] Such exaggerations were typi-

[5]   Quoted in William F. Adams, *Ireland and Irish Emigration to the New World from 1815 to the Famine* (New Haven, 1932), pp. 234–35. Similar advice is in a Dutch guidebook, *De Vereenigde Staten van Noord-Amerika en de landverhuizing derwaarts* (Tiel, 1846).
[6]   Florence E. Janson, *The Background of Swedish Immigration, 1840–1930* (Chicago, 1931), pp. 233–34. The same point is made in George M. Stephenson, "The Background of the Beginnings of Swedish Immigration, 1850–1875," *American Historical Review* 31 (July 1926): 717–18.
[7]   A list of all Swedish guidebooks is in Oscar F. Ander, *The Cultural Heritage of the Swedish Immigrant: Selected References* (Rock Island, 1956), pp. 36–53.
[8]   John B. Newhall, *The British Emigrants' Handbook and Guide to the New States of America* (London, 1844), p. viii.
[9]   Quoted in Bertus Wabeke, *Dutch Emigration to North America, 1624–1860* (New York, 1944), p. 98.

cal. Strive though they might for objectivity, few guidebook authors could resist a bit of "puffing" now and then.

This was even more the sin of promoters seeking to peddle the 180,000,000 acres awarded the land-grant railroads. The first of these lines, the Illinois Central Railroad, set the pattern in 1854 when it named an emigration agent for Sweden and Norway with instructions to travel about the rural counties, lecturing, distributing promotional literature, placing advertisements in newspapers, and mingling with prospective customers at social gatherings. A similar campaign in Germany was expanded to include bribing German-American clergymen to speak glowingly of western farming when vacationing in their homelands, and employing an eminent geographer, Dr. J. G. Kohl, to exaggerate the richness of the company's territories in a supposedly impartial guidebook: *Reisen im Nordwesten der Vereinigten Staaten.*

The results were so spectacular that in 1862 the Illinois Central embarked on a major expansion program, thus setting a pattern that other railroads were to imitate. This included full-time agents in Germany, the Scandinavian countries, and Great Britain, each with a sizable budget and a share of the profits on every acre sold. Their first step was to hire small armies of salesmen to canvas the countryside for recruits; within four years eighty thousand acres of frontier land in Illinois had been sold in Germany alone. They also were given free rein to employ less-publicized devices. Thus the Scandinavian agents persuaded the Augustana Synod of the Luthern Church, then seeking funds to build Augustana College, to glorify the profits to be made on an Illinois farm in return for a percentage of the returns on all acreage sold. Agents in England not only launched the usual propaganda barrage but hired a member of Parliament, James Caird, to publicize the railroad's lands after a visit there; his report, published as *Prairie Farming in America*, not surprisingly found that the Illinois Central bordered "the greatest tracts of fertile land on the surface of the globe," all so rich that no manuring was necessary.[10]

This campaign was to be copied by all major land-grant railroads built west of the Mississippi, but on a far more grandiose scale. The Burlington, with three million acres of Iowa farmland, was operating on a full scale by the end of 1870, with agents in Germany, Holland, and England distributing posters and handbills, placing newspaper advertisements, and scattering colorful circulars about the table in hotels and rooming houses where emigrants gathered. In England alone 150 were operating by the

[10] James Caird, *Prairie Farming in America* (New York, 1859), p. 37. The campaign of this pioneer railroad for emigrants is admirably described in a major book and an article by Paul W. Gates: *The Illinois Central Railroad and Its Colonization Work* (Cambridge, 1934), pp. 188–219, and "The Campaign of the Illinois Central Railroad for Norwegian and Swedish Immigrants," *Norwegian-American Historical Association Studies and Records* 6 (1936): 66–88.

end of 1871, lecturing, buttonholing prospects and displaying a 250-foot-square "Sylphorama" picturing the lush Iowa countryside. Others in Germany labored valiantly to convince peasant farmers that Americans were so interested in speculation and mechanical gadgets that they would abandon all agriculture to newcomers from Europe.[11]

The railroad image-makers reached their zenith in late 1871 when the Northern Pacific Railroad launched its Bureau of Immigration. By 1883 its agents—carefully selected from the ranks of successful immigrants willing to return to their homelands for a fat fee—numbered no less than 831 in Britain, with another 124 scattered over Norway, Sweden, Denmark, Holland, Germany, and Switzerland. In all they distributed 632,500 publications that year, as well as a specially printed magazine called the *Northwest*. Five years later Northern Pacific agents were advertising in 3,385 newspapers; they were also circulating each year 500,000 maps, 650,000 circulators, the *Northwest* magazine, and several local newspapers, all picturing the northern Great Plains as the Garden of the World, a Land of Opportunity unmatched in all the universe.[12]

Other western railroads fell into line as the campaigns of the Burlington and Northern Pacific lured unexpectedly large numbers of immigrants to their lands: the Santa Fe, the Union Pacific, and the Southern Pacific maintained armies of agents in Europe and squandered gallons of printer's ink on gaudy posters and temptingly worded circulars. Even the smaller lines, unable to afford separate European agencies, sought to tap this bonanza; the railroads of Texas in 1881 created the "Southwest Immigration Company" with each contributing twenty-five dollars for each mile of track they operated to support the propaganda machine it established.[13]

The network of image-makers spread across Europe by the western railroads suffered under a serious handicap: even the most gullible peasant realized that their purpose was to sell land, and hence that their advertising was suspect. The agents did their best to offset this impression, assur-

---

[11]   An excellent account of the Burlington's campaign is in Richard Overton, *Burlington West: A Colonization History of the Burlington Railroad* (Cambridge, 1941). The operations of the London office are described in Ian McPherson, "Better Britons for Burlington: A Study of the Selective Approach of the Chicago, Burlington and Quincy in Great Britain, 1871–1875," *Nebraska History* 50 (Winter 1969): 373–407.
[12]   A standard work on this railroad is James B. Hedges, "The Colonization Work of the Northern Pacific Railroad," *Mississippi Valley Historical Review* 13 (December 1926): 311–42. The firm's London office is described in the *American Settler*, 2 September 1872.
[13]   *American Settler*, 17 September 1881. Efforts of western railroads to attract immigrants are described in: Glenn D. Bradley, *The Story of the Santa Fe* (Boston, 1920), pp. 111–34; William S. Greever, *Arid Domain: The Santa Fe Railway and Its Western Land Grant* (Stanford, 1954); Barry B. Combs, "The Union Pacific Railroad and the Early Settlement of Nebraska, 1868–1880," *Nebraska History* 1 (Spring 1969): 1–26; and Edna M. Parker, "The Southern Pacific Railroad and the Settlement of Southern California," *Pacific Historical Review* 6 (June 1937): 103–19.

ing prospective emigrants: "we have the largest and keenest interest in your welfare and prosperity, both present and future, for upon your welfare and success, year after year, depends our own success and prosperity."[14] Disillusioned settlers, bitter over misleading claims, could do more harm than the railroads could afford.

And why gloss the lily? The truth was sufficiently appealing to need no exaggeration. When a landless laborer in Sweden feasted his eyes on a poster proclaiming HOMES FOR ALL! MORE FARMS THAN FARMERS! MORE LANDLORDS THAN TENANTS! WORK FOR ALL WORKERS, he wanted to believe too much to doubt; when a British cottager opened his paper to an advertisment assuring him that "many men who came here ten or fifteen years ago with little livestock besides a span of horses, a waggon, a plough, and a little livestock, are today quite wealthy and independent" he needed little faith to realize that the door to opportunity was ajar.[15] The American West was a haven for the dispossessed, and the railroads were performing a public service by awakening Europe to its opportunities.

Particularly when they operated side by side with agents of the western states and territories. That governments there should be eager to attract emigrants from Europe was easy to understand: every new settler meant money for the state's coffers in tax payments and support for its economy in exportable agricultural surpluses. Each male immigrant, it was estimated in 1866, was worth $1,500 to the community in the taxes his family would pay and the economic activity he would generate as consumer and producer—with Germans somewhat more valuable and Irish considerably less.[16] These were prizes worth seeking.

And seeking was a recognized necessity, for by the 1850s competition for immigrants between states, railroads, and land companies was at fever pitch. "The means by which emigration is directed to particular quarters of the United States," wrote an expert in 1855, "is now almost reduced to a system."[17] This operated on the sensible belief that European peasants and laborers knew so little about the United States that they could be persuaded to go almost anywhere; "their minds," an agent opinioned with better understanding than grammar, "is a blank sheet."[18] Only a small expenditure in agents and propaganda was needed to bring tax dollars to one community rather than another. The result was a network of conflicting

[14] *American Settler*, 1 August 1883.
[15] Overton, *Burlington West*, p. 267. Printed in this volume, p. 443, is a circular *Das Südliche Nebraska*, describing Nebraska lands. The quotation is from the *American Settler*, 9 October 1880.
[16] David M. Emmons, *Garden in the Grasslands: Boomer Literature of the Central Great Plains* (Lincoln, Nebr., 1971), pp. 48–49.
[17] Quoted in Livia Appel and Theodore C. Blegen, "Official Encouragement of Immigration to Minnesota during the Territorial Period," *Minnesota History* 5 (August 1923): 191.
[18] Quoted in Emmons, *Garden in the Grasslands*, p. 68.

agencies that spread across Europe and influenced the decision of virtually every newcomer on his choice of a home site. And, perhaps equally important, that hurried his departure by painting an unrealistically glowing picture of the frontier Land of Opportunity.

The states entered this competition in 1845 when Michigan named a European agent to advertise for settlers in German newspapers and circulate promotional literature in villages there. Wisconsin followed by appointing a commissioner of immigration in 1852, to be supplemented a decade later by a board of immigration. Within a few months this agency was advertising in fifty-two German newspapers, distributing twenty thousand pamphlets and nine thousand maps yearly. One by one the other states and territories fell into line, with Minnesota's agency under Hans Mattson reaping a particularly impressive crop.[19] By 1870 only Iowa among the states of the Upper Mississippi Valley was making no official effort to lure immigrants, but when figures were released showing that newcomers to Wisconsin were importing $1,045,661 in cash yearly while the few bound for Iowa carried only $248,355, the state awakened to its opportunity. Over the next years every state and territory in the Far West created an immigrant bureau, with California the sole exception.[20]

Most agencies attempted a degree of truth in their propaganda, but with their salaries dependent on a head-count of those they influenced, the temptation to exaggerate was irresistible. Why write that Iowa corn lands produced "forty" bushels to the acre when "eighty" could be written just as easily? Why picture Dakota's winter climate as bone-chilling when "bracing and invigorating" was equally accurate?[21] The agents' principal sin was to print as typical the life-stories of the most successful emigrants; these Horatio-Algerish testimonials were their principal stock in trade, distributed widely in pamphlets, magazines, and newspapers. Although purposely selected "at random," their tales of universal success seemed

[19] The creation of the immigration agencies is well described in ibid., pp. 44–77; their impact is appraised in Merle Curti and Kendall Birr, "The Immigrant and the American Image in Europe, 1860–1914," *Mississippi Valley Historical Review* 37 (September 1950): 207; and Theodore C. Blegen, "The Competition of the Northwestern States for Immigrants," *Wisconsin Magazine of History* 3 (September 1919): 3–29. Mattson's activities are stressed in Lars Ljungmark, *For Sale—Minnesota: Organized Promotion of Scandinavian Immigration, 1866–1873* (Chicago, 1971) and Hans Mattson, *Reminiscences: The Story of an Emigrant* (St. Paul, 1891), pp. 97–99.
[20] Activities in western states are described in Marcus L. Hansen, "Official Encouragement of Immigration to Iowa," *Iowa Journal of History and Politics* 19 (April 1921): 159–95; Orville H. Zabel, "To Reclaim the Wilderness: The Immigrant's Image of Territorial Nebraska," *Nebraska History* 46 (December 1965): 315–24; Arthur J. Brown, "The Promotion of Emigration to Washington, 1854–1909," *Pacific Northwest Quarterly* 36 (January 1945): 3–17; Herbert S. Schell, "Official Immigration Activities of Dakota Territory," *North Dakota Historical Quarterly* 7 (October 1932): 5–24; and Warren A. Henke, "Imagery, Immigration, and the Myth of North Dakota, 1890–1933," *North Dakota History* 38 (Fall 1971): 413–91.
[21] *American Settler*, 4 August 1883.

Die
Apachen am Rio grande.

Eine Erzählung

aus dem Indianerleben

von

W. Frey.

Mülheim a. d. Ruhr,

Verlag von Julius Bagel.

From cover of original edition of Wilhelm Frey, *Die Apachen am Rio Grande*. (From the collections of the University of Texas Library.)

more than coincidental. The farmer who swore that he had arrived in Dakota three years before with nothing save a debt of $5,000 and now owned an 840-acre farm and stock worth $12,000 may have been telling the truth, but he was hardly the run-of-the-mill plains newcomer.[22]

Truthful or not, the agents of land companies, railroads, and the western territories were wonderously effective. Their impact can be measured by the hue and cry raised against them by upper-class Europeans fearful that needed laborers were being drained away by their propaganda. How expect the truth from these hirelings, they asked; "you might as well expect a horse dealer to dwell on the faults of the animal for sale."[23] Their sole purpose was to seduce honest Europeans into buying worthless lands; they were little better than "serpents crawling among naive people under a deceptive name"; "their propaganda was "slow poison . . . introduced into many peaceful and happy families."[24] Even this defense failed, for many a would-be emigrant convinced himself that these wealthy overlords were trying to keep the American West for themselves, and decided to migrate in consequence.

Nor were all upper-class Europeans eager to dam the emigrant tide. Those who sought to keep the labor supply at home were more than balanced by others who believed Europe to be overpopulated, and that its salvation depended on the export of its surplus population. Their concern was not with peopling the United States, but with de-peopling the Old World. Overcrowding lowered living standards and bred poverty and crime, and must be lessened before prosperity and morality could be restored. This was the belief of the editors of the emigration newspapers that multiplied across the Continent. "Here," one wrote, "enforced idleness in the foul haunts of vice; there, healthful employment in the fresh, pure air, face to face with the bountiful provisions of Nature. Here hunger, want and misery; there plenty and prospective independence."[25] Such statements might be inspired by the need to better Europe, but their effect was to picture frontier America as a modern Eden, overflowing with opportunity for the unfortunate.

Most of the emigration newspapers that preached this message were published weekly, sold at a pittance, and filled with information about the American West: how to get there, where to settle, how to obtain land, how to farm. All paraded their objectivity, but most of their information on agricultural conditions and opportunities came from successful emi-

[22] Henke, "Imagery, Immigration, and the Myth of North Dakota," pp. 414–17.
[23] *American Settler*, 13 November 1880.
[24] Sygurd Wiśniowski, *Ameryka 100 Years Old: A Globetrotter's View* (Cheshire, Conn., 1972), p. 14; Friedrich Gerstäcker, *Nach Amerika* (Leipzig, 1855), 4: 86; Malcolm Macleod, *Practical Guide for Emigrants to the United States and Canada* (Manchester, 1870), p. 11.
[25] *Emigration*, 9 March 1891.

grants eager to enhance land values by attracting newcomers to their communities—"to point out to their countrymen the most eligible parts of America for settlement," as one tongue-in-cheek editor put it.[26] Hardly impartial information, certainly, but still more widely believed than that of self-serving railroad or land agents.

Most of the emigration newspapers were published in the countries most likely to contribute to the emigrant system: Germany, the Scandinavian nations, and Great Britain. Some were widely known: in Germany *Die Süddeutsche Auswanderung's Zeitung, Die Hansa,* and *Die Allgemeine Auswanderung's Zeitung;* in Switzerland *Die Schweizer Auswander's Zeitung;* in England *The American Settler, America,* and *Emigration;* in Scotland *Chambers' Information for the People* and *Chambers' Edinburgh Journal.*[27] All, even those in England that preached Malthusian doctrines and tub-thumped for settlement in Britain's own colonies, saw the American West as the nearest and most convenient outlet for Europe's excess citizenry.

And why not? Could distant Australia or South Africa, or even Canada offer a temperate climate, adequate rainfall, and (in the words of the editor) "hundreds of millions of acres of fertile ground, magnificent forests abounding in game, and beneficent streams of incalculable value to the farmer."[28] Pluck and industry would surely be awarded with prosperity beyond the imagination of the Old World. The emigration newspapers that trumpeted this message across northern Europe were immensely popular; they sold at a penny a copy, were passed from hand to hand, and often ended in the libraries of workingmen's clubs where they were read and reread until worn to shreds.[29] Scarce a prospective emigrant in the late nineteenth century but knew the American West as a land of hope and promise. When a traveler in Scandinavia recorded that in peasant home after peasant home he found the promotional literature of states, railroads, and immigration companies "standing in the little bookshelf side by side with the Bible, the prayer-book, the catechism, and a few other reminiscences,"[30] he was offering testimony to the success of the image-makers.

The "America Letters"

Yet the influence of promotional agents was dwarfed by that of the "America Letters" that spanned the Atlantic by the thousands and hundreds of thousands, each bearing word of the success of a friend or rel-

[26] Quoted in Appel and Blegen, "Official Encouragement of Immigration to Minnesota," pp. 193–94.
[27] Hansen, *Atlantic Migration,* p. 150. The purpose of the papers was usually stated in their first issues: *American Settler,* 1 January 1872; *Emigration,* 9 March 1891.
[28] *America,* 2 October 1883.
[29] *American Settler,* 1 February 1782.
[30] Quoted in Curti and Birr, "Immigrant and the American Image in Europe," p. 208.

ative in his New World home; over two million reached the United Kingdom in 1854 alone and nearly half a million were received in tiny Denmark in 1883.[31] All were unabashedly boastful of the writer's wealth and
good fortune; all piled evidence on evidence that any industrious person
could find his pot of gold if he migrated to the Land of Promise. That they
were written in such numbers was tribute to the psychological needs of
the emigrants. All harbored an unconscious fear that they had been exiled
from the homelands, and must justify their move: many suffered from a
compelling urge to appear better than those left behind—the "Royal
Swedish Jealousy" this malady was called—and were incapable of admit-
ting error or lack of success.[32] As each demonstrated the wisdom of his
move by enameling his own triumphs, he convinced his readers that the
America of their dreams was worthy of any sacrifice.

The arrival of every "America Letter" in an Old World village was a
major community event, to be celebrated by the entire populace. The
precious document was hurried to the local minister or schoolmaster first
of all, to be read to the family and a few friends, then read again to a wider
circle or at church services to the entire congregation, then read once more
by relatives and friends attracted from miles away by news of its arrival,
until it literally crumbled away. For days all talk in the hamlet was of
what Michael or Hans or Tobias had said; for weeks every villager
dreamed longingly of the riches waiting beyond the seas.[33]

Their tone varied little, although Germans and Norwegians were
more inclined than Britons to stress the liberties that had been denied
them in their homelands. All dwelt glowingly on the riches accumulated
by the writer, and waiting others bold enough to migrate. Such evidence
was not to be dismissed lightly. Guidebooks or emigration newspapers
might stretch the truth now and then, but who could doubt the word of
friends or relatives? Here was the gospel, not to be questioned. And here
was a new world of reality suddenly opened. Until that letter arrived Ohio
or Nebraska had been distant mirages, mere names on a map. Now Peter
or Ulrich were there and the vision cleared to reveal a bustling village, a
forest cabin, a "spread" on the vastness of the plains. "The people for the
first time," wrote a Norwegian editor, "learn from those of their own
milieu, in their own language, their own way of thinking."[34] The collec-

[31] Kristian Hvidt, *Flight to America* (New York, 1974), pp. 185–86; Arnold Schrier, *Ireland and the American Emigrants, 1850–1900* (Minneapolis, 1958), pp. 21–22.
[32] H. Arnold Barton, *Letters from the Promised Land: Swedes in America, 1840–1914* (Minneapolis, 1975), pp. 16–17.
[33] Accounts by contemporaries of the excitement caused by the arrival of "America Letters" are in Schrier, *Ireland and the American Emigration*, pp. 40–41, and Hans A. Foss, *Tobias: A Story of the Northwest* (Minneapolis, 1899), p. 9.
[34] Quoted in Ingrid Semmingsen, "Emigration and the Image of America in Europe," in *Immigration and American History: Essays in Honor of Theodore C. Blegen*, ed. Henry S. Commager (Minneapolis, 1961), pp. 40–41.

tive effort of the "America Letters" was the rediscovery of America, not by the learned and wealthy who profited from Columbus's landfall, but by the common people who saw the New World as it really was for the first time.

And what a heartening vision that was. Most "America Letters" provided essential information: the cost of the land, the nature of the soils, the wages paid, the conditions of labor. Most, too, told the writer's success story in simple prose: "I have eighty acres fenced, and the grass looking as green as an English lawn"; "I have a small farm of about eighty acres, twenty-four head of cattle, thirty pigs, and two horses and I'm doing all right."[35] An educated Pole who had lived in the West recalled writing hundreds of letters for his illiterate countrymen, all beginning "Praised be . . ." and going on to catalogue the wealth they had amassed down to the last calf and scythe.[36] Mingled with these success stories was word of the opportunity awaiting those bold enough to follow: "I know of eighty acres not far away for sale cheap," or "my Yankee neighbor wants to move; he is asking ten dollars an acre for his farm."[37] Nearly all closed on a note of assurance: "One thing is certain, you can be your own master a good deal sooner."[38]

Their impact was phenomenal. Emigrants repeatedly testified that an "America Letter" from a friend or relative decided their move to the West; one told of word from a former neighbor of an hundred-acre farm on virgin land that "produced such an effect on my mind, that from that moment the desire to cross the Atlantic haunted me like a passion."[39] To those thus afflicted life in the Old World lost its charm. A novelist sensed that transition: "Tobias began to dislike the potato-planting and seeding in the hills around his house; he felt as though he could no longer live exclusively on fish; his house at once became strangely low and narrow, the fjord looked dark and dismal; the boat would no longer cleave the waves as before."[40] Tobias was a victim of the "American Fever" and could never recover. One steerage passenger on an emigrant ship found that each of his fellow travelers, when questioned as to why he was migrating, pulled from his pocket a letter from a son or brother or neighbor and said, "Read this."[41] "Typhoid Mary" was an amateur in spreading a virulent disease when compared with the "America Letters."

Contemporaries who escaped the virus themselves gave ample evi-

---

[35] *American Settler*, 7 August 1880.
[36] Wiśniowski, *Ameryka 100 Years Old*, p. 7.
[37] Quoted in Marcus L. Hansen, *The Immigrant in American History* (Cambridge, 1940), p. 71.
[38] Quoted in Schrier, *Ireland and the American Emigration*, p. 24.
[39] John Regan, *The Emigrant's Guide to the Western States of America* (Edinburgh, 1852), p. 10.
[40] Foss, *Tobias*, pp. 6–7.
[41] Hansen, *The Atlantic Migration*, p. 287.

dence of its fatal impact. A Dutch editor bore witness that each fresh batch of "America Letters" in a village was responsible for a general exodus; a London newspaper blamed the departure of a sizable portion of the population of Cork and Galway on assurance from friends in the West that jobs were plentiful there;[42] a Polish scholar was convinced that the basis of the "mad emigration" from his country that he deplored was "less the promises of foreign agents than the word sent home and the letters written in boastful speech, striking directly to the heart, telling of the success of persons they knew."[43] Here was an appeal difficult to resist for those wanting change.

Particularly when it was reinforced by the direct testimony of "returnees"—successful emigrants who visited their old homes to flaunt their success before jealous friends and relatives. They came by the thousands, clad in carefully selected clothes that radiated affluence, gold watch and chain dangling conspicuously from vest pockets, boots shined to radiance, a hat that only a sheriff or landlord would dare wear in Europe. Often they carried with them examples of the crops their virgin lands had produced, carefully selecting the most gigantic ear of corn, the largest turnip, the most meaty potato, the plumpest grains of wheat.[44]

Their coming created a sensation not unlike that which (one Norwegian villager wrote) "one might imagine a dead man would create were he to return to tell of life beyond the grave"—and could picture Heaven in terms as tempting as the returnees pictured western America.[45] Women vied for the privilege of cooking their meals; they were fawned over by local dignitaries who would have scorned them as menials a year before; strangers came from miles around to gape and to marvel. Day after day, night after night, on the streets or in the homes of friends, they were plied with questions about the riches and liberty of that land of wonders beyond the seas. And when they returned to America, many followed. One Croation lad remembered that when a former fellow townsman visited his village, his pockets overflowing with cash and his clothes mirroring his lavish new way of life, he had scarcely departed when half the townsmen began packing to move.[46] The success stories of the returnees were as irresistible as the tales told by writers of "America Letters."

---

42   Wabeke, *Dutch Emigration to North America*, p. 98; Schrier, *Ireland and the American Emigration*, p. 18.
43   Wiśniowski, *Ameryka 100 Years Old*, p. 8.
44   *American Settler*, 1 January 1872.
45   Theodore C. Blegen, ed., *Ole Rynning's True Account of America* (Minneapolis, 1926), p. 17.
46   Louis Adamic, *From Many Lands* (New York, 1930), p. 56.

The Travelers

The role of travelers as image-makers was less rigidly patterned, for their accounts of western America varied from ecstatic praise to vitriolic denunciation. In sum, however, they must be ranked among those who etched a favorable opinion of frontier opportunity on the European mind, partly because the majority sympathized with the American democratic experiment and deliberately sought to prove its success, partly because would-be emigrants chose to believe those they wished to believe.

Certainly there was no dearth of enthusiastic reporters. Many a hostile witness would have been needed to refute the rapturous picture of western life painted for Germans (and most other Europeans) by Gottfried Duden in his widely translated *Bericht eine Reise nach den Westlichen Staaten Nordamerikas*. Building upon his own experiences as a pioneer in Missouri in the 1820s, Duden described in down-to-earth prose how he cleared the land, the cabin-raisings and play-parties, the enormous yields of his virgin fields, the joys of life without tax collectors, the sense of freedom that he experienced as he realized he could vote and worship as he pleased.[47] Many a German emigrant later testified that he had been moved to migrate by reading that volume.[48]

Few travelers rivaled Duden as propagandists for western America, but their role as image-makers cannot be disputed. Some began arriving early in the nineteenth century, but the mass migration did not begin until the 1840s. By this time the transatlantic crossing was losing some of its terrors as steam-driven vessels replaced the older sailing ships and regularly scheduled packets brought order to the haphazard sailings of the past; the Cunard Line inaugurated regular service from England in 1841 and the Compagnie Génèrale Transatlantique from the Continent a few years later, assuring regular sailings and reducing the passage time from months to nine or ten days. At the same time the railroad network was displacing the slow-moving stagecoaches in spanning the vast distances of western America. Travelers could now visit every nook and cranny of that little-known land without risking life and limb or squandering an undue number of months and dollars.

[47] Gottfried Duden, *Bericht eine Reise nach den westlichen Staaten Nordamerikas und eines mehrjährigen Aufenthalts am Missouri (1824, 1827)* (Elberfeld, 1829). Duden's favorable account was attacked by Gustav Körner, *Beleuchtung des Duden'schen Berichtes über die westlichen Staaten* (1834). Duden answered this attack in his *Die nordamerikanische Demokratie und das von Tocquevillesche Werk darüber als Zeichen des Zustandes der theoretischen Poltik* (1837). The controversy is described in Lawrence M. Price, *The Reception of United States Literature in Germany* (Chapel Hill, 1966), pp. 30–31.
[48] William G. Bek, "Followers of Duden," *Missouri Historical Review* 14 (October 1919): 29–72 to 19 (January 1925): 338–52, reprints diaries and letters from immigrants who testified that they came to America under his influence.

These changes coincided with a growing curiosity about the United
States as evidence mounted that the democratic experiment was succeed-
ing. By mid-century writing travel accounts was becoming a major industry in England, with the Continent not far behind. More than two
hundred were published in Britain in the quarter century before the Civil
War, fifty in Germany between 1815 and 1850, fifty-six in Norway, fourteen in Italy, and eight in Hungary all before 1865.[49] So many were read
in England that they ranked only below "Divinity" in the listings of the
London Catalogue, while critics agreed that the average Londoner knew
more about Chicago and St. Louis than he did about Manchester or
Leeds. Such was the interest in France that two magazines—*Le Tour du
Monde* and *Le Journal des Voyages*—enjoyed brisk sales by concentrating on
articles about the American West.[50]

Nor was the circulation of travel books confined by national boundaries. Mrs. Frances Trollope's *Domestic Manners of the Americans*, an ill-tem-
pered criticism of western society, went through ten editions in England
within a year of its publication in 1832, and within three years was translated into French, Dutch, Spanish, and German.[51] Books by Americans
were equally popular. Edwin Bryant's *What I Saw in California* was offered
in two French and two English editions within a year after it appeared in
1848.[52] Many a Netherlander gained his first impressions of the Far West
from reading Richard Henry Dana's *Twee Jaren voor den Mast* or Balduin
Möllhausen's *Reis van den Mississippi naar de kusten van den Grooten Oceaan*
without realizing that the author of the first was a Yankee and the second a
German.

Read they did, but the question remains: how accurate was the image
projected by travelers? There can be no simple answer to that question.
Visitors to the United States saw not what was there, but what their experiences, beliefs, prejudices, and convictions convinced them should be
there. Their books reflected their diverse personalities, dissimilar backgrounds, conflicting ideologies, and individual loyalties so accurately that
to generalize from their findings would be to deny the reality of human
diversity. Two basic factors, however, seemed to shape the views of most
visitors.

[49] Philip Taylor, *The Distant Magnet: European Emigration to the U.S.A.* (New York, 1971),
pp. 65–66; Andrew J. Torrielli, *Italian Opinion on America, As Revealed by Italian Travelers,
1850–1900* (Cambridge, 1941), pp. 3–4; Anna Katona, "Hungarian Travelogues on the Pre–
Civil War U.S.," *Hungarian Studies in English* 5 (1971): 51–56; Max Berger, *The British Traveller in America, 1836–1860* (New York, 1943), pp. 19–20.
[50] W. S. Shepperson, *Emigration and Disenchantment: Portraits of Englishmen Repatriated from
the United States* (Norman, 1965), p. 11.
[51] Antonello Gerbi, *The Dispute of the New World: The History of a Polemic, 1750–1900* (Pittsburgh, 1973), pp. 477–88.
[52] Doyce B. Nunis, Jr., *Books in Their Sea Chests: Reading Along the Early California Coast*
(Berkeley, 1964), pp. 4–5.

One was personal experience. Those who arrived in the West with open minds and were successful in winning the friendship of the frontiersmen were inclined to overstate the advantages of life along the borderlands; those who expected too much and found too little or who were hostilely received overemphasized the disadvantages. Travelers anticipating a fairyland of abundance and democracy tended (as one guidebook author noted) "to discharge themselves of their ill-natured spleen, by traducing the country and the people."[53] Those with less-elevated expectations, or who were greeted beyond their hopes, leaned too far in the other direction. A would-be emigrant, reading all that had been written about a settlement that interested him, found that "one traveller described it as an earthly paradise, another as a miserable, unhealthy swamp." The truth, he correctly concluded, "is midway between these extremes."[54] When a Norwegian urged his countrymen to beware of English travel accounts "partly on account of British prejudice," he was capsulizing a legitimate criticism of image-makers from all lands.[55]

Ideological and political preconceptions were as destructive of accuracy as personal prejudices. Most nineteenth-century visitors arrived determined to prove or disprove the virtues of democracy, particularly on the frontiers where its extremes—both good and bad—were best exhibited. They came with fixed views, for or against, and both consciously and subconsciously selected evidence to prove their cases. When an Italian visitor "stooped reverently to kiss the land sacred to liberty" on his arrival in the United States,[56] his reaction to frontier life was predictable; he would either venerate each square inch of the West as a cradle of freedom or be so disillusioned by frontier crudity and barbarism that he would overreact negatively.

Those who reached the West with preconceived notions of the frontier as an Eden of democracy included British Whigs, French and Italian idealists, Scandinavians and Germans laboring for greater popular rule in their homelands, and intellectuals from the despot-ridden nations of eastern Europe questing for examples of democracy's success. When the Polish traveler Jakub Gordon dedicated his *Podróż do Nowego Orleanu* (1867) to "the defenders of freedom" he inadvertently proclaimed that his purpose was not an accurate description of his journey to New Orleans but to pen a polemic against the despotic rulers of his country. Books of this ilk may have played their role in mankind's struggle for liberty, but they hardly cast an accurate image of western America.

[53] Calvin Colton, *Manual for Emigrants to America* (London, 1832), pp. 1–2.
[54] William N. Blane, *An Excursion through the United States and Canada, during the Years 1822–23* (London, 1824), p. 157.
[55] Ole Munch Raeder, *America in the Forties: The Letters of Ole Munch Raeder* (Minneapolis, 1929), p. 79.
[56] Henry T. Tuckerman, *America and Her Commentators* (New York, 1864), pp. 344–45.

Nor did those whose authors argued the other side of the case. These were British Tories, Scandinavian aristocrats anxious to protect the labor supply, German disciples of the Metternich school of politics, and French and Italian royalists. Most made no effort to hide their prejudices. "My object," wrote Frederick Marryat whose *Diary in America* (1839) set a pattern for antidemocratic rhetoric, "was to do injury to democracy."[57] Mrs. Frances Trollope, who was even more famed for her acid denunciations, admitted that her chief desire was to persuade Britons "to hold fast by a constitution that ensures all the blessings which flow from established habits and solid principles."[58] She and Marryat were dyed-in-the-wool conservatives yet their invective was matched by Charles Dickens, an avowed liberal. His *American Notes* (1842), and his novel *Martin Chuzzlewit* (1844) expressed his deep frustration when he found the American frontier to be far less than the paragon of equality and culture he had anticipated.[59]

The principal weapon of the antidemocratic critics was to picture the frontier, the acknowledged source-head of American liberty, as a cultural backwash, peopled by tobacco-spitting, dollar-grabbing illiterates whose principal sport was gouging out each other's eyes and biting off each other's noses. "Crakeyrs" and "Gaugeurs," one French visitor labeled them.[60] Travelers such as Thomas Ashe who lavished pages on gory descriptions of nose-biting, ear-clawing, eye-gouging frontier brawls were unblushingly propagandists for aristocratic rule, and were not above stooping to invention to accomplish their purpose. "The stories of shooting men, gouging out their eyes, biting off their noses, etc.," wrote a more sensible observer, "are all romances of times, which if they ever existed, were before my remembrance."[61] Or of the remembrance of anyone, for that matter, for they were the inventions of antidemocratic aristocrats or imaginative frontier tall-tale tellers pulling the leg of a foreign greenhorn by spinning impossibly gory yarns.[62] The result, however, was to convince readers that the West was a land of decadence where brutality reigned.

[57]   Frederick Marryat, *A Diary in America* (London, 1839), 1: 132.
[58]   Frances Trollope, *Domestic Manners of the Americans* (London, 1832), preface.
[59]   Robert B. Heilman, "The New World in Dicken's Writings," *Trollopian* 1 (September 1946): 30–31. Gerbi, *Dispute of the New World*, pp. 468–508, discusses British criticism of this period as a logical continuation of the attacks of de Pauw and others in the seventeenth century.
[60]   Quoted in Durand Echeverria, *Mirage in the West: A History of the French Image of American Society to 1815* (Princeton, 1957), p. 240.
[61]   *Sequel to the Counsel for Emigrants* (Aberdeen, 1834), p. 36.
[62]   Friendly travelers pointed out that American visitors to England could find comparable examples of decadence and brutality in London slums, but that they were hardly typical. Wrote one: "If an American traveler in England were to do the same [seek out instances of violence] he would have no difficulty in proving us the most profligate, unmoral and cheating nation on the face of the earth." Blane, *An Excursion through the United States*, p. 147. A similar comment is in William A. Baillie-Grohman, *Camps in the Rockies* (New York, 1882), p. 27.

"No ye don't." From Mayne Reid, *The Headless Horseman* (London, 1865), 2, opposite p. 313. (From the Special Collections of the University of California at Los Angeles.)

That travelers were as unreliable as land agents or guidebook authors in describing the American frontier seems clear; indeed none among the image-makers could be judged a fountain of truth and accuracy. This was unimportant. What did matter was that millions of Europeans, whatever their reading tastes, were confronted with two diametrically opposed pictures of the successive Wests, one the Land of Savagery projected by novelists and hostile travelers, the other the Land of Promise envisioned by promoters and idealists. This dual image was to persist throughout the nineteenth century, and was to govern the impression of Europeans on the landscape, the Native American peoples, and the frontiersmen themselves.

IV

The Look of the Land

PERSONAL TASTE IS INEXPLICABLE; each of us approves or disapproves of a painting, a poem, or a landscape because of a complex of factors that defy explanation. Many of those have to do with the psychology, temperament, training, and body chemistry of the viewer. Others are the product of the environment in which the viewer has been raised, for "taste" is governed by social mores no less than by individual likes and dislikes. All of us see the world around us through eyes that have been programmed by the prevailing mood. Our views are "learned reactions"; we like what we have been taught to like, and approve what we have been conditioned to approve.

During the late eighteenth century, and well into the nineteenth, Europeans equated Nature wiith beauty. In their reaction against the cold formalism of the Age of Reason they glorified the Creator's splendors, untainted by the artifices of man; the unspoiled wilderness, the mountain cataract, the natural garden unsullied by the human touch, the Noble Savage blessed with virtues drawn from daily contact with the creations of a benevolent Deity. So long as Romanticism shaped Europe's attitudes, the untamed frontiers of the New World would be seen as attractive Edens, needing only the industry of man to rival in beauty and usefulness Europe itself.

Living in such an atmosphere, the tendency of the image-makers was to glorify western America as a land of beauty and rejuvenation, where Nature played a larger role in the purification of man than in decadent Europe. Countering this impression, however, were their own prejudices and misconceptions. Each was inclined to assess frontier America in terms of his own standards and purposes. This allowed each to alter the landscape to suit his own needs. A guidebook author might picture a forested valley as a sylvan paradise only awaiting the plow to blossom with Nature's bounties; a hostile traveler might describe the same spot as a dank swamp, unsuited to human habitation; a sensational novelist might transform it into a horror-land infested with the savage beasts and hostile savages needed to test the bravery of his hero. In other words, the purpose of the image-makers, no less than the prevailing taste in the Old World, helped shape the impression of the frontier held by generations of Europeans.

The result was a multifaceted image of the successive America Wests—hostile or friendly, peaceful or warlike, beautiful or ugly, inviting or repelling, as the whims and prejudices and needs of the image-makers dictated. These images were further distorted by the westward movement of the frontier, for the forests of the East, the prairies of the Midwest, and the plains and deserts of the Far West stirred differing reactions among those who described them. A traveler accustomed to life in wooded areas might view the Great Plains as a barren wasteland, whatever its potential for civilization's use.

Despite the kaleidoscopic patterns that emerged from the variety of influences on the image-makers, they increasingly agreed on one cardinal point: that Nature was an evil to be subdued, not a god to be worshiped. The abrupt about-face from eighteenth-century beliefs was the product of a transformation in popular taste that was itself a by-product of the industrial revolution. As machines increasingly assumed the burdens of production and opened new opportunities for self-advancement, progress and utilitarianism were enshrined as mankind's goals, to be achieved by exploiting, not venerating, Nature. Coal must be ripped from the bosom of the earth, mountains raped of their precious metals, forests leveled to provide fuel. Imperial-minded novelists no longer saw distant lands as pastoral Edens but as sources for raw materials, primitive peoples not as freedom-blessed children of the forest but as potential customers for textiles and shoes and gimcracks.

As the century progressed and the material benefits of industrialization multiplied, men in Europe and America enshrined the machine as their new god. Why worship the creations of Nature when the creations of industry promised to end all want? Nature was weak and impotent, unworthy of the adoration lavished by eighteenth-century romanticists, useless until it had been made useful by man. When travelers could write rap-

turously of the beauty of forests fires as they destroyed virgin timber—
"Where surging flames advance amidst extraordinary crackling"[1]—or note
depreciatingly that "the fruits of the earth are only excellent when subject
to culture,"[2] popular standards had changed mightily since the Age of
Romanticism.

This new mood vastly altered the image of the frontier demanded by
Europeans. The forests and the grasslands of the West were transformed
from beckoning Edens cleansing mankind of the evils of civilization to forbidding barriers to progress—hostile, evil, unwanted—existing only to be
destroyed. So, too, were the Indians converted from Noble Savages to
fossilized relics of an outworn culture blocking civilization's advance—
dirty, slovenly, lazy, indolent—so incapable of adjustment to the modern
world that their elimination was justified. This was the image that deepened steadily as the image-makers followed settlement westward, across
the woodlands and plains and deserts toward the distant Pacific.

The Woodlands Frontier

Nowhere was this transformation better illustrated than in the changing
view of the woodlands frontiers of the eastern United States. To the
romanticists of the eighteenth century the dense forests were bowered
wonderlands, overpowering, in their splendor, the ultimate example of
God's creative genius. François-René, vicomte de Chateaubriand, of
Noble Savage fame, pictured the woodlands as wilderness grottoes where
wild vines twined amidst dazzling festoons of flowers, where flaming cardinals and purple woodpeckers warbled hymns to the glory of their Creator as they flitted from jessamine flower to jessamine flower, where blue
herons and rose-shaded flamingos sported beneath the warming sun.[3]
Here was Nature run riot; here was romanticism unabashed.

The romantic tradition was too strong to succumb immediately to materialism, and for some years after Chateaubriand poets and novelists paid
emotion-laden tribute to the glories of America's wilderness. German
writers especially sang of Nature's wonders; they saw the forests as "more
beautiful than the lovely gardens and fields which men create."[4] Friedrich
Armand Strubberg could sing of a sylvan paradise:

[1] Paul Wilhelm, Duke of Württemberg, *Travels in North America, 1822–1824* (Norman, 1973), p. 383. A similar comment is in Ernest Duvergier de Hauranne, *A Frenchman in Lincoln's America* (Chicago, 1974), 1: 210–11.
[2] Elias P. Fordham, *Personal Narrative of Travels in Virginia, Maryland, Pennsylvania, Ohio, Indiana, Kentucky; and of a Residence in the Illinois Territory, 1817–1818* (Cleveland, 1906), p. 225.
[3] François-René, vicomte de Chateaubriand, *Atala: or, The Love and Constancy of Two Savages in the Desert* (1802; reprint ed., Stanford, 1930), pp. 14–16, 20–21, 44.
[4] Albert Stifter, quoted in D. L. Ashliman, "The American West in Nineteenth Century German Literature" (Ph.D. diss., Rutgers University, 1969), p. 60.

Far from humanity's restless, bewildering pomp
Where never the white man's axe fells the trees.
He could be echoed by Nikolaus Lenau whose verse glorified the wood-
land depths:

Where in marvelous splendor
The trees climb heavenward,
Rearing around the virginal night
They entwine their giant arms.[5]

In these natural wonderlands "the light melted: here glowing and flashing,
there swimming in soft shades while the slim young hickory trunks protruded like flaming golden lanterns in the background," all so breath-
takingly beautiful that the "eye was blinded . . . and scarcely able to comprehend the wonders of the new world."[6] In such rapturous prose there
was no hint of the spirit of materialism that would soon transform beauteous Nature into an unwanted harlot.

Nor were the Germans unique in clinging to the romantic tradition or
glorifying the frontier forest in purple-hued adjectives. Staid British novelists could be just as effusive as they described the "sublimity" of a western world where "the loftiness of the mountains, the grandeur of lakes and
rivers, the majesty of the rocks shaded with a picturesque variety of beautiful trees" testified to Nature's elegance,[7] or as they glorified a sylvan
scene where myriads of "bright-plumed choristers were giving full play to
their untutored melody, . . . while the fall of the cataract . . . sounded
with the solemn unvarying tone which emanates from all things that we
are conscious have been in action since the creation."[8]

In that forested paradise,

Every sound of life was full of glee,
From merry mock-bird's song, or hum of men,
While hark'ning, fearing naught their revelry,
The wild deer arch's his neck from glades, and then
Unhunted, sought his woods and wilderness again.[9]

Here was the glorification of the Earth Goddess writ large. The spirit of
romanticism died hard in Europe.

But die it did, as the materialistic mood gained credence with the century's advance. It was expressed first in descriptions of western rivers, for
here image-makers had their first glimpse of the real West from the decks
of the riverboats that carried them inland. They saw not flower-decked

[5] Quoted in ibid., pp. 68, 94–95.
[6] Friedrich Gerstäcker, quoted in Bjorne Landa, "The American Scene in Gerstäcker's
Fiction" (Ph.D. diss., University of Minnesota, 1952), p. 27.
[7] G. Imlay, *A Topographical Description of the Western Territory of North America* (London,
1792), p. 40; Frances Brooke, *The History of Emily Montague* (London, 1769), 3: 23–25.
[8] Percy St. John, *The Trapper's Bride: A Tale of the Rocky Mountains* (London, 1845), p. 76.
[9] Thomas Campbell, *Gertrude of Wyoming: A Pennsylvania Tale* (London, 1809), pp. 6–7.

bowers and sylvan glades riotous with bloom, but sluggish streams, their banks piled high with rotting timber and the rank scent of decay everywhere. Dante, wrote one, might have described the road to Hell as such a waterway;[10] added another: "all is dull, solitary, gloomy—nothing to cheer, nothing to enliven the mind."[11] Nothing would improve such desolation but the frontiersman's ax. "It will be a long time," wrote a Norwegian visitor longingly, "before the dreary monotony of the woods will be enlivened by the appearance of neat little towns and smiling landscapes with cheerful houses."[12] Man's creations were more desirable than God's.

If the river bottoms were repelling to the image-makers, they found the ultimate in desolation in the depths of the forests. There where arched branches shut out the sun, where the dank ground was cluttered with "fallen masses of wood, often half rotten," where the withered arms of dying trees stretched their naked arms toward the sky, all entwined with creeping plants, all was deadly still, all bespoke death rather than life;[13] "not a breath of wind blows here in the summer, and scarcely a solitary bird is to be heard."[14] Wrote a Norwegian visitor: "You have to have lived in the American primeval forest to realize what solitude and silence is."[15] The hushed stillness, the sense of isolation, created a "strange, almost uncanny, impression," a "mysterious awe" that struck all who ventured into the shady vastness of the woods.[16] When an emigrant experiencing that sensation for the first time exclaimed, "I had imagined the thing quite different from this," he spoke for a Europe sadly misinformed by the romanticists.[17]

None expressed this new realism more scathingly than Charles Dickens when he described the journey of Martin Chuzzlewit to the farm he had purchased unseen in a promotion called "the Valley of Eden." As Martin approached the end of his dreary trip the montonous desolation of the wilderness recalled to his mind the grim domain of Giant Despair.

A flat morass, bestrewn with fallen timber; a marsh on which the good growth of earth seemed to have been wrecked and cast away, that from its decomposing ashes vile and ugly things might arise; where the very trees

[10] Kalikst Wolski, *American Impressions* (Cheshire, Conn., 1968), p. 120.
[11] William Savage, *Observations on Emigration to the United States of America* (London, 1819), p. 12. A similar opinion is expressed in Friedrich Gerstäcker, *The Wanderings and Fortunes of Some German Emigrants* (New York, 1848), p. 117, and the same author's *Nach Amerika* (Leipzig, 1855), 4: 2–3.
[12] Ole Munch Raeder, *America in the Forties: The Letters of Ole Munch Raeder* (Minneapolis, 1929), p. 127.
[13] Gerstäcker, *Wanderings and Fortunes of Some German Emigrants*, p. 131.
[14] *Sequel to the Counsel for Emigrants* (Aberdeen, 1834), p. 21.
[15] "Sketches from Life in North America," *Børnenes Blad* (Norway) 13 (1873), no. 16.
[16] Gerstäcker, *Wanderings and Fortunes of Some German Emigrants*, p. 131; Johannes Scherr, *Die Pilger der Wildnis, historische Novelle* (1853; reprint ed., Hanover, 1917), 1: 101.
[17] Gerstäcker, *Wanderings and Fortunes of Some German Emigrants*, pp. 132–33.

took the aspect of huge weeds, begotten of the slime from which they spring, by the hot sun which burnt them up; where fatal maladies, seeking whom they might infect, came forth at night in misty shapes, and creeping out upon the water, hunted them like spectres until day; where even the blessed sun, shining down on festering elements of corruption and disease, became a horror; this was the realm of Hope through which they moved.[18]

Eden, of course, proved to be a fetid swamp with a few half-finished cabins and a handful of famished outcasts. Martin Chuzzlewit's fate was that predicted by Dickens for all foolish enough to venture onto the frontier.

As if the gloomy forests with their interminable bogs and pestilential swamps were not enough, the image-makers filled the American woodlands with a whole zooful of beasts and reptiles that would test the bravery of a Hercules. True, friendly travelers and guidebook authors dwelt more often on the abundance of edible wildlife than on the predators who menaced settlers; their books were filled with tales of prairie chickens and plump pigeons in flocks so dense that they blotted out the sun, of wild hogs "enjoying unchecked the republican freedom of going at large" and readily available for the family table, of deer so numerous that eight or ten could be counted in the middle of any road, of turkeys and ducks and geese in noisy profusion.[19] Now and then a novelist added a cougar or two to menace the heroine—"slowly advancing along the dead-wood, not by bounds or paces, but with the stealthy tread of a cat"[20]—but this was to be expected more than believed.

No so the accounts of the reptiles that threatened settlers everywhere along the frontiers. Snakes were commonplace; even the authors of guidebooks and "America Letters" admitted that a rattler as large as one's arm might suddenly emerge in a pioneer's cabin after tunneling through a dirt floor,[21] and cautioned newcomers to wear buckskin stockings and boots when walking in the woods.[22] Here was grist for less friendly authors who filled their accounts with hair-raising yarns: of poisonous black snakes

[18] Charles Dickens, *The Life and Adventures of Martin Chuzzlewit* (London, 1844), pp. 284–86.
[19] Mayne Reid, *The Hunters' Feast; or, Conversations around the Camp-fire* (London, n.d.), p. 109; Charles Hooten, *St. Louis Isle, or Texiana* (London, 1847), p. 47; Jean-B. Bossu, *Nouveaux Voyages aux Indes occidentales* (Paris, 1768), 1: 128. A Norwegian guidebook assured emigrants that they needed only a good rifle to supply food for the family for at least two years after the first settlement. Theodore C. Blegen, ed., *Ole Rynning's True Account of America* (Minneapolis, 1926), p. 80.
[20] Mayne Reid, *The Wild Huntress* (London, 1861), 1: 194.
[21] Theodore C. Blegen, ed., *The Land of Their Choice: The Immigrants Write Home* (Minneapolis, 1955), p. 184.
[22] Gustave Unonius, *A Pioneer in Northwest America, 1841–1858: The Memoirs of Gustaf Unonius* (Minneapolis, 1950–51), 1: 287; Wilhelm, *Travels in North America*, p. 114.

who wrapped themselves around their victims' legs, of a campsite where a dozen rattlers had to be killed before tents could be raised, of armies of poisonous snakes infesting every frontier community, of a rattler killed in Illinois found to have 140 young rattlers in its belly, some with even smaller snakes in theirs.[23]

Such stories were hair-raising enough, but even they were embroidered by tall-tale tellers among the image-makers. Europeans learned of a "glass snake" that shattered when struck but immediately reassembled itself to hunt down its attacker, of a "horned hoop-snake," which grasped its tail in its teeth and rolled after its victim with incredible speed, of a monstrous black-spotted yellow serpent called the *piscobia*, which was more deadly than the rattler because it struck without a warning, of giant serpents that could hypnotize their victims with their magnetic gaze.[24] One hunter who took refuge in a hollow log to escape an Indian found himself staring into the beady eyes of such a reptile: "they seemed to emit a magnetic ray—thin, pointed and palpable, that pierced right into his brain."[25] Fortunately the Indian broke the spell by kicking the log, but many a reader shuddered over his possible fate.

The terrors of frontier life amidst this herpetological nightmare were greatest on the southwestern frontier where the slime covered bogs and swamps hid a variety of reptilian horrors: black water snakes, savage turtles, water moccasins, and above all "voracious and ugly alligators" in such numbers that many a hunter lost his life when he made a false step. They were everywhere, sunning on the banks of every stream, "lazily wallowing in the mud" of every swamp, ready to swallow the unwary in a single gulp.[26] As one band of woodsmen made their wary way across a treacherous bog, "alligators raised their hideous snouts from the green coating of the swamp, gnashing their teeth and straining toward us, while the owls and other birds circled round our heads, flapping and striking us with their wings as they passed."[27] The forests of the Southwest were not for the timid: "at your feet, over your head, at your side, everywhere danger lurked."[28]

Not only danger, but intolerable discomfort. Even the most ardent promoters of frontier settlement could not deny that the woodlands and

[23] Rebecca Burland, *A True Picture of Emigration; or, Fourteen Years in the Interior of North America* (London, 1848), p. 40; Blegen, ed., *Ole Rynning's True Account of America*, pp. 19–20; Jacob H. Schiel, *Journey through the Rocky Mountains to the Pacific Ocean* (Norman, 1959), p. 28; J. C. Beltrami, *Pilgrimage in Europe and America* (London, 1828), p. 162.
[24] Beltrami, *Pilgrimage in Europe and America*, 2: 149; *Emigrant Life in Kansas* (London, 1886), p. 66; *American Settler*, 15 March 1884.
[25] Edward S. Ellis, *Seth Jones; or, The Captives of the Frontier* (London, 1861), p. 90.
[26] Gustave Aimard, *The Prairie Flower: A Tale of the Indian Border* (London, n.d.), pp. 2–3.
[27] Charles Sealsfield, *Frontier Life; or, Scenes and Adventures in the Southwest* (New York, 1855), pp. 30–31.
[28] Paul Duplessis, *Le Batteur d'estrade* (Paris, 1862), 1: 23.

clearings teemed with blood thirsty insects that plagued man and beast: ticks that burrowed beneath the flesh of their victims, horseflies whose bite sent farm animals into tantrums of kicking, and above all the ever-present mosquitoes. Those tiny pests were a greater menace to the pioneers than man-killing tigers; "hardly anyone," wrote a visitor to Missouri, "thinks about snakes, wolves, bears, or tigers," but all were terrified by those ravenous bloodsuckers.[29] Well they might be, for with swamps everywhere mosquitoes swarmed in such numbers that they literally covered every inch of flesh that was not protected, and formed clouds so thick that objects twenty feet away were hidden.[30] "They were that thick, boys," testified one character, "that if you had stuck your arm in among'em so—and pulled it back again—you'd have seen a hole the shape o' your arm! Ain't that so Cord?" Cord allowed it was so.[31] In such exaggeration there was truth.

And how annoying they were. "On land and water, while hunting or fishing, plowing or sowing, by day and by night, they torture us," complained a newcomer.[32] Their sting might not pierce heavy boots as some insisted, but they could penetrate ordinary clothing, leaving painful blisters that persisted for days on end. Now and then an overenthusiastic promoter would insist that they were disappearing as settlement thickened, or that a form of wasp known as the "mosquito hawk" was rapidly depleting their numbers, but this was only wishful thinking.[33] The mosquito would torture pioneers for generations to come, and no amount of partisan testimony could hide the fact from Europeans.

Disease, too, was the inevitable lot of newcomers to the woodland frontier, and again no chorus of rebuttal from emigration-minded image-makers could conceal its ravages. Most agreed that the climate was partly to blame; Europeans accustomed to the ocean-moderated weather of the Continent were unable to adjust to the rapid fluctuations in interior America from "Siberian winter cold to African heat" (as one German editor put it).[34] Who could be healthy when "a person dripping with sweat

[29] Alice H. Finckh, "Gottfried Duden Views Missouri, 1824–1827," *Missouri Historical Review* 44 (October 1950): 24.
[30] Schiel, *Journey through the Rocky Mountains*, p. 15; Wilhelm, *Travels in North America*, p. 272.
[31] John Regan, *The Emigrant's Guide to the Western States of America* (Edinburgh, 1852), pp. 380–81.
[32] Unonius, *Pioneer in Northwest America*, 1: 281.
[33] Reid, *The Hunters' Feast*, p. 89; Charlotte Erickson, *Invisible Immigrants: The Adaptation of English and Scottish Immigrants in Nineteenth Century America* (London, 1972), p. 154.
[34] William G. Bek, trans., "Nicholas Hesse, German Visitor to Missouri, 1835–1837," *Missouri Historical Review* 42 (April 1947): 178. A similar view is expressed in Gunnar J. Malmon, ed., "The Disillusionment of an Immigrant: Sjur Jørgensen Haaeim's 'Information on Conditions in North America,' " *Norwegian-American Historical Association Studies and Records*, 3 (1928): 5–6.

"Borne Off." From Mayne Reid, *The Death Shot* (Beadle's Dime Novel Library, New York, n.d.), p. 41. (From the Special Collections of the University of California at Los Angeles Library.)

from the heat scarcely had time to pull on his jacket before he feels the harmful effects of the surprisingly sudden cold"?[35] Propagandists might counter that frontiersmen lived longer than Europeans, or insist that "the more you travel westward, the more mild and temperate the climate grew";[36] they might cast doubts on their own veracity by holding that in mid-America winter only lasted from January to February and was so mild that a small fire would be enough to warm an average family.[37] This was nonsense, and most Europeans were right when they pictured the Mississippi Valley as a land of debilitating winter cold and energy-sapping summer heat.

They were also right when they recognized that frontier diseases were less a product of fluctuations in climate than of the swamps that were a normal feature of the western landscape. Hostile image-makers saw each as a death-dealing pesthole, reeking "with pestilent carbonic acid, emitted imperceptibly through the myriad pores of the earth's surface," and spreading over the neighborhood. There it formed a death-dealing layer so foul that torches burned pale or were extinguished, and men walked about as though weighted down by chains.[38] Woe unto all who breathed its poisons by night; a fatal illness usually struck within an hour. "Forsake those poison-impregnated swamps," emigrants were warned, "where a German, unless already acclimated, cannot exist."[39]

Nor were the swampy lowlands the only dangerous spots along the frontiers. Everywhere, even in the hill country, Mother Earth waited her victims. For centuries vegetation had been rotting on the forest floors, forming deadly gasses that were trapped just beneath the surface. With the first plowing they were released in an odoriferous cloud that carried death as it spread. Newcomers lacking the immunity developed by American pioneers were doomed to dangerous illness and possible death if they ventured into the danger zone within the five years needed to dissipate the "deadly miasmate."[40] "It seems that the earth," a Polish visitor observed,

---

[35] Johannes Johansen and Søren Bache, "An Imigrant Exploration of the Middle West in 1839. A Letter of Johannes Johansen and Søren Bache," *Norwegian-American Studies and Records* 14 (1944): 46. Similar opinions are in H. Smith Evans, *A Guide to the Emigration Colonies* (London, 1852), p. 22; and *Cassell's Emigrants' Handbook: Being a Guide to the Various Fields of Emigration in All Parts of the Globe* (London, 1852), pp. 23–24.

[36] *Cassell's Emigrants' Handbook*, pp. 24.

[37] Ibid., pp. 21–22; William G. Bek, ed., "Gottfried Duden's 'Report,' " *Missouri Historical Review* 13 (January 1918): 87.

[38] Hooton, *St. Louis Isle*, pp. 64–65; *Advice to Emigrants Who Intend to Settle in the United States of America* (Bristol, 1832), pp. 12–13; Sealsfield, *Frontier Life*, p. 26.

[39] Sealsfield, *Frontier Life*, p. 26; Gerstäcker, *Wanderings and Fortunes of Some German Emigrants*, p. 137.

[40] Franz Löher, *Land und Leute in der Alten und Neuen Welt* (Göttingen, 1860), p. 163; *To the Emigrant Farmer: A View of the Advantages, Climate, Soil, Product, Government and Institutions of Texas* (London, 1848), pp. 12–13; Bek, tr., "Nicholas Hesse, German Visitor to Missouri," pp. 27–28.

"jealous of her treasures, sentences to death the bold one who dares to be the one to tear open her breast."[41]

The most common—and dreaded—of the diseases spread by these miasmatic gases, the image-makers agreed, was the ague, or "shaking fever," known today as malaria, and carried not by released vapors but by the myriads of mosquitoes that swarmed out of the swamps with their death-dealing cargoes. This was the universal plague of the frontier, inflicting on its victim alternate chills and raging fevers accompanied by uncontrollable shaking, "so violent as to make the sufferer feel as if his bones were dislocated."[42] There was no escaping its ravages; so universal was malaria that a phrase book used by Norwegians on their way west taught them to say: "Ai aemm naat uell aet aell. Mei hedd is giddi, aand ai keenn haerdli staend onn mei leggs" ("I am not well at all. My head is giddy, and I can hardly stand on my legs").[43] Promoters might list remedies guaranteed to cure, or urge newcomers to avoid swampy lands, shun whiskey, and settle well behind the cutting edge of the frontier, but they could not hide the fact that pioneering was a dangerous profession for Europeans.[44]

The image of the woodlands frontier as a land of comfort and plenty that had been popularized by the romanticists eroded rapidly before this barrage of realistic reporting. The West was no sylvan paradise, but a testing ground for the strong and the brave and the foolhardy. Even such a tub-thumper for frontiering as Germany's Gottfried Duden admitted that he must combat an image well planted in the minds of his countrymen—most of them knew, he wrote, of "the terror of hostile Indians; the dread of beasts of prey, of poisonous serpents, of scorpions, or tarantulas and various insects, such as mosquitoes and so forth, and finally the host of maladies that are caused by the climate and the conditions of the soil."[45] The image-makers had done their work too well. Nature was an enemy, not a friend; perhaps the realists overexaggerated the perils of pioneering, but Europeans who chose migration to the frontier were better adjusted to the actualities of life there than had been their counterparts a century before.

[41] Julian U. Niemcewicz, *Under the Vine and Fig Tree: Travels through America in 1797–1799, 1805* (Elizabeth, N.J., 1965), p. 262.

[42] *Tegg's Handbook for Emigrants; Containing Useful Information & Practical Directions* (London, 1839), p. 160. Hair-raising accounts of the ravages of the disease are also in C. F. Volney, *A View of the Soil and Climate of the United States of America* (Philadelphia, 1804), pp. 285–86; and R. G. A. Levinge, *Echoes from the Backwoods; or, Sketches of Transatlantic Life* (London, 1846), 2: 212.

[43] Quoted in Theodore C. Blegen, *Norwegian Migration to the United States* (Northfield, Minn., 1931–40), 1: 255.

[44] *Tegg's Handbook for Emigrants*, p. 161; Calvin Colton, *Manual for Emigrants to America* (London 1832), p. 25; *Cassell's Emigrants' Handbook*, p. 21; *Wiley and Putnam's Emigrant's Guide* (London, 1845), pp. 81–82.

[45] Bek, ed., "Gottfried Duden's 'Report,' " pp. 258–59.

The Prairies and Plains

By the 1840s the frontier of settlement was emerging on the lush grass-lands of the western Mississippi Valley and the interminable Great Plains of the Far West. Here was a wondrous new landscape to be described by the image-makers, a strange world to be explored by the armchair voyagers of Europe. Authors, however, could no more agree when they pictured the prairies and plains than they had when describing the wood-land frontiers. To some they were flower-decked Edens, waiting only the plow to be transformed into the Garden of the World. To others they were barren wastelands, overwhelming in their vastness, their emptiness defying the puny efforts of man. Here, as in the East, a dual image emerged, attracting or repelling as the image-maker willed.

All agreed that Nature's grandeur was nowhere better revealed than in the awesome emptiness, the limitless horizons. To the pious and romantic the prairies were the ultimate symbols of God's ever-presence, humbling mere humans by their infinite magnitude, reminding man of his insignificance when contrasted with his Creator's powers. "You are alone with God," wrote one, "and you tremble in His presence."[46] In that wondrous temple there was no trace of man's sinful hand; all about was "the beautiful, immaculate work of God."[47] Even the hardened reprobates in European novels felt the hand of the Almighty on them when they journeyed across the grasslands: "No longer did a single one of them use profane language or revel in obscenity. They behaved like Puritan church-goers on Good Friday. And indeed it was as though we were moving slowly on hallowed ground toward the Lord's temple."[48]

To the less reverent the vastness of the prairies signified the limitless space of America itself, an awesome sight to Europeans whose horizons were bounded by the hills that rimmed the tiny valleys where they were born. Authors never tired of describing the interminable distances: of enjoying a twenty-five-mile canter before breakfast, of newcomers who wandered from their camps and searched for days before finding their companions; of government surveyors who "lost" a four-million-acre tract that was left without government until they discovered their error.[49] Not a European but sensed the limitless vistas of the West as he read these accounts.

The image-makers agreed that Nature offered no grander sight than

[46] Reid, *The Hunters' Feast*, p. 25.
[47] Sealsfield, *Frontier Life*, p. 77.
[48] Ulrich S. Carrington, *The Making of an American: An Adaptation of Memorable Tales by Charles Sealsfield* (Dallas, 1974), p. 27.
[49] Mayne Reid, *The Headless Horseman: A Strange Tale of Texas* (London, 1865), p. 76; Karl May, *Der Schatz im Silbersee* (1894; reprint ed., Bamberg, West Germany, 1973), pp. 144–45.

the prairies dappled with spring wild flowers. Even the most cynical realists taxed their rhetorical powers as they described "the multicolored carpet . . . of bright flowers entangled amidst the grass . . . bloom upon bloom in a joyful, loving delirium," all swaying before the wind "like billows on a golden sea."[50] Surely that vision was of beauty beyond Eden and Elysium (or so one guidebook judged);[51] Harriet Martineau wondered if Milton had seen the prairies in a springtime before he wrote of the Garden in *Paradise Lost*.[52]

The pious and the romantic might glorify the springtime splendors of the grasslands, but more realistic image-makers were less sure. They saw the mere vastness as repelling rather than attracting, the distances overwhelming as well as inconvenient, and the sense of loneliness oppressing. In the forests men were not aware of their complete isolation; on the plains where only emptiness stretched to the distant horizons they were terrifyingly aware that they had forsaken civilization and stood alone against Nature. In that empty sea "a sickly sense of loneliness" became unbearable to some.[53] Typical was a German traveler who was gripped by a terrible sense of horror, of foreboding, as he made his solitary way across the vast plain: "I felt my connection with the past was broken—the first symptom of various kinds of madness—when the meaning of life becomes so tragic that there was no rescue."[54] To men accustomed to the companionship of their fellows in thickly settled Europe the feeling of aloneness that oppressed them in the grasslands could be a horrifying experience.

Nor did the realists among the image-makers find the prairies attractive save when clothed in the sparkling verdure of spring. For most of the year they were monotonous wastelands—"a desolate plain without a single tree," a "yellow, sealike plain of grass," and rank weeds.[55] Karl May, usually a staunch defender of anything western, saw the plains as a monotonous ocean: "Nothing, absolutely nothing around save for those undulating waves all the way to the horizon, as far as weary eye can see."[56]

[50] Levinge, *Echoes from the Backwoods*, 2: 199; Henryk Sienkiewicz, *Portrait of America: Letters of Henryk Sienkiewicz* (New York, 1959), pp. 74–75; Bek, ed., "Gottfried Duden's 'Report,'" pp. 258–59.
[51] Regan, *Emigrant's Guide to the Western States*, p. 42.
[52] Harriet Martineau, *Society in America* (New York, 1837), 1: 241. Another traveler, Patrick Shirreff, reported in his *A Tour through North America* (Edinburgh, 1835), p. 219, that he had met a farmer who told him that Pigeon Prairie was the place where Adam and Eve had lived.
[53] Frederick Marryat, *Narrative of the Travels and Adventures of Monsieur Violet, in California, Sonora, and Western Texas* (London, 1843), 2: 93–94; Sealsfield, *Frontier Life*, p. 77; Thoralv Klaveness, *Blandt Udvandrede Nordmaend* (Oslo, 1904), pp. 74–75.
[54] Otto Ruppius, *Der Präirieteufel* (1861; reprint ed., Berlin, 1974), p. 373.
[55] Ernst Graf zu Erbach-Erbach, *Reisebriefe aus Amerika* (Heidelberg, 1873), p. 143; Paul Wilhelm Herzog von Württemberg, *Erste Reise nach dem Nördlichen Amerika in den Jahren 1822 bis 1824* (Stuttgart, 1835), p. 254.
[56] May, *Der Schatz im Silbersee*, pp. 107–8.

Charles Dickens, who could be depended on to take a hostile view, described the prairie as not only "lonely and wild, but oppressive in its monotony."[57] Russian travelers were reminded of the steppes of Siberia, Italians of the Sahara desert.[58] Said a little girl in Conan Doyle's *Study in Scarlet* when she voiced her stout belief that God had nothing to do with creating the Great Plains, "He made the country down in Illinois, and He made the Missouri, but I guess somebody else made the country in these parts. It's not nearly so well done."[59] Civilized Europeans saw the grasslands of western America not as Nature's fairylands, but as depressing reminders of man's inferiority, burdensome to the soul and offensive to the eye.

A people-killing climate made them even less attractive. The most scrupulous promoters could not hide the fact that the extremes of heat and cold would test the endurance of a Superman, even though they insisted that the dry air and the constantly blowing breeze assured year-around comfort.[60] Most image-makers disagreed. They pictured the summers as smelting-furnace hot, with a relentless sun beating from copper-hued skies, withering the grass and cracking the earth with its rays. "Not even an insect crawls about," wrote a Polish traveler. "No bird is on the wing, and even the wild animal rests in its lair throughout the day."[61] On such days, one visitor was told, the railroad tracks moved over into the shade until they heard the train approaching.[62] Thunderstorms offered occasional relief, but they themselves were terrifying examples of Nature's fury: "vast masses of inky darkness crowding in wild and furious tumult aloft, mountain upon mountain of towering clouds; . . . a sheet of flame, perfectly awesome in its intensity, pouring its fury over all, illuminating the wild scene, and for a moment hushing even the raging wind." Then came the thunder: "the mighty roar of a battlefield where a hundred cannon poured forth their belching fury," and "the rain in cold shivering floods."[63]

Even such displays were preferable to the "Northers" that ushered in winter's blasts. "There's death in yonder shadow," an old plainsman told his British companions. "If you do not make haste it will be too late. . . . Quick, sir, I entreat you! The sky—heaven itself—commands you."[64]

[57] Charles Dickens, *American Notes* (London, 1842), pp. 264–65.
[58] A. Bykova, *The North American United States*, 3d ed. (St. Petersburg, 1909), p. 46; Frederick G. Bohme, trans., "Vigna dal Ferro's un viaggio nel Far West Americano," *Colorado Magazine* 35 (October 1958), p. 296.
[59] Arthur Conan Doyle, *The Annotated Sherlock Holmes* (New York, 1967), p. 199.
[60] E. A. Curley, *Nebraska, Its Advantages, Resources and Drawbacks* (London, 1875), pp. 102–3; *American Settler*, 18 September 1880.
[61] Sienkiewicz, *Portrait of America*, pp. 70–71.
[62] Quoted in Robert G. Athearn, *Westward the Briton* (New York, 1953), p. 53.
[63] St. John, *The Trapper's Bride*, pp. 43–46.
[64] Paul Duplessis, *Les Mormons* (Paris, 1859), 8: 66–67.

Woe unto those who failed to listen. Screaming winds tossed trees about as they would bits of straw, lifted streams from their beds, and even leveled mountains. Then came the snow, driven so furiously that wayfarers were blown for leagues before it, and wagons rolled into giant snowballs that were trundled irresistibly down the steppes.[65] As the winds died, numbing cold followed, freezing men and horses in their tracks, stopping watches, solidifying the ink and coffee in settlers' cabins, turning horses' ears—and farmers' noses—so brittle that they broke off when touched.[66] After such a storm, one hero in a French novel confessed, "it will be almost a treat to be roasted at a redskin's torture fire."[67]

Nature's extremes made life on the Great Plains both unpleasant and hazardous, but there was compensation in the thin, invigorating air. This was an elixir beyond compare; tales were told of consumptives magically cured after a week in the high country; of an invalid who arrived "so kinder coffiny-looking that he appeared to walk about only to save funeral expenses" and within a few days was chasing bears up trees; of an old-timer so curious to know what sickness felt like that he lived on fat pork and lemonade for a week but still suffered no ill effects.[68] These relatively creditable tales led to others less believable: on the high plains men grew younger rather than older with each passing year, horse thieves had to be hung five minutes longer than in the lowlands to kill them, natural deaths were so few in one town that the inhabitants had to shoot a man to start a cemetery; in another the only persons who died were doctors who starved to death.[69] The climate might be rugged, but the champagne air worked wonders.

There were compensations, too, in the abundance of game waiting the hunter's gun; quail in such numbers that eighteen were usually killed with a single shot, turkeys so numerous that their flocks darkened the skies; passenger pigeons in such abundance that a single flock might number a billion and consume eighteen million bushels of feed daily; so many elk and deer that their tracks formed labyrinths in which unskilled hunters wandered for days before finding their way out; wild horses in gargantuan

[65] Gustave Aimard, *The White Scalper: A Story of the Texan War* (London, 1861), p. 281; Gustave Aimard, *The Red River Half-Breed: A Tale of the Wild North-West* (London, n.d.), pp. 42–43; Reid, *The Headless Horseman*, p. 23; *American Settler*, 11 February 1888.
[66] H. Arnold Barton, ed., *Letters from the Promised Land: Swedes in America, 1840–1914* (Minneapolis, 1975), p. 147; Ebbutt, *Emigrant Life in Kansas*, p. 79; *American Settler*, 14 March 1885; Ronald A. Wells, "Migration and the Image of Nebraska in England," *Nebraska History* 54 (Fall 1975): 475–87.
[67] Aimard, *The Red River Half-Breed*, p. 45.
[68] James F. Muirhead, *America: The Land of Contrasts* (London, 1902), p. 202; William A. Baillie-Grohman. *Camps in the Rockies* (New York, 1882), p. 4; James Burnley, *Two Sides of the Atlantic* (Bradford, England, 1880), p. 141.
[69] *American Settler*, 1 March 1873; 3 December 1881; Baillie-Grohman, *Camps in the Rockies*, p. 4; *Counsel for Emigrants, and Interesting Information from Numerous Sources, with Original Letters* (Aberdeen, 1834), p. 128.

herds that galloped about with manes fluttering and tails like plumes in the wind.[70] Coyotes were everywhere in the West, but they were usually pictured as slinking cowards, harmless to men, but incredibly smart. One was seen chewing through a lasso that held a bundle of meat suspended and making off with his prize, another twisted and rolled on his back until he lured a curious antelope near enough to be attacked.[71]

Two animals intrigued the image-makers particularly: prairie dogs and buffalo. Prairie dogs were described as unbelievably numerous, living in villages covering 625 square miles, and so extensive that plainsmen rode all day to reach their limits.[72] They were friendly little creatures, gathering after the day's work for spirited conversation or "visiting about from hole to hole, to gossip and talk over one another's affairs." Their social life was highly organized under an elected mayor who assigned such tasks as well-digging or burrow-repairing, and served as arbiter in disputes.[73] They were also extremely shy, but so curious that Karl May's hero, Old Shatterhand, discovered a way to approach their towns, performing "all kinds of leaps and gyrations, crouched, then leaped high in the air, turned around and spread his arms like a windmill" until he was in their midst.[74] Not even a prairie dog could outwit Old Shatterhand.

Buffalo fascinated Europeans even more than prairie dogs. Millions of these shaggy beasts, each combining "the ferocious intelligence of the tiger and the indominable brutality of the bull," ranged the prairies, trampling grass and shrubs and earth into a solid mass.[75] Plainsmen knew that to be caught in the path of a stampeding herd—"great living wave which sweeps along with the power of a tornado"[76]—was sure death. Few would have the luck of the hunter who was tossed high in the air by the horns of the lead buffalo, landed on its back, and used his bowie knife to goad the

[70] John (János) Xantus, *Letters from North America* (Detroit, 1975), pp. 32–33; Reid, *The Hunters' Feast*, pp. 39, 41, 49; Gabriel Ferry, *Le Coureur des bois* (1850; reprint. ed., Paris, 1932), 2: 203; Gustave Aimard, *The Pirates of the Prairies: Adventures in the American Desert* (London, 1862), p. 66; Karl May, *Winnetou I. Ungekürzte Ausgabe* (reprint ed., Vienna, 1953), p. 46; Gustave Aimard, *The Trail Hunter: A Tale of the Far West* (London, n.d.), p. 84.
[71] Mayne Reid, *The Boy Hunters; or, Adventures in Search of a White Buffalo* (London, 1853), pp. 166–67; G. A. Henty, *Captain Bayley's Heir: A Tale of the Gold Fields of California* (London, 1889), p. 172.
[72] Xantus, *Letters from North America*, pp. 111–12; Reid, *The Boy Hunters*, pp. 196–97; Charles W. Webber, *Old Hicks the Guide; or, Adventures in the Comanche Country in Search of a Gold Mine* (New York, 1848), p. 48.
[73] Chamber's Journal, *Journey from New Orleans to California, 1849, and Other Excerpts from Chamber's Journal* (Edinburgh, 1849–57) 101 (8 December 1855); Marryat. *Narrative of the Travels and Adventures of Monsieur Violet*, 1: 184–86.
[74] May, *Der Schatz im Silbersee*, p. 283.
[75] Paul Duplessis, *Les Peaux-Rouges* (Paris, 1864), pp. 102–3.
[76] Gustave Aimard, *The Border Rifles: A Tale of the Texan War* (Philadelphia, n.d.), p. 39. See also Reid, *The Boy Hunters*, pp. 27–28; and the *American Settler*, 12 February 1881.

frightened animal into outrunning its followers, then when a mile ahead slipped from its back and climbed a convenient rock to safety.[77]

During the latter years of the century Europeans watched the slaughter of the buffalo with an occasional twinge of conscience—a German confessed remorse after killing a stately bull weighing a thousand pounds and taking only its tongue[78]—but with little genuine compassion. They agreed with the American frontiersmen that the animals would soon be extinct, and felt that this was as it should be. The buffalo occupied land that could be used for farming, just as did the Indian, and as a nonuseful species must be sacrificed to progress. "The sooner the bears and cougars and buffalo are killed the better," quoth a character in a British novel; "the land is not for dumb brutes, but for men."[79] When Nature stood in men's way, Nature was doomed.

Mountains and Deserts of the Far West

The image-makers paid less attention to the Rockies and Sierras than to the Great Plains, probably because Europe's own Alps robbed mountains of some of their awe, but they did allow them sufficient notice to misinform a good many readers. This was a largely unknown country they were describing, unsettled and crossed only by a few trails. Hence they could not be challenged when they peopled the Kansas River Valley with Blackfoot Indians,[80] described a journey from San Diego to Santa Fe made entirely by boat,[81] scattered dense forests of oak and sycamore across west Texas,[82] and filled the upper Missouri Valley with "palms and magnolias; the latter shaped like a perfect cone, stood in lustrous verdure against the dazzling whiteness of the flowers which, despite the lateness of the season [October was well along] were still blooming."[83] The "middle course" of the Missouri was also a spectacular beauty land, dazzling with the blossoms of date plums and giant "Rowan trees" from whose "forty foot high crown big white flower clusters hung in profusion."[84]

---

[77] Mayne Reid, *The Scalp Hunters; or, Romantic Adventures in Northern Mexico* (London, 1851), 1: 44–48. In Marryat, *Narrative of the Travels and Adventures of Monsieur Violet*, 2: 246–47, a band of hunters divide a charging herd by exploding a whiskey bottle in front of the leaders.

[78] Balduin Möllhausen, *Reisen in die Felsengebirge Nord-Amerikas bis zum Hoch-Plateau von Neu-Mexico* (Leipzig, 1861), 1: 372.

[79] Sealsfield, *Frontier Life*, p. 45.

[80] "The Beaver Trappers: A Story about Indians," *For Ungdommen*, n.s., 3 (Oslo, 1870): 45–50.

[81] G. A. Henty, *The Golden Canyon* (New York, 1899), pp. 35–36.

[82] Etienne Marcel, *Un Chercheur d'or* (Limoges, 1881), p. 28.

[83] Aimard, *The Prairie Flower*, pp. 160–61.

[84] Wilhelm Frey, *In Indianerhänden* (Mülheim, n.d.), pp. 3–4.

If these natural marvels were not enough, the image-makers invented a dozen new species that lent interest to the mountains and plateaus: the compass plant whose leaves pointed exactly north and south and allowed many a lost hunter to find his way to safety,[85] the "angry tree," which ruffled its leaves and gave forth an unpleasant odor when annoyed,[86] the "jocuistle plant" whose bananalike fruit sobered the most drunken inebriate with a single mouthful,[87] the "candle tree" whose resinous branches would burn for hours as torches,[88] the "oregano plant" whose fruit pounded to a pulp and applied as a poultice would heal any wound,[89] and the "gem bush" whose berries "turned to petrification" as they matured, the red to form rubies, the blue turquoises, and the colorless into flawless crystal. A lucky trapper who stumbled on one of these marvels filled his pouch with precious stones that he later sold to a Jewish peddler for 800 dollars.[90] Mayne Reid was not far wrong when he told his British readers that the Far West was a "cornucopia of plenty."[91]

The mountain country also teemed with wild life: lions, wolves, coyotes, rattlesnakes, and a zooful more. Some were remarkable creations. The bighorn sheep who thrived there could leap from cliffs seventy-five feet high, land on their horns, bounce two or three times, and trot away unharmed.[92] Even more unusual were the herds of ostriches found in the Blackfoot Indian country. These remnants of the millions who had once covered the Far West were rapidly being exterminated, partly by mountain lions who had learned to attract the curious birds by twitching their tails while lying on their backs, partly by humans for "the ostrich is excellent eating, and the Indians prepare, chiefly from the meat on the breast, a dish renowned for its delicacy and exquisite flavor."[93]

Of all the animals of the high country the beaver and the grizzly bears fascinated the image-makers. They pictured the beavers as industrious little creatures who had perfected a cooperative social order that man might envy; they worked as teams when building their dams and homes, some mixing mortar as fine as the best Roman cement, others gnawing through trees, still others directing the tree cutters by slapping the water to indicate the course of the fall. Each band had its own territory and elected ruler who kept order, handed down judgments, and punished

[85]   F. M. Holmes, *Raff's Ranche: A Story of Adventure among Cow-Boys and Indians* (London, 1901), p. 128. The plant is also described in the *American Settler*, 22 October 1892.
[86]   *American Settler*, 13 June 1891.
[87]   Gabriel Ferry, *The Wood Rangers* (London, 1860), 2: 49.
[88]   Gustave Aimard, *The Smuggler Chief* (London, n.d.), p. 201.
[89]   Ferry, *The Wood Rangers*, 2: 70.
[90]   Aimard, *The Red River Half-Breed*, p. 46.
[91]   *Boy's Illustrated News*, 18 May 1881, p. 74.
[92]   Mayne Reid, *The Desert Home; or, The Adventures of a Lost Family in the Wilderness* (London, 1852), p. 124.
[93]   Aimard, *The Prairie Flower*, pp. 242–45.

marauding beavers from other colonies by biting off their tails—"the greatest disgrace to which a beaver can be exposed." When war broke out between two bands the chiefs either directed their troops in skillful tactics or settled the argument by personal combat as the two armies watched.[94]

The grizzly's appeal to storytellers was natural, for few other animals were so capable of eliminating villains or testing the prowess of heroes. Standing ten feet tall, with enormous claws that could rip a man apart as a terrier could a rabbit, and thick fur so matted that it would deflect a bullet, these fearsome beasts were so speedy that they could outrun the fastest horses and so powerful that they could carry a buffalo in their jaws. Their favorite food was the buffalo; "he pounces on their backs, presses them in his iron arms, breaks their skulls with his teeth, and more often than not kills quite a few for pleasure before he decides to eat one."[95] "Its cruelty," wrote a French novelist, "is equal to all other cruelties put together."[96] Authors agreed that these monsters could only be killed by a perfectly placed shot, either in the center of the right eye, or in a vulnerable square-inch spot on the nape of the neck.[97]

Here was a foe to test the bravest hero, particularly when the hero's Winchester had jammed as did that of Snap, the idol of a generation of British schoolboys: "Grasping the barrel with both hands, he had just time to hurl the useless weapon with all his strength at the head of the grizzly and spring to one side. He had a glimpse of the devilish head, with ears laid back and fiery eyes, and long white fangs gleaming from a shaggy mass of fur, going over him at railroad speed."[98] Snap managed to escape that time, but the next he might not. This suspense was the stuff of which stories are made, and the storytellers saw their chance. "The grizzly," Mayne Reid noted, "is becoming [in England] almost as much an object of interest as the elephant, the hippopotamus, and the king of beasts himself."[99]

If the mountains and the high country challenged the imagination of the image-makers, the deserts of the Southwest provided them an even more spectacular opportunity for inventive genius. Unlike mountains, deserts were *terra incognita* to Europeans and usually envisaged, if at all, in terms of the Sahara. Too, the Southwest was off limits for travelers, with transportation facilities few and the Comanches and Apaches dangerous through most of the nineteenth century. This was no handicap to novel-

---

[94] Gustave Aimard, *The Trappers of Arkansas; or, The Loyal Heart* (London, 1864), p. 155.
[95] *Boy's Illustrated News*, 18 May 1881.
[96] Duplessis, *Les Peaux-Rouges*, p. 106.
[97] Ferry, *Le Coureur des Bois*, 2: 203; Gustave Aimard, *The Trapper's Daughter: A Story of the Rocky Mountains* (London, 1877), p. 124.
[98] C. Phillipps-Wooley, *Snap: A Legend of the Lone Mountain* (London, 1899), p. 79.
[99] Reid, *The Hunters' Feast*, pp. 60–61.

ists. The result was a never-never land of their own invention where armchair voyagers could thrill to impossible adventures and the most refined tastes in exotica be satisfied.

There was but scant appeal in the landscape sketched by the image-makers. The desert soil was either so powdered that it rose in clouds of choking dust when stirred, or so flinty-dry that it rang like metal under horses' hooves; not even iron tent stakes could penetrate its surface.[100] Over all the sun spread its searing heat, so furnace-hot that travelers heard plants crackle as they rode by. Not an insect crawled, not a bird was on the wing. Thirst was a constant menace to man and beast; "in the wild western desert," warned Mayne Reid, "it is the *thirst that kills*."[101] When there was no water "the throat is on fire, the eyes are suffused with blood, and the wretched man, a prey to horrible delirium . . . at length dies in atrocious agony." Death was everywhere; "it meets the eye everywhere without intercession in its most fearful guise," observed one hero, and no European reader of Westerns would disagree.[102]

Something more than a monotonous landscape was needed by the novelists; they must have oases where adventurers could find haven from desert heat, caves to shelter them from marauding Apaches, towering cliffs where hero and villain could battle with bowie knives, raging rivers where bad men could be swept to their deaths. Hence writers performed feats of geographic legerdemain remarkable to behold as they transformed the Southwest to suit their needs. At their command placid streams and glimmering lakes appeared in unlikely spots; Karl May's Old Shatterhand discovered such a haven near the Pecos River where shimmering waters "shone with silver-grey beauty, undisturbed by even the slightest breeze as they reflected the oak and pecan trees that lined their banks;[103] a band of plainsmen finding a similar spot threw themselves down amidst the flowering shrubs to drink their fill, then "bound the grape clusters to our foreheads like bacchanals, and tied great bunches of the orange-tree round us as scarves."[104] Oases were oases in those days.

They were rare, however; over miles of desert landscape not a bush or a tree or a blade of grass was to be seen. "Dead, dead, dead was everything about us," mourned Old Shatterhand as his eyes searched the horizon, "not a single trace of life showed itself."[105] Yet life was there for those who

[100] Ruppius, *Der Präirieteufel* p. 460; St. John, *The Trapper's Bride*, pp. 40–41; Schiel, *Journey through the Rocky Mountains*, pp. 25, 35. Mayne Reid, in *The Desert Home*, pp. 1–16, devotes a whole chapter to describing the desert.
[101] Reid, *The Scalp Hunters*, 1: 128.
[102] Aimard, *The Trapper's Daughter*, p. 109.
[103] May, *Der Schatz im Silbersee*, p. 476; Karl May, *Old Surehand: Erster Band* (Vienna, 1953), p. 51.
[104] Charles J. Lever, *Confessions of Con Cregan: The Irish Gil Blas* (London, 1849–50), 2: 52–53.
[105] Karl May, *Im Tal des Todes* (Vienna, 1951), pp. 214–15.

"Stir a Finger and I Spur On." From Mayne Reid, *The Headless Horseman* (London, 1865), 1 opposite p. 217. (From the Special Collections of the University of California at Los Angeles.)

could see: here and there a lonely mesquite bush—"a mockery to the eye searching for a splash of green"—a sickly green artemisia, fetid creosote plants, a few ball-like globe cacti that yielded gallons of water when slashed open—all reasonable facsimilies of actual desert growth.[106] Now and then a tree grew inexplicably, many of them concealing canoes hidden by the Apaches who knew that sudden rainstorms could flood the countryside to depths of five or six feet.[107] Occasionally, too, plainsmen encountered giant clumps of cactus, hundreds of feet in circumference and so tightly packed that only a skilled *Westmann* could find the secret passage to the "hide-spot" in the interior.[108]

The Gila River formed a boundary that every plainsmen knew. To its north lay the dread Llano Estacado, the West's most fearful desert, shunned by even the bravest frontiersmen for the certain death that lurked there.[109] Just south of the Gila the landscape changed dramatically; there lush prairies where birds sang joyously alternated with dense forests of trees so large that they sank the earth a dozen feet when they fell and formed river-rafts two miles long and half-a-mile wide. Spanish moss—*barbe d'Espagne*—hung in festoons from the topmost branches to the ground, while vines and creepers entwined in luxurious profusion among their trunks.[110] To enter this stately woodland from the desert wastes was a solemn experience; even hardened plainsmen felt "a gentle melancholy at the sight of those thousand arches of foliage, intertwined like the ceiling of an old Gothic church."[111]

So tightly packed were the trees that travel was easier above ground than below. Skilled *Westmanner* soon learned to lasso a branch, ride upward with it as it sprang back in place, and travel for miles eighty feet above the ground, dropping down now and then to knife an unfriendly Apache or rescue the heroine from a fate that in those days was considered worse than death. Now and then a villain used this route to escape pursuers: "While they are seeking our trail on the ground," Red Cedar hissed, "we will slip through their hands like serpents, passing from tree to tree, from branch to branch, thirty yards above their heads."[112] Or to outwit justice; a Mexican outlaw, pursued by a posse of avenging trappers, sud-

[106] May, *Old Surehand, pp.* 82–83; Reid, *The Desert Home,* pp. 91–92.
[107] Gustave Aimard, *Stronghand: A Tale of the Disinherited* (London, 1878), p. 44.
[108] May, *Old Surehand, pp.* 106–7.
[109] Reid, *The Scalp Hunters,* 2: 206; Gustave Aimard, *The Tiger Slayer* (New York, n.d.), pp. 98–99.
[110] Aimard, *The Tiger Slayer,* pp. 53, 63, 98–99; Aimard, *The Trail Hunter,* pp. 20–21; May, *Im Tal des Todes,* pp. 71–72; Thomas Krag, *Fældejægeren eller Skovløberens Forræderi: Fortælling Fra Colorados Vildnis* (Oslo, 1890), p. 3; Sealsfield, *Frontier Life,* p. 87; Charles W. Webber, *The Prairie Scout; or, Agatone, the Renegade* (New York, 1852), p. 10.
[111] Gustave Aimard, *The Freebooters: A Story of the Texan War* (London, n.d.), p. 35.
[112] Aimard, *The Trapper's Daughter,* p. 122. Another such escape is described in Gustave Aimard, *The Red Track* (New York, 1884), pp. 20–21.

denly stood in his saddle, grabbed a vine that hung from a branch, and swung himself upward amidst the leaves and moss.[113]

Along the limpid streams on the forest edge, and on the prairies that opened now and then, wild flowers grew in dazzling abundance: dahlias flaunting flowers "each full of as much honey as Hercules could drain at a draught, whiter than Chimborazo's snow, or rudier than the tiger-lily's blood-splashes, . . . immense lianas twineing and circling . . . the fan-leaved *abanijo*, the *pirijao* languidly swinging its enormous golden fruit in clusters, . . . the guave, the banana, the intoxicating *chirinoya*, the cork-oak, the Peruvian tree, the war-palm."[114] Birds were everywhere, lifting their voices in a torrent of melodious harmony: tanagers, curassow, chattering *lloras*, *haras*, flycatchers, toucans with their enormous beaks, parrots and parakeets, *trogons*, hummingbirds flitting from flower to flower like sparkling gems, elegant rose flamingos, swans balancing and sporting in the streams.[115] Nature ran riot in the Southwest of the image-makers' imaginations.

On the ground could be found more terrifying examples, of the earth's abundance: "the *cotejo* with its venomous bite; the chameleon whose skin reflects every hue; the green lizard, and the basilisk crawling silent and sinister beneath the leaves; the monstrous boa, the coral snake so small and yet so terrible; the *cascabel*, the *macaurel*, and the great striped serpent."[116] Giant iguanas sprawled in the sun, and now and then a hunter came across a great armadillo that had wedged itself between the rocks so tightly that it could be extracted only by tickling until it relaxed and could be pulled out. Scorpions and centipedes so poisonous that they could inflict fatal wounds simply by crawling across a man's body were plentiful; so were hairy-legged spiders larger than a hand, and tarantulas whose bite "was not only fatal but extremely rapid."[117]

Snakes were commonplace in the deserts, of course, basking on the roadways in such numbers that horsemen had to pick their way among them, "slithering through the prairie grass," or lurking beneath mesquite bushes, always ready to coil and strike.[118] Here and there lay an immense swamp, such as the *El Voladero de las Animas*, that literally teemed with cobras, coral snakes, rattlers, and the tiny ribbon snake. "Bitten by him,"

[113] Charles W. Webber, *The Gold Mines of the Gila: A Sequel to Old Hicks the Guide* (New York, 1849), p. 161.
[114] Gustave Aimard, *The Treasure of Pearls: A Romance of Adventures in California* (London, n.d.), p. 6; Aimard, *The White Scalpers*, p. 51; Aimard, *The Pirates of the Prairies*, pp. 19–20.
[115] Aimard, *The Pirates of the Prairies*, p. 20; Gustave Aimard, *The Indian Scout; or, Life on the Frontier* (Philadelphia, n.d.), p. 20; Reid, *The Desert Home*, p. 135.
[116] Reid, *The Desert Home*, pp. 102–3; Aimard, *The Border Rifles*, p. 153.
[117] Edward S. Ellis, *Across Texas* (Philadelphia, 1893), pp. 40–52; Reid, *The Headless Horseman*, pp. 46–48.
[118] János Xantus, *Utazás Kalifornia déli részeiben* (Pest, 1860), pp. 11–12; Wilhelm Frey, *Die Apachen am Rio Grande* (Mülheim, n.d.), p. 1; Aimard, *The Prairie Flower*, p. 170.

an old hunter warned, "you have eleven minutes to live. You grow first yellow, then green; then you begin to swell and it is all over."[119] Fortunately skilled *Westmanner* knew how to protect themselves, either by rubbing their bodies with the Mikania plant that neutralized all venom, or by luring the serpent from its victim with milk. One Norwegian party, threatened by a cobra in a cave where they had sought refuge, saved themselves by placing a saucer of milk (conveniently on hand) on the floor, then escaped while the reptile was drinking.[120] A Mexican wet-nurse was less fortunate; the rattler released by the villain to kill the child she was feeding "seized the nipple the little creature had let go of and glued its hideous mouth to it." The nurse died, but she was only a Mexican; Mexicans always surrendered to death when bitten and made no effort to save themselves.[121]

This reptilian assemblage made life hazardous in the Southwest, but the dangers there were multiplied fullfold by the menagerie of carnivorous animals that haunted forest and desert. The usual assortment of carnivores lurked there, of course: bears, wolves, coyotes, panthers, and a dozen more, all ferociously savage. Two were especially dangerous: cougars and peccaries. Cougars were fearsome beats, nine feet long and so powerful that they killed by leaping on the back of a horse or buffalo, crushing the neckbone in their jaws, and sucking the blood until their prey dropped dead.[122] One hunter, surprised by two of the giant cats, used the single shot in his gun to kill one, then knelt to wait the attack of the other, a blanket folded over his left arm, his knife in his right hand. The beast sprang—"man and tiger writhed together in a deadly embrace, and after a few seconds only one of the adversaries rose; it was the man. The tiger was dead; the hunter's machete, guided by a firm hand, had passed right through its heart." "Splendidly played," shouted the hunter's British companion. "It was one of the best double strokes I ever saw in my life."[123]

Peccaries—piglike horrors with razor-sharp hooves and tusks six inches long—hunted in packs of twenty or more, and could rip a cougar to shreds in seconds. One hunter witnessed an unfortunate cougar who made the mistake of pouncing on a lone peccary. The victim's squeals brought the whole pack in a furious charge that surrounded the lion in less than a

---

[119] Gustave Aimard, *Stoneheart: A Romance* (London, 1868), pp. 98–99.
[120] "The Cobra," *Norske Gutter* (Oslo, 1898), 1, no. 16. Gustave Aimard, *The Bee-Hunter: A Tale of Adventure* (London, 1868), p. 14, and Aimard, *Stoneheart*, p. 98, describe cures for snakebite.
[121] Gustave Aimard, *The Queen of the Savannah: A Story of the Mexican War* (London, n.d.), pp. 45–47.
[122] Reid, *The Hunters' Feast*, p. 59; Aimard, *Stronghand*, pp. 8–9; Ferry, *The Wood Rangers*, 1: 178.
[123] Aimard, *The Trail Hunter*, pp. 22–23.

minute: "we could see the blood streaming from his flanks. He now seemed as if he wished to make his way through them and escape; but the peccaries, as active as himself, hemmed him in their midst, surrounding him with a dense mass of bodies and snapping jaws. Twice or three times the cougar sprang into the air—as if to leap beyond the circle of antagonists—but at the same time several of these were also seen to rear upward and intercept him in the spring."[124] That cougar met his fate, as would any beast or man who fell prey to these savage animals. Not even hunters were safe when attacked, for those who stood their ground succumbed to the mere weight of numbers and those who climbed to safety were besieged, with day-and-night peccary guards who watched until their victim fell. They could be hunted only at night, for peccaries slept by backing one by one into a hollow tree until only the snout of the last guarded the entrance; when he was shot the one behind moved into the guard position until all were killed.[125]

Still more fearsome enemies lurked beneath the slimy surface of rivers and bogs in the Southwest. Alligators haunted every lake and stream, wallowing in the mud of the Gila and basking in the swamps of the San Joaquin Valley, ready to snatch any man or animal that came within reach of their deadly jaws. Many a hunter paid with his life when he stepped on an alligator, thinking it a log.[126] Alligators were not without their uses, however; California ranchers killed them by the thousands for their fat, which was used to grease wagon wheels. One hero put them to another service when he was marooned on an island; killing a dozen or so he removed their intestines, and using a bird quill as a straw inflated them into sausage-shaped balloons. Fastening them to his body he floated to safety, apparently ignored by the other alligators who filled the stream.[127]

He was unbelievably lucky, for the image-makers filled the waterways of the Southwest with a variety of man-eating monsters capable of disposing of a man in seconds: Devil Jack Diamond Fish weighing four hundred pounds, Saw Fish eight feet long, with a toothed snout that could cut through a human leg in moments, Horn Fish that ripped their victims apart with a bony protuberance on its upper jaw, and Blanket Fish—loathsome creatures who smothered their victims by wrapping their flabby bodies about them. Even more feared were the Gar Fish, ten feet long and covered with scales so hard they deflected rifle bullets and were

---

[124] Reid, *The Desert Home*, pp. 422–23.
[125] Aimard, *The Trail Hunter*, p. 28; Reid, *The Boy Hunters*, pp. 131–32; Reid, *The Hunters' Feast*, p. 115.
[126] Aimard, *The Pirates of the Prairies*, pp. 100–101; Aimard, *The Bee-Hunter*, p. 8; Gustave Aimard, *The Gold Finders: A Romance of California* (New York, n.d.), p. 44.
[127] Alexander Dumas, *A Gil Blas in California* (San Francisco, 1848), pp. 114–15; Reid, *The Hunters' Feast*, pp. 33–34.

used as flint and steel to light fires. Witnesses saw one Gar Fish snap an alligator in two, then tow the two halves to the depths to be devoured.[128]

Most dangerous of all were the *carvanas*, or *carwans*, hideous monsters twenty feet long with a snout like an alligator's and a shell as impenetrable as gunboat armor. No traveler was safe when fording a stream, for a *carvana* might be lurking on the river bottom, ready to swallow horse and rider at a single gulp. None was ever seen, although their dried shells, measuring more than eight feet across, were found occasionally. The Army Corps of Engineers, determined to capture one of the reptiles after it had killed an officer, baited a specially made hook with the body of a sheep, which was dropped in a hole where one was known to hide. It took the bait but two teams of horses and a brace of oxen failed to dislodge it. After an hour's struggle "the surface of the slime was shaken by a submarine trembling, as the animal's jaw's appeared," but then the hook was jerked violently loose, its prongs warped and twisted.[129] That was enough. Man was destined never to see a *carvana*.

This array of ferocious beasts and reptiles scattered about the Southwest by the image-makers exaggerated, but still typified in European minds, the brutality of Nature along the American frontiers. The picture was a repelling one, hardly designed to lure newcomers to the Land of Promise. But more was to come, for the West was the home of not only savage animals but of Indians who were still more savage. Such was the message spread by the blood-and-thunder tales of novelists and travelers, to create an indelible image of the American West as a Land of Savagery.

[128] Marryat, *Narrative of the Travels and Adventures of Monsieur Violet*, 3: 291–92; *American Settler*, 22 October 1887.
[129] Dumas, *Gil Blas in California*, pp. 114–16; Marryat, *Narrative of the Travels and Adventures of Monsieur Violet*, 3: 279–83.

V

Native Americans:
From Noble to Ignoble Savagery

THE INDIAN was the most tragic victim of the spirit of progress and utilitarianism that shaped social thought in Europe and America during the nineteenth century. His fall from grace was an inevitable by-product of changing attitudes toward Nature. So long as the wilderness was seen as a purifying Eden where men were cleansed of their sins by nearness to their Creator, the Native American could be viewed as the most envied of all people, bathed in righteousness and free of oppression—a true Noble Savage to be envied and imitated. Even the most ardent Rousseauist realized that this idealized image, exaggerated beyond credibility as it was, could not long endure, but few could anticipate the violence of the revolution in thought that toppled the Noble Savage from his pedestal as the Age of Romance gave way to the Age of Utilitarianism in the early years of the nineteenth century.

Responsible for this catastrophic change were the linked forces of industrialization and urbanization. As life in a metropolis rather than a forest became the ideal, and as factories opened new avenues to wealth and comfort for the masses of Europe, utilitarian progress increasingly became the goal of men and women. If they were to achieve the position and comforts of their dreams, untamed Nature must be subdued. Forests must give way to the farms and factories that were monuments to mankind's creative skills and symbols of civilization's progress. "There prevails in all directions," remarked a character in a German novel, "a principle of Utility." So it did. When Americans could seriously contemplate ruining the beauty of Niagara Falls by attaching a waterwheel to tap its power, the spirit of romanticism was dead.[1] Mother Nature was a bitch goddess, and must be conquered by the ruthless advance of materialistic culture.

This meant that the Indian must be sacrificed, for his way of life was geared to the preservation, not the destruction, of the wild. He was an outlived fossil, destined to extinction in the evolutionary progress of civilization. Arnold Guyot spoke for much of the western world in the prestigious Lowell Lectures of 1849 when he characterized the Indian as an insensitive, melancholy relic of the past, whose "vegetative" nature made him unfitted for the modern world.[2] He had played his role and must go. Said a character in a mid-century novel: "He hath a pioneer mission, to prepare the wild for the superior race; and, this duty done, he departs."[3] The Indian had had a chance to follow Thomas Jefferson's advice and fall in step with progress by adopting the white man's way; he had chosen instead to dispute for control of the continent, and in so doing had deliberately signed his own death warrant. His fate was sealed.

The Indian's demise was hurried by the reports of travelers. Visitors from Europe, nurtured on the Noble Savage tradition, came in increasing numbers during the first half of the nineteenth century, expecting to find godlike Children of Nature living amidst abundance and freedom. When they found instead a primitive people just emerging from the Stone Age and untutored in the refinements of civilization, their reaction was normal to those misled by exaggeration. Stung by their own gullibility, they leaned too far in the opposite direction in picturing the Indians as slovenly, dirty, lazy, uncultured barbarians. "We have made them models of humanity," complained the editor of the *Tour du Monde* in 1860, "with all the enchanting virtues of the Golden Age. . . . As a reaction today we hardly see in these primitive peoples anything but an awesome mixture of madmen, thieves, assassins, and cannibals of a nature inferior to human beings."

An emerging generation of scientists deepened the shadow. Generally sympathetic in their findings, they were still too untrained in scientific methodology and too culturally biased to present a fair picture of the Native Americans they described. In all their works the assumption persisted that the Indians were basically different from whites, the products of a lower civilization. Studies such as Lewis Henry Morgan's *The League of the*

---

[1]   J. C. Biernatzki, *Der braune Knabe* (1840), quoted in Paul C. Weber, *America in Imaginative German Literature in the First Half of the Nineteenth Century* (New York, 1926), pp. 188–89.
[2]   Arnold Guyot, *The Earth and Man* (Boston, 1863), pp. 216–18.
[3]   Quoted in Roy H. Pearce, *The Savages of America: A Study of the Indian and the Idea of Civilization* (Baltimore, 1953), pp. 219–20.

Iroquois (1851) might attempt an objective appraisal, but they were inclined to debate whether the red men were examples of arrested progress or had descended to their low state through contact with Europeans, rather than to describe them as they were: the products of environmental challenges and the cultural shock they faced in a Europeanizing United States.

Their inferior rung on the ladder of life was underlined as Charles Darwin's evolutionary theories gained credence. To Darwinians the red men were retarded offshoots of the mainstream of human evolution, a living example of a species destined to extinction in the continuing struggle of the survival of the fittest. Thomas H. Huxley, Darwin's principal popularizer, saw them as existing in perpetual savagery where "the Hobbesian war of each against all is the normal state."[4] Such barbarians had no place among civilized peoples. To the scientists, no less than to unsympathetic travelers and progress-minded materialists, there was no such thing as a "good" Indian. All were cultural deviates and must go.

These findings posed problems for European novelists. Both "good" and "bad" Indians were essential to their plots, the "bad" to test the prowess of the hero and invent the sadistic tortures demanded by sensation-seeking readers, the "good" to serve as faithful companions for their heroes, for the Natty Bumppo-Uncas relationship was to persist through the nineteenth century and beyond—as witness the Lone Ranger and Tonto. Where could authors find red men who met the standards demanded by Europe's moralists and utilitarians?

One obvious solution was to recognize that not all Indians were the same; some were cruel sadists and others gentle humanitarians as their personalities and environment dictated. This differentiation was accomplished in a number of ingenious ways. Some authors separated whole tribes as had James Fenimore Cooper; in Karl May's stories all Apaches were good and all Comanches bad; Gustave Aimard exactly reversed their roles, while Frederick Marryat cast the Shoshones as loyal friends and the Crows as implacable enemies—"thieves never known to keep a promise or do an honourable act."[5] Readers meeting villainous Apaches in one novel and encountering them in another as staunch fighters for justice had every reason to be confused.

Those who were bad, the image-makers generally agree, were bad because they had been brutalized by contact with whites on the outer

---

[4] George Woodcock, "The Lure of the Primitive," *American Scholar* (Summer 1976): 390. This article expertly examines the attitude of scientists toward the Indian, as does Antonello Gerbi, *The Dispute of the New World: The History of a Polemic, 1750–1900* (Pittsburgh, 1973), pp. 452–53.
[5] Frederick Marryat, *Narrative of the Travels and Adventures of Monsieur Violet, in California, Sonora, and Western Texas* (London, 1843), 1: 116.

frontiers: soldiers, squatters, greedy speculators, and traders. Traders especially were pictured as the dregs of society—"more ferocious than the Indians," the "least industrious and most dissolute white men on the continent," hovering "like hawks upon the outskirts of civilization."⁶ Traders were the profligate outcasts who cheated the red men of their furs, besotted them with whiskey, raped their wives, and left a residue of hatred that turned the kindliest Indian into a savage barbarian. Only in the deepest wilds could red men be found who still clung to their noble ways; "the less the Indians have communicated with the civilized nations," a traveler noted, "the more they are good, kind, and generous."⁷ Heroes had to travel far to find their faithful companions, but the result was worth the search.

Whether good or bad, the red men deserved the compassion, not the censure, of Europeans. Their plight would be laid at the door of the federal government that had wrenched them from their tribal homelands, driven them westward to the desert territories beyond the Mississippi, herded them onto reservations, and condemned them to menial servitude as wards of a heartless bureaucracy. Here was a theme to stir the blood—and sympathy—of Europeans: a free people living in a state of perfect equality reduced to serfdom simply because they were unwilling to agree that one man should serve another "merely because he had a few pieces of shining metal."⁸ They might be out of tune with "progress" but they still deserved the tearful understanding of Europeans.

The image-maker's favorite device to drive this point home was the allegorical tale of the dying Indian whose death symbolized the passing of his race. These usually involved beauteous young maidens named "Startled Fawn," or "the fairest of the Oneidas," with "ripe pouting lip and dimpled cheek," who spoke perfect Hiawathese and had been driven to suicide by the sufferings of their people. Typical was the tearful story of Powontanomo, the mighty chief of the Mohawks, whose lovely daughter Soonseetah and Adonis-like son died of the white man's diseases. He planted a tree above their graves, then fled westward. When he returned he found that the tree had been chopped down by a frontiersman; "a deep groan burst from the soul of the savage" as he broke his bow and arrows, scattered the bits over the graves of his children, and departed forever—

⁶   Charles Mackay, *Life and Liberty in America* (London, 1859), p. 93; George Featherstonhaugh, *Excursion through the Slave States* (New York, 1844), p. 311.
⁷   François Perrin Du Lac, *Travels through the Two Louisianas and among the Savage Nations of the Missouri* (London, 1807), p. 63. Similar views are in Thomas Hamilton, *Men and Manners in America* (Edinburgh, 1833), 2: 240–41, and Frederick Marryat, *A Diary in America* (London, 1839), 1: 144.
⁸   Thomas Day, *The History of Sandford and Merton* (London, 1818), 2: 166–67. For a summary of comparable expressions on the subject see Weber, *America in Imaginative German Literature*, pp. 79, 112, 180–81.

"Wolves on the Trail." From Mayne Reid, *Adventures among the Indians*
(London, n.d.), opposite p. 282. (From the Special Collections
of the University of California at Los Angeles Library.)

the sad victim of a civilization that had condemned his people to oblivion.[9]

Indians who behaved in this way were true noblemen, knighted by Nature rather than a king, but deserving all the sympathy that Europeans could summon. Clearly "good" Indians deserved to escape the brutality of the federal government. But they must also be worthy of survival. How justify their continued existence in a world that had enshrined materialism and progress? At first, early in the century, authors could endow them with traits of Noble Savages and picture them as models of compassion, loyalty, and nobility, but with the passing years this fantasy proved increasingly unacceptable to Europeans. "After having been with the Indians in their village," a Norwegian realist confessed, "and having had my nose inside the chief's wigwam, I am convinced that Cooper was one of the greatest liars that ever existed."[10] The Age of Romanticism was dying, and the "splendid myth" of the Noble Savage dying with it.[11]

Europeanizing the Noble Savage

But good Indians were needed. How provide them in a form acceptable to nineteenth-century utilitarianism? The novelists' solution was ingenious. They would "Europeanize" their "good" Indians, endowing them with traits and ideals drawn from civilization, yet still possessing the natural nobility that made them valuable allies. They would dress them in a blend of their native costumes and white men's clothes, picture them as properly pious, and recast them as honest, compassionate, and trustworthy friends of Europeans and progress. Thus all that was "good" about the red men would be traceable to civilization, all that was "bad" to Nature. They would blend Noble Savagery and utilitarianism to form a new breed of Indian, usable in fiction, but as unrealistic as the Noble Savage of Chateaubriand and Rousseau.

There was little savagery in these Europeanized red men, with their splendid foreheads, aquiline noses, faintly bronzed skin, and eyes "dark and flashing, when excited, but otherwise mild, with a soft twinge of melancholy."[12] One Apache was so perfectly formed that "he would make Apollo envious"; his Comanche opponent "presented the most perfect

[9] Lydia Maria Child, *Coronal: A Collection of Miscellaneous Pieces* (Boston, 1832), pp. 4–5, 16–17. The extracts are from a story, "The Indian Wife," that was widely reprinted in German magazines. For similar tales see James A. Jones, *Traditions of the North American Indians* (London, 1830), 2: 139–40, and Fredrika Bremer, *The Homes of the New World: Impressions of America* (New York, 1853), 2: 30.
[10] Magnus B. Olsen, *Min Amerikafærd* (Copenhagen, 1900), unpaged. Comparable comments on Cooper are in Theodora Guest, *A Round Trip in North America* (London, 1895), pp. 85–86, and Charles R. Russell, *Diary of a Visit to the United States of America in the Year 1883* (New York, 1910), p. 71.
[11] Richard F. Burton, *The City of the Saints* (London, 1861), pp. 103.
[12] Marryat, *Narrative of the Travels and Adventures of Monsieur Violet*, 2: 111.

build a sculptor could have dreamed of."[13] "There was," wrote a novelist of a Delaware brave, "nothing savage either in his speech or bearing."[14] Their haughty aloofness reminded writers of Europe's noblest crowned heads, exhibiting "more *éclat* and majesty than are possessed by sceptered kings."[15] One Shoshone when speaking to his assembled warriors reminded an observer of "those sages of ancient Greece inculcating to their disciples those precepts of wisdom which have transmitted their names down to us, bright and glorious."[16] Karl May's Old Shatterhand was sure that if his Apache companion, Winnetou, "were the son of a European ruler, he would be a great general, or an even greater prince of peace."[17]

They were worthy of such roles, for they had mastered the most difficult art of civilization: to keep their emotions in check. None acted precipitously in war or peace, but deliberated at length before striking an enemy or bestowing a blessing. Indian chiefs were also immensely learned, "far ahead of our philosophers in the laws of physical life and the processes of inductive reason."[18] All, chiefs and followers alike, were natural gentlemen, fully aware of the deference due their social superiors, and expecting proper recognition in turn. Old Shatterhand was delighted when a young Apache bowed low on meeting him, confessing, "I am not yet a warrior and may not speak to you."[19] Here was respect without humility.

Their speech was that of Europe's chivalrous, worthy of the elevated thoughts they expressed. Mere declaratory sentences would never do; instead Comanches and Apaches spoke in romantic symbolism, rich in metaphor. "You left the village of the Flowers," one Apache chief told a hunter, "to follow the hunting path at daybreak of the third sun of the moon of the falling leaves; thirty suns have passed since that period, and we are hardly at the moon of the passing game."[20] Indians, to other Indians, were "Arabs of the South," whites "Long Knives of the West." A mere "thank you" would never suffice; when a Tuscarora maiden thanked a trapper who had saved her from the Sioux she exclaimed soulfully: "The heart of the Tuscarora girl is glad. The sun has opened the first bud of the Rose." And when Jack Harkaway tried to thank a chief who had saved his

---

[13] Thomas Krag, *Fældejægeren eller Skovløberens Forræderi: Fortælling fra Colorados Vildnis* (Oslo, 1890), p. 44; Paul Duplessis, *La Sonora* (Paris, 1858), 2: 168–69.
[14] Mayne Reid, *The Scalp Hunters; or, Romantic Adventures in Northern Mexico* (London, 1851), 1: 279.
[15] J. C. Beltrami, *Pilgrimage in Europe and America* (London, 1828), 2: 173.
[16] Marryat, *Narrative of the Travels and Adventures of Monsieur Violet*, 2: 18.
[17] Karl May, *Winnetou I: Ungekürzte Ausgabe* (Vienna, 1953), p. 69.
[18] Charles W. Webber, *Old Hicks, the Guide; or, Adventures in the Comanche Country in Search of a Gold Mine* (New York, 1848), p. 305.
[19] Karl May, *Canada Bill: Including the Talking Leather and 'One-Eyed' Joe Burkers* (London, 1971), p. 119.
[20] Gustave Aimard, *The Freebooters: A Story of the Texan War* (London, n.d.), p. 54.

life he was reminded: "A word of kindness is a seed which is sure to spring up in flower."²¹ No mere savage ever spoke in such golden phrases.

Or dressed as did the Europeanized red men of the novelists, blending as they did the barbaric splendor of primitivism with the latest in European fashions. The women, all ravishingly beautiful and resembling Arabian queens or the Florentine Venus, were exquisitely gowned in tunics of fawnskin adorned with colorful quills, their shapely limbs enclosed in scarlet velvet.²² One, a Comanche princess named White Gazelle, outshone her companions with her "loose Turkish trowsers made of Indian cashmere, fastened at the knee with diamond garters, . . . a jacket of violet velvet buttoned over the bosom with a profusion of diamonds, . . . a brilliant-hued Navajo zarape, and a Panama hat of extreme fineness (*doble paja*) decorated with an eagle plume."²³ Here was splendor to outshine Europe's royalty.

White Gazelle was rivaled in garish costume by the warriors of the Southwest. Eagle Wing, chief of the Cora Apache, wore a rattlesnake skin in his plaited hair, "a blouse of striped calico, adorned with a profusion of bells, descended to his thighs, which were defended from the stings of mosquitoes by drawers of the same stuff. He wore moccasins made of peccari skins, adorned with glass beads and porcupine quills. To his heels were fastened several wolves' tails, the distinguishing mark of renowned warriors."²⁴ Like other chiefs, his neck was adorned with a necklace of grizzly-bear claws and buffalo teeth. Some wore bright ornaments of silver about their necks and carried fans made of a single wing of an eagle; a few of the greatest were allowed to wear a falcon feather as testimony of their bravery.

This rainbow raiment was justified, for they boasted a noble ancestry. The archaeologists of that day had decided that the prehistoric ruins scattered over the Southwest had once housed Aztec Indians who, in an early era, had been driven southward into Mexico by the fierce plains tribes. This was evidence enough for the novelists. The primitive pueblos of the region were transmuted into Americanized Pompeian splendors, with

²¹ Charles W. Webber, *Tales of the Southern Border* (Philadelphia, 1853), p. 218; Gustave Aimard, *The Border Rifles: A Tale of the Texan War* (Philadelphia, n.d.), p. 44; Percy St. John, *The Trapper's Bride: A Tale of the Rocky Mountains* (London, 1845), pp. 86–87.
²² Duplessis, *La Sonora*, 2: 264; Marryat, *Narrative of the Travels and Adventures of Monsieur Violet*, 1: 131–32; Bénédict-Henry Révoil, *Le Bivouac des trappeurs* (Paris, 1864), pp. 133–34.
²³ Gustave Aimard, *The Pirates of the Prairies: Adventures in the American Desert* (London, 1862), pp. 50–51. Similar elaborate costumes are described in St. John, *The Trapper's Bride*, pp. 81–82; Reid, *The Scalp Hunters*, 1: 288–89.
²⁴ Gustave Aimard, *The Trail Hunter: A Tale of the Far West* (London, n.d.), p. 48. Comparable descriptions are in the same author's *The Prairie Flower: A Tale of the Indian Border* (London, 1878), pp. 9–10; and *The White Scalper: A Story of the Texan War* (London, 1861), p. 98; and in Franz Löher, *Land und Leute in der Alten und Neuen Welt* (Göttingen, 1860), pp. 169–70.

"fountains, aqueducts, heavy domes and long graceful obelisks, rising at the foot of massive pyramids," where lived the descendants of Montezuma and his noble followers.[25] They had spread northward with the Spanish invasion of Mexico, carrying the sacred fire, some to settle on the plains as ancestors of the Blackfeet and Sioux, others in the Southwest as Comanche and Kiowa and Apache. In each nation the fire still burned, hidden deep in lofty temples or sacred caves; one hero stumbled on such a cavern near the Gila River, its white walls splendid with sculptured figures, lighted by torches in iron brackets that had been burning steadily since the days of Montezuma.[26]

The cities that surrounded these temples were worthy of their noble inhabitants. The tribes that had drifted farthest from their Aztec ancestors—the Blackfeet of the upper Missouri and the plain dwellers—lived in wigwams of buffalo hides, many thirty feet or more tall with roofs of finely woven white straw, grouped about a central plaza where stood the "Ark of the First Man." All were neatly arranged along well-ordered streets. Beyond the residential area was the *Machotlé* where the dead were laid to rest, and beyond this, racks filled with drying meat, all ringed by palisades of earth or tree trunks rising twelve feet tall.[27] Within all was bustle as squaws hurried about with dog-drawn sleds laden with foodstuffs and warriors busied themselves cleaning their rifles or polishing the blades of their tomahawks.

These villages of the Great Plains were dwarfed by the metropolises of the Southwest where Comanaches, Navajos, and Apaches best perpetuated the Aztec traditions. They lived in towering apartmentlike dwellings along the Gila River, each with twin towers rising two hundred feet high and connected by bridges, or in mammoth cities where ordered streets radiated from a central "Square of the Sun." This central plaza was bordered by four palaces grouped about a lofty temple, its inner walls draped with tapestries of embroidered feathers and in its center a *teocalí*, or altar, surmounted by a glittering sun fashioned of gold and precious stones. Before the altar stood a marble sacrificial table, and at its rear a secret pas-

[25] Marryat, *Narrative of the Travels and Adventures of Monsieur Violet*, 1: 47–48. Josiah Gregg, *Commerce of the Prairies* (Norman, 1954), pp. 188–89, reports having seen such a fire in the kiva of an old Pueblo chief.
[26] Aimard, *Pirates of the Prairies*, pp. 46–47. Similar accounts are in Aimard's *The Prairie Flower*, pp. 134–40, and *Stronghand: A Tale of the Disinherited* (London, 1878), p. 97.
[27] Such villages are described in Bracebridge Hemyng, *Jack Harkaway Out West amongst the Indians* (London, n.d.), p. 32; Marryat, *Narrative of the Travels and Adventures of Monsieur Violet*, 2: 73–75; Heinrich Luden, ed., *Reise Seiner Hoheit des Herzogs Bernhard zu Sachsen-Weimar-Eisenach durch Nord-Amerika* (Weimar, 1828), 2: 30, as well as in several books by Gustave Aimard: *The Bee-Hunter: A Tale of Adventure* (London, 1868), p. 79, *The White Scalper*, pp. 95–96, and *The Prairie Flower*, p. 185, and in Karl May, *Old Surehand: Erster Band* (Vienna, 1953), p. 57.

sage led to the hidden vault where burned the sacred fire of Montezuma.[28] Edifices such as these were worthy of the supermen who built them.

They also symbolized the deep religious beliefs of the Europeanized Indians. Only a few accepted conversion to Christianity, an unhappy fact that image-makers bemoaned, but all were unquestionably pious and all engaged in religious ceremonies as elaborate as those of Rome itself. Typical were the Apaches. Each day they gathered in the central square of their villages where the sachem greeted the rising sun by sprinkling holy water to the four corners of the world, at the same time intoning: "Wacondah! Wacondah! thou unknown and omnipotent spirit, whose universe is the temple, Master of the life of man, protect thy children." The Apaches responded by bowing respectfully and repeating in chorus: "Master of the life of man, protect thy children." Then, at a signal, the sachem tossed the remainder of the holy water in his calabash toward the sun, proclaiming: "Oh, sun! thou visible representative of the Invisible Master of Life, protect us on this commencing day! Give us water, air and fire, for the earth belongs to us, and we can defend it." With these words all uttered a loud shout and scattered to begin their day's activities.[29] Indians such as these baptized their newborn with all the faithfulness of Christians and never entered battle without kneeling to seek God's blessing.[30] Their piety would put to shame most Europeans.

Marriage was a sacred covenant among them. Warriors courted their brides as arduously as Frenchmen, although with less orthodox techniques; an Apache brave proposed by killing his horse, plucking out the heart, and nailing it to the door of his intended's home. If she accepted, she roasted the heart and divided it equally with her lover, thus sealing the compact.[31] A Comanche courtship ended when a suitor seized his would-be bride, plunged his knife into his horse's neck, ripped out the heart, and touched it to her forehead, shouting: "This is my squaw; woe to the man who touches her."[32] Among the Shoshone the groom staged a lavish banquet in a flower-decked lodge, and at its climax grasped his would-be bride's hand as he proclaimed his love; the marriage was sealed if she answered: "Faithful, ever faithful, in joy and in sorrow, in life and in death."[33] The Shoshone ceremony may have been less glamorous than

[28] Aimard, *Stronghand*, p. 56. Similar cities are described in the same author's *Pirates of the Prairies*, p. 90, and *The Indian Scout; or, Life on the Frontier* (Philadelphia, n.d.), pp. 239–45, and in Reid, *The Scalp Hunters*, 2: 259–61.
[29] Aimard, *The Freebooters*, p. 28; Aimard, *The White Scalper*, p. 128. A note in Jones, *Traditions of the North American Indians*, 1: 143–44, suggests that the name "Wacondah" was taken from Edwin James, *Account of an Expedition from Pittsburgh to the Rocky Mountains, Performed in the Years 1819, 1820* (Philadelphia, 1823), 1: 251.
[30] Aimard, *The Bee-Hunter*, pp. 80–81; Révoil, *Le Bivouac des trappeurs*, pp. 113–14, 139–40.
[31] Aimard, *Pirates of the Prairies*, p. 62.
[32] Aimard, *The White Scalper*, p. 138.
[33] Marryat, *Narrative of the Travels and Adventures of Monsieur Violet*, 1: 135–36.

those of the Comanches and Apaches, but it was less destructive of horses.

Once the bond was sealed, the wife was expected to obey her husband just as in Christian countries of that day, but she was never reduced to the servile drudgery of non-Europeanized Indians. Ladies were ladies, whether white skinned or red, and deserved to be treated as such. Stoutly insisted one of Karl May's warrior heroes as he prepared to marry the lovely Mola: "She will not be a slave in the wigwam of Falkenauge, but a lady of the hut and tent, as the women of palefaces. Howgh."[34] Most image-makers dared not defy reality to the degree that they claimed equality among the sexes in the Indians they pictured, but they could voice their indignation at the usual treatment of the women. Gustave Aimard, proper Frenchman that he was, railed now and then that Indian women were "condemned, by the laws that govern their tribe, to remain constantly bowed beneath a yoke of iron, to be reduced to the most complete abjectness, and devote themselves to the harshest and most painful tasks,"[35] but he could do nothing but proclaim his dissatisfaction. Not even the most imaginative novelists could deny customs too well known to be questioned.

They could, however, endow their Europeanized red men with a knowledge of military tactics that would put many an Old World general to shame. Napoleon was their model; his picture hung in every lodge in Apacharia, while every chief from Winnetou to Sitting Bull studied his campaigns.[36] They learned their lessons well. Shoshones charged in squadrons, formed squares, and wheeled with precision against their enemy's lines.[37] Both Comanche and Apaches used maneuvers "frequently employed in Europe"; a Comanche army, surprised by an Apache attack, "broke up into platoons, and vigorously returned the fire" as they deployed into a circle, but the Apaches quickly "formed their ranks, and marched in excellent order on the Comanches."[38] On another occasion two hundred Comanches marched into Santa Fe in close columns, flanked on either side by troops of forty horsemen, and with Chief Unicorn twenty paces in front.[39] "The red man," wrote one novelist, "no longer

[34] Karl May and Gabriel Ferry, *Der Waldlaufer* (Bamberg, 1877), p. 272.
[35] Aimard, *The Indian Scout*, p. 229. A similar comment is in St. John, *The Trapper's Bride*, p. 9.
[36] Aimard, *The White Scalper*, p. 114. According to Joseph Bournichon, *Sitting Bull, le héros du désert* (Tours, 1879), p. 60, Alexander read Homer, Caesar read Alexander, Napoleon read Caesar, and Sitting Bull, "the Alexander and Napoleon of the desert," read Napoleon.
[37] Marryat, *Narrative of the Travels and Adventures of Monsieur Violet*, 1: 152.
[38] Aimard, *The White Scalper*, pp. 223–24, 228.
[39] Aimard, *The Trail Hunter*, p. 142. Indians were also described as experts in siege tactics, digging trenches, posting guards, and throwing up earthworks. Sieges against the California missions lasted as long as three years. Gustave Aimard, *The Trapper's Daughter: A Story of the Rocky Mountains* (London, 1877), pp. 43–4; Edward S. Ellis, *Teddy and Towser: A Story of the Early Days in California* (Philadelphia, 1904), pp. 273–74.

goes to war as a mere savage. He . . . possesses a military system as complete as that of the most civilized nation."[40] The irrepressible Jack Harkaway paid the ultimate tribute after witnessing an engagement: "They were splendid fellows. . . . The Old Guard couldn't do better."[41]

So Europeanized were some favored tribes that they instinctively reverted to the tournaments of medieval times when settling disputes or choosing a new chief. These were colorful affairs, supervised by a sachem clothed in regal robes, and opened by a procession of dancing girls carrying garlands of flowers. The spectators seated, combat began with two mounted Indian charging full-tilt, the well-poised lance of each aimed at the other's shield. After each exchange each turned to salute the other "as a mark of esteem from one brave foe to another."[42] Witnesses to such encounters, noting the noble warriors clad in bucklers and with long spears leveled, felt that they had been transported back to King Arthur's Court. "I doubt much," one wrote, "whether in the tournaments of the days of chivalry, the gallant knights could show their lady-love greater skill."[43]

Their skill in warfare was matched by their compassion in peace. Prisoners were treated as humanely as in Europe, with death only decreed after a proper trial and rendered as painless as possible. "With the Apaches," one novelist assured his readers, "there were no murders in cold blood, no abuse of the prisoners; a captive knows that he will either suffer death or be adopted in the tribe; but he has never to fear the slow fire."[44] Women prisoners were particularly respected; "there is too much chivalry among them ever to kiss or misuse a female prisoner."[45] "The red man has a heart, too, just like a paleface," Old Shatterhand was told. "He wishes to punish swiftly, but he will not torture slowly."[46] Such was the Indian's humanity that a white settlement was never attacked without proper warning, usually in the form of a bundle of arrows with their points dipped in blood. "The redskins," one explained, "have an eminently chivalrous character, and never . . . will they attack an enemy without warning."[47].

Their exemplary behavior marked the councils where terms of peace or war were debated. These were dignified assemblages, presided over by the principal chiefs carrying the silver mounted canes that were their

[40] Mayne Reid, *The Wild Huntress* (London, 1861), 3: 22–23.
[41] Hemyng, *Jack Harkaway Out West amongst the Indians*, p. 20.
[42] Reid, *The Scalp Hunters*, 3: 137–39, 141; Marryat, *Narrative of the Travels and Adventures of Monsieur Violet*, 2: 114.
[43] Marryat, *Narrative of the Travels and Adventures of Monsieur Violet*, 2: 2–3.
[44] Ibid., 2: 210.
[45] Weber, *Old Hicks, the Guide*, pp. 27–28.
[46] May, *Canada Bill*, p. 140. Similar comments are in Paul Duplessis, *Les Peaux-Rouges* (Paris, 1864), p. 172.
[47] Aimard, *The Border Rifles*, p. 64.

badge of office, and speaking "with a majesty equal to that of European kings sitting in parliament."[48] As the speakers rose, "bowing their heads in stately recognition," they were heard amidst a religious silence and never interrupted, for each was free to express himself unchecked, no matter how unpopular his ideas. The debate over, the principal chief summed up the arguments and the warriors voted, either by nodding their heads or by uttering the word *Aschest*, meaning "It is well."[49] Their decisions were recorded in resplendent phrase: "The chiefs and sachems assembled round the council fire . . . have formed the following resolutions, which will be executed with the aid of the Wacondah. . . ."[50] Little wonder that a Norwegian trapper who was present could write: "If this had not been beneath the open sky, . . . I would have imagined that I witnessed a judicial procedure in a civilized society."[51]

The Europeanized Indians of the image-makers' creation might have born slight resemblance to actual Native Americans, but they cast a long shadow over the attitudes and beliefs of many Europeans. Those who read of these noble creatures could not escape a vital question: how could the United States treat such gentle people so cruelly, robbing them of their lands, herding them westward, driving them onto unwanted reservations? The persisting view of the American government as a ruthless persecutor of minorities was grounded in this image, and has endured to this day. It was partially offset, however, when the same authors who glorified the Europeanized red men described the "bad" Indians, so necessary to their tales.

"Bad" Indians: Evil Incarnate

If the "good" Indians were metamorphosed into unbelievable saints by the image-makers, the "bad" were transformed into equally improbable devils. Treacherous, vindictive, cruel, many of them cannibalistic, they spent their lives scalping travelers, abducting heroines, battling with white hunters, and devising torture techniques that would have shocked the Marquis de Sade. Their roles in European "Westerns" were essential, for they provided expendable opponents for the heroes and the sensationalism demanded by the Wild West tradition from that day to this. And what monsters they were.

Their savagery, dating back to the Spanish defeat of the Aztecs, was a passion of hatred, kept alive by the struggle of successive generations to

48 Gustave Aimard, *The Tiger Slayer* (New York, n.d.), p. 61.
49 Aimard, *Stronghand*, pp. 56–61.
50 Gustave Aimard, *The Queen of the Savannah: A Story of the Mexican War* (London, n.d.), pp. 255–56.
51 E. A. Hagerup, "The White Steed of the Prairies," *Børnenes Blad* (Norway) 12 (1872), nos. 1–26.

protect their lands from advancing frontiersmen.[52] The mere sight of a white man stirred the urge for revenge, to be satisfied only by killing two Americans for every Indian who had died. No red man was to be trusted; a friendly native who smoked the pipe of peace with his white "brother" one moment was likely to cut his heart out the next. Such was their hatred that all whites—men, women, and children—were fair game, to be killed on sight whether innocent or guilty of wrong.[53] American pioneers had learned this lesson; old-timers on the frontier advised newcomers to shoot on sight when they saw an Indian: "for if you don't he will shoot you; show him no mercy for he will show you none."[54] One might expect to find more humanity in a rattlesnake than in a redskin.

All were instinctively sadistic, unrestrained by the traditions of humanity. Their cruelty was shown in their treatment of their animals. Their dogs were starved, mercilessly flogged, and sometimes eaten; their horses were whipped and ridden until near death; their cattle killed slowly and painfully with their torturers "laughing, yelling, hooting at the evident suffering of their victim."[55] "An Indian," wrote a Norwegian novelist, "has compassion for neither humans nor animals."[56] Captives were tortured to death only to satisfy their captor's blood-lust; enemy dead deliberately hacked to pieces or left unburied on the battlefield to be picked clean by vultures.[57] Indians found their greatest pleasure in cruelty, not compassion.

The image-makers disagreed on which tribe was the most brutal, but agreed that savagery was common to all. Some ranked the Sioux, Arikaras, and Blackfeet as most barbaric—"torturing captive warriors with studied cruelty"; others assigned this role to the Apaches—"the most eager to fight among all the Indians of North America."[58] Still others believed that the Comanches, Cheyenne, and Pawnee deserved the crown. Whatever their differences, most felt that the cruelest savages of all belonged to no one tribe but were half-breeds, "especially when the father is a Negro."[59] These were academic quarrels. When the red men were on

[52] Johannes Scherr, *Die Pilger der Wildnis, Historische Novelle* (1853; reprint ed., Hanover, 1917), 2: 18; Duplessis, *La Sonora*, 2: 146–47; Reid, *The Scalp Hunters*, 1: 251.

[53] Robert M. Ballantyne, *Digging for Gold: Adventures in California* (London, n.d.), p. 63; Friedrich Gerstäcker, *Roovers en Regters, of zoo Gaat in Amerika* (Haarlem, 1847), p. 58; William Savage, *Observations on Emigration to the United States of America* (London, 1819), pp. 41–42; Charles J. Latrobe, *The Rambler in North America* (London, 1835), 2: 256–57.

[54] *American Settler*, 24 October 1874.

[55] *American Settler*, 11 April 1874.

[56] O. V. Falck-Ytter, *Aslaug og Elling Blandt Indianerne* (reprint ed., Oslo, 1913), p. 71.

[57] May, *Winnetou I*, p. 241; Friedrich Armand Strubberg, *Bis in die Wildnis* (Breslau, 1858), p. 199; Robert M. Bird, *Nick of the Woods: A Story of Kentucky* (London, 1837), 2: 149–50.

[58] Paul Wilhelm, Duke of Württemberg, *Travels in North America, 1822–1824* (Norman, 1973), pp. 337–38; E. Riedel, "En Vinter hos Apatsche-Indianerne," *Folkevennen* (1890): 1–2.

[59] Eilert Storm, *Alene i Urskogen: Fortælling fra Amerika* (Oslo, 1899), pp. 135–36; Hemyng, *Jack Harkaway Out West amongst the Indians*, p. 5.

the warpath, as they normally were, a sadistic bloodletting was to be expected, whatever the tribe.

All prepared for combat by whipping themselves into a frenzy of hatred. The Comanches, one of the most feared tribes, named a war chief for each battle, with instructions to recruit his followers from among his most savage tribesmen. When all were armed and ready, a medicine man, weirdly garbed in discordant colors, sprinkled wormwood to the four cardinal points, shouting: "Wacondah! Thou seest these warriors; be favourable to them, blind their enemies, and remove any snares in their paths!" Each then held the point of his knife against the tribal emblem tattooed on his naked chest, swearing to follow the leader, even to his death. A war dance followed, the warriors leaping and singing to animalistic drumbeats as they whipped themselves in a fury of passion.[60]

Then the march into the enemy territory, carefully avoiding skirmishes that would interfere with their main purpose, for their motto was: "A brave man on the warpath avoids all useless fights which might tire him out before he encounters the real enemy."[61] Their purpose was to ambush their foes or to cut down small parties of the enemy without risking their own lives; their wars consisted of a succession of tricks and surprises designed to win victories rather than glory. But what formidable antagonists they were as they rushed into battle shouting their fearful war cry of "How-ow-owgh-aloo-loo-lo," their bodies painted to resemble wolves and bears, their breasts and shields hideous with garish death-heads and crossbones, their savage eyes gleaming with hatred. "All these," Norwegians were told, "created the impression that hell itself had broken loose."[62]

Once the enemy was engaged, tactics were supervised by three chiefs, two on the field of battle, one posted on a prominence with an overall view of the field where he could direct strategy.[63] The Indians avoided hand-to-hand conflict and favored small encounters where victory was certain, for to engage in battle without being sure of success was considered madness. When the tide turned against them they saw no disgrace in flight, to regroup and attack again. "They disappear as if by enchantment," wrote one novelist, "and without any shame, begin watching again for a more favorable moment."[64]

In these battles customary weapons were used—arrows, tomahawks, rifles, even the crossbow—but the Apaches and Sioux were also masters of

[60]   Aimard, *Queen of the Savannah*, pp. 260–61.
[61]   Paul Duplessis, *Le Batteur d'estrade* (Paris, 1862), 1: 7.
[62]   "From the Indian Uprising in Minnesota, 1862: the Siege of Fort Ridgley," *Børnenes Blad* (Norway) 14 (1874): 105.
[63]   Duplessis, *Le Batteur d'estrade*, 5: 21. Karl May, *Der Schatz im Silbersee* (reprint ed., Bamberg, 1973), pp. 452–53, describes similar tactics in a battle between the Navajo and Ute indians.
[64]   Aimard, *The Prairie Flower*, p. 77.

the lasso; they could send a coil of rope hissing through a hundred feet to entwine about the neck of an enemy.[65] Poisoned arrows and spears were commonly used, the poisons so subtly brewed that they killed in seconds. Among the Apaches a secret sect known as the "Poison Hatchets," distinguished by the emblem of a rattlesnake tattooed on their chests, was able to compound poisons so lethal that to cure the victim, "the united faculties of Europe would be baffled."[66]

As soon as the fighting ended the combatants retired in order, the losers slapping their breechclouts as they rode away—"the last indignity an Indian can offer to a foe"[67]—the winners hurrying back to their villages, to march triumphantly through the ranks of their assembled tribesmen. Mourning came first, as the wives of slain warriors at their chief's command cut off several joints of their own fingers, then scarred their faces, arms, and bosoms with sharp knives until they were bathed in blood. As this went on the triumphant warriors had assembled before an altar where a naked prisoner was stretched. As all watched, the chief sachem plunged his knife into the victim's chest, laid open the ribs with a single slash, and tore out the palpitating heart, while his assistants caught the dripping blood. When this was scattered over the watchers, "the red skins, frenzied with excitement, rent the air with deafening clamor."[68]

This ceremony only whetted the Indians' appetite for the sadistic orgy that followed. This was described with obvious relish by the image-makers. Scalping was a favorite theme and vividly depicted: "three quick cuts, a pull on the hair, a horrible scream from the prone victim, and the chief rose with the bloody scalp in his hand."[69] White prisoners fared no better than red. In one typical passage a French sergeant unfortunate enough to be captured by a band of Mixteca was thrown to the floor by the chief who knelt on his chest and cut through the skin on his forehead as the Frenchman screamed in agony. "Don't cry, you dog," said the chief, "this cut doesn't hurt yet. It will only begin to hurt when I take down your hide. Then you will start to sing. Just watch." He grabbed the hair and slowly pulled the scalp loose. The sergeant could not move his head, and the upper part of his body, because the Mixteca knelt on him, but his legs were free. With them he thrashed the air and floor in boundless ter-

[65] Karl May, *Captain Caymen* (London, 1971), p. 154.
[66] Gustave Aimard, *The Treasure of Pearls: A Romance of Adventures in California* (London, n.d.), p. 7.
[67] Charles W. Webber, *The Texan Virago* (Philadelphia, 1852), p. 50.
[68] Aimard, *The White Scalper*, pp. 234–35; Gustave Aimard, *Stoneheart: A Romance* (London, 1868), pp. 81–82.
[69] May, *Der Schatz im Silbersee*, pp. 320–21. Similar gruesome descriptions are in Karl May, *Im Tal des Todes* (reprint ed., Vienna, 1951), p. 242; Jens Tvedt, *Sihasapa-Indianerne: Norske Udvandreres Hendelser i Amerika* (Stavanger, 1887), p. 92; and Gabriel Ferry, *The Wood Rangers* (London, 1860), 2: 251–52.

"The Toughest Struggle of My Life." From Mayne Reid, *Adventures among the Indians* (London, n.d.), opposite p. 106. (From the Special Collections of the University of California at Los Angeles Library.)

ror. "Cowardly you are, and a sissy," said the Indian in disgust as he thrust the knife into the captive's heart."[70]

A "scalp dance" usually followed a battle, with the enemy scalp fastened to a pole as the warriors, naked to the waist and with a death's-head painted on their chests, danced wildly about, waving knives and tomahawks, and either howling at the tops of their voices or hissing like snakes. As they danced they tore at the bloody relic with their hands and teeth, or spit on it with vindictive scorn.[71] Some were saved for decoration; Old Shatterhand met a chief "the fringes of whose suit were comprised of fourfold braids of human hair; the tuft of hair on his head was decorated with scalps; his shoulder piece was of scalps and the lower thighs were fringed about with scalps."[72] A whole enemy village must have been sacrificed to clothe such a dandy. Sometimes trappers survived a scalping and forever afterward took malicious delight in snatching off their wigs to show their mutilated heads to horrified greenhorns.[73]

Their fate was to be envied when compared with that of most captured by Indians, for "to kill an enemy as cruelly as possible was victory's greatest reward" among them.[74] The image-makers vied in devising tortures to shock—and delight—their readers: captives were nailed to trees to be consumed by animals, skinned alive, roasted over slow fires, buried in the arms of an already dead comrade, their flesh sliced off and eaten as they watched, sulphur matches lighted between their fingers, wooden splinters thrust under their nails, their faces coated with honey to lure bees that would sting them to death, molten gold poured into their mouths (a favorite means of disposing of miners), thongs slipped through gashed skin and used to suspend the sufferer, eyes plucked from their heads and the sockets filled with live coals.[75] All as watchers shouted their joy. "Indians engaged in the delights of torturing a prisoner," one writer explained with masterful understatement, "are without heart."[76]

One favored device was to paint a circle on the victim's chest, strap him to a cross, and use him for target practice. Warriors shot in turn, each careful to avoid a fatal spot that would end the suffering. Wrote one novel-

---

[70] Printed in translation in Ernst A. Stadler, "Karl May: The Wild West under the German Umlaut," *Missouri Historical Society Bulletin* 21 (July 1965): 304–5.
[71] Révoil, *Le Bivouac des trappeurs,* pp. 201–2; *Boy's Illustrated News,* 25 May 1881.
[72] Quoted in Richard H. Cracroft, "The American West of Karl May" (M.A. thesis, University of Utah, 1963), p. 135.
[73] Robert Watt, *Hinsides Atlanterhavet: Skildringer fra Amerika* (Copenhagen, 1874), p. 23; May, *Der Schatz im Silbersee,* p. 325.
[74] "The Beaver Trappers: A Story About Indians," *For Ungdommen* (Norway) 3 (1870): 373–74.
[75] May, *Winnetou I,* pp. 197–98; Aimard, *The White Scalper,* pp. 326–40; Gustave Aimard, *The Trappers of Arkansas; or, The Loyal Heart* (London, 1864), p. 99; Aimard, *The Trail Hunter,* pp. 39–40; Scherr, *Der Pilger der Wildnis,* 2: 92–93.
[76] Bird, *Nick of the Woods,* 3: 215–16.

ist describing such a scene: "Gradually the disk on the breast is seen to darken, turning red, till at length not a spot of white is visible."[77] Occasionally this torture misfired; when one band of Arapaho proved to be such poor shots that they failed to kill the white hunter they were tormenting they asked the hunter's companion to fire the fatal bullet. Instead that sure-shot plainsman shot away his friend's thongs and both dashed to freedom.[78]

Most to be dreaded were tortures known as the "Apache Death" and "Death at the Post." In the former a tourniquet was tightened about the skull until the scalp literally popped from place; in the latter tribesmen tried out "all the tortures which their blood-thirsty imaginations could invent." In one such episode, which the writer described "with the utmost horror and disgust only because we are committed to telling the truth," one warrior cut away the victim's eyelids to expose his eyes to the sun, another stuck a rod of red-hot iron into his flesh until it touched the bone, another sawed off fingers and toes with a dull knife, one by one, a fourth used a stone to break off his teeth.[79]

Even that unfortunate sufferer fared better than a Sioux who had been captured by a band of Chippewa. He was first tied to the ground and a coal fire lighted on his stomach: "His tongue lolled out of his mouth. A horrid smell arose from the charred flesh . . . which could be heard crackling under the heat." Next he was unbound and used as a target by knife throwers who sliced off slivers of flesh with each throw, then a thong tightened about his forehead until his eyeballs protruded. The chief tormentor, taking his knife, "scooped out the eyeballs and threw them on the ground. First the right eye, then the left." When this forced a groan of agony from the sufferer he was scalped, and his fingers cut off, one after the other. "Then they took him up and cast him into the blazing fire, where he writhed and squirmed like a crushed worm" until "his charred and blackened limbs gave a compulsive twitch, and all was over."[80] Surely Indians guilty of such cruelty were less than human.

Particularly when the victim was often eaten, for nearly all tribes living near the Colorado River were cannibalistic. Santa Fe traders reported seeing Navajo who eyed small boys hungrily; "Lucky for the urchin it's broad daylight," one observed, "or he might get chucked under one of

---

[77] *Boy's Illustrated News*, 25 May 1881. Similar scenes are described in May, *Winnetou I*, pp. 200–1, and Reid, *The Wild Huntress*, p. 251.

[78] Reid, *The Wild Huntress*, p. 266. The *American Settler*, 15 August 1874, reported that a body had been found near Fort Sill so full of arrows that it obviously had been used for target practice.

[79] Duplessis, *Les Peaux-Rouges*, p. 166.

[80] Hemyng, *Jack Harkaway Out West amongst the Indians*, pp. 72–73. After this gruesome description the author adds: "Were these the 'poor Indians' that the United States government has so long fed and pampered?"

those striped blankets."[81] Arapaho were equally fond of human flesh, and had been known to pick human bones clean with as much relish as "the wings of a pheasant would have been by an European epicure."[82] So were the Apaches; a trapper testified that he had seen "les sauvages manger—eat—one—deux—tre—tre enfants rotis, like hump rib of de buffle."[83]

Perhaps these fantasies were disbelieved by more sensible Europeans, but the oft-told tales of Indian savagery left their mark. Certainly the gullible were convinced that the frontier was a land of danger and death suited only to the most reckless adventurers, and that at least half of the red men were sadistic monsters, unworthy of the name of human, and fit only for extermination. Yet the degrading of the Native Americans was still incomplete. Another group of image-makers whose testimony was far more believable, were to administer the coup de grace.

The Ignoble Savage

Travelers in the American West during the middle and late nineteenth century usually saw the Native Americans as neither "good" nor "bad," but as something far worse than either. The image that they projected was of a decayed race, steeped in vice and indolence, unable and unwilling to adjust to the modern world, and hence doomed to rapid and justifiable extinction. When one visitor described the Indians as "the worthless relics of the primeval race which so aptly succeeded to the reptiles of the antediluvian world," he was only slightly less harsh in his judgment than his contemporaries.[84]

Such a verdict was unfortunate yet understandable. European visitors were subconsciously mirroring the sentiments of their hosts at a time when pro-Indian sentiment among Americans was at its lowest ebb. They were subjected to endless newspaper accounts of "atrocities" and "massacres" in the warfare that flamed as the red men made their last stand against reservation life; they were bombarded by statements that equated the Indians with savagery and cast them as perpetual enemies to progress. Not the fate of the Indian was in the balance, but the fate of civilization.

Travelers were also misled by the Native Americans that they saw. By mid-century railroads were opening the West to visitors, funneling them not to the wilds but to the frontier towns and forts that were most accessible. The dregs of the Indian people were concentrated in these out-

[81]   Reid, *The Scalp Hunters*, 1: 81.
[82]   Marryat, *Narrative of the Travels and Adventures of Monsieur Violet*, 1: 172.
[83]   Reid, *The Scalp Hunters*, p. 81. Among other references to cannibalism were those in *Der Hollandsche Illustratie* 2 (1865): 274, and M. Cohen Stuart, *Zes Maanden In Amerika* (Haarlem, 1875), 3: 36.
[84]   C. G. F. Berkeley, *An English Sportsman in the Western Prairies* (London, 1861), p. 98.

posts—the maladjusted discontents who sought escape in liquor from the culture shock that was a tragic by-product of their forced transition to a reservation life-pattern. To judge these sad victims of the government's Indian policy as typical was as false as to see the derelicts on today's skid rows as typical of all Americans. Some few travelers were wise enough to see this; only on the seldom-visited remote frontiers, one conceded, could be found "native manners and customs in their utmost purity."[85] Such disclaimers did little good. The image of a decayed race was too firmly planted to be questioned.

And what a tragically distorted image it was. Travelers saw the Indians not as the bronzed demigods created by Fenimore Cooper, but as "a dirty army of indescribably greasy, degenerate people, covered with pests,"[86] their matted hair as coarse and uncombed as a horse's mane, their clothes encrusted with filth, their eyes lusterless and sullen, animated "only when they saw in the trader's stores the red-striped whiskey jug."[87] Time and time again vistors were reminded of animals rather than humans; one felt after visiting an Indian village that he had been at a zoo peopled by animated apes "as greasy as if drawn from a cesspool";[88] another described those he saw as "but a few degrees removed from the orang-outang."[89] These were a different breed than those pictured in romantic novels; again and again travelers complained that "they had nothing in common with tribes described in Indian novels."[90]

If the Indian men were disillusioning, the Indian women were positively disgusting to image-makers who expected to find the fawn-eyed beauties described by the romanticists. Instead they found ugly, dirt-encrusted hags: "hideously ugly, and filthy to the extreme; wrinkle upon wrinkle covered their faces, and layer upon layer of dirt covered the wrinkles,"[91] or "a hideous picture of ugliness and dirt; . . . discharges ran out of her mouth, nose and eyes."[92] There was nothing of the Noble Sav-

[85] Ole Munch Raeder, *America in the Forties: The Letters of Ole Munch Raeder* (Minneapolis, 1929), p. 145.
[86] Jacob Schiel, *Reise durch die Felsengebirge und die Humboldtgebirge nach dem Stillen Ocean* (Schaffhausen, 1859), pp. 12–13.
[87] Ernest Duvergier de Hauranne, *A Frenchman in Lincoln's America* (Chicago, 1974), 1: 206–7; Edward S. Ellis, *Across Texas* (Philadelphia, 1893), p. 33; Ernst Graf zu Erbach-Erbach, *Reisebriefe aus Amerika* (Heidelberg, 1873), p. 146.
[88] Erbach-Erbach, *Reisebriefe aus Amerika*, p. 146.
[89] William Kelly, *An Excursion to California over the Prairie, Rocky Mountains, and Great Sierra Nevada* (London, 1851), 1: 253.
[90] O. Drevdahl, *Fra Emigrationens Amerika* (Oslo, 1891), unpaged; a similar opinion is in Henryk Sienkiewicz, *Listy z Podróży: Koleja Dwóch Oceanów Szkice Amerykańskie* (Warsaw, 1898), 4: 57–58.
[91] John T. Irving, *Indian Sketches, Taken during an Expedition to the Pawnee and Other Tribes of American Indians* (London, 1835), 1: 170.
[92] Jacob Schiel, *Journey through the Rocky Mountains to the Pacific Ocean* (Norman, 1959), p. 97.

age in these caricatures. "Horrible, more horrible—most horrible," one characterized them, and few disagreed.[93]

Both men and women were incredibly lazy, content to spend their days "in slothful ease and idleness," and so indolent that they would rather starve than lift a hand in their own behalf.[94] Like animals, they made no plans for the future. "They live they know not how," wrote a visitor among the Pawnee, "and they care not where. A little suffices them; if they can get it, they are satisfied; if not, they are satisfied without it."[95] The mark of the civilized man was his concern for the future; in their indifference to their fate the Indians proved themselves beasts rather than humans.

Their total lack of morality proved the point. Visitors were repeatedly shocked by what they viewed as sexual promiscuity; girls gave or sold themselves to anyone they chose, and even a proud warrior was willing to "consign his wife or daughter for the gratification of anyone, for merely a few baubles."[96] One German barely escaped with his honor when "a number of young Indian girls fell upon me, ripped at my clothes and allowed themselves the most embarrassing grasps of the hands."[97] He escaped by flailing about with his fists, but such liberties were not allowable in Victorian Europe.

Indians showed their moral weakness particularly by their insatiable craving for alcohol. The sights recorded by travelers were ample evidence of their inhumanity: half-drunken Indians shouting "Whiskey, Whiskey," at passing stagecoaches; once proud warriors bartering away their total possessions for a bottle, mere youths "drinking themselves into a stupor, reeling to their feet, and beginning drinking again," young and old wallowing in the mud like pigs, uttering half-choked sounds, men brawling and murdering each other in drunken frenzy.[98] "Confronted with the pos-

[93] Latrobe, *The Rambler in North America*, 1: 160. Similar opinions are in Löher, *Land und Leute in der Alten und Neuen Welt*, p. 173, and Paul Wilhelm, Herzog von Württemberg, *Erste Reise nach dem Nördlichen Amerika in den Jahren 1822 bis 1824* (Stuttgart, 1835), p. 179.
[94] Julian Thoulet, "Seven Months with the Chippeways," *Tygodnik Ilustrowany* 13 (1874): 63; *American Settler*, 9 February 1889.
[95] Irving, *Indian Sketches*, 1: 23–24.
[96] Isaac Holmes, *An Account of the United States of America, Derived from an Actual Observation during a Residence of Four Years in that Republic* (London, n.d.), p. 33. Similar comments are in Storm, *Alene i Urskogen*, p. 51; Marryat, *Diary in America*, 2: 96–97, and Francesco Arese, *A Trip to the Prairies in the Interior of North America* (New York, 1934), p. 373.
[97] Löher, *Land und Leute in der Alten und Neuen Welt*, p. 174.
[98] *Chamber's Journal* 100 (1 December 1885): 340; *American Settler*, 5 November 1887; Patrick Shirreff, *A Tour through North America: Together with a Comprehensive View of the Canadas and United States* (Edinburgh, 1835), pp. 98–99; Carl D. Arfwedson, *The United States and Canada in 1832, 1833, and 1834* (London, 1834), 2: 23. An excellent discussion of this subject is in Gary C. Stein, "A Fearful Drunkness: The Liquor Trade to the Western Indians As Seen by European Travelers in America, 1800–1860," *Red River Valley Historical Review* 1 (Summer 1974): 109–21.

sibility of Fire Water," wrote a Norwegian traveler, ". . . a mother will let her infant cry with hunger and a husband will sell his wife to the first one who offers him a bottle."[99]

Indians, the image-makers agreed, drank solely to get drunk; civilized humans drank for pleasure or companionship. They, unlike the whites, could not resist temptation, a sure indication of their animalistic natures. Only a few observers were willing to admit that drinking was an escape-hatch from the poverty and humiliation that accompanied the shattering of their culture, or that the true villains were the storekeepers and traders who plied them with liquor to cheat them of their lands and goods. "When I see an Indian groveling in the dirt, with a helpless body and a reeling brain, and uttering thick and half-choking sounds," a British traveler wrote, "I cannot help thinking that we have done this!—We, who boast of our civilization."[100] Few were that understanding. The image projected by travelers was of an inferior race, lacking the self-restraint that separated man from beast, and doomed to extermination.

The ultimate degradation of the red men was the public humiliation they suffered at the hands of travelers or promoters. Oft-told were tales of visitors who plied young Indians with liquor until they made spectacles of themselves; of tourists who bribed tribesmen to stage a "war dance," then urged on the performers as they would trained dogs; of campers who tossed scraps of meat and watched the red men battle for them; of the mighty Sitting Bull peddling his photograph at carnivals for a dollar.[101] Nor were these spectacles confined to the American West. From the 1840s on, troupes of Indians were regularly displayed on the Continent, re-cruited by promoters with the open connivance of federal agents who believed that "they were better off in a show making money than at home fighting or doing nothing."[102] Londoners or Parisians who gaped at once-proud warriors peddling patent medicines or staging their "war dances" at carnivals were witnessing the final degradation of the Noble Savage.

Thus were the mighty fallen, toppled from their pedestals by image-makers unwilling to question or understand the reason for their sad fate. Most Europeans accepted their judgment. Charles Dickens spoke for many when he wrote in 1853: "I call him a savage, and I call a savage something highly desirable to be civilized off the face of the earth."[103]

[99] Arfwedson, *The United States and Canada*, 2: 23.
[100] Eneas Mackenzie, *An Historical, Topographical, and Descriptive View of the United States of America, and of Upper and Lower Canada* (Newcastle-upon-Tyne, 1819), p. 702.
[101] Duvergier, *A Frenchman in Lincoln's America*, 1: 222; Nicolaus Mohr, *Excursion through America* (Chicago, 1973), p. 112.
[102] *American Settler*, 6 June 1891. An account of the role of Indians in traveling shows is in Carolyn T. Foreman, *Indians Abroad, 1493–1938* (Norman, 1943), pp. 120–73.
[103] Quoted in Robert B. Heilman, "The New World in Dickens' Writings," *Trollopian* 1 (September 1946): 41.

Others, more charitable, mourned the passing of a proud race but accepted its passing as inevitable. They were a doomed species, by-passed in society's evolution. Karl May wrote their epitaph when he described the mighty warriors of the past who now crept about like mangy dogs, begging and stealing: "Yes, he is a sick man, and with sympathy we stand by his bedside to close his eyes for him."[104] The end of an era, and of a race was at hand.

[104] Quoted in Cracroft, "The American West of Karl May," p. 128.

VI

Native Americans:
Doomed to Extermination

THE EUROPEAN IMAGE-MAKERS might differ in describing the Native American as Europeanized Noble Savages or as bloodthirsty barbarians but they all agreed on one point: that all, "good" and "bad" alike, were doomed to rapid extermination. Their fate was decreed by a heartless federal government whose deliberate policy was to kill as many as possible in needless wars, then drive the remainder onto barren reservations where they would soon perish. Underlying this program was the demand of the frontiersmen for the Indians' lands; the red men were to be sacrificed on the altar of the Almighty Dollar. They deserved the pity of Europeans, just as the government deserved contempt for its inhuman policies.

Some of the image-makers were honest enough to admit that a modicum of logic underlay the "removal" policy of Andrew Jackson and his successors; by being transplanted to reservations beyond the Mississippi they would be separated from the contaminating impact of the white man's greed, liquor, and land hunger. Beyond this point Americans and Europeans disagreed. To Americans, or at least American humanitarians, the reservation system was needed to preserve the red men's culture. To Europeans this was a shoddy subterfuge: its real purpose was to drive them from lands wanted by frontiersmen. As the century progressed, and the tragedy of the removal policy became more and more clear, this opinion deepened. The enduring European belief that the United States was a predatory nation, willing to exploit helpless minorities that stood in the way of its manifest destiny, was rooted in resentment against its policies during the "century of dishonor."

Frontier Savagery: The European View

This resentment was heightened by the image of frontiersmen popularized by novelists and hostile travelers. Europeans were taught that every pioneer was a born-again Indian hater who saw the red men as an inferior species, incapable of accepting civilization, and fit only for extermination. Westerners, they were told, would as soon shoot an Indian as a wildcat— or a raccoon, or a deer, or a bear, or a coyote, depending on the time and the place.[1] In their eyes all red men were worse than vermin—"nothing better than a destructive, ravenous, wild beast, without reason, without a soul, that ought to be hunted down like a wolf."[2] To wipe them out would be to serve humanity. "According to the philosophy of the frontier," a Polish visitor recorded, "the white man has the same right to exterminate Indians as he would rattlesnakes, grizzly bears, and other harmful creatures."[3] Among the frontiersmen pictured by the image-makers there was no sympathy for an endangered species.

To make matters worse they practiced what they preached. Travelers' tales were filled with stories of frontiersmen who killed Indians in cold blood: one who instinctively raised his rifle to shoot an Indian before he realized that he was in a town;[4] another who killed an innocent red man to get the turkey he had just killed;[5] two more who gunned down two passing Indians for sport, "as casually as if shooting two crows."[6] Even more

[1] This remark appeared, with different animals each time, in such accounts as Francis Baily, *Journal of a Tour in the Unsettled Parts of North America in 1796 and 1797* (London, 1856), pp. 220–21; William N. Blane, *An Excursion through the United States and Canada, during the Years 1822–23* (London, 1824), p. 301; Philip S. Robinson, *Sinners and Saints: A Tour Across the States, and Round Them* (London, 1883), p. 273; Carl of Solms-Braunfels, *Texas, 1844–1845* (Houston, 1936), p. 40; and Moritz Busch, *Wanderungen zwischen Hudson und Mississippi 1851 und 1852* (Tübingen, 1854), pp. 305–6.
[2] Isaac Weld, *Travels through the United States of North America and the Provinces of Upper and Lower Canada* (London, 1807), 2: 217–18.
[3] Henryk Sienkiewicz, *Listy z Podróży: Koleja Dwóch Oceanów Szkice Amerykańskie* (Warsaw, 1899), 4: 60.
[4] J. E. Alexander, *Transatlantic Sketches, Comprising Visits to the Most Interesting Scenes in North and South America and the West Indies* (London, 1833), 2: 82. Many other examples, with an admirable discussion of the subject, are in Gary C. Stein, "Federal Indian Policy As Seen by British Travelers in America, 1783–1860" (Ph.D. diss., University of New Mexico, 1975).
[5] Charles A. Murray, *Travels in North America during the Years 1834, 1835, and 1836* (London, 1839), 2: 96–97.
[6] Quoted in Alan Conway, ed., *The Welsh in America: Letters from the Immigrants* (Minneapolis, 1961), pp. 241–42.

"Basil and the Bison Bull." From Mayne Reid, *The Young Voyagers*
(London, 1854), opposite p. 123. (From the Special Collections
of the University of California at Los Angeles Library.)

tragic were accounts of gangs of California miners who slaughtered whole villages for no reason—"mothers with infants at their breasts, pleading for their lives, were killed while the infants had their skulls smashed with stones"—then staged a "victory celebration" to burn the bodies of the dead, including several boys and girls who were still alive.[7] Those who escaped such massacres were worked unmercifully as slaves, then butchered. "If any of them displease us," one traveler was told, "we take them out doors and kick them a little, for they are like dogs, and so will love you the better for it."[8]

Nor were these isolated bursts of sadism; they were not only common but vigorously defended by western opinion and the western press. The brutal Chivington Massacre was hailed by western newspapers as "a good and wholesome act of severity—one that ought to be repeated twice a year"[9]—while the defeat of Colonel Custer's forces at the Battle of the Little Big Horn stirred a universal demand for an all-out war of extermination. "There will be no treating or temporizing with the red brutes," proclaimed a San Francisco newspaper widely quoted in Europe, "whose fiendish atrocities and mutilations of the dead on the field of the Little Big Horn stamp them as worse than wild beasts."[10] The West would not be satisfied until every Indian was dead. "We can destroy them by the laws of war," quoth one frontiersman, "or thin 'em out by whiskey; but the thinning process is too plaguy slow."[11] Europeans who heard this savage litany were convinced that along the frontier the only good Indian was a dead Indian.

That image was heightened by sensation-peddling novelists who seized on the revenge theme as made to order for their needs. A favorite plot sent the white hero, whose wife and children had been killed by Indians, on a one-man crusade against the whole race—"Sending all those red devils to hell," in the words of one whose family had been wiped out by Comanches in Kentucky [sic].[12] They carried on their quests with insatiable intensity; declared one: "Hundreds must die, thousands, before my revenge is satisfied." Merely slaughtering redskins was not enough for that

[7] Theodor Griesinger, *Land und Leute in Amerika: Skizzen aus dem Amerikanischen Leben* (Stuttgart, 1863), pp. 476–77.
[8] Fortesque Cuming, *Sketches of a Tour to the Western Country* (Pittsburgh, 1810), pp. 238–39.
[9] William Hepworth Dixon, *New America* (London, 1867), 1: 61.
[10] *San Francisco Chronicle*, quoted in Robert A. Trennert, "Popular Imagery and the American Indian: A Centennial View," *New Mexico Historical Review* 51 (July 1976): 225.
[11] Robert Watt, *Hinsides Atlanterhavet: Skildringer fra Amerika* (Copenhagen, 1874), p. 31. The quotation is from Charles W. Dilke, *Greater Britain: A Record of Travel in English-Speaking Countries during 1866 and 1867* (London, 1872), pp. 85–86.
[12] P. M. Petersen, *Grændsejægerens Datter: Skuespil i tre Akter* (Oslo, 1877), pp. 31–32.

doughty hero who planned to circulate smallpox-infested blankets among them until all were dead.[13]

So persuasive was the practice of Indian killing among American frontiersmen that even visiting Europeans adopted the habit—at least in European fiction. Gustave Aimard's alter ego, Valentine, thought nothing of counseling a companion who had captured an Indian: "Thrust your knife into the scoundrel's breast, and that's an end to him."[14] Jack Harkaway felt the same way and "thought no more of drawing a bead on a redskin than he did of kicking over the house of a prairie-dog." His trusted companion, Billy Shoot-Dead, went even farther: "I've no sort of respect for a man who hasn't killed his Injun," said he.[15] Only Karl May's characters, suffering as they did from overdoses of Teutonic morality, could not bring themselves to cold-blooded murder; Old Surehand found himself despised as a "greenhorn" when he showed a touch of compassion.[16]

After a diet of such sensationalism, two British schoolboys (fictional, but probably true to life) fell to discussing a trip West just to kill Indians:

"We could each take a gun along," one declared, "and every day we'd go out and shoot Injuns. You and me would keep tally and see who could drop the most." "I wonder how long it would take us to shoot 'em all?" the other asks. "Oh, we wouldn't be mean enough to have all the fun by ourselves; after we had plugged two or three hundred, we'd hunt up other boys and join together; we'd just march through the country and clean 'em all out. It's our duty to do that for then it would be safe for other boys and their little brothers and sisters and mothers to go out West."[17]

Gross exaggeration, perhaps, but in such impressions there was a grain of truth.

Such attitudes were savage enough, but even more shocking to proper Europeans was the universal frontier practice (in novels that is) of scalping Indian victims; frontiersmen were pictured as just as adept at lifting-hair as the most ferocious redskins. Many a tale was told of professional scalp hunters who lived on the government bounties paid for hair, the price ranging up to fifty dollars for an Apache. "Counts six," declared such a character, ". . . six at fifty—three hundred shiners for Pash hair; beats

[13]   Friedrich Gerstäcker, *Mississippi-Bilder, Licht-und Schattenseiten transatlantischen Lebens* (Jena, 1847–48), p. 540. A similar account is in Gabriel Ferry, *The Wood Rangers* (London, 1860), I: 241–42.
[14]   Gustave Aimard, *The Gold Finders: A Romance of California* (New York, n.d.), pp. 55–56.
[15]   Bracebridge Hemyng, *Jack Harkaway Out West amongst the Indians* (London, n.d.), pp. 3, 6.
[16]   Karl May, *Old Surehand: Erster Band* (Vienna, 1953), pp. 15–16.
[17]   Edward S. Ellis, *Teddy and Towser: A Story of the Early Days in California* (Philadelphia, 1904), pp. 14–15.

beaver trappin' says I.''[18] When Jack Harkaway protested the mutilation of the dead he was assured: "More don't they. That's why we do it. They think if we raise their har that they'll go baldheaded into the happy-hunting grounds."[19] That convinced Jack; from then on he scalped with the best of them.

Seasoned plainsmen could only keep track of the number of Indians they killed by cutting notches on their gun stocks. Old Rube Hawkins's rifle, "Tar-Guts," was solidly covered with symbols: crosses for Apaches, double crosses for Sioux, triple crosses for Pawnees, stars for Crows, parallel notches for Flatheads, and circles for Blackfeet.[20] Among themselves they boasted of the number they had shot down, each vehemently defending his own record: "Each notch here stands for a redskin's soul," Old Reuben declared. "Look here! There are many! Here are fifteen, here are twenty."[21] Nor were the Indian dead safe from frontier brutality; those killed on the battlefield were left to rot there ("Bury a dead Injun: My word, you'll talk of burying a dead donkey next!")[22] or when burial was necessary, the graves were intentionally left so shallow that the remains could be scattered and devoured by wolves.[23] Here was inhumanity carried to the ultimate power.

Official Savagery: Federal Indian Policy

Tolerant-minded Europeans fed on a diet of Westerns might expect half-savage frontiersmen to be mercilessly cruel toward the Indians, but none could forgive the federal government for its heartless policies. Indian removal to the barren lands beyond the Mississippi and Indian concentration on arid reservations there were very much part of the image-makers' story. Grossly distorted to favor the red men, these tales pictured the United States as a merciless enemy of a helpless minority: fracturing the Indians' social structure, and relentlessly eroding their numbers by warfare, vice, and starvation, with the avowed purpose of eliminating the entire race.

Many Americans, and a few Europeans, believing that Christianity would so benefit the red men in heaven that any suffering on earth was justified, saw American policy as both necessary and beneficial. To their

[18] Mayne Reid, *The Scalp Hunters; or, Romantic Adventures in Northern Mexico* (London, 1851), 2: 166–67. A similar story of scalp hunters is in Gustave Aimard, *The Queen of the Savannah: A Story of the Mexican War* (London, n.d.), pp. 7–8.
[19] Hemyng, *Jack Harkaway Out West amongst the Indians*, p. 12.
[20] Gabriel Ferry, *Le Coureur des bois* (reprint ed., Paris, 1932), 1: 152.
[21] Petersen, *Grændsejægerens Datter*, pp. 34–35.
[22] Hemyng, *Jack Harkaway Out West amongst the Indians*, pp. 14–15.
[23] Jakub Gordon, *Podróż do Nowego Orleanu* (Leipzig, 1867), pp. 157–58.

mind the Indians must be taught to worship the true God and to enrich themselves by tilling the soil,[24] but with this view the vast majority of image-makers differed completely. Instead they saw both Indian removal and isolation as deliberately planned to rob Native Americans of their cultural traditions, induce psychological maladjustment, and leave them so unfit for assimilation that their extermination would be justified. The United States was doing little more than place its stamp of approval on the land hunger of the pioneers.

Basic to the majority view in Europe was the belief that Indians were human beings, not a subspecies, and hence capable of assimilation. "There is no deficiency in their intellect," one traveler insisted, "that would consign them to perpetual degradation."[25] With proper care they could be taught the manual arts and converted into useful citizens. "They are idle," a British commentator insisted, "—let us present them with the inducements of industry; they have been cut off from the chase—let us give them a knowledge of the useful arts; they are spiritless and disheartened—let us cheer them with the hope of present comfort and future happiness."[26] Here was the platform on which sympathetic Europeans placed their understanding. A platform obviously the opposite of that accepted by the frontiersmen and the American government.

For so long as the red men were repeatedly harrassed from their lands they would be incapable of such blessings. "One who is being slowly but surely driven to extinction," Winnetou explained to Old Shatterhand, "cannot believe that the teachings of the executioner are teachings of love."[27] But give the Indian half a chance and he was as capable of civilization as the white man. That chance would be forever denied them so long as they occupied land wanted by the greedy pioneers. "The pale faces are insatiable," complained an Indian in a French novel, ". . . and seek continuously to rob and dispossess us."[28] So long as they held an inch of territory wanted by frontiersmen the fatal cycle would continue: "They drive us far off; we become settled, they disturb us, and drive us farther off again, because they want our lands for themselves."[29] Not until the last was killed would the pattern of aggression end.

Until that day the Americans would use any means, fair or foul, to seize the Indian lands, from open warfare to maneuvering tribes into

[24] Comments supporting this generalization are in Stein, "Federal Indian Policy As Seen by British Travelers," pp. 122, 149.
[25] Quoted in ibid., pp. 133–34.
[26] John M. Duncan, *Travels through Part of the United States and Canada in 1818 and 1819* (Glasgow, 1823), 2: 90.
[27] Karl May, *Winnetou I: Ungekürzte Ausgabe* (reprint ed., Vienna, 1953), p. 212. A similar comment in a Dutch journal is in *Vragen van de Dag* 3 (1888): 399.
[28] Gustave Aimard, *The Tiger Slayer* (New York, n.d.), p. 60.
[29] James S. Buckingham, *America* (London, 1841), 1: 110–11.

weakening conflicts.[30] A character in a French novel was guilty of only slight exaggeration when he gunned down the inhabitants of a Pawnee village after failing to negotiate its purchase; "I had the right to do so," he explained, "since the redskins refused to surrender it to me."[31] The government land-grabbers might use more subtle methods, but the results were the same. Alexis de Tocqueville, who understood American motivation better than most Europeans, told his fellow Frenchmen that "it was impossible to destroy a man with more respect for the laws of humanity," than did the federal government in dealing with the Indian.[32]

Europeans accepted this verdict, and adopted an I-told-you-so attitude as they learned of each new aggression. Andrew Jackson's removal policy was generally condemned: "an unwarranted exercise of *power* against *right*"; "one of the most painful chapters in the history of America"; "a tragic example of inhuman egoism and greed."[33] More protests were stirred as the army drove the southern tribesmen across the Mississippi at bayonet point, or entrusted their removal to unscrupulous contractors who amassed small fortunes while their charges died of starvation and neglect. "My heart bled for them in their delocation and decline," a British observer moaned, and his tears were shared by many a European as he read of their fate.[34]

The story of Indian removal provided a tempting theme for sentimental novelists, and they responded by the score. Typical was Charles Sealsfield's *Der Legitime und die Republikaner*, published in English as *Tokeah; or, The White Rose*, a story of the lifelong struggle of the Oconee chief, Tokeah, to defend his people's lands against the white aggressors. He failed, of course, and was himself driven westward into a dreary wilderness. In its tragic conclusion the novel described Tokeah's return to retrieve the bones of his ancestors, only to die himself and be carried westward to a country so distant that his body would never be molested. Sealsfield's symbolism was clear; only by fleeing to the most distant and unwanted reaches of the West could the red men escape "the glaring avarice of our squatters and shop-keepers."[35]

With the inauguration of the reservation policy after the Civil War, the image-makers focused on the plight of tribesmen uprooted from their

[30] *American Settler*, 2 October 1886; *De Hollandsche Illustratie* 10 (1873): 5; and Pierre Maël, *Les Derniers Hommes rouges* (Paris, 1896), pp. 161–62, report such tactics as used by the United States.
[31] Gustave Aimard, *The Border Rifles: A Tale of the Texan War* (Philadelphia, n.d.), p. 60.
[32] Alexis de Tocqueville, *Democracy in America* (New York, 1904), 1: 385–86.
[33] Excellent quotations on this subject are in Stein, "Federal Indian Policy As Seen by British Travelers," pp. 87–99, 110–16, 310–12.
[34] Charles J. Latrobe, *The Rambler in North America* (London, 1835), 2: 158.
[35] Charles Sealsfield, *Der Legitime und die Republikaner: Eine Geschichte aus dem amerikanisch-englischen Kriege* (Zurich, 1833), introduction.

homes and forced to become begging vassals of a cruel government. Degraded as wards of a corrupt bureaucracy, they were pictured as victims of the misery and despair natural among people wrenched from their traditional culture; emaciated, dirty, sullen, lifeless—escaping into strong drink to forget their humiliation, dying from the white man's diseases and vices—"living in poverty on the products of a land which they know not how to cultivate and over which they used to roam as masters."[36] "We want to live as we have been raised," a chief told a visitor, "hunting the animals of the prairie. Do not speak to us of shutting us up on reservations and making us cultivate the land. Let us follow the buffalo."[37] Here was a tortured call for freedom bound to touch any European.

In all of this literature of protest, however, there was no suggestion that the Indians should be allowed to retain their lands and culture. This was a materialistic century, in Europe as in the United States, and to waste land on hunting that could be cultivated was unthinkable. Europeans might weep over the plight of red men, but they agreed that to survive they must accept instruction in farming and craftmanship until able to support themselves as the white man supported himself. They must, in other words, acknowledge "the duties and responsibilities of intelligent citizenship,"[38] and consent to instruction in the ways of an utilitarian world. Image-makers noted with delight that the first thing little Indian girls who had been schooled did when they returned to their reservations was "to transform the lodge of filth into one that is neat and tidy."[39] Educate all red men and they would be fitted into American society; isolate them on reservations and they would vegetate in ignorance until fit only for roles in Wild West shows.

This was whistling in the wind, and most of the image-makers said so. Not only were many Indians emotionally and physically incapable of walking the white man's road, but the frontiersmen would never accept them as equals.[40] The red men had only two choices: they could stage a hopeless war that would end with their extermination, or they could waste away on reservations until filth, disease, and a broken heart carried off the last survivor. Whatever their choice, their fate was sealed. All would vanish from the earth within a century. "They can," wrote a Polish observer, "neither resist civilization nor support its heavy burden upon their weak shoulders."[41]

36   Fernand Hué, *Les Coureurs de frontières* (Paris, 1889), p. 219.
37   Louis L. Simonin, *The Rocky Mountain West in 1867* (Lincoln, 1966), p. 111.
38   *American Settler*, 8 March 1888.
39   *American Settler*, 27 October 1888.
40   Paul Duplessis, *La Sonora* (Paris, 1858), 2: 216–17; Jens Tvedt, *Sihasapa-Indianerne: Norske Udvandreres Hendelser i Amerika* (Stavanger, 1887), 71; Bénédict-Henry Révoil in *Journal des voyages et des adventures de terre et de mer*, no. 188 (13 February 1881): 87.
41   Sienkiewicz, *Listy z Podróży*, 4: 64.

Inevitably their plight was linked with that of the animals that stood in the way of civilization's progress, and particularly with that of the buffalo. As these shaggy beasts were slaughtered, the Indians' staff of life went with them; soon the "great savage poem" of the hunt would give way to "the prose of cultivated land, of cattle, and of Yankee workers."[42] Both were victims of the great chain of evolution and had outlived their purposes. "Primitive man," a French visitor wrote, "will disappear with the primitive animal."[43] Where civilization was progressing, "the uncultivated must give place to the cultivated."[44] As easily stop the course of the stars in their firmament as challenge this law of Nature. The Indian, like the buffalo, must go.

During the latter half of the century this dire prophecy was universally accepted; journalists and novelists and letter writers, British and German and Norwegian and Hungarian commentators, all chorused the early demise of the Indian race. They spoke in many tongues but their words had a common ring: "It is as certain as any human event can be, that they are destined to be displaced by the Anglo-Saxon race";[45] "the remains of the ancient inhabitants of America will soon be completely destroyed";[46] "it is unanimously agreed that the Indian race must end . . . and will cease to exist once the Europeans reach the Pacific Ocean";[47] "the red men . . . is doomed to be wiped from the roll of peoples."[48] The fate of all was sealed, even those who tried to walk the white man's path. They had been, as one image-maker put it, "improved off the face of the earth."[49]

Tragically, the Indians were aware of their fate, and said so in many a tearful dialogue with the image-makers. "The days of my people are almost numbered," sighed one chief; "already they are dropping off like the rays of the sunlight in the western sky."[50] "We are melting like snow before the sun," added another.[51] This was the fate they had chosen, for death was preferable to becoming vassals of the whites, grubbing in the land over which they had roamed so widely. "The proud Indian will die of

[42] Most novelists and travelers linked the extermination of the buffalo with the fate of the Indians.
[43] Simonin, *Rocky Mountain West in 1867*, p. 22.
[44] *American Settler*, 11 June 1881.
[45] James S. Buckingham, *The Eastern and Western States of America* (London, 1842), 3: 112.
[46] A. S. Pushkin, "John Tanner," in *Complete Works*, 12 (Moscow, 1949): 104–5.
[47] Ludwik Powidaj, "Polacy i Indianie," *Dziennik Literacki* 56 (1864): 835.
[48] Hans J. S. Astrup, *Blik paa Amerikanske forhold, særlig med hensyn paa fra Norge indvandrede* (Oslo, 1893), pp. 49–50. A number of quotations from English travelers on this theme are in Stein, "Federal Indian Policy As Seen by British Travelers," pp. 232–36.
[49] David W. Mitchell, *Ten Years in the United States* (London, 1862), p. 62; Albert de Chenclos, "Peaux-Rouges et visages pales," *Revue des deux mondes* (May–June 1889), p. 858.
[50] *American Settler*, 27 October 1883.
[51] Francis B. Head, *The Emigrant* (London, 1847), p. 146.

hunger rather than serve a white man," said one.[52] Every schoolboy on the Continent knew of the last red man on earth who wept as he chanted the death song that would waft him to his happy-hunting ground, and the boy wept with him, partly out of sympathy, partly because that Indian might not live long enough for the boy to go west and shoot him as had the hero of *The Trapper's Guide; or, Ten-Fingered Jake, the Silent Terror of the Tuscaroras.*[53]

Here was another theme that lent itself to sentimentalism, and one that few novelists could resist. Their villains were the frontiersmen—ruthless landgrabbers driving the Indians from their ancestral hunting grounds, "pursuing them like wild beasts whenever they met them, burning their callis and dispersing the bones of their ancestors to the four winds of heaven."[54] No desert was too remote to escape these dollar-worshiping Yankees. "Soon we will be crowded against the rocks," mourned an old chief, "and there we shall die in snow and ice for want of food."[55] Jack Harkaway listened sadly as an aging Soux counted on his fingers: "One, two, three. In three generations the red men and the buffalo will be no more."[56] No matter what he read, the European heard that sad message over and over again. The death of a race was near.

Extermination Justified: The Imperialistic View

The image-makers might agree that the Indian was doomed, but they differed sharply on whether his fate was justifiable. Some mourned his passing and pictured his tragic plight in verse and story; those who held this belief were largely—but not exclusively—eastern Europeans who equated the plight of the red men with their own struggles for freedom and survival, or southern Europeans strongly influenced by the romantic tradition. Others viewed the extermination of the Indians as not only inevitable but desirable. This view was most strongly represented among British, Germans, and Scandinavians whose countries had contributed so largely

---

[52] Sándor Farkas, *Journey in North America, 1831* (Santa Barbara, 1978), p. 63. Similar sentiments are expressed in Béla Szécheny, *Amerikai utam* (Pest, 1863), p. 42, and Chenclos, "Peaux-Rouges et visages pales," p. 859.

[53] *American Settler,* 18 January 1890.

[54] Gustave Aimard, *The Indian Scout; or, Life on the Frontier* (Philadelphia, n.d.), p. 237.

[55] Gustave Aimard, *The Red River Half-Breed: A Tale of the Wild North-West* (London, n.d.), p. 357. The same opinion was expressed by Aimard in *The Trappers of Arkansas; or, The Loyal Heart* (London, 1864), p. 87; *The Pirates of the Prairies: Adventures in the American Desert* (London, 1862), p. 20; *The Queen of the Savannah,* pp. 6–7, and other books, as well as in the works of many other writers, including William Black, *Green Pastures and Piccadilly* (London, 1878), p. 386, and Friedrich Gerstäcker, *Gold! Ein californisches Lebensbild aus dem Jahr 1849* (Leipzig, 1858), 2: 431, 432.

[56] Hemyng, *Jack Harkaway Out West amongst the Indians,* p. 34.

to the immigrant stream then flowing toward the frontiers. This division revealed something of the influence of national traits in image-making.

Those who believed the Indian unassimilatable, and hence expendable, held that the red man was a subhuman barbarian and would remain so forever. Over and over again the image-makers reiterated this message: "Indians are incapable of civilization";[57] "they are like gypsies; nature's wildness is in their blood";[58] "wolves by nature, by the instincts implanted by centuries of savage life";[59] "blood-thirsty brown animals who are best destroyed."[60] Incapable of learning civilization's ways, stubbornly determined "never to be torn from the breast of their barbaric mother,"[61] they should be allowed to vanish from the scene. "As well persuade the eagle to descend from the lofty region in which he exists and live with the fowls of our court-yards," an English publicist wrote, "as to prevail upon the red men of North America to become what we call civilized."[62] One symbolized savagery, the other civilization, and never could the twain meet.

One needed only to visit a reservation to realize the truth of that statement. The Indians were a sad lot, suspended between the past and present, unable to hunt and unwilling to farm.[63] "If they were to dig in the ground," one warrior proudly asserted, "their sight would become weak, and their enemies would say they were moles or badgers."[64] The white man's ways were not for them; they were born to the chase and to the broad horizons of Nature. "His pride and untamed freedom are in harmony with the lonely mountains, the rivers, and the waterfalls that surround him," wrote a Norwegian novelist.[65] Those who tried to adjust to civilization were "dying out quietly, defeated by the reservation to which they have been assigned."[66]

Their fate demonstrated one indisputable fact: that the Indians had been outmoded by the evolution of higher social forms and were as doomed to extinction as the dinosaur or the dodo bird. They were incapable of survival when pitted against Europeans who represented a higher

---

[57]   Károly Nendtvich, *Amerikai utazásom* (Pest, 1858), 1: 202.
[58]   Kristofer Janson, *Amerikanske forholde: Fem foredrag* (Copenhagen, 1881), pp. 101–2.
[59]   *American Settler*, 19 December 1885.
[60]   *De Hollandsche Illustratie*, 7 (1887): no. 28.
[61]   Eilert Storm, *Alene i urskogen: Fortælling fra Amerika* (Oslo, 1899), p. 53. A similar opinion of an Hungarian traveler is in Jenö Bánó, *Úti képek Amerikából* (Budapest, 1890), p. 70.
[62]   Head, *The Emigrant*, p. 124.
[63]   Griesinger, *Land und Leute in Amerika*, pp. 462–63, and Paul Duplessis, *Le Batteur d'estrade* (Paris, 1862), 4: 41, are typical of travelers, nearly all of whom expressed this view.
[64]   Frederick Marryat, *Narrative of the Travels and Adventures of Monsieur Violet, in California, Sonora, and Western Texas* (London, 1843), pp. 23–24.
[65]   Storm, *Alene i urskogen*, p. 13.
[66]   Alajos Izsóf, *Tul a nagy vizeken* (Budapest, 1916), p. 34.

level in the evolutionary scale. The skills needed for survivial in the modern world were beyond them. "Their sense of inferiority to the white man in these arts," wrote a commentator, "drives them to despair."[67] The two races—one superior, the other inferior—could no more live together than crabbed old age and innocent youth, or black and grey rats. One must go, and under the laws of evolution, that must be the inferior.

On this point there was no wavering among the image-makers. They saw European civilization as the crowning achievement of the evolutionary chain, and agreed that its progress must not be slowed to accommodate a lesser people. "The process of modernization," a traveler wrote, "possesses an inalienable right to go ahead and is entitled to push away whatever stands in its way."[68] There should be no sentimental tears shed for the victims, for there was too much to gain by those who benefited. Europeans wrote of "the triumph over violence," and of "savages giving way to more enlightened inhabitants."[69] The basic laws of civilization must be obeyed.

Those "enlightened inhabitants" were those who could use America as God intended: for farms and homes and factories. If the red men would forsake the hunt for farming and herding, they could remain, but they were either incapable or unwilling to do so. Why set aside millions of fertile acres needed by industrious white men? "Such extravagances cannot be afforded in the modern household of the world. . . . As they seem to be without a function in the developing economic life, they must be destroyed."[70] That was the Divine Will; God in His infinite wisdom would never allow a few hundred savages to monopolize lands "on which hundreds of millions of industrious men could dwell and support themselves."[71] Their elimination was demanded "by the ineluctable nature of things, or rather by the law of progress and civilization, which is the only law of history."[72] Nor could the Indians claim that the land was theirs. They had no more right to the soil than the beasts of the field; they were merely "tenants at will" intended by the Divine Plan to occupy the land only until it was needed by a more advanced civilization. The whole human race had an inherent right to all natural resources that would benefit mankind; hence the American government was guilty of neither illegality nor inhumanity when it seized the red men's lands for a better

---

[67]   George D. Warburton, *Hochelaga; or, England in the New World* (New York, 1846), 2: 164–65.
[68]   Nendtvich, *Amerikai utazásom*, 1: 200–201.
[69]   Frances Wright, *Views of Society and Manners in America* (London, 1821), p. 106, and Priscilla B. Wakefield, *Excursion in North America* (London, 1806), p. 133.
[70]   Henrik Gevling, *Fra Amerika* (Copenhagen, 1897), 2: 407–8.
[71]   Frederick L. G. von Raumer, *America and the American People* (New York, 1846), p. 138.
[72]   Louis L. Simonim, "Les Derniers Peaux-Rouges," *Revue des deux mondes* (March–April 1874), p. 79.

use.[73] "By right," according to a French observer, "the land belonged to the more intelligent race who cleared it, who made it valuable, who watered it with the sweat of the brow, who held it in the name of God and of the King, and who would not give it up."[74] The law of might was the law of right.

This was the message preached by image-makers over all of northern and western Europe, but never more vehemently than by the British. This was understandable. England's empire was spreading across the world, usually at the expense of peoples whose color and culture differed from her own. Expansion could be justified only by extolling the virtues of the Anglo-Saxon race, and degrading the "lesser" races who stood in its way. To picture one such people—the Native Americans—as inferior was to justify imperialism everywhere.

This note ran through much British writing in the late nineteenth century, but was expressed nowhere more stridently than in the novels of Mayne Reid, England's leading Western writer. Reid refused to accept the verdict that the Indians were a doomed race; after all, natives were needed to generate wealth in the colonies. "There is," he wrote, "not the slightest danger of such a destiny for the Indian; his race is not to become extinct."[75] It should, and would survive, but only if recast in the white man's mould. This was the true mission of the Anglo-Saxon: to transmute lesser people into civilized citizens useful to mankind. The miracle could be accomplished by elevating them from the "hunter stage" of their evolution to the "farming stage" overnight.

Without that change, Reid argued, the red men had neither the right nor the chance to survive. Where the agriculturist could produce abundance from a small patch of land, the hunter-savage must command a whole domain for mere subsistence. Such an extravagant use of Nature's heritage had been outmoded by the spread of Europe's superior races; in the modern competitive world all peoples, whatever their cultural level, must contribute food and raw materials or surrender their right to exist. "No handful of men," Reid declared, "have the right to hold from the great body of mankind a valuable portion of the earth's surface, without using it."[76] Here was the loud voice of imperialism. Native peoples—

[73] Francis J. Grund, *The Americans, in Their Moral, Social, and Political Relations* (Boston, 1837), pp. 225–26; Mayne Reid, *The Headless Horseman: A Strange Tale of Texas* (London, 1865), p. 338; Charles V. C. de Varigny, "Les Fins d'une race: L'Insurrection des Sioux," *Revue des deux mondes* (January–February 1891), p. 915, and many other writers express this sentiment.
[74] Charles V. C. de Varigny, *The Women of the United States* (New York, 1895), pp. 20–21.
[75] Mayne Reid, *The Boy Hunters; or, Adventures in Search of a White Buffalo* (London, 1853), p. 295.
[76] In his novel *The Scalp Hunters*, 3: 291–94, Reid digresses at length to express his views on this subject.

"The Eyes Are Not Closed, Not Glassed." From Mayne Reid, *The Death Shot* (Beadle's Dime Novel Library, New York, n.d.), front cover. (From the Special Collections of the University of California at Los Angeles Library.)

whether in India or Africa or the United States—must accept the ways of Europe's superior races or surrender their right to survive.

Extermination Deplored: The Humanitarian View

This harsh judgment was rejected by the larger group of European image-makers who saw the Indians as tragic victims of frontier greed, and hence deserving of sympathy and aid. Many of their arguments were borrowed from American reformers who in the late century were forming the Indian Rights Association and pressuring the government to restore property and dignity to the red men. On one point, however, Americans and Europeans differed. While American reformers urged congressional appropriations of federal land to lure Native Americans into farming, the European image-makers offered no practical solution for their plight. Instead they resorted to pure sentimentalism to evoke sympathy, glorifying primitivism, and dipping into the rhetoric of Noble Savagery to extol the Indian's way of life.

Most, but by no means all, of this school were from southern and eastern Europe, with a liberal sprinkling of French and German among them. The motive of French and German authors was largely emotional; they knew that tearful accounts of the plight of the poor Indian would open the hearts—and pocketbooks—of sentimental readers. So they associated their heroes with proud warriors—Old Shatterhand often proclaimed that the red men "are also sons of the Great Spirit whose children the palefaces also are"—[77] and in tear-dripping prose mourned their passing. Authors also devised special means to tug at the heartstrings of their countrymen, again revealing something of their national traits.

French writers, most notable, Gustave Aimard, deplored the certain extermination of the Indians as deeply as any author, but voiced a slight irritation that it must be so. He saw the red men as victims of their own weaknesses; instead of uniting against their aggressors under the leadership of French generals, as they could have during the imperial wars of the eighteenth century, they chose to squander their energy in intertribal wars and dissipation until so weakened that they could be herded onto reservations like cattle. They had stirred the implacable wrath of the Wacondah and must pay the penalty; "ere a century has elapsed," he predicted, "not a single native will be left in this territory of the Union."[78]

The German image-makers were just as certain of the red men's extermination, but they were hopeful that the end would come gloriously.

[77] May, *Winnetou I*, p. 93.
[78] Gustave Aimard, *The White Scalper: A Story of the Texan War* (London, 1861), pp. 226–27. Aimard's changing views are discussed in William P. Dallman, *The Spirit of America As Interpreted in the Works of Charles Sealsfield* (St. Louis, 1935), pp. 670–71.

Their deep sympathy was undisguised. Charles Sealsfield was openly emotional as he described the exodus of the Five Civilized Tribes to the Indian Territory: "it was a painful sight to see them staring across upon the eastern shore of the Mississippi, some stretching out their hands toward it."[79] Karl May, too, was tearfully sympathetic. Over and over again Old Shatterhand deplored the greedy avariciousness of Yankee land grabbers ("white men came with sweet words on their lips, but simultaneously with sharp knives in their belts and loaded guns in their hands"),[80] or railed against a government policy that demanded instant civilization as the price of survival. "How," he asked, "do you send a six year old boy to school, and then hit him over the head when after fifteen minutes he is not a professor."[81]

All this could not save the Indian; "he is meant to die, and so he will," Karl May wrote sadly.[82] But he still deserved a better fate than to fade into oblivion. May's hope was that the southern and northern plains tribes would unite for a final bloodbath in the canyons and gorges of the Rockies, with Comanche and Apache and Sioux fighting side by side, "wading in the gore of their enemies until the last of them is slain."[83] Such an end would be worthy of such a noble people.

Eastern Europeans were even more sympathetic to the Indian, even though they imagined no such triumphant end for the race. Many of the image-makers there were expatriates, driven from their homelands by the failure of the liberal revolutions of mid-century and hopeful that they could stir world sympathy for their oppressed countrymen by comparing them to the American Indians. So they expressed a common message, even though they wrote in Hungarian or Austrian-German or Polish. The red men and their compatriots were one, both victims of despotic overlords. "You are truly my *nekam* (good friend)," a chief told an Hungarian traveler, "because you, like ourselves, were driven off your lands."[84] Tears should be shed for Europeans and Native Americans alike. "Has not," one asked, "the same thing that we see here before us in Europe been carried out there to the ultimate extreme?"[85] The oppressed peasant and the oppressed Indian were one, equally deserving of sympathy and aid.

[79] Quoted in Bernhard A. Uhlendorf, *Charles Sealsfield: Ethnic Elements and National Problems in His Works* (Chicago, 1922), pp. 48–49.
[80] May, *Winnetou I,* introduction.
[81] Karl May, *Der Schatz im Silbersee* (reprint ed., Bamberg, 1973), pp. 62–63.
[82] Karl May, *Canada Bill: Including the Talking Leather and 'One-Eyed' Joe Burkers* (London, 1971), p. 148.
[83] Ibid., p. 149.
[84] John Xantus, *Letters from North America* (Detroit, 1975), p. 34. Similar views by a Russian visitor are in Nikolaj Slavinskij, *Letters on America and Russian Immigrants* (St. Petersburg, 1873), p. 188, while the opinion of other Russians are described in I. I. Uspenskij, *Russian Writers in America* (Moscow, 1952), p. 23.
[85] Quoted in Uspenskij, *Russian Writers in America,* p. 21.

This approach was so effective that by the 1850s a popular subject of conversation in the Vienna salons, according to one witness, was "the cruel tricks which allowed those in the free states to rob the poor Indians of their country."[86] Grist for these intellectual mills was provided by dozens of writers, typified by the Polish patriot, Ludwik Powidaj, whose article on "Poles and Indians," was published in a Lvov journal, *Dziennik Literacki*, shortly after the defeat of the Polish insurrection of 1863. Recalling the ill-natured jibe of Frederick II—"I am trying to teach European civilization to those hapless Iroquois (meaning Poles)"—he traced the similarities between his countrymen and the Indians: both were unable to adapt to modern life, both dreamed of past greatness, both were destined to cultural oblivion. Powidaj's pessimistic obituary stirred a storm of controversy among Polish intellectuals, with some denying, others defending his comparisons, but the fact remains that the comparison was made, and that Polish sympathy for the red men was heightened as they grasped its meaning.

The tragedy of eastern Europeans and the red men was compared in many literary works, but in none more effectively than in Henryk Sienkiewicz's moving short story, "Sachem." This tale began with the extermination of the Black Snake Indians of Texas by a colony of Germans who wanted their land for the village of Chiavatta. Fifteen years later a circus arrived at the town, with its principal attraction "The Sachem of the Black Snakes"—an Indian who had been rescued from the slaughter as a ten-year-old boy and was now a gifted acrobat. Sienkiewicz movingly described the scene as the sachem balanced on a high-wire far above the heads of the wrapt audience, telling of the peace and happiness his people had known, the coming of the German colonists, and of "how they stole into Chiavatta by night, like coyotes, and their knives were plunged into the breasts of sleeping men, women and children."

Then, suddenly, his voice rising to a scream, his body twisting in satanic anger, the sachem howled: "Out of an entire tribe, only a single child remained. He was small and weak, but he had made a vow to the Earth Spirit that he would be avenged. That he would see the corpses of the white men, women, and children—in a conflagration, blood." Below him the audience cowered in terror. Would he spill oil from the burning lamps and consume them in a giant holocaust? Then, abruptly, the sachem disappeared. A moment of terrified waiting and he was among them, passing a tin plate, and whining: "was gefällig für den letzten der Schwarzen

Schlange" ("something, please, for the last of the Black Snakes"). Relieved, they opened their pocketbooks, just as he had planned.[87] Sienkiewicz's message was clear. The Indians had been robbed not only of their land but of their spirit by docile submission. Such would be the fate of the Poles unless they threw off the yoke of their oppressors.

Eastern European image-makers might have a unique purpose in stirring sympathy for the Indian, but they were by no means alone in accomplishing their desire. Throughout Europe during the late nineteenth century sentimental appeals deploring the sad plight of the Native Americans were a regular part of the literary diet. These all made clear that the Indians themselves did not deserve their tragic fate. All were noble, kind and true, generous to a fault, and utterly loyal to their friends. Over and over again storytellers dwelt upon their laudable traits. One typical tale, this one in a Norwegian boys' magazine, told of a Huron caught in a blizzard who sought refuge in a trapper's cabin. The trapper refused— "damned Huron! How dare you dirty up my floor and ask me for shelter? Go, before I put a bullet through your head." The Huron vanished into the storm, but a few days later had an opportunity to rescue the trapper from another howling blizzard. "Do not be afraid," he assured him, after serving him milk for breakfast, "I only want to show you that I am better than you are." That tale, the young readers were told, would show them "the good-nature and kindness of these savages."[88]

So would the barrage of pro-Indian comment loosened against European readers throughout the latter decades of the nineteenth century, whatever their country or literary taste. Novelists agreed upon a common point: the red men were blameless of any wrong, the frontiersmen solely responsible for their plight. Whites had "chased them from their birthplace like animals,"[89] they had "deceived them in every way; made drunkards of them; armed them against each other, and declared unjust wars against them."[90] "A gallant little people," they had made no mistakes and done no wrong.[91] They were the victims of human greed and nothing more.

The most eloquent witnesses for the red men were the red men themselves, real and fictional, and they were called upon to testify to their virtues in novel after novel. Each placed the blame squarely where it belonged; on the frontiersmen. "They teach our people to drink vodka and

[87] This story appears in translation in Henryk Sienkiewicz, *Western Septet: Seven Stories of the American West* (Cheshire, 1973), pp. 145–51. It is brilliantly interpreted in Jerzy Jedlicki, "Images of America," *Polish Perspectives* 18 (November 1975): 29–30.

[88] "The Huron," *Børnenes Blad* (Norway) 8 (1869): 172.

[89] Slavinskij, *Letters on America and Russian Immigrants*, p. 171.

[90] A. Bykova, *The North American United States*, 3d ed. (St. Petersburg, 1909), p. 13.

[91] Ulrik Sverdrup, *Irokeserne: Et Indianerfolks Historie* (Oslo, 1897), pp. 126–27.

insult our women," one Russian writer insisted;[92] another—Chief White
Falcon of the Narraganset tribe of Colorado [*sic*]—held that "the Palefaces
have crept into our country like rats in a granary. . . . When the wind
blows across the prairie, we hear our brothers' death cry sound to us from
many fallen warriors."[93] Chief Red Wolf, speaking the Norwegian tongue
in this case, testified that the pale faces had poisoned his tribesmen just as
would "the frozen rattlesnake that strikes poison into the breast that has
thawed its frozen body."[94] Reading these laments, the faults of the pioneers burdened the consciences of many a European reader.

So determined were European novelists to prove that the Indians were
innocent victims of white greed that they rewrote history to make their
points. At least two novels were built on the premise that the Indian attack
on Custer's forces at the Little Big Horn was justified and humane. One, a
French work, made Sitting Bull its hero, faithfully holding his followers
in check until the last hope of a peaceful settlement had vanished, then
leading them reluctantly into battle. A tragic hero, as befitting his race,
and forced to flee into Canada to regroup his forces. There he remained,
"waiting for the appropriate time to renew his fight and seek revenge for
the terrible tortures and miseries and sufferings of his oppressed brothers."[95]

Sitting Bull was cast in an equally favorable role by a Norwegian storyteller: a mighty warrior who rallied his people to resist only to save their
own lives, and to win back the hunting grounds that were rightfully
theirs. When this gave the white men an excuse to strike back, this mighty
leader led his people to their greatest moment of glory on the Little Big
Horn.[96] Here was a new hero, made to order for European youth, one
worthy of their adulation. Nor was he adored by the young alone. One
Dutch newspaper compared him to the nobility of Europe, and branded
his death at Wounded Knee a "foul murder" by the whites.[97]

The impact of these emotionally charged views on Europeans was far
from insignificant. They heard but one side of the story. From novels,
newspapers, travelers, letter writers—whatever they read—they learned
that the red man was a blameless victim of land-hungry exploiters who
would stop at nothing to rob him of his homeland. Thus did the image
emerge of the American frontiersmen—and to a lesser degree of the Amer-

[92] Slavinskij, *Letters on America and Russian Immigrants*, p. 175.
[93] Thomas Krag, *Fældejægeren eller Skovløberens Forræderi: Fortælling fra Colorados Vildnis* (Oslo, 1890), p. 9.
[94] Petersen, *Grændsejægerens Datter*, p. 91.
[95] Joseph Bournichon, *Sitting-Bull, le héros du désert* (Tours, 1879), pp. 223–24.
[96] L. A. Stenholt, *Sitting Bull: Billeder fra den sidste Indianerkrig* (Oslo, n.d.), passim. A similar flattering view of Sitting Bull was in the *Nieuwe Rotterdamse Courant*, 21–28 November and
2–17 December 1890.
[97] *Het Nieuws van der Dag*, 18 November 1890.

ican people as a whole—as heartless predators, stripping a defenseless mi-nority of its birthright, condemning them to reservations that were little better than prison camps, and dooming them to early extinction. This was an image that was to haunt the United States for generations to come.

VII

The Frontiersmen:
Heroes vs. Villains

THE IMAGE-MAKERS whose sentimental description of the last days of the red men sent waves of sympathy coursing across Europe should logically have cast all frontiersmen as villains, for all played a role in goading the government into robbing the Indians of their lands. Fiction writers, however, found this impossible. They needed white as well as red heroes to carry on the battle against untamed Nature, and these had to be recruited from among the variety of frontiersmen carrying the banner of civilization westward. Their qualifications were easily defined: those selected for the heroes' roles must be sufficiently glamorous to be appealing, sufficiently civilized to symbolize the triumph of man over Nature, and sufficiently primitive to cater to European tastes for savagery. But who to single out for this role?

The hardworking farmers and merchants who were the true tamers of the West would not do, for there was little glamour in their necessary tasks. Nor would the backwoodsmen, or squatters, whose half-cleared fields and tumbledown cabins heralded the first coming of civilization on all frontiers. The squatters clearly deserved a hero's role in an age when utilitarianism was venerated, for theirs was the first genuine effort to conquer the wilderness, but they were guilty of one unpardonable sin. They failed in their conquest; instead of dominating Nature they were dominated by Nature, reverting to primitivism at a time when primitivism was unpopular. Hence they were ignored by the novelists and deplored by the travelers who pictured them as the dregs of society—slothful, ignorant, dirty, lazy—a despicable lot unworthy of human companionship.

Passing over both pioneer farmers and squatters, the storytellers selected their heroes and villains from among those advance agents of civilization who ranged far ahead of the frontier of settlement. Some were drawn from real life; hunters, fur trappers, government agents, soldiers, ranchers, plainsmen, eastern "greenhorns," and a host more who usually appeared in European novels as reasonably accurate facsimilies of the models on which they were based. Others were invented for the occasion: the *batteurs d'estrade* and bee hunters and wood runners who sprang from the imaginations of their creators untouched by reality. Of these the hunters and plainsmen were favored for heroes' roles by most writers, for Leatherstocking and his ilk were too popular with readers to be discarded.

Villains were also easy to identify, for they must pass only two tests: they must be sufficiently unsavory and cruel to deserve the fate sure to await them on the last page, and they must symbolize primitivism by their savage behavior, thus allowing civilization to triumph over Nature in every penny dreadful. Some were based on real-life characters: half-breeds—"untiring plunderers like the Indians"[1]—who combined the ferocity of red men with the skills of whites; renegades who had fled the East with the law at their heels—"the scum of society, people with a far harder and crueller heart than the red warriors," who sought a savage life "to slake a rampant thirst for blood";[2] buffalo hunters—"selfish, money-making, pitiless slaughterers"[3]—who were mercilessly exterminating helpless animals for their own gain.

Others more favored by writers were villains who bore such faint resemblance to real life that their behavior could never be questioned. Included in this rogues' gallery were Mormon elders, all of them lecherous sex fiends seeking innocent virgins (usually the hero's sister) for their harems; "pirates of the prairies" who had adopted all the vices of both whites and Indians without retaining any of the virtues—"pitiless men, a hundred-fold more ruffianly than the most ferocious red-skins";[4] and Yankees, universally described as scrawny-necked, hawk-nosed, watery-eyed, broomstick-thin money grabbers who would slit the throat of their dearest

---

[1] Gabriel Ferry, *Le Coureur des bois* (reprint ed., Paris, 1932), 1: 67–68.
[2] "The Adventures of the Two Norwegian Boys on the American Prairies," *Børnenes Blad* 12 (Norway, 1872): 262; Charles W. Webber, *Old Hicks the Guide; or, Adventures in the Comanche Country in Search of a Gold Mine* (New York, 1848), p. 205.
[3] Gustave Aimard, *The Red River Half-Breed: A Tale of the Wild North-West* (London, n.d.), pp. 100–101.
[4] Gustave Aimard, *The Pirates of the Prairies: Adventures in the American Desert* (London, 1862), p. 35.

friend for the slightest gain. Karl May's favorite villain's were tramps who roamed the West in gangs of ten thousand or more, murdering and raping and pillaging—until Old Shatterhand and Winnetou came to the rescue.[5] And, in the Southwest of course, ferociously bearded Mexican robbers and plunderers waited to murder every white man who came their way.

Ranged against this improbable assemblage in European novels were two hero-types who proved indestructible: the hunter who dominated the scene until mid-century, and the leather-clad plainsman who assumed his role when the frontier pushed westward beyond the woodlands. Both were ideally suited to their parts. Glamorous demigods in buckskin shirts and fringed leggings, skilled with knife and rifle, and bearing civilization's banner high as they marched against the evils of primitivism, they were sufficiently Europeanized to appeal to readers who worshiped at the throne of the Great God Progress, yet sufficiently uncivilized to captivate those eager to wallow vicariously in the gore of villains. Natty Bumppo had only to be updated and freed of the moral restraints that hindered his blood-letting instincts to be the ideal hero.

Hunters and Plainsmen

The Hunter-Hero did not spring full blown from the imagination of Europe's image-makers, but evolved rapidly during the first half of the nineteenth century. His model was the Daniel Boone created by John Filson in his *Life and Adventures of Colonel Daniel Boon*, an imaginative biography published in Paris in 1785 and in London a short time later.[6] Filson's Boone was the logical counterpart of the Noble Savage then so popular— an idealized Child of Nature unrestrained by the pressures of civilization. He could properly be pictured by the editor of the French edition as blessed with intellectual and spiritual superiority solely through his contacts with the unblemished wild. That editor might cluck disapprovingly at Boone's habit of killing Indians—"les Naturels," he called them, not "les Sauvages" of later usage—but that was Nature's way.[7] Boone was worthy of Byron's designation: "the happiest among mortals, anywhere," his companions " a sylvan tribe of children of the chase" who meant no evil.[8]

[5] Karl May, *Der Schatz im Silbersee* (reprint ed., Bamberg, 1973), p. 221.
[6] This account appeared first as an appendix to John Filson, *The Discovery, Settlement and Present State of Kentucke* (Washington, 1784). Its foreign editions, including one in Germany in 1785, are described in John Walton, *John Filson of Kentucke* (Lexington, 1956), pp. 43–44.
[7] Henri Parraud's "Préface" in John Filson, *Histoire de Kentucke, nouvelle colonie à l'ouest de la Virginie* (Paris, 1785).
[8] Excellent discussions of these points are in Richard Slotkin, *Regeneration through Violence: The Mythology of the American Frontier, 1600–1800* (Middletown, 1973), pp. 390–92; and Hoxie N. Fairchild, *The Noble Savage: A Study of Romantic Naturalism* (New York, 1928), pp. 241–42.

This idealized version of the Hunter-Hero was too romanticized to survive the growing realism of the nineteenth century; audiences demanded less godlike adventurers who could symbolize the triumph of civilization by slaughtering a few red men now and then without suffering any qualms of conscience. By the 1830s the image-makers had discovered a fresh prototype in Mike Fink, the legendary Mississippi River keelboatman. Mike was still an idealized superman as he first appeared to Europeans—"a figure cast in a mould that added much of the symmetry of an Apollo to the limbs of Hercules"[9]—but he could also shoot an Indian without suffering twinges of remorse. Readers approved when he saw one about to draw a bead on a deer, timed his own shot so exactly that he killed the Indian just as the Indian killed the deer, and returned to camp with a good meal and another scalp. Shooting an enemy in the back was an act of savagery rather than civilization, but it was also a way of removing a bad Indian, and the end justified the means.

European authors sensed this changing taste as the Age of Romanticism waned, and rose to the challenge with unwarranted enthusiasm. Their first Hunter-Heroes were still touched with romanticism, but had moved far along the road to realism. Most were patent-office models of Daniel Boone himself, roaming widely through the woodlands in search of redskins and adventure, but others were introduced of sufficient variety to titillate the reader's fancy.

Foremost among these were the "wood rangers" or *coureurs des bois*, who frequented the northern borderlands just as had their ancestors in the days of New France. A reckless breed of men, they ranged the forests "with no other object than that of living and dying unrestrained by any other will save their own."[10] They blended savagery and civilization in their dress as they did in their lives, wearing caps of beaver skin, shirts of cotton or calico fastened around the waist with a rattlesnake skin belt, leather trousers, and either Indian moccasins or stout iron-studded shoes.[11] All were incredibly skilled in woodcraft, able to tell by the sighing of the wind, the motion of a branch, the rustle of grass, or the murmur of water over pebbles whether a passer-by was a friend or foe.[12]

The counterparts of the *coureurs des bois* in the Southwest were the *gambusinos*, or vaqueros of the Mexican borderlands, who loved the deserts no

[9]   Morgan Neville, "The Last of the Boatmen," in *The Western Souvenir for 1829*, ed. James Hall (Cincinnati, 1829), p. 117. This article on Mike Fink was translated into German and reprinted in numerous European magazines.
[10]   Gustave Aimard, *The Border Rifles: A Tale of the Texan War* (Philadelphia, n.d.), pp. 23–24. A similar description is in Ferry, *Le Coureur des bois*, 1: 75.
[11]   Their clothes are described in Aimard, *Border Rifles*, p. 23; Gustave Aimard, *The Missouri Outlaws* (London, n.d.), p. 19; and Percy B. St. John, *The Trapper's Bride: A Tale of the Rocky Mountains* (London, 1845), p. 78.
[12]   Gustave Aimard, *The Queen of the Savannah: A Story of the Mexican War* (London, n.d.), p. 243.

"Besieged by Peccaries." From Mayne Reid, *The Desert Home*
(London, 1852), opposite p. 433. (From the Special Collections
of the University of California at Los Angeles Library.)

less fervently than their northern cousins loved the forests. Colorfully clad
in shirts of rich cloth laced with gold, white pantaloons decorated with
buttons of filigreed gold, a scarf of silver fringed with gold about the
waist, their heads protected from the sun's rays by a large *paño de sol* of
Arab design, their boots of cordovan leather stitched with gold and silver
wire, tiny bells that tinkled as they rode attached to their spurs, these
bedouins of the Southwest were unsurpassed horsemen and formidable
foes of all evil.[13] They differed from their fellow frontiersmen only in
their love of gold—the "gold-seekers of the New World," they were
called—and their passion for gambling. This was bred into them by the
dangerous lives they led, risking death daily in their sweeps across the
deserts where brutal Nature was a constant hazard.

The *coureurs des bois* and the *gambusinos* bore some faint relationship to
actual frontiersmen on the Canadian and Mexican borderlands, but the
same could not be said for a gallery of plainsmen invented by the image-
makers; the *batteurs d'estrade*, the bee hunters, and the wood runners. The
batteurs d'estrade were the least improbable of this trio; serving as scouts for
less venturesome plainsmen, they operated only in the most remote areas
of the West, spying out Indian marauders, locating game, marking trails,
and generally lessening risks for their followers by risking their own lives
daily.[14] Their companions, however, were somewhat less probable.

The bee hunters' task was to keep pace with advancing swarms of bees,
for these industrious insects ranged far ahead of the frontier of settlement,
seeking virgin sources for their honey; when an Indian sighted a bee he
prepared to move, knowing that whites would soon appear.[15] Facing constant danger, boasting "all the vices of whites and redskins, and without
the virtues of either,"[16] bee hunters were despised for their rough manners
and crude speech, and were universally feared. They were sometimes
sighted by the "wood-runners" who served as couriers in the West, running on foot from settlement to settlement, carrying messages and pack-
ages. Negroes were usually chosen for this task because of their greater
speed and endurance. One of the most famous ran in less than a month
from the Gila Country to Colorado, bearing news of an impending attack
on the settlements by the Narraganset Indians of Colorado [*sic*].[17]

These exotic specialists were far outnumbered in European novels by

[13]   Karl May, *Old Surehand: Erster Band* (reprinted ed., Vienna, 1953), p. 169; Gustave
Aimard, *The Trail Hunter: A Tale of the Far West* (London, n.d.), pp. 20, 24.
[14]   Paul Duplessis, *Le Batteur d'estrade* (Paris, 1862), 1: 11.
[15]   Edward S. Ellis, *Life and Adventures of Colonel David Crockett* (London, n.d.), p. 70. The
bee-hunters are also described in Carl of Solms-Braunfels, *Texas, 1844–1845* (Houston,
1936), p. 31.
[16]   Gustave Aimard, *The Bee-Hunter: A Tale of Adventure* (London, 1868), pp. 63–64.
[17]   Thomas Krag, *Fældejægeren eller Skovløberens Forræderi: Fortælling fra Colorados Vildnis*
(Oslo, 1890), passim.

run-of-the-mill plainsmen, all cast from a common mould, and differing only in their Teutonic, or French, or Norwegian, or British mannerisms as the nationality of their creators dictated. All were of gigantic stature, their arms and legs like young oaks, their skin bronzed by exposure to sun and wind and so toughened that it resembled the shell of a turtle or a dried buffalo hide. All boasted the strength of Hercules, with fists that could crush a puma's skull, and endurance to outlast the strongest Indian. Their giant strength endowed them with a calm sense of self-assurance that other men lacked.[18] They were of the stuff of heroes, perfectly cast in heroes' roles.

Even the clothes they wore symbolized the blending of the two cultures that they represented. Most favored hunting jackets of fringed leather, vests made of white fawnskin, and a coat of buckskin or buffalo hide. Their legs were encased either in leather leggings that had been "worked up" with grease so that they would not stiffen when wet, or in well-worn cloth pants. A few sported old felt hats, but most preferred caps of beaver pelts with the tail still attached, not as an ornament but as protection from a blow from behind. About their necks were silk handkerchiefs fastened with a gold clasp, or more often necklaces of grizzly-bear claws.[19] On their feet they wore heavy boots to withstand the desert heat. All were abundantly bearded, and all were walking arsenals, their otter-skin belts stuffed with revolvers and knives, a rifle cradled in their arms. These guns were fearsome weapons, impossibly accurate, and so endeared by their owners that they were treated as companions and addressed by favorite names.[20] Despite their ferocious appearance, the plainsmen were gentle souls, overflowing with kindness to their fellowmen, and with soft eyes that radiated warmth and friendship.

They were superbly mounted, for a good horse meant the difference between life and death on the plains. Horses were treated as friends in return; Old Shatterhand's "Hatatitla" was such a faithful companion that "there developed a feeling of belonging, so that we were ever ready to place our lives in each other's hands."[21] On the rare occasions when *West-*

[18] Charles Sealsfield, *Courtship of George Howard, Esquire* (New York, 1843), pp. 42–43; Charles W. Webber, *The Gold Mines of the Gila: A Sequel to Old Hicks the Guide* (New York, 1849), p. 120.
[19] Good descriptions are in May, *Der Schatz im Silbersee*, pp. 152–53; Karl May, *Winnetou II* (reprint ed., Vienna, 1951), p. 129; Johannes Scherr, *Die Pilger der Wildnis, Historische Novelle* (Hanover, 1917), 1: 23–24; Friedrich Armand Strubberg, *An der Indianergrenze* (Hanover, 1859), 1: 2; Friedrich Gerstäcker, *Nach Amerika* (Berlin, 1855), 5: 34–35; Otto Ruppius, *Der Präirieteufel* (Berlin, 1861), p. 348; Moritz Busch, *Wanderungen zwischen Hudson und Mississippi 1851–1852* (Tübingen, 1854), p. 316; Mayne Reid, *The Scalp Hunters; or, Romantic Adventures in Northern Mexico* (London, 1851), 1: 262–65.
[20] Karl May, *Winnetou I: Ungekürzte Ausgabe* (reprint ed., Vienna, 1953), pp. 20–21; Fredrich Armand Strubberg, *Bis in die Wildnis* (Breslau, 1858), pp. 112–13.
[21] May, *Winnetou II*, p. 192.

manner stopped at inns they demanded care for their animals before asking for help for themselves. "From your care of these animals," one innkeeper told a group, "I can see that you are good men."[22] Proper care of animals was the sign of a gentleman in those days, and the plainsmen passed the test.

They also lived as gentlemen, if the quantity rather than the quality of their eatables was judged, feasting often on buffalo meat "until their faces shone with grease and happiness."[23] And what quantities they consumed! "I have seen an old trapper eat eight pounds of meat at one sitting," Old Shatterhand testified, "and when I asked him if he were full, he answered, with a grin, 'I have to be, for I don't have any more.' "[24] Always the choice pieces were eaten first, "for fear some sulkin' Redskin should kill me before we've had time to enjoy them."[25] Buffalo meat was all they needed, but now and then their diet was supplemented with berries and roots, or with specialties of the countryside; beaver tails, or grizzly-bear paws or the flesh of a puppy dog in the northern Rockies, cakes of *hautle* made from the eggs of species of waterbugs on the southwestern deserts.[26]

Most plainsmen preferred to sleep under the open skies even when visiting villages, but now and then one built a mountain-valley home that rivaled in splendor the palaces of Arabian princes. One such mansion deep in the Rocky Mountains was centered about a recreation hall that would outshine any Moorish creation: floors of yellow ochre, a sky-blue ceiling, walls of light green decorated with flutings of yellow and blue separated by bands of red, a chandelier of sun and stars commingling and surmounted by fruits and fanciful cupids, the room amply furnished with blue chairs, red ottomans, and yellow tables.[27] That monstrosity outshone most homes, but the plainsmen were so accustomed to comforts that they often carried with them the furniture needed "to transform a cave or a hut into a nest of luxury." One such cavern was complete with rugs, blankets, and furs, in its center a table bearing a large silver chafing dish where the occupants gathered for meals.[28]

These elaborate trappings made clear that *Westmanner* were the products of Europe's rich cultural traditions; their wilderness skills showed how thoroughly they had mastered the arts of savagery. "There is no In-

[22] Karl May, *Winnetou III* (reprint ed., Vienna, 1951), p. 45.
[23] Robert M. Ballantyne, *Tales of Adventure, by Flood, Field, and Mountain* (London, 1885), p. 38. Ballantyne borrowed this phrase, word for word, from Thomas J. Farnham, *Travels in the Californias, and Scenes in the Pacific Ocean* (New York, 1844), p. 235.
[24] May, *Winnetou I*, p. 43.
[25] Ballantyne, *Tales of Adventure, by Flood, Field, and Mountain*, pp. 36–37.
[26] Aimard, *The Bee-Hunter*, p. 36; May, *Der Schatz im Silbersee*, p. 460; Louis L. Simonin, *The Rocky Mountain West in 1867* (Lincoln, Nebraska, 1966), p. 97.
[27] Robert M. Ballantyne, *The Wild Man of the West: A Tale of the Rocky Mountains* (Boston, 1864), pp. 192–93.
[28] Aimard, *The Red River Half-Breed*, p. 48.

dian," a novelist wrote, "who is a match for him in those things at which the Indians are masters."[29] They learned those arts from each other and from their Indian companions; Old Shatterhand was forever indebted to Winnetou for teaching him how to survive in a desert: never let your water pouch go dry, never waste a bullet for that very one might be needed to save your life, never sleep beside a fire that could be detected by an enemy, never overtire your horse lest he be unable to flee from danger, never relax your constant vigilance, always follow a circuitous route to avoid ambushes, remain constantly alert, and above all keep calm in the presence of danger.[30] A sharp eye and a steady hand were the plainsman's most reliable weapons. "Life in the wilderness," wrote Karl May, "sharpens a man's senses to the highest degree."[31]

Those who succeeded learned these lessons so well that they far outshone the most skilled Indians. A well-trained plainsman could determine the tribe of a raiding party by its horses' footprints, decide from a single track how many hours ago a deer had passed, determine whether a twig had been bent by a passing red man or animal, scent a campfire three miles away, and detect an enemy's approach by the almost imperceptible change in air pressure.[32] Said a French hero on hearing a distant flurry of shots from a friend's weapon: "That man is in danger at this moment. He is fighting Apaches, who have surprised and attacked him during sleep. The number of shots leads me to suppose that my friend has only one or two companions with him; if we do not go to his help, he is lost, for his adversaries are numerous."[33] Anyone who could deduce so much from so little deserved the title of *Westmann*.

So did those whose instincts and skills meant survival amidst the constant dangers. Plainsmen learned how to leave no trail by walking backward in their own footsteps, to build fires of dry wood that would give off no telltale smoke, to fashion a cache for their valuables by scooping the earth onto a buffalo robe, then returning it to leave no trace. They learned, too, not to disturb such a cache, for according to the law of the prairies, such an act was punishable by death.[34] All knew how to heal

[29] Friedrich Spielhagen, *Deutsche Pioneer* (Berlin, 1871), quoted in D. L. Ashliman, "The American West in Nineteenth Century German Literature" (Ph.D diss., Rutgers University, 1969), p. 182.
[30] May, *Winnetou I*, p. 217; May, *Der Schatz im Silbersee*, p. 248; Aimard, *The Bee-Hunter*, p. 3; Strubberg, *Bis in die Wildnis*, pp. 173–74.
[31] *Winnetou III*, p. 120.
[32] May, *Winnetou II*, p. 297; Karl May, *Canada Bill; Including the Talking Leather and 'One-Eyed' Joe Burkers* (London, 1971), p. 152; Friedrich Gerstäcker, *Mississippi-Bilder: Licht-und Schattenseiten transatlantischen Lebens* (Jena, 1847–48), p. 493.
[33] Gustave Aimard, *The Indian Scout; or, Life on the Frontier* (Philadelphia, n.d.), pp. 29–30.
[34] Gustave Aimard, *The Prairie Flower: A Tale of the Indian Border* (London, 1878), p. 25; Gustave Aimard, *The Treasure of Pearls: A Romance of Adventures in California* (London, n.d.), pp. 20–21.

knife wounds with herbs, and how to hurl a lasso with unerring accuracy; they realized that their enemies always carried knives to cut the rope, but that seventy-five percent were strangled before they could bring the blade into play. Most were able to throw a tomahawk with such precision that it made several circles on the way to its target, then struck with the handle up or down as they wished.[35]

Above all the plainsmen could shoot with unerring accuracy. One, challenged to a match by a gang of ruffians, calmly put a bullet through each hole that his opponent had made in the target, explaining, "It's a trick of mine. I caught it from shootin' varments in the eyes."[36] Old Shatter-hand had perfected the "knee shot" to be used when surprised by an In-dian while sitting by his campfire; carefully lifting his knee until a line along his thigh pointed straight at the enemy's heart, he could snatch up his rifle, slap it against his leg, and fire in the fraction of a second. Nor-mally his bullet found its target directly through the heart or between the eyes.[37] "Can a prairie hunter shoot?" he once exclaimed. "That's almost as bad as asking if a bear can eat."[38]

Indians might occasionally—very occasionally—perfect such skills, but they could never rival the plainsman in ingenuity. Here the white man was clearly superior. Old Shatterhand once saved his life by hastily sketching a picture of the old chief who had captured him and threatened to destroy the chief's soul by throwing it in the fire unless released.[39] Another *Westmann* attempting to steal a horse from an Indian herd rubbed his body with mugwort plants to conceal his own scent, wrapped himself in an Indian's blanket, and approached without stirring an alarm.[40] When "Oregon Olive" sensed that an Indian was hidden in the brush near his camp he clicked his gun barrel with a fingernail, at the same time releasing a mouthful of tobacco smoke near its firing pan. The Indian, thinking he had fired his last shot, rose with a shout of triumph, only to be met with a bullet in the chest.[41] These were feats of woodmanship that no 'tarneled red skin' could rival.

Yet the plainsmen of the image-makers were not savages, even though their dangerous lives forced them to master the arts of savagery. They were Europeans to the core, even though some strange instinct had driven them to rebel against the restraints of European society. All had fled their

---

[35] Gustave Aimard, *The White Scalper: A Story of the Texan War* (London, 1861), pp. 215–16; Aimard, *The Indian Scout*, p. 142; Busch, *Wanderungen zwischen Hudson und Mississippi*, p. 314.
[36] Charles W. Webber, *Jack Long; or, Shot in the Eye: A True Story of Texas Border Life* (New York, 1846), p. 8.
[37] May, *Winnetou I*, pp. 247–48.
[38] May, *Der Schatz im Silbersee*, pp. 114–15.
[39] May, *Winnetou III*, p. 124.
[40] May, *Old Surehand*, pp. 144–45.
[41] Aimard, *The Treasure of Pearls*, p. 64.

homelands in search of freedom from social tyranny; each sought a lonely land where (as one fictional hunter put it) he could be "a king in the wilderness."[42] All had been tested against Nature's dangers, and all had proven themselves. In doing so each had "discovered a peace which is only given a man who has felt more than a match for the dangers and frustrations which threaten him."[43] That sense of inner security brought with it a sense of self-confidence, of security against social pressures and obligations. Charles Sealsfield, one of the few European writers who knew the breed well, saw the plainsmen as "a vast community of separate existences—each, in a sense, independent of every other thing, except God."[44] Only those who had braved the dangers and hardships of the desert could attain such heights of individual satisfaction.

They experienced, too, a spiritual uplift, a sense of well-being that made any sacrifice worthwhile. Theirs was a world that "exalts the spirit, rendering it . . . as well as the body, energetic and firm."[45] A world where even the insensitive must sense "the finger of God imprinted in an indelible way on the broad and grand scenery."[46] That glorious sight was overwhelming; it was also sobering as men realized their own insignificance in the vastness of space, and exalting as they sensed that they alone among humans comprehended that infinity. Man became, as one French novelist put it, "what really the Supreme Being meant to make him; that is to say the king of the creation."[47]

This did not mean that the image-makers pictured the plainsmen as pantheistic Natty Bumppos, finding in Nature the revealed will of God. All were unwavering Christians, shaping their behavior by the code of European churchgoers; no proper plainsman would strike an enemy from behind, hunt on the Sabbath day (although even Old Shatterhand had to admit that "a westerner doesn't ask if it is Sunday when he sees a buffalo before him"),[48] neglect his regular prayers, or seek every opportunity for worship. Instead they found in the unspoiled magnificence of the wild additional proof of the might of Europe's God, and through this an understanding and strength denied the less fortunate. "The primitive-strong,"[49]

[42] Duplessis, Le Batteur d'estrade, 1: 7.
[43] Strubberg, An der Indianergrenze, pp. 24–25.
[44] Charles Sealsfield, Life in the New World; or, Sketches of American Society (New York, 1844), p. 269.
[45] Quoted in George R. Brooks, "The American Frontier in German Fiction," in The Frontier Re-examined, ed. John F. McDermott (Urbana, 1967), pp. 161–62. Charles Sealsfield is quoted.
[46] Aimard, The Border Rifles, pp. 37–38.
[47] Gustave Aimard, The Trappers of Arkansas; or, The Loyal Heart (London, 1864), pp. 157–58.
[48] May, Winnetou I, p. 34.
[49] Quoted in Augustus J. Prahl, "America in the Works of Gerstäcker," Modern Language Quarterly 4 (June 1943): 224.

one German novelist called them; "among them," added another, "I have observed a genius which could have done honor to the greatest philosophers of ancient and modern times."[50]

This was the ultimate in unreality. Even Europeans with the most remote acquaintance with the American West must have realized that the plainsmen of the image-makers bore not the faintest resemblance to the trappers and Mountain Men who served as their models. Thus the invented *Westmanner* of fiction spurned wealth; in novel after novel one was offered a gold mine by a friendly chief only to answer angrily: "What the deuce would you have me do with the gold? I am a hunter, whom his horse and rifle suffice."[51] No actual frontiersmen would be guilty of such lofty nonsense; they risked their scalps and their lives daily simply because such risks were necessary if they were to amass the fortune of their dreams. The crude, materialistic, half-civilized illiterates who roamed the advance frontiers in real life were neither Olympian philosophers nor noble humanitarians. The image-makers who created the Hunter-Plainsmen of fiction had further distorted the picture of frontier America seen by Europeans.

Squatters and Backwoodsmen

If the image-makers trifled with the truth in glorifying the Hunter-Plainsmen, they were equally guilty of distortion when they described the next wave of pioneers who followed the hunters westward. These were the squatters, or backwoodsmen, who normally served as advance agents for the agricultural frontier. Admittedly these seminomadic half-hunters, half-farmers were less glamorous than the hunters that preceded them and less effective as pioneers than the equipped farmers that followed. They were restless outcasts, fleeing the responsibilities of society, and content to live slovenly lives as they made the first forest clearings or turned the first prairie sod. But neither were they the savage semibarbarians seen by the image-makers—wild, lawless, indolent, useless—the scum of America, shunned by white man and red alike, and worthless to themselves and their fellowmen.

That they should be pictured by novelists and travelers as such despicable subhumans can be explained partly by the state of scientific thought in the nineteenth century, partly by the misunderstandings among social philosophers, and partly by the eagerness of hostile observers to degrade frontier democracy by exaggerating the social disintegration of the borderlands. The eagerness of the conservative travelers to picture the semi-

[50] Sealsfield, *Courtship of George Howard*, p. 42.
[51] Gustave Aimard, *The Tiger Slayer* (New York, n.d.), p. 118.

savage backwoodsmen as products of frontier equality is readily understandable; the state of scientific and social thought as it influenced their
evaluation requires more explanation.

Scientists through much of the nineteenth century saw society as constantly evolving, moving over the course of centuries from barbarism to
universal enlightenment. They believed, too, that this evolution occurred
in well-defined phases easily discernable to scholars. Ten of these were
identified by the French philosopher, the Marquis de Condorcet, whose
Progress of the Human Mind was a bible for European thinkers, the first the
state of savagery, the last an age of reason, equality, and cultural outpouring. Between were the stages of agriculture, commerce, industry, and
their subclassifications.[52]

In casting about for a laboratory where these concepts could be tested,
scientists naturally fastened on the United States, for here civilization was
evolving from primitive to complex forms within a definable time span.
Unfortunately their theories were applied with more enthusiasm than
knowledge by dozens of visitors to western America. Each saw the
frontier as evolving in precise stages from the lowest social forms represented by backwoodsmen to the highest in the cultural elite of urban
areas. Talleyrand, commenting on their findings, concluded that a journey westward from the Atlantic seaboard cities to the crude cabins of the
squatters was "traveling backward over the progress of the human
mind."[53]

This succession placed the backwoodsmen at the bottom level of the
evolutionary process—the mudsill against which the whole story of civilization could be measured. The squatter was the least civilized of all humans; he had, as one British traveler put it, "attached himself to a life of
savage independence," and hence was incapable of progress, doomed forever to a state of near-savagery.[54] Why waste sympathy on a lowly creature who had sealed his own fate by adopting a life-pattern that made him
the stepping-stone for the advance of others, but from which he could
never rise?

The squatter was also the victim of changing European views on the
nature and benefits of society. So long as romanticism reigned the yeoman
farmer was the philosophers' ideal, and the squatter best represented that

[52] These views are described in Henry Nash Smith, *Virgin Land: The American West as Symbol and Myth* (Cambridge, 1950), p. 219.
[53] Quoted in ibid., p. 220. Dozens of travelers noted the stages of civilization as they trav-
eled westward toward the frontier. Typical were: Elias P. Fordham, *Personal Narrative of
Travels* (Cleveland, 1906), pp. 125–27; James Flint, *Letters from America* (Edinburgh, 1822),
pp. 206–9; Francis Baily, *Journal of a Tour in the Unsettled Parts of North America in 1796 and
1797* (London, 1856), pp. 216–18; and John Melish, *Travels through the United States of America
in the Years 1806 & 1807, and 1809, 1810, & 1811* (London, 1818), pp. 256–57.
[54] Daniel Blowe, *A Geographical, Historical, Commercial, and Agricultural View of the United
States of America* (London, 1820), p. 745.

stereotype in the United States. But when the excesses of the French Revolution cast doubts on the ability of natural man to restrain his savage instincts, European intellectuals began to question the virtues of natural man everywhere. Thoroughly disillusioned on the benefits of primitivism, and overreacting in their disillusionment, they degraded the backwoodsmen to a "degenerate race," traitors to progress, and "little above the beast of the field."[55] The squatters were society's outcasts, deserving of neither praise nor pity.

Their supreme crime in the eyes of European intellectuals was to surrender to, rather than triumph over, Nature. There was evidence of their failure in every forest opening where they made their homes: half-cleared fields, a tumbledown cabin still uncompleted, a dilapidated fence that would keep out nothing, and everywhere the weeds and second growth that marked the retriumph of Nature. The squatter had tried, in a first burst of ambition, but had surrendered. This was unpardonable in an age when the great god Progress had been sanctified. Those unwilling or unable to carry on civilization's battle were little better than the savage whose lands they had usurped—a "disconnecting link between the Indians and the settlers"—but with lower moral standards than even the Indians, and equally deserving of extermination.[56]

In giving up their war against Nature, they had revealed a fundamental weakness that made them less than human. One German storyteller drove this point home in the tale of a small child, the son of a French trapper and an Indian wife, who strayed from his village and grew up by himself in the forest depths. Years later he was discovered by a band of hunters, crouched in a tree, half-man and half-beast. For a time they debated whether to shoot him or lure him down, deciding on the latter course. His appearance was shocking: "his whole body was coated with a fine mantle of gleaming black hair, while the hair on his head hung like a mane over his shoulders and neck. A monstrous beard reached below his chest, and under his bushy eyebrows his eyes glowed darkly with anxiety and terror."[57] The lesson was clear. Unaided Nature produced animals, not men, and the closer to Nature the more animalistic the person. Such were the backwoodsmen.

And what complete traitors to progress they were. The image-makers vied in coining phrases insulting enough to describe them: "one-eyed sav-

---

[55] George W. Featherstonhaugh, *A Canoe Voyage up the Minnay Sotor* (London, 1847), 1: 152. A similar view is expressed in William Faux, *Memorable Days in America: Being a Journal of a Tour to the United States* (London, 1823), pp. 240–41.

[56] William Savage, *Observations on Emigration to the United States of America* (London, 1819), pp. 32–33.

[57] Strubberg, *Bis in die Wildnis*, 2: 23.

ages,"[58] "blackened with iniquity,"[59] "men of morose and savage disposition, the very outcasts of society,"[60] "the scum, the dregs, of civilized society,"[61] "rude and even abandoned characters,"[62] "the dregs, repelled by a civilized society,"[63] "the refuse of all nations . . . , the shame and scum of the North-American population."[64] The squatter was a glaring example of mankind regressing toward savagery under Nature's savage influence. "Indifferent to any motive of honor," wrote a British visitor to backcountry Missouri, "occupied by mean associations without solicitude for the future, and incapable of foresight and reflection, they pass their lives without thinking, and are growing old without getting out of their infancy."[65]

The dwellings of the squatters revealed the degradation. They lived in ramshackle log hovels with dirt floors, often so poorly built that wind blowing through the chinks extinguished candles within. All were decaying away, with broken windows, doors dangling from hinges, piles of litter all about, and rank weeds growing everywhere. Nearby was a half-cleared field planted to an untended crop surrounded by a worn fence of rails so twisted that escaping hogs who thought they had made their way outside found themselves still within.[66] These tumbledown shanties offered no protection from the mosquitoes that swarmed by the billions, carrying malaria in its most virulent form. Not a backwoodsman but was wracked with ague.

Their squalor was reflected in their appearance. All were clay colored or "tallow white" as might be expected among those who lived in constant shade; one image-maker described them as "tall and pale, like vegetables that grow in a vault, pining for light."[67] Squatters commonly wore dirty leather jackets, ragged pants held by a single gallus, and a hat misshapen by years of abuse. All went barefooted the year around. Their women were slatternly caricatures of female beauty and their swarms of children,

[58] Richard Weston, *A Visit to the United States and Canada in 1833, with a View to Settling in America* (Glasgow, 1836), p. 124.
[59] Frederick Shirreff, *A Tour through North America: Together with a Comprehensive View of the Canadas and United States* (Edinburgh, 1835), p. 428.
[60] Isaac Weld, *Travels through the United States of North America, and the Provinces of Upper and Lower Canada, during the Years 1795, 1796, and 1797* (London, 1807), 2: 326–27.
[61] Sealsfield, *Courtship of George Howard*, pp. 212–14.
[62] Morris Birkbeck, *Notes on a Journey in America* (London, 1818), p. 92.
[63] Charles Sealsfield, *The Courtship of Ralph Doughby, Esquire* (New York, 1844), p. 235.
[64] Aimard, *The Trappers of Arkansas*, pp. 87–88.
[65] Flint, *Letters from America*, p. 145.
[66] William Black, *Green Pastures and Piccadilly* (London, 1878), p. 108; Edward S. Ellis, *Across Texas* (Philadelphia, 1893), p. 11.
[67] Sealsfield, *Courtship of George Howard*, pp. 44–45. Similar descriptions are in Melish, *Travels through the United States of America*, p. 372; and Birkback, *Notes on a Journey*, p. 125.

largely naked even in cold weather, resembled pigs more than humans.[68] The comforts of life were unknown and unwanted.

Nature was to blame for their plight, for they lived amidst such abundance that there was no need to work. Why extend a clearing or cultivate a field when plentiful game was within rifle shot? "Where Nature is bountiful," a visitor reported, "man is apt to be indolent."[69] Nature's cupboard provided most of their needs without effort, and they could always swap a few pelts for other necessities: powder, lead, a little coffee and tobacco, and once in awhile a jug of corn whiskey. Their easy lives drained them of all ambition; "many," wrote a traveler, "become listless and unenterprising, and lose that energy which alone can secure riches."[70]

Evidence of the squatters' laziness was everywhere in the backwoods; weed-choked fields, homes and fences needing repair, dirty water dipped from a stream to avoid digging a well, a fallen tree blocking a road for months because no one could summon the energy to drag it away.[71] A traveler stopping at a tumble-down cabin was told that the husband was seldom home long enough to make needed repairs; "right now he has gone off to help a neighbor to hunt up an old painter that's been arter all the pigs; he ain't been home in a week, and I reckon he's stopt somewhar to help *shuck* corn."[72] Humdrum tasks were outlawed so long as Nature's cafeteria was well stocked.

Just as shocking to the European image-makers was the lawlessness of the backwoodsmen. The much-boasted freedoms so admired during the Age of Romanticism were less acceptable now; instead property accumulation was the ambition of most individuals and property protection the principal duty of society. The backwoodsmen refused to play by these rules. Rebels against the social system themselves, they saw no reason to follow codes that easterners and Europeans found acceptable. "They shun everything that appears to demand of them law or order," a traveler reported, "and dread anything that breathes of restraint. They hate the name of justice."[73] To them each man should make and enforce his own law. "This is my Christ," one shouted, waving his rifle. "He's my savior.

[68] Matilda J. F. Houstoun, *Hesperos; or, Travels in the West* (London, 1850), 2: 49; Gustaf Unonius, *A Pioneer in Northwest America, 1841–1858: The Memoirs of Gustaf Unonius* (Minneapolis, 1950–51), 1: 206; Albert C. Koch, *Journey through a Part of the United States of North America in the Years 1844 to 1846* (Carbondale, 1972), p. 81; Sealsfield, *Courtship of George Howard*, p. 45.
[69] Robert Barclay-Allardice, *Agricultural Tour of the United States and Upper Canada* (Edinburgh, 1842), pp. 137–38.
[70] Charles J. Latrobe, *The Rambler in North America* (London, 1835), 1: 139. Countless other travelers made this same observation.
[71] Fordham, *Personal Narrative of Travels*, p. 156; George W. Featherstonhaugh, *Excursion through the Slave States* (New York, 1844), p. 104.
[72] Featherstonhaugh, *Excursion through the Slave States*, pp. 81–82.
[73] Johan D. Shoepf, *Travels in the Confederation, 1783–84* (Cleveland, 1911), 1: 338–39.

"The Skulkers." From Mayne Reid, *The Death Shot* (Beadle's Dime Novel
Library, New York, n.d.), p. 34. (From the Special Collections
of the University of California at Los Angeles Library.)

He'll save me from evil."[74] Might, not right, was their guiding principle.

Especially in obtaining land, for none would think of buying a farm; they lived up to their names by "squatting" on any piece of real estate that pleased them, then defending it against its rightful owners. Europeans, long accustomed to viewing property rights as sacred, judged this practice the ultimate in lawlessness. Fiction writers particularly gloried in describing the conflicts between lawless occupants and real owners. "Not my clarin'?" one backwoodsman shouted. "Shew me the man who says it's not! Shew'm to me! By the Almighty eternal, he won't say't twice." Had he bought the land, he was asked. "Neer a mind for that, mister. I've *made* it: that's my style of purchase, an' by G——! it'll stan' good, I reck'n."[75] Possession to the backwoodsman was ten-tenths of the law, a shocking concept to those bred in the belief that the law was sacred.

This attitude was enough evidence of the squatters' surrender to savagery, but even worse was their inability to conquer Nature. Once a civilized man had made his first clearing and built his cabin he would defend his possessions against any odds. Not so the backwoodsmen, who at the first setback would move on to begin the process anew. This constant moving about, this "restless temper" as Tocqueville called it, could have been excused if its purpose was to quest for better opportunity elsewhere. Instead, the squatters were retreating before advancing civilization, symbolized by the neighbors who moved in about them. Each move was an escape from the responsibility of contributing to the nation's prosperity. The image-makers chronicled these retreats endlessly: "the sound of the axe in the woods is hateful to him; and no sooner does the smoke of a settler's fire become frequent in his neighborhood, than, packing up his scanty moveables . . . he, with his family seeks a more congenial home in those solitudes where nature holds undisputed sway."[76]

The typical backwoodsman surrendered to his own failure seven or eight times during his lifetime, selling only his "improvements" to later comers, for he had nothing else to sell. "As the population advances," a visitor recorded, "these wild spirits melt away before it"—a "froth and scum" of society boiling away to make room for civilization.[77] So they moved, on and on, to span the Mississippi Valley and invade the Southwest. Travelers in Texas found them hovering along the western borders of the settlements, "too indolent either to plant vegetables, shoot game, or

[74]   Ulrich S. Carrington, ed., *The Making of an American: An Adaptation of Memorable Tales by Charles Sealsfield* (Dallas, 1974), pp. 40–41.
[75]   Mayne Reid, *The Wild Huntress* (London, 1861), 1: 220; a similar statement is in Aimard, *The Prairie Flower*, p. 64.
[76]   William Oliver, *Eight Months in Illinois* (Newcastle-upon-Tyne, 1843), pp. 154–55.
[77]   Tyrone Power, *Impression of America during the Years 1833, 1834, and 1835* (London, 1836), 2: 139.

catch fish," "willing and able to engage in anything except what might demand steady and settled habits of industry."[78]

The backwoodsmen were creatures of the forested frontiers, for the game on which they subsisted was less easily available on the arid plains of the Far West. Imaginative novelists, however, were not content to end their westward march in the Mississippi Valley or eastern Texas. Instead that same breed appeared now and then in the Rocky Mountains. "Squatting" on land that belonged to others, and defying the true owners with rifle and bowie knife. Their homes bore little resemblance to the ramshackle cabins on the actual frontier. One, built in three weeks on the upper Missouri River in 1801 by two brothers, contained a cluster of log cabins held together by iron clamps and surrounded by a palisade that was in turn encircled by a moat ten feet wide and fifteen feet deep. A single drawbridge, guarded by giant dogs trained in killing Indians, provided the only entrance. Once completed this elaborate establishment was legalized in a proper ceremony: an American flag was planted in the soil and a proclamation read aloud by the owner: "I take possession of this wild territory by the right of first occupant, and proclaim myself its sole lord and master," wheron the assembled servants shouted, "Hurrah; Long Live America," and the titled was assured.[79]

The frequent stress on the illegal use of land by squatters was a fair indication of the reaction of property-conscious image-makers to a common frontier practice. To them, denial of the right of an owner to his possessions was a denial of all civilization. Their European readers agreed with them. When they read of a Texan landlord whose valuable forests were being destroyed by a gang of loggers, they aligned themselves with the landlord, not with the loggers who protested: "God gave the ground to man that he might labor on it. Every proprietor that does not fulfill this condition tacitly renounces his rights, and the earth becomes the property of the man who tills it with the sweat of his brow; so go to the Devil."[80] Skeptical Europeans might question the eloquence of such language from an illiterate backwoodsman, but they did not miss the point he was making. American squatters were not only crude, vulgar, outcasts, but were proven enemies of the concept of private property on which civilization was based. In painting them in these harsh colors, the image-makers added a new dimension to the frontier as a land of violence and lawlessness, unsuited to men and women who had advanced beyond savagery.

---

[78] Houstoun, *Hesperos*, 2: 120–21.
[79] Aimard, *The Missouri Outlaws*, p. 31.
[80] Aimard, *The Trail Hunter*, p. 42.

Enter the Cowboy

Still another dimension was to be added in the 1880s and 1890s with the emergence of a new type of hero in European fiction, destined within a remarkably short time to push the backwoodsmen and Hunter-Heroes from the stage. This was the cowboy.

The cowboy did not come upon the scene until late in the century largely because he had to live down an unsavory reputation before he was to be fitted for a hero's role. The name was first used during the American Revolution, and by mid-century was universally accepted as synonymous with villains and outlaws. "Cow-boys" were generally centered along the southwestern frontier where they preyed on legitimate ranchers, stealing their cattle, plundering and murdering on both sides of the border. They were universally condemned as outlaws: "the plague of the West . . . too idle to work . . . invariably drunk and a terror to the inhabitants."[81] There was little of the stuff of which heroes are made in the cowboy of fact or legend during most of the nineteenth century.

He made his first appearance in fiction during the early 1880s as authors of American dime novels sought to profit by the popularity of Buffalo Bill's Wild West show. During the first years of the decade cowboys were still pictured as unsavory reprobates, always boisterous and often profane and lawless. "The cowboys are coming," shouts a character in an early dime novel; "Git to hidin'! Thar on a tear."[82] Gradually this image changed; cowboys were still too given to rambuctious conduct to don the hero's garb, but authors were increasingly inclined to blame not them but the saloon keepers in the cattle towns who plied innocent young men with "prussic acid bug juice" and the gamblers who cheated them of their pay.

They were rescued from their unhappy past by Colonel Prentiss Ingraham, the author of hundreds of dime novels. Casting about for a new hero type, Colonel Ingraham happened on Buck Taylor, a leading actor in Buffalo Bill's show, whose only qualifications were a ruggedly handsome face and an ability to stay aboard a bucking bronco. From the day when *Buck Taylor, King of the Cowboys; or, The Raiders and the Rangers* appeared in Beadle's Half Dime Library in 1885, Taylor was assured a place in the sun of legendary heroes and the cowboy a role as the principal hero of Westerns. And what a popular hero he was. Over the coming years cowboys were to dominate American dime novels, reign supreme in the pulp magazines that appeared in the twentieth century, and stir the blood of millions

---

[81] Edmond, baron de Mandat-Grancey, *Cowboys and Colonels: Narrative of a Journey across the Prairie and over the Black Hills of Dakota* (London, 1887), p. 27. A similar hostile view is in Charles W. Webber, *The Texan Virago* (Philadelphia, 1852), p. 6.
[82] Quoted in Warren French, "The Cowboy in the Dime Novel," *Studies in English* 30 (1951): 227–28. The emergence of the cowboy in dime novels is admirably described in this article.

of viewers of films and television programs. With the publication of Owen Wister's *The Virginian*, in 1902, they entered the realm of respectable fiction. Their triumph as the greatest of frontier heroes was complete.[83]

There was little of the true cowboy—"the hired hand on horseback" of the real world—in these tales. Their authors saw him as he ought to be, not as what he was; they simply created a new hero-type to fit a role. A blend of Hercules and Tristam, riding tall in the saddle against the forces of evil, gunning down villains and rescuing blonds, he symbolized to millions of Americans and Europeans the ultimate in righteousness and modern chivalry. He symbolized, too, the supremacy of the Nordic race; the Negroes and Mexican-Americans who were almost as numerous as white cowboys in real life never appeared on the pages of dime novels. The fictional cowboy might bear but scant resemblance to his model, but he became to millions of readers the hero of the conquest of Nature's last stronghold—"the Hector of our ignored Iliad," as Frank Norris put it— representing the triumph of civilization over the primitive lawlessness that stood in the way of progress.[84]

This was a role that guaranteed his success with European audiences. Travelers began introducing the cowboy to Europeans in the 1880s, but their judgment was mixed. Some found these "centaurs on horseback" a "wild and crude race" who "behaved like wild animals in their excesses," and "whose only law is the revolver, whose only god is whiskey, and whose only prayer is foul-mouthed blasphemy."[85] Others were more generous, reporting that their manners were not offensive and that they washed their hands before eating; they might occasionally stage barroom brawls or shoot up a town but this was only the exuberance of youth—no more than "a band of college boys from Harvard or Cornell, or Princeton might do."[86] Still other critics found them a noble race, the true stuff of classic heroism. "The first breath they breathe is one of freedom, of infinity," intoned an Hungarian visitor. "Their cradle is the saddle, the heavens their blanket, storms their music, cold winters and hot summers harden them. They are a special race."[87] A British editor agreed: "As a class there are no nobler-hearted or honourable men in the world. Brave to rashness, generous to a fault, if you should be thrown among them you

[83] Ingraham's works are described in ibid., pp. 229–31.

[84] The connection between classical heroes and cowboys is made in John B. Jackson, "Ich bin ein Cowboy aus Texas," *Southwest Review* 38 (Spring 1953): 158–63.

[85] Carl S. Andersen, *Det Store Vesten: Kolonisationen af Nordamerikas indland imellem Mississippi-floden og Rocky Mountains* (Copenhagen, 1883), p. 52. Similar views are in A. O. Ansnes, *Amerikanske streiftog: Oplevelser og indtryk fra de forenede stater* (Kristiansund, 1889), p. 111; O. Drevdahl, *Fra Emigrationens Amerika* (Oslo, 1891), ch. 3., and William A. Baillie-Grohman, *Camps in the Rockies* (New York, 1882), p. 363.

[86] *American Settler*, 9 May 1885.

[87] Alajos Izsóf, *Tul a nagy vizeken* (Budapest, 1916), p. 36.

would find them ready to share their last crust with you, or lie down at night with you on the same blanket."[88] One Hungarian traveler was delighted to meet a cowboy who read Horace in Latin as he tended his herd.[89]

The cowboy, clearly, was ready to emerge in European fiction as a full-blown hero. He assumed this role gradually; the force of tradition on the Continent was so strong that the hunter-plainsmen remained dominant until well into the twentieth century. In Great Britain, however, imported American dime novels set an example that was followed by a few writers during the 1890s. Their cowboys established a pattern that helped shape the European image of the frontier for generations to come.

All were spare of build, with muscles of whipcord, eyes keen and watchful, and faces ever alert to danger. They wore wide-brimmed hats made of stiff felt and ornamented with a band of gold or silver, flannel shirts with a colorful silk handkerchief knotted about the neck, trousers of tanned leather protected by chaparajos, jackets adorned with fringes, high boots cut away at the knees in back, and a bright Mexican sash into which were stuffed an arsenal of bowie knives and six-shooters.[90] All were brave to the point of recklessness; "we don't place much valley on our lives," one told a British schoolboy, "seeing as we risk them every day. We know they ain't likely to be long anyhow."[91] All were dedicated, hard-working young men, accustomed to incredible hardships. "I have gone twenty hours without a mouthful," said one, "for the simple reason that I hadn't had time to ride to the cook wagon and get it."[92]

Above all the cowboys that sported through the pages of British boys' novels were models of virtue, honesty, and decorum. Their exemplary conduct was easily explained: many were the younger sons of British noblemen seeking their fortunes, or English schoolboys in quest of excitement. These lads made fine cowboys, partly because of their English pluck and valor, partly because they had perfected their riding skills while fox hunting. To such younsters, life as a cowboy was an irresistible lark. "Of course I know, as well as anyone," one novelist confessed, "that to a hot-blooded English boy, roughing it, and facing dangers which he just manages to overcome, are fun and frolic."[93]

Fun and frolic might add joys to cowboy life, but their real contribution was to bring law and order to the West. True, they might play a bit rough at times, roaring through towns with guns blazing, shooting out

[88] *American Settler*, 9 May 1885.
[89] Ferenc Pulszky, *Életem és Korom* (Budapest, 1880–82), 1: 117.
[90] G. A. Henty, *Redskin and Cow-Boy: A Tale of the Western Plains* (London, 1891), p. 125.
[91] Ibid., pp. 186–87.
[92] Ellis, *Across Texas*, p. 92.
[93] C. Phillipps-Wolley, *Snap: A Legend of the Lone Mountain* (London, 1899), is built on this theme. The quotation is from p. 146.

saloon windows, knocking pipes from the mouths of strangers with a well-placed shot, forcing a greenhorn to dance by raining bullets about his feet. But this was only boyish exuberance. Doing good was their business, and they blazed a path of virtue through the West. "If it wasn't for cow-boys," one hero explained, "there wouldn't be no living in the border settlements. . . . Who is to keep the Injuns in order? Do you think it is Uncle Sam's troops? Why the Red-skins just laugh at them. It's the cow-boys."[94] Yet they always fought fair and never killed unless killing was justified. When a man whose wife and children had been massacred by the redskins wanted to kill Indian woman and children in return, he was told by Bronco Harry: "We have come here to help you, and we are risking our lives pretty considerable in this business, but afore we ride into that village we are going to have your word that there ain't going to be a shot fired at a squaw or child. Those are our terms."[95] Chivalry was the foundation of the cowboy code—in British Westerns.

The image of the cowboy as a western hero was just emerging in England at the close of the nineteenth century, and had hardly begun to infiltrate Continental fiction, but the model was already taking shape: the lone avenger with muscles of steel and heart of gold, quick to kill bad men whether red or white, but staunchly committed to the laws of decency that governed civilized men. Clearly marked as the hero of the future, he was ready to intensify the European image of the frontier as a land of blood and violence, where individual justice usurped the ordinary functioning of the law and where the six-shooter and the lyncher's rope were needed to keep order and protect lives and property. During the twentieth century the cowboy of film and fiction was to play a major part in deepening the impression of the West as a center for savagery where ordinary mortals were unwelcome and unsafe.

[94]   Henty, *Redskin and Cow-Boy*, p. 186.
[95]   Ibid., p. 228.

VIII

Pioneer Farmers: Unsung Heroes

IF THE IMAGE-MAKERS HAD BEEN TRUE to their prejudices, they would have glorified the pioneer farmers as the true heroes in the conquest of the frontier. These were the hardworking men and women who transformed forest and plain into productive farms, built sturdy houses and barns, laid cultural foundations, demanded trade links with eastern markets, and exported the first surpluses. They were, in other words, the final victors in the battle against Nature, completing the process that hunters and plainsmen and squatters had begun. Yet their fate was to be scorned as undesirable inferiors unfit for the company of civilized men, partly because they had not advanced far enough along the road to civilization to meet European standards, partly because they provided a convenient foil for novelists and travelers debating the virtues of democracy.

Travelers conceded that the pioneer farmers had surpassed the backwoodsmen in their social evolution, recognizing that they made farming, not hunting, their principal occupation.[1] In doing so they had acquired

[1] This distinction was made by numerous travelers. Typical were the comments of Jacques-Pierre Brissot de Warville, *New Travels in the United States of America, Performed in 1788* (London, 1792), pp. 331–32; John Bernard, *Retrospections of America* (New York, 1887), pp. 178–80; Victor Collot, *A Journey in North America* (Paris, 1826), 1: 109–10; Henry B. Fearon, *Sketches of America* (London, 1818), pp. 224–25; William N. Blane, *An Excursion through the United States and Canada, during the Years 1822–23* (London, 1824), pp. 179–80; and Dominique de Blackford, *Précis de l'état actuel des colonies angloises dans l'Amérique septentrionale* (Milan, 1771), pp. 13–15.

the sedentary habits of civilized men and the ambitions of incipient capitalists, both essential virtues in an age when wealth was the measure or worth. Yet they lacked the basic qualities that differentiated the civilized and uncivilized. Thus they might aspire to learning and good manners, but they had achieved neither. Their battle against Nature had so robbed them of their sensitivity that they were incapable of good taste, aesthetic appreciation, or acceptable social conduct. Men who were unable to recognize the beauty of a tree, and were concerned only with the number of strokes needed to cut it down, were (as Talleyrand noted) hardly suited to the company of Europe's intellectuals.[2] They were winning the continent to civilization, but they had been permanently brutalized in doing so.

Most image-makers agreed that the pioneers would eventually regain the sensitivity and cultural sophistication that were the marks of civilization; Alexis de Tocqueville put the matter well when he wrote that they displayed "the inexperience and the rude habits of a people in their infancy."[3] They agreed also that that day would not come until the pioneering process was completed. Until then they would remain subhuman—"half-civilized and half-savage"[4]—crude in speech and manners, deficient in literature and the arts, only a step above the backwoodsmen in cultural expression and appreciation. So long as this was their status they would continue as fair game for image-makers seeking examples to prove their own preconceptions. To some the pioneers would continue to be social and cultural outcasts, to others they would shine as self-sacrificing heroes who had temporarily forsaken a better life to win a continent for civilization—"obscure soldiers of progress," as one called them.[5] The result was a dual image of the pioneer farmer that persisted for most of the nineteenth century.

Portrait of the Pioneer

Whatever their predilections, however, virtually all image-makers pictured the pioneer farmers as victims of the cultural lag normal among those who had forsaken the centers of civilization. This was evidenced by

[2]   Quoted in Durand Echeverria, *Mirage in the West: A History of the French Image of American Society to 1815* (Princeton, 1957), p. 205. A similar point was made in Charles J. Latrobe, *The Rambler in North America* (London, 1835), 2: 139.
[3]   Alexis de Tocqueville, *Democracy in America* (Cambridge, 1865), 2: 322. The same views are expressed in John Woods, *Two Years' Residence in the Settlement on the English Prairie in the Illinois Country* (London, 1822), pp. 288–89, and Frederick Marryat, *A Diary in America* (London, 1839), 3: 265.
[4]   P. I. Pierre Poletica, *A Sketch of the Internal Condition of the United States . . . by a Russian* (Baltimore, 1826), p. 109.
[5]   Louis L. Simonon, *The Rocky Mountain West in 1867* (Lincoln, Nebr., 1966), p. 30.

Front cover of Mayne Reid, *The Hunters' Feast*
(London, n.d.). (From the Special Collections
of the University of California at Los Angeles Library.)

their appearance. The men were shabbily dressed, wearing threadbare coats, patched trousers stuffed into boot tops, battered felt hats, and down-at-the-heel shoes innocent of all polish; the women favored shapeless homespun dresses bare of all ornamentation. Most housewives were of sallow complexion, their hands roughened by labor, their features sad and resigned.[6] Most had lost their teeth while still in their teens, a misfortune that some travelers blamed on tea drinking, others on their failure to blow their noses, allowing accumulated mucus to eat away the enamel, and one Polish visitor on their smoking and excessive consumption of "vodka."[7] Yet they were generally better appearing than the wives of European peasants, with an air of self-assurance and hopefulness.

Men and women alike showed the effects of their lonely lives, distant from towns and even neighbors. More kindly image-makers saw their isolation as planned self-sacrifice; they had deliberately seceded from the world of friendship and pleasures to join the army of conquest that was winning the West. Educated newcomers and recent arrivals from Europe were sometimes not sure that they had not sacrificed too much, for most found that even when neighbors were nearby they were too uncultured to provide proper companionship. "There is no society even to quarrel with, to rouse the dormant faculties," complained one commentator; "no social neighbor to chat with on passing events."[8] Life in a social vacuum was hardly the bed of roses sought by most emigrants.

Recent arrivals felt even less secure as they observed the remarkable skills of the practiced American pioneers. Image-makers never ceased to marvel at the speed with which they transformed a wilderness into an established community; the succession from a virgin forest to a neat farm with a frame house and a cluster of barns seemed to take place in the twinkling of an eye.[9] Even more remarkable was the growth of towns. Promoters had only to lay out a few paths through the unbroken forest and label them "Main Street" and "Walnut Street" to attract a swarm of buyers who as though by magic cleared away the trees and built their houses. "The blows of hammer and axe are heard all day long and into the

[6]   Typical descriptions are in George W. Pierson, ed., *Tocqueville and Beaumont in America* (New York, 1938), pp. 244–45, and François, duc de La Rochefoucauld-Liancourt, *Voyage dans les Etats-Unis d'Amérique fait en 1795, 1796, et 1797* (Paris, 1799), 3: 104.
[7]   François Marie Perrin Du Lac, *Travels through the Two Louisianas and among the Savage Nations of the Missouri* (London, 1807), pp. 104–5; Henryk Sienkiewicz, *Western Septet: Seven Stories of the American West* (Cheshire, Conn., 1973), p. 124.
[8]   William Savage, *Observations on Emigration to the United States of America* (London, 1819), p. 31. The lonely life of the pioneers is also stressed in Friedrich Armand Strubberg, *An der Indianergrenze* (Hanover, 1859), 1: 194–95; Michel-Guillaume St. John de Crèvecoeur, *Voyage dans la haute Pennsylvanie et dans l'état de New York* (Paris, 1801), 1: 81–82.
[9]   Fredrika Bremer, *America of the Fifties: Letters of Fredrika Bremer* (New York, 1924), p. 246.

evening," wrote a recent arrival in such a village.[10] Within weeks a brand new "city" had emerged, complete with a few dozen cabins, a church, an inn or two, and perhaps an academy to lure more settlers. One traveler watched in amazement as a steamboat disgorged two dozen passengers into a dense woodland, carrying with them a mahogany piano and elegant furniture ornate with plush and silk upholstery. He was, he realized, witnessing the birth of a new community.[11] So hurried was the transformation that in such a city the scream of the woodpecker mingled with the melodies of the pianoforte and visitors could step from an untamed forest into a store stocked with silks from Paris.[12]

Now and then a romantic European visitor sighed with regret as he watched civilization advancing with railroad speed. A German novelist captured the disappointment of those idealists in the reactions of his hero, Farnwald, to the coming of civilization. Farnwald had fled westward seeking the loneliness of isolation, the solitude of the primeval forest, the undisturbed happiness and contentment of those who shaped their own destinies. Yet within months his life had changed—"with the growth of the settlement, with the fights over mine and thine, with envy, betrayal and hatred. . . . Once again seized by the turmoil of so-called civilized life, he had to swim with the current."[13] Europeans could never quite forget that primitivism had its rewards as well as its hardships.

Cultural Decay—or Renaissance?

The image-makers might disagree on the rewards of pioneering but they stood shoulder to shoulder in their belief that the pioneers suffered from a severe case of cultural retardation. Beyond this point they divided sharply. Some with conservative and monarchistic prejudices, insisted that the first settlers had severed the ties of civilization so completely that the West was doomed forever to cultural darkness. Others, with liberal and democratic leanings, argued that the low state of learning along the frontiers was temporary, and would be followed by a glorious renaissance once men and women had completed the material tasks essential to pioneering. Image-makers of this bent inclined to exaggerate the significance of every scrap of evidence that showed that cultural stirrings did exist along

10 Quoted in Theodore C. Blegen, ed., *The Land of Their Choice: The Immigrants Write Home* (Minneapolis, 1955), p. 253. See also Elias F. Fordham, *Personal Narrative of Travels in Virginia, Maryland, Pennsylvania, Ohio, Indiana, and Kentucky; and of a Residence in the Illinois Territory, 1817–1818* (Cleveland, 1906), p. 158, and Count Adelbert Baudissin, *Der Ansiedler im Missouri-Staat* (Iserlohn, 1854), pp. 67–68.
11 János Xantus, *Xantus János levelei Északamerikából* (Pest, 1857), p. 134.
12 Latrobe, *The Rambler in North America*, 2: 139.
13 Strubberg, *An der Indianergrenze*, 2: 260–61.

the frontiers, and to insist that frontiersmen were more culturally sophisticated than European peasants who lived under despots. Those conflicting images must have confused readers in the nineteenth century, just as
they have confused scholars ever since.

The conservatives—those who held that civilization and primitivism
was irreconcilable—stated their case plainly: "Bring the polished man in
contact with savage nature . . . and the one must succumb to the other, or
both will undergo a change. As man civilizes the wilderness, the wilderness more or less brutalizes him."[14] This was inevitable, for along the
frontiers the urge to hurry the coming of material civilization was so compelling that there was no leisure for cultural pursuits. Time was an essential commodity if the battle against Nature was to be won, so important
that every pursuit was judged in terms of the minutes and hours that it
required; portrait painters in the West complained that custom forced
them to charge by the hour, and at a rate substantially below that of car-
penters.[15] The finer things of life must wait on the necessities. "We are a
busy people, sir," said an American to Charles Dickens's Martin Chuzzlewit, "and have no time for reading mere notions. We don't mind 'em if
they come to us in newspapers along with almighty strong stuff of another
sort, but darn your books."[16] Such a philosophy outlawed a cultured elite;
in the West "every man of liberal education must have an occupation,"[17]
and to westerners an occupation meant performing tasks that would improve the physical lot of mankind. Yet the cultivation of the arts required
a class who "possess leisure and means of subsistence independently of
labour."[18] Here was a dilemma that doomed the West to perpetual cultural deprivation.

Not so, answered more friendly observers. They admitted that learning underwent an eclipse along the frontiers, but insisted that this lasted
only until the material base for a cultural outpouring had been laid. "The
Westerner," wrote one image-maker "is rough because he has not had
time to soften his voice and cultivate the graces of manner. . . . He has
been obliged to occupy himself much more with the cultivation of the
earth, than of himself."[19] But let the pressing tasks of pioneering lessen
and westerners would not only overtake but pass the nation in cultural

[14] Alexander Mackay, *The Western World* (Philadelphia, 1849), 2: 119.
[15] Marryat, *A Diary in America*, 2: 176–77.
[16] Charles Dickens, *The Life and Adventures of Martin Chuzzlewit* (London, 1844), p. 207.
[17] *Blackwood's Edinburgh Magazine*, March 1819, p. 223.
[18] Poletica, *Sketch of the Internal Condition*, p. 116.
[19] Michel Chevalier, *Society, Manners and Politics in the United States: Being a Series of Letters on North America* (Boston, 1839), p. 220. Similar views are in Bremer, *America of the Fifties*, p. 246; William A. Baillie-Grohman, *Camps in the Rockies* (New York, 1882), p. 22; John Melish, *Travels through the United States of America, in the Years 1806 & in 1807, and in 1809, 1810 & 1811* (London, 1818), p. 435; and Charles Sealsfield, *The United States of America As They Are* (London, 1827), 1: 31–32.

achievement as the dynamic energy bred of conquering the wilderness was released in this new direction. Let critics beware! A lusty infant was aborning in the West, and would someday guide the world into new frontiers of art and learning.

That revival might come, pessimists answered, but generations, even centuries, must await its arrival. As Tocqueville admitted, educational opportunity in the United States diminished directly in proportion to distance from the seaboard.[20] This seriously blighted prospects for the future; eons must pass before young men and women could be properly trained to shoulder cultural progress. For so long as pioneering remained the principal occupation, there would be little interest in schooling. As an early Illinois settler told a visitor: the people there "don't calculate that books and the sciences will do as much for a man in these matters as a handy use of the rifle."[21] Even with the best of will schools must lag, for frontier farms provided few tax dollars for their support.

Moreover, the problem was certain to compound itself. Properly trained teachers were virtually nonexistent, and would be as long as the educational process lagged. One being examined for a post as local schoolmaster was able to read a line or two and cipher simple sums, but then came to a dead standstill. "I never was much to school in my life," he explained. "I cyphered as fur as division, an' it wa'n't long till I forgot it all. I don't pretend to much school larnin nohow."[22] Yet he was given the job, for there were no other candidates. As a friendly commentator remarked sadly, generations yet unborn along the frontier would grow to manhood "with scarcely any other intelligence than that they derived from the feeble light of nature."[23]

More optimistic image-makers refused to accept this gloomy estimate. The West was certain to experience a renaissance within a brief time, they argued, because it was already well stocked with intellectual leaders eager to build there a patent-office model of the society they had known in the East. They might be vastly outnumbered, and they might meet stubborn opposition from their less-lettered neighbors, but these "men of education and manners"[24] were an influential lot, and would succeed. These "western pilgrims" lived in homes well stocked with books, read eastern journals, gathered for intelligent social discussions, and listened enraptured to classical music whenever opportunity offered. "Visit any log cabin you please," wrote a recent arrival from Sweden, ". . . and you will find the man who wields the axe and guides the plow civilized and able to express

20 Tocqueville, *Democracy in America*, 1: 405.
21 Eliza Farnham, *Life in Prairie Land* (New York, 1846), p. 330.
22 John Regan, *The Emigrant's Guide to the Western States of America* (Edinburgh, 1852), p. 241.
23 James Flint, *Letters from America* (Edinburgh, 1822), p. 128.
24 Fordham, *Personal Narrative of Travels*, p. 175.

his ideas on a variety of subjects in grammatical language and with intelligence and insight."[25] This was gross exaggeration, of course, just as was Tocqueville's claim that the average frontier community supported more intellectual activity than the most enlightened and populous districts of France.[26] Yet there was a grain of truth in that overstatement, as the testimony of a legion of travelers makes clear.[27]

This rosy picture was further magnified by promoters seeking to lure immigrants to their western holdings. If they were to be believed, a westward-rolling tide of arts and letters kept pace with the surging population; there was no reversion to savagery along the frontiers, not even for a moment. "There is no relapsing into barbarism," one guidebook insisted, "—the schoolmaster follows close behind."[28] Newcomers should not be misled by the raw appearance of the country and its people. Within the rough cabins were all the refinements of civilization; men with hands callused from holding plows were capable of discussion on the highest literary and artistic levels, while many women busy with household tasks were competent "to write a treatise on some abstruse subject, requiring thought and research."[29] Western communities, too, supported "theatrical entertainments, concerts, lectures, festivals, balls, and other amusements" just as did those in the East.[30] Emigrants willing to believe these tub-thumpers reached the frontier anticipating no lessening of the literary and social entertainments they had known in their homelands.

Underlying this cultural outpouring—according to the less scrupulous promoters—was the universal frontier belief that schools were essential not only to assure an intellectual renaissance, but for the survival of democracy. Hence they would always be well supported. Time and time again the image-makers told of tiny communities, boasting only a dozen families, whose menfolk contributed their labor to build a schoolhouse and their spare earnings to support a teacher. "Schools spring up like mushrooms whenever a dozen house can be found within a mile of each other," a visitor to Kansas in the 1860s reported.[31] Others commented happily that the first harvest had scarcely been reaped from freshly

[25]   H. Arnold Barton, ed., *Letters from the Promised Land: Swedes in America, 1840–1914* (Minneapolis, 1975), pp. 26–27. Harriet Martineau, *Retrospect of Western Travel* (London, 1838), 2: 54, makes the same point.
[26]   Tocqueville, *Democracy in America*, 1: 407.
[27]   See for example: Pierson, ed., *Tocqueville and Beaumont*, pp. 236–38; Napoléon-A. Murat, *A Moral and Political Sketch of the United States of North America* (London, 1833), p. 63; Basil Hall, *Travels in North America, in the Years 1827 and 1828* (Edinburgh, 1829), 1: 156; Matilda J. F. Houstoun, *Hesperos; or, Travels in the West* (London, 1850), 2: 126–27; and János Xantus, *Utazás Kalifornia déli részeiben* (Pest, 1860), pp. 37–39.
[28]   *Sequel to the Counsel for Emigrants* (Aberdeen, 1834), 53.
[29]   A. R. Fulton, "An Invitation to Immigrants," *The Palimpsest* 18 (July 1937): 241.
[30]   *American Settler*, 1 October 1872.
[31]   William A. Bell, *New Tracks in North America* (London, 1869), 1: 15.

plowed fields before the community's energy was directed toward a schoolhouse.[32] These reports were certainly accurate, but they were far from typical. Reality hardly sustained the image of an educational renaissance among ill-trained and practical-minded frontiersmen.

This same conflict of opinion blurs the image of the reading tastes of the frontiersmen. Hostile travelers found the West a literary desert; "I have not seen a book in the hands of any person since I left Philadelphia," one reported, while another concluded that any bookstall in England contained more reading matter to the square inch than could be found in any square league in Texas.[33] Friendly travelers, on the other hand, found books aplenty; frontier cabins filled with the works of Shakespeare or Milton; an Indiana lad who gathered nuts each year to be able to buy books by Dante, Plato, and Milton; a Louisville pioneer whose copy of *Ivanhoe* was in such demand that one or two persons an hour called to borrow it; a bookshop in a frontier hamlet well stocked with current novels, the classics, and such unlikely volumes as *The Pirates Own Book* and *The Language of the Flowers*.[34] They also testified that circulating libraries were commonplace in the smallest western communities, and that they were widely patronized; one traveler saw a shabbily clad pioneer enter such an establishment, learn that the book he wanted was out, and settle down to wait its return days hence, for he knew he could not face his family without it.[35] Such episodes were certainly not common in the West, but by picturing them as typical, friendly image-makers created an impression of the frontier as a fountain of learning and culture.

They also glorified the cultural role of pioneer newspapers. Hostile critics might insist that the sensational weeklies that purveyed a modicum of news and a maximum of the editor's political prejudices were "rags of the most miserable description," and that they sold only because their readers were too illiterate to read books,[36] but they could not gainsay the fact that the newspaper played an essential role in pioneer life, or that the tiniest western hamlet supported at least one. A favorite device was to

[32]   Károly Nendtvich, *Amerikai utazásom* (Pest, 1858), 1: 20–21; Adam Hodgson, *Letters from North America, Written during a Tour in the United States and Canada* (London, 1824), 1: 143–44; William Oliver, *Eight Months in Illinois* (Newcastle-upon-Tyne, 1843), p. 112; Gustaf Unonius, *A Pioneer in Northwest America, 1841–1858: The Memoirs of Gustaf Unonius* (Minneapolis, 1950–51), 1: 135.
[33]   Fearon, *Sketches of America*, pp. 252–53; Charles Hooton, *St. Louis Isle, or Texiana* (London, 1847), p. 10.
[34]   John Parsons, *A Tour through Indiana in 1840* (New York, 1920), pp. 120–21; Flint, *Letters from America*, pp. 272; Karl Bernhard, duke of Weimer, *Travels through North America, during the Years 1825 and 1826* (Philadelphia, 1828), 1: 70.
[35]   Morleigh (pseud.), *Life in the West: Back-Wood Leaves and Prairie Flowers* (London, 1842), p. 249. For a similar episode see Fortesque Cuming, *Sketches of a Tour to the Western Country* (Pittsburgh, 1810), pp. 166–67.
[36]   Hooton, *St. Louis Isle*, p. 10; Frances Trollope, *Domestic Manners of the Americans* (London, 1832), pp. 92–93.

parade statistics on the small number of settlers needed to support a news-paper: a town of thirty houses with a weekly already circulating; a news-paper in a village four months old with only four hundred inhabitants; three newspapers in an Arkansas community with six hundred resi-dents.[37] This was the stuff of legend, but it ignored the fact that quantity did not always indicate quality, and that there was little of literary quality in frontier journalism.

Religious Fanaticism

There was less dispute among the image-makers as they described the religious practices of the frontier. To Europeans accustomed to es-tablished churches with well-ordered practices and unquestioned ortho-doxy there was little of true religion in the emotionalism of western wor-ship. The frontiersmen were pious enough—no one questioned that—but their inspiration was drawn from the Devil, not God, and their ministers were cunningly disguised disciples of Satan bent on undermining true religion. How else explain the wild emotionalism of the congregations, unlettered preachers who brayed from their pulpits, the complete lack of discipline? The West was either a religious desert or a land where Satan had triumphed in the eternal battle between good and evil.[38]

The so-called ministers made this clear. They were described as misguided illiterates who found preaching easier than work, or as de-praved scoundrels capitalizing on the gullibility of their congregations; many were out-and-out horse thieves and murderers hiding beneath the cloak of religion, or degenerate sex fiends who used their churches to seduce innocent women. European novelists frequently cast ministers as villains or pictured them as degenerates parading in ministerial garb: a Yankee swindler, an unsavory scissors-grinder from Germany, a cutthroat who used his office to steal gold and horses from his trusting flock.[39] One typical character in a German novel displayed not a single trace of spiritu-ality; "his empty blue-gray eyes revealed nothing save extreme wicked-ness, appearing like the poisonous glare of a businessman who does not get rich enough from his milking cow."[40] Hardly the sort of man to serve as a guide on the road to salvation.

Or to conduct services on true spirituality. Most of the image-makers

[37] Moritz Busch, *Wanderungen zwischen Hudson und Mississippi 1851 und 1852* (Tübingen, 1854), pp. 287–88; Harriet Martineau, *Society in America* (New York, 1837), 1: 273; George W. Featherstonhaugh, *Excursion through the Slave States* (New York, 1844), p. 96.
[38] Unonius, *A Pioneer in Northwest America*, 1: 337–38; Calvin Colton, *Manual for Emigrants to America* (London, 1832), p. 136.
[39] Bjorne Landa, "The American Scene in Gerstäcker's Fiction" (Ph.D. diss., University of Minnesota, 1952), pp. 66–68, describes the use of such characters by German novelists.
[40] Ferdinand Kürnberger, *Der Amerika-Müde* (Frankfurt, 1850), p. 377.

agreed that westerners sincerely sought God's guidance and were generous in supporting churches, but that they were misled by their corrupt
and misinformed clergy. Some were seduced into eccentric sects; one
Hungarian writer described with obvious relish the "Adamites" who
bathed together in the nude, staged lecherous dances, offered young girls
to visitors, and drank quantities of "arrack."[41] Others were led down Satan's path by untrained clergymen in more traditional churches; uneducated and unorthodox, they corrupted traditional teachings, spoke in un-
learned jargon, grimaced and contorted their bodies in the pulpit, and
roared their messages as might have the priests of Baal. All were more notable for their "bellowing utterances" than for the wisdom of their teachings.[42]

With such guidance, the congregations surrendered completely to
practices that bore faint resemblance to proper worship. As the spirit
gripped them during worship they succumbed to animalistic emotionalism, swaying, groaning audibly, sighing deeply, weeping, and
showing every symptom of madness. This was conduct unbecoming true
believers. "What European German," asked a visitor from the Fatherland,
"who was suddenly taken from his well-ordered Sunday worship proceedings according to strict rules, and was thrown into the bedlam and confusion of a Methodist minister . . . would not like to grasp his cross and cry
out: 'I thank thee God, that I am not like these.' "[43]

The camp meetings that brought worship to the isolated frontiers were
even more vigorously condemned. Travelers and novelists alike were fascinated by these gatherings and devoted pages to vivid descriptions of
their wild emotionalism. They described with loving detail the prepara-
tion of the campgrounds, the gathering of thousands of worshipers from
miles around, and batteries of ministers who assembled to address them.
They dwelt with exquisite pleasure on the services themselves: the singing
of hymns, the shouted "amens," the preacher weaving in the log pulpit,
his voice rising higher and higher, the terrifying picture that he painted of
the hellfire that waited all unbelievers, the tortures that those before him
would surely suffer for none was worthy of eternal glory—"they were all
sinners, bad, miserable, despicable sinners before God—no one of them
worthy of God's righteousness, and when they died they would only have
one day of rest before they were cast deep, deep, into the bowels of hell
where all was wailing and gnashing of teeth forever and ever." Above all,
the image-makers savored the plight of the congregations as they were
swayed into emotional frenzies by these words, uttering anguished

41 Ferenc Belányi, *Vadonban: Regények az Észak Amerikai Államokból* (Pest, 1865), p. 21.
42 Flint, *Letters from America*, p. 169.
43 Busch, *Wanderungen zwischen Hudson und Mississippi*, p. 126.

screams, moaning, and crying out: "Be gracious, Looooord. Mercy, mercy, mercy! Salvation! Be good to us God, be good to us."[44]

Shocking as these practices were to Europeans, readers were even more disturbed by accounts of the physical excesses of the frontiersmen under sway of religious emotionalism. These were hard to believe: women jumping wildly into the air clapping their hands, and crying out "Oh Lord, glory, glory, glory, glory, happy, glory" until they fell exhausted; others fainting from the excitement and carried beyond the camp-meeting grounds to be laid like logs "heaving the most lamentable sighs"; still others screaming or jerking uncontrollably, some dancing through the crowds singing, or falling on their knees to run about like barking dogs.[45] This was neither religion nor Christianity. The camp meetings were indisputable proof that the frontiersmen had succumbed to barbarism and were beyond the pale of civilization. Some might read newspapers or stock their cabins with books but more had forsaken their birthrights. They had succumbed to Nature and Satan until they were no longer worthy of the company of civilized men.

Uncivilized Manners

The boorish mannerisms and antisocial conduct of the pioneers made them even less desirable neighbors—or so most of the image-makers agreed. There was little question on the basic point: the typical frontiersman was slovenly in his manners, unclean in his person, taciturn in his speech, rude in his relationship with others, and disgusting in his personal habits. Even the most sympathetic Europeans could do no better than explain, not condone, his peculiar ways. This they did by recognizing his social immaturity—"he has not had time to refine his manner of speaking and has not learned to move in a refined way"[46]—or by pointing out that he lacked proper examples of correct etiquette; lack of politeness was natural in a near-empty countryside where social pressures for conformity were lacking. These defects would be remedied as population thickened.

---

[44] Friedrich Gerstäcker, *Nach Amerika* (Leipzig, 1855), pp. 34–35; Moritz Beyer, *Das Auswanderungsbuch oder Rührer und Ratgeber bei der Auswanderung nach Nordamerika und Texas* (Leipzig, 1846), pp. 133–34.
[45] Clarence Evans and Liselotte Albrecht, eds., "Friedrich Gerstaecker in Arkansas: Selections from His *Streif-und Jagdzeuge durch die Vereinigten Staaten Nordamerikas*," *Arkansas Historical Quarterly* 5 (Spring 1946): 44; François-A. Michaux, *Travels to the Westward of the Allegheny Mountains, in the States of Ohio, Kentucky, and Tennessee in the Year 1802* (London, 1805), pp. 80–81. Among the best descriptions of camp meetings by European travelers are: Flint, *Letters from America*, pp. 231–36; Marryat, *Diary in America*, 2: 180–89; Michaux, *Travels to the Westward of the Allegheny Mountains*, pp. 242–43; Simon A. O'Ferrall, *A Ramble of Six Thousand Miles through the United States of America* (London, 1832), pp. 71–78; and Regan, *Emigrant's Guide to the Western States*, pp. 173–88.
[46] Gábor Fábián, "Travels by Steamer in the United States," *Athenaeum* 2 (1838): 345–46.

More perceptive—and democratically inclined—image-makers recognized that standards of behavior differed in Europe and America, and would continue to differ so long as current political and social differences remained. When a rough-mannered pioneer with dirty boots, unwashed hands, and filthy shirt slapped a stranger on the back and treated him as a friend he was simply proclaiming the equality that was a part of the frontier creed. No sense of humility restrained him from acting the equal of any man, no matter how different their stations in life. He was equally at home in his humble cabin or a palaced salon, as he must be to practice his democratic beliefs. "He enters with complete self-assurance," a traveler noted, "his hat on his head, hoisting his boots onto the armchair and spitting on the floor," for such was the right of every freeborn American.[47] Treat him as an equal and he would be your friend; lift nose in air in affected superiority and his boorishness would intensify in retaliation.

Explaining the pioneer's crude manners was one thing, living with them was quite another. Few Europeans could restrain their disgust when they watched a frontiersman clean his teeth and fingernails with his pocketknife, prop his wet boots so close to the fire that a choking cloud of mist filled the room, use his handkerchief "only after the major operation had been performed with the fingers," borrow a stranger's comb for his hair and brushes to clean his coat, or help himself to a companion's toothbrush and express delight when told that he could keep it.[48] Brazen violations of the rules of hygiene and etiquette such as these forced many a European to shun the West and to escape what one called "the vulgar effrontery of men who mistake lawless license for liberty."[49]

Particularly when that "lawless license" took the form of a relentless grilling by the insatiably curious westerners. This "impertinent inquisitiveness" was readily explained by the less hostile image-makers; they saw it as a natural malady of the remote settlements where loneliness converted all into persistent busybodies and where happenings and ideas were so few that every event was worth infinite discussion,[50] but these rationalizations did not make the inquisitorial techniques of the frontiersmen any easier to endure. "Call it impertinence, and curiosity, and such-like," explained Colonel Quackinboss to a fellow character in a British novel, "but it ain't anything of the kind. No sir. It simply means what sort of

47 Ernest Duvergier de Hauranne, *A Frenchman in Lincoln's America* (Chicago, 1974), 1: 253–54.
48 Gustaf Unonius, *Minnen från en sjuttonårig vistelse i Nordvestra Amerika* (Uppsala, 1862), 1: 339; Ole Munch Raeder, *America in the Forties: The Letters of Ole Munch Raeder* (Minneapolis, 1929), p. 149; William Hepworth Dixon, *New America* (London, 1867), 2: 292.
49 E. Howitt, *Selections from Letters Written during a Tour through the United States, in the Summer and Autumn of 1819* (Nottingham, 1820), p. 200. A similar opinion is in Aurél Kecskeméthy, *Éjszak-Amerika 1876-ban* (Budapest, 1877), p. 413.
50 William Chambers, *Things As They Are in America* (London, 1854), p. 147; Isaac Candler, *A Summary View of America* (London, 1824), pp. 482–83.

knowledge, what art or science or labour, can you contribute to the common stock? I want to know whether you and I . . . can't profit each other; whether either of us mayn't have something the other has never heard before."[51] That was all logical enough, but logic did not ease the lot of travelers subjected to what one of them called "pitiless questioners."[52]

The prying techniques of a gifted frontiersman were awesome to behold. Charles Dickens recorded the tactics of one: "I wore a fur coat at that time, and before we were clear of the wharf, he questioned me concerning it, and its price, and where I bought it, and when, and what the fur was, and what it weighed, and what it cost. Then he took notice of my watch, and asked what *that* cost, and whether it was a French watch, and where I got it, and how I got it, and whether I had bought it or had it given to me, and how it went, and where the keyhole was, and when I wound it, every night or every morning, and whether I ever forgot to wind it at all, and if I did, what then?"[53] And so and on. There was no end to the questioning, no satisfying this raging curiosity.

So traveler after traveler testified. They told of being accosted by strangers in the manner of highwaymen solely to be questioned about their personal affairs; of being plied with whiskey to loosen their tongues; of merciless grillings that went on for hours and hours.[54] Woe unto those who refused to answer; such ill-mannered conduct was seen as aristocratic snobbery and might lead to assault or mayhem—one visitor to a Colorado mining camp who sought a little privacy by pinning a shirt over his window had it ripped away with a rude "I want to see what there is that is so damned private in here."[55] Foreigners were even more rudely questioned than natives; wherever they appeared crowds gathered to finger their clothing, marvel at their speech, and ply them with inquiries about events in Europe.[56] Only rarely were the inquisitors outwitted; a one-legged traveler was so bothered with questions about how he lost his limb that he promised to tell *only* if he were asked no more questions. When all had sworn he confided: "It was bitten off."[57]

Almost as annoying to the image-makers as the persistent questioning was the incessant whittling that seemed a trademark of all frontiersmen.

[51]   Charles Lever, *One of Them*, in his *Novels of Charles Lever* (Boston, 1904), 31: 394–95.
[52]   Pierson, *Tocqueville and Beaumont*, pp. 246–47.
[53]   Charles Dickens, *American Notes* (London, 1842), 2: 55–56.
[54]   Isaac Weld, *Travels through the United States of North America, and the Provinces of Upper and Lower Canada, during the Years 1795, 1796 and 1797* (London, 1807), 1: 124, 234–35; Michaux, *Travels to the Westward of the Allegheny Mountains*, pp. 240–41; Featherstonhaugh, *Excursion through the Slave States*, p. 91; Flint, *Letters from America*, p. 143; Richard G. A. Levinge, *Echoes from the Backwoods; or, Sketches of Transatlantic Life* (London, 1846), 2: 25; Hodgson, *Letters from North America*, 2: 32–35; and many others.
[55]   *American Settler*, 19 June 1886.
[56]   Unonius, *Pioneer in Northwest America*, 1: 116.
[57]   Charles Lyell, *A Second Visit to the United States of America* (New York, 1849), 2: 167–68.

"Dogs Defending a Child from Wolves." From Mayne Reid,
The Desert Home (London, 1852). (From the Special Collections
of the University of California at Los Angeles Library.)

Let one seat himself for a moment and his first move was to pull a knife from his pocket and begin whittling—on the arm of his chair, on a nearby table, on the woodwork, on the porch railing, on a chunk of wood carried specifically for the purpose. "The urge to whittle," a Norwegian observed, "seems irresistible."[58] Nothing was safe: church pews were notched and slashed, school desks initialed and engraved, jury boxes and even the judge's bench bore the mark of incessant attack. No trial could proceed unless judge, jury, attorneys, and plaintiff were provided with raw material for their knives; no business transaction could be conducted without both contenders busily plying their weapons. A knife suddenly closed was the signal that an agreement had been reached.[59] Whittling might serve as a palliative to overly energetic frontiersmen, but travelers found it excessively annoying.

Yet less so than the eating habits of the pioneers. The food was repulsive enough—enormous quantities served with a complete lack of delicacy and washed down with great gulps of ice water—but the table manners of the frontiersmen were even less appealing. Speed was the sole guide to behavior at the dining table; every call to dinner at a frontier inn or on a steamboat touched off a mob scene as the customers hurtled themselves toward the door, shoving and elbowing and trampling in a mad scramble to reach the laden table. One of Charles Dickens's characters almost lost his life when an umbrella he had forgotten to unfurl temporarily blocked the doorway, spreading panic among those struggling to enter the dining room as they saw the food disappearing, and threatening the digestion of those already there as they choked down giant mouthfuls in an effort to consume more than their share before the barrier was broken.[60]

Once at table, frontiersmen heaped their plates sky-high, plunging their forks into the serving dishes, and piling meat, vegetables, potatoes, salads, fruit—everything indiscriminately together. And in gargantuan quantities. One visitor, watching a pioneer cut slice after slice of steaming turkey and delighted to find at least one man willing to carve for the whole table, was astounded to see the whole mass shoved onto the carver's plate, covered with an entire jar of cranberries, and demolished in a few moments.[61] Politeness was outlawed; those who waited for others to be

---

[58] Unonius, *Minnen från en sjuttonårig vistelse,* 1: 339. A similar statement is in Henryk Sienkiewicz, *Portrait of America: Letters of Henryk Sienkiewicz* (New York, 1959), p. 19.
[59] Unonius, *A Pioneer in Northwest America,* 1: 256; Houstoun, *Hesperos,* 2: 171–72, 187.
[60] Dickens, *Life and Adventures of Martin Chuzzlewit,* p. 154. Similar scenes are described in John (János) Xantus, *Letters from North America* (Detroit, 1975), p. 78; and Francis and Therese Pulszky, *White, Red and Black: Sketches of Society in the United States* (London, 1853), 2: 232.
[61] Frederick Marryat, *Narrative of the Travels and Adventures of Monsieur Violet, in California, Sonora, and Western Texas* (London, 1843), 3: 12.

served before helping themselves were likely to starve to death, for even in private homes the food was transferred to the plates in the twinkling of an eye. "Politeness at meals may be and is practiced in Europe, and among the Indians," a visitor recorded sadly, "but among the Americans it would be attended by starvation."[62]

Frontier manners might be judged deplorable, but the image-makers saved their principal invective for the three basic sins of all pioneers; swearing, drinking, and tobacco chewing. Profanity was so universal that the typical frontiersman was unable to speak without packing every sentence with a variety of expletives so meaningful and diabolic that the Goddess of Depravity herself could have taken lessons.[63] So traveler after traveler reported, sometimes with a trace of awed envy at the wonderous originality of the word combinations and the skill with which they were packed three or four to the sentence when one would have sufficed for ordinary mortals. Moralistic visitors and novelists clucked their disapproval, of course, and bemoaned the fact that men could stoop so low that they swore from habit rather than necessity, but they could not conceal a touch of envy now and then. "They had," one novelist reported, "evidently ceased to be aware that they were using oaths—so terribly had familiarity with sinful practices blunted the consciences of men, who in early life, would probably have trembled in this way to break the law of God."[64] Alas, the moral standards of that day forbade authors to use examples of the "shocking profanity," a loss to culture that can never be overestimated.

The image-makers were under no such restraint when they launched their barbs against the pioneers' excessive drinking. Some were generous enough to advance some explanations for what they saw as universal drunkenness: liquor at thirty or forty cents a gallon was too cheap to be resisted; it was less harmful than the water in many communities; it stilled the qualms of loneliness and restored bodies ravaged by excess labor; it was the only possible stimulant in a land where wine and beer were almost unknown.[65] Such explanations, however, did not excuse the remarkable thirst of the frontiersmen. A land where drunkenness was "almost the nor-

[62]   Ibid., 3: 13.
[63]   Eugene L. Schwaab, ed., *Travels in the Old South: Selected from Periodicals of the Times* (Lexington, K., 1973), 1: 151; Hooton, *St. Louis Isle*, p. 23.
[64]   Robert M. Ballantyne, *The Golden Dream; or, Adventures in the Far West* (London, 1861), p. 85. Other authors who paid particular attention to western profanity included: William H. Barneby, *Life and Labour in the Far, Far West: Being Notes on a Tour of the Western States, British Columbia, Manitoba, and the North-West Territory* (London, 1884), p. 174; Hodgson, *Letters From North America*, 2: 250; Melish, *Travels through the United States of America*, p. 208; and Candler, *A Summary View of America*, p. 453.
[65]   Francis Wyse, *America: Realities and Resources* (London, 1846), 2: 159; Michaux, *Travels to the Westward of the Allegheny Mountains*, p. 49; Melish, *Travels through the United States of America*, pp. 312–13.

mal condition," and where "liquoring up" began before breakfast, was continued through the day, and began again with renewed vigor at sunset, had clearly abandoned its place among the civilized nations of the world.[66]

So Europeans argued as they pictured the frontier as a carnival of overindulgence. Visitors to the eastern frontiers during the early years of the nineteenth century described inns where the rooms, staircases, and courtyards were strewn with men too drunk to stand or speak; travelers in the Far West at the century's end pictured saloon brawls and drunken shootings on the streets of cattle towns as they bemoaned the tendency of all frontiersmen to drink themselves into near-oblivion.[67] Authors fastened with delight on such terms as "eye-opener," "corpse-reviver," and "widow's smile"; they took malicious pleasure in describing the gargantuan consumption at pioneer dances—on one such occasion fiddler after fiddler had to be carried out after consuming a full bottle of whiskey, with the party only ending as the last succumbed.[68] Repeating frontier tall tales was one of their stocks in trade; one told of a wake where the mourners took up a collection of forty-one dollars, sent a member to buy food and liquor, and when he returned with forty dollars' worth of whiskey and one of bread, angrily asked, "what in thunder made you want to waste all that money on bread."[69]

Despite such an occasional dip into caricature, the image-makers found little amusing in the drunkenness that they described as universal along the frontiers. They were particularly concerned that every possible occasion—from a casual meeting to a wedding or ministerial ordination—was seized upon as an excuse for overindulgence. "If you meet," one noted, "you drink; if you part, you drink; if you close a bargain, you drink."[70] To refuse a drink offered by a friend or a stranger was the supreme insult in the West, and might lead to insult or injury; a common greeting was "stranger, will you drink or fight?"[71] Even Old Shatterhand, brave as he was and a virtual teetotaler, never dared turn down such an invitation. "That would be a great insult," he explained to a greenhorn, "for, as you know, he who refuses to drink in this land can be answered with a knife or pistol."[72] British schoolboys were warned never to enter a west-

---

[66] Alexandre André, *A Frenchman at the Trinity River Mines in 1849* (New York, 1957), p. 7; Bell, *New Tracks in North America*, 2: 90.
[67] Michaux, *Travels to the Westward of the Allegheny Mountains*, pp. 36–40; Paul Bourget, *Outre-Mer: Impressions of America* (New York, 1895), pp. 251–52.
[68] Bourget, *Outre-Mar*, p. 252; Evans and Albrecht, eds., "Friedrich Gerstäcker in Arkansas," p. 52.
[69] Walter Besant and James Rice, *The Golden Butterfly* (New York, n.d.), p. 211.
[70] Quoted in Max Berger, *The British Traveller in America, 1836–1860* (New York, 1943), p. 64.
[71] Ibid., p. 65. A similar comment is in Ference Pulszky, *Eletem és Korom* (Budapest, 1880), p. 115.
[72] Karl May, *Winnetou III* (reprint ed., Vienna, 1951), p. 146.

ern bar lest a villain invite them to drink solely to pick a fight when they refused.[73] Excessive drinking was the way of life along the frontiers where Nature's freedom transcended the restraints imposed by civilization.

Deplorable as was this state of affairs, it remained for the tobacco chewers to stir the image-makers to the ultimate in disgust. All agreed that day and night, year in and year out, every frontiersman's jaws were in constant motion—"chew, chew, and chew; spit, spit, and spit, all the blessed day and most of the night," all moving their jaws rhythmically "as though they were some species of ruminating animal," all unrelentingly, mercilessly, spitting and spitting and spitting—that was the image of the typical frontiersman accepted by Europeans.[74] Charles Dickens believed that they must expectorate in their dreams.[75] Farmers chewed as they went about their chores, tradesmen as they served their customers, legislators as they made the laws, judges and juries as they administered justice, governors as they sat in their executive offices. Even the army was addicted; soldiers were seen offering their officers a hank of tobacco during inspections.[76] "Ef you get hungry, take a chew," one old timer told Jack Harkaway, "ef you get thirsty, take a chew; and ef yer feel as ef there was nothing left to live for, take a chew, and you'll consider the matter."[77]

Many had perfected such dexterity with tobacco juice that they stirred the reluctant admiration of their harshest critics who could only gape in wonder as they watched the brown stream arch in a perfect parabola into a distant cuspidor. "I can," said a frontiersman to Martin Chuzzlewit, "calc'late my distance, Sir, to an inch. I require, Sir, two foot clear in a circ'lar di-rection, and can engage my-self to keep within it. I *have* gone ten foot, in a circ'lar di-rection, but that was for a wager."[78] Skilled as the spitters were, those about them were in a constant state of apprehension as the brown stream narrowly missed their persons time and time again. "True," one observer noted, "they are good shots, and one can make sure to three square inches of the spot they aim at; still, when you are surrounded by shooters . . . you feel nervous."[79] Just as when you noted a sign in your hotel room saying, "Don't spit on the blankets," you began to wonder about the cleanliness of the establishment.[80]

The inevitable result of universal tobacco chewing was a blanket of

[73] G. A. Henty, *Captain Bayley's Heir: A Tale of the Gold Fields of California* (London, 1889), p. 286.
[74] Francis C. Sheridan, *Galveston Island; or, A Few Months off the Coast of Texas* (Austin, 1954), p. 37; Sienkiewicz, *Portrait of America*, p. 20; Raeder, *America in the Forties*, p. 122.
[75] Dickens, *American Notes*, 2: 52.
[76] Charles Sealsfield, *Der Legitime und die Republikaner: Eine Geschichte aus dem lezten amerikanisch-englischen Kriege* (Zurich, 1833), 2: 254.
[77] Bracebridge Hemyng, *Jack Harkaway Out West amongst the Indians* (London, n.d.), p. 31.
[78] Dickens, *Life and Adventures of Martin Chuzzlewit*, p. 389.
[79] Edward Money, *The Truth about America* (London, 1886), p. 129.
[80] James S. Buckingham, *The Eastern and Western States of America* (London, 1842), 2: 277.

dried, brown juice that inundated all the West. Floors and carpets of homes and inns, boarding houses, stagecoaches, river steamboats, theaters, courtrooms, legislative chambers, even churches, were so filthy that one's boots were soiled with every step.[81] Even the physical appearance of the westerners showed their addiction to chewing. Frontiersmen, travelers noted, had thin, tight lips because they were constantly pursed to spit and twangy voices because their mouths were always so filled with juice that they were forced to talk through their noses.[82] Shrewd merchants always watched the mouths of rivals while bargaining, knowing the intensity of the rhythm would reveal their emotions.[83]

Europeans who read of western table manners, inquisitiveness, drunkenness, swearing, and tobacco chewing in books by travelers and novelists (guidebook authors were understandably reluctant to discuss such matters) gained the impression of a primitive society where crudity and bad manners were accepted behavior, and where properly bred men and women would be repelled rather than attracted. Immigrants who ventured along the frontiers could expect not only danger to their lives and property, but to associate with ill-mannered individuals whose scale of civilization was different from their own. They could also expect to mingle with a people whose values and ambitions so differed from their own that they seemed a different race, and a far less pleasant one.

[81] Patrick Shirreff, *A Tour through North America: Together with a Comprehensive View of the Canadas and United States* (Edinburgh, 1835), p. 269; Martineau, *Society in America*, 2: 200; Barton, ed., *Letters from the Promised Land*, pp. 63–64.
[82] Trollope, *Domestic Manners of the Americans*, p. 234.
[83] William G. Bek, tr., "Nicholas Hesse, German Visitor to Missouri, 1835–1837," *Missouri Historical Review* 42 (April 1947): 191.

IX

Europeans View
the Western Character

THE IMAGE-MAKERS MIGHT ARGUE over the state of culture along the frontiers, but they agreed on one thing: that the westerners were a race apart, as different from easterners as they were from Londoners or Parisians. They agreed, too, that the characteristics that set them apart were exactly those that distinguished Americans from Europeans, appearing now in exaggerated form. What those image-makers were noting was the emergence of a unique "American character," which was clearly evident everywhere in the United States but most of all in the emerging Wests. They were telling their readers that "the West was the most distinctly American part of America" (in Lord Bryce's phrase) precisely because the traits responsible for the uniqueness of that character were a product of the frontier environment, and most strongly apparent along the borderlands.

In defending their position, the image-makers made clear that East and West were worlds apart, separated by a discernible boundary that shifted constantly westward with each new advance of the frontier. That line divided two different peoples; the population of the western territories, one wrote, "is as unlike that of the eastern states as if they were of different nations."[1] There the ties with the past were most completely broken; there men and women were least respectful of tradition and most

[1]   William Oliver, *Eight Months in Illinois* (Newcastle-upon-Tyne, 1843), p. 68.

inclined to adjust their behavior and thought to the demands of the time and place. There, as a German novelist put it, they "began to reason quite differently concerning things of the past and future."[2] The image-makers who noted these changes were watching the emergence of "that new man, the American," and a fascinating personage they found him to be.

What were the marks of that "new American character" they observed? What traits distinguished westerners from easterners and easterners from Europeans? European visitors, whether travelers or novelists or guidebook authors, wasted a great deal of thought and ink trying to answer these questions. Most contented themselves with isolating and describing certain traits that they identified as peculiarly American and that appeared in most observable form along the frontiers. These were many, ranging from open-handed hospitality and money-mad materialism to a restless inclination to be always on the move, peculiar inventive skills, starry-eyed optimism, a senseless dedication to hard work, and the irritating habit of "puffing" the glories of their nation. Few writers attempted to merge these characteristics into a composite portrait of the pioneer character, but together they present a fair image of the frontiersman as he appeared to Europeans.

Frontier Materialism

Every visitor to the frontiers, and every storyteller who exploited the western scene, agreed that the Almighty Dollar was "the only divinity that in reality" was worshiped by the pioneers, the "end and aim of their lives, their daily and nightly thought,"[3] the ultimate goal of their ambitions. One novelist believed that the national bird should have been a vulture rather than an eagle; another that westerners' hearts rattled rather than beat.[4] Even the language of the frontiersmen mirrored their determined quest for gain. One of every three words they uttered was "I calculate,"[5] while they reserved their most flattering term, "elegant," for money-making projects such as "an elegant improvement," or "an elegant mill."[6] "Dollars," wrote a British traveler, "were in everyone's mouth, whether they were in their pockets or not."[7]

[2]   Charles Sealsfield, quoted in Bernard A. Uhlendorf, *Charles Sealsfield: Ethnic Elements and National Problems in His Works* (Chicago, 1922), p. 127.
[3]   James Bryce, *The American Commonwealth* (New York, 1888), 2: 895; Gustaf Unonius, *A Pioneer in Northwest America 1841–1858: The Memoirs of Gustaf Unonius* (Minneapolis, 1950–51), 1: 335–36.
[4]   Mayne Reid, *The Child Wife* (London, 1868), 2: 41; Charles Sealsfield, *Der Legitime und die Republikaner; Eine Geschichte aus dem amerikanisch-englischen Kriege* (Zurich, 1833), 3: 163.
[5]   Paul Duplessis, *La Sonora* (Paris, 1858), 2: 192–93.
[6]   Morris Birkbeck, *Notes on a Journey in America* (London, 1818), p. 133.
[7]   R. G. A. Levinge, *Echoes from the Backwoods; or, Sketches of Transatlantic Life* (London, 1846), p. 2.

When a newcomer appeared in any frontier community he was questioned not about the state of the arts or sciences in the world without, but about the prices of commodites in the communities he had visited: "How much is meat selling for in Helena?" or "What is the price of fur in Virginia City?"[8] Let him reply with a high figure and like as not a dozen suppliers in his audience would be on their way to take advantage of the news. A traveler who questioned another coach passenger why he sat silent during a spirited discussion of the price of corn and wheat was answered with: "But you have not spoken of hides yet." That opened the gates for a flood of words on the profits he had made trading in leather.[9] "If anything is characteristic of the New World," a German novelist believed, "it is the tendency of the Americans to fix a value on everything in heaven and on earth."[10]

So deeply etched on the European mind was the image of the frontiersman as a money-mad materialist that novelists based entire plots on the theme. In one an impracticable German farmer who read Latin verse instead of cultivating his fields in the homeland lost his farm, migrated to frontier America, and returned a few years later such a hardheaded success that he won his farm back again;[11] in another an idealistic political refugee whose dream of freedom lured him to the West was converted into a materialist with enough brazen self-confidence that he convinced the maiden of his heart to marry him.[12] The message was clear: a few years among the dollar-hungry pioneers would convert a civilized dreamer into a ruthless money grabber. "He will," a Norwegian novelist warned, "immediately develop an irresistible zeal to earn money, his eyes take on a more lively, audacious, searching look, on the street he begins to move at a fast pace, he becomes unconsciously prone to unrestrained boasting and bombastic exaggeration."[13] Those seeking to nurture their cultural sensitivities should avoid the frontier.

They would pay the price if they did not, for dollar chasing was so all-important to the pioneers that they sacrificed comfort and pleasure to the pursuit. Frontiersmen were willing to live in miserable hovels, eat repulsive food, and dress like derelicts in order to save a few pennies to invest in

[8] Sygurd Wiśniowski, *Ameryka 100 Years Ago: A Globetrotter's View* (Cheshire, Conn. 1972), p. 57.
[9] Zsigmond Vékey, *Utazásaim a föld körül* (Pest, 1885), p. 227.
[10] Karl Gutzkow quoted in Paul C. Weber, *America in Imaginative German Literature in the First Half of the Nineteenth Century* (New York, 1926), p. 250.
[11] Wilhelm Raabe, *Alte Nester* (1880), summarized in D. L. Ashliman, "The American West in Nineteenth Century German Literature" (Ph.D. diss., Rutgers University, 1969), p. 175.
[12] Gustav Freytag, *Die Valentine* (1848), in Ashliman, "The American West in Nineteenth Century German Literature," p. 177.
[13] Anders Ahlin, *En Gröngölings Romans*, quoted in Dorothy B. Skårdal, *The Divided Heart: Scandinavian Immigrant Experiences through Literary Sources* (Bloomington, 1974) p. 139.

property and production. Nor did the amassing of wealth change their attitudes. The more the accumulated fortune, the greater was the urge to sell more goods, make greater profits, and set aside less and less for personal comforts. Men and women in comfortable circumstances lived on salt meat, stale bread, and decayed vegetables rather than spend surpluses that might be invested.[14] Even families were sacrificed on the altar of gain. Reported an English lady from the Far West: "Hard greed, and the exclusive pursuit of wealth . . . are eating up family love and life throughout the West."[15] Such an atmosphere doomed all artistic or literary enterprises. Why waste time on pleasing the eye or ear or palate when money was to be made? "We cannot avoid thinking," quoth a frontiersman in a German novel, "that a man might employ his time and powers to much better advantage."[16] A Norwegian short story captured the spirit of western materialism when it described a highly cultured man and woman who were forced to bake in the sun outside a frontier inn while a crowd of bearded ruffians caroused on the shaded porch and a small group of heavily armed aristocrats sat in the cool but stuffy parlor, smoking cigars and discussing the price of land. The story's symbolism was obvious. Culture waited in discomfort without, while coarseness and brute strength enjoyed the shade of the veranda, and wealth was palisaded within, fully armed to protect itself.[17] In the scale of frontier values, wealth ranked first, strength second, and culture only third.

That same spirit was reflected in a conversation between a traveler and a pioneer farmer:

"This is really a beautiful country of yours."

"Oh yes, sir; the crops are wonderfully beautiful; but you should have seen them last year. I reckon there's not a more beautiful valley in America, at least for wheat; and it's considerable of a corn country."

"Yes, it seems to possess a rich soil, but I was not alluding to its fertility—I meant that it was a fine country to look at; that it has some very fine prospects."

"Oh yes, sir; I would not wish for better prospects, if this weather does but hold till harvest; last year our prospects were not half as good, but we got an abundance."[18]

[14] Isaac Weld, *Travels through the United States of North America, and the Provinces Of Upper and Lower Canada, during the Years 1795, 1796, and 1797* (London, 1807), 1: 292. Similar descriptions are in George W. Featherstonhaugh, *A Canoe Voyage up the Minnay Sotor* (London, 1847), 2: 119–20; Balduin Möllhausen, *Riesen in die Felsengebirge Nord-Amerikas bis zum Hoch-Plateau von Neu Mexico* (Leipzig, 1861), 2: 304–5; Frances Trollope, *Domestic Manners of the Americans* (London, 1832), 1: 43; and John (János) Xantus, *Letters from North America* (Detroit, 1975), p. 179.
[15] Isabella L. Bird, *A Lady's Life in the Rocky Mountains* (London, 1879), p. 53.
[16] Quoted in Weber, *America in Imaginative German Literature*, p. 150.
[17] Harald Meltzer, *Skizzer: Til oq fra Amerika* (Oslo, 1860), pp. 82–83.
[18] Adam Hodgson, *Letters from North America, Written during a Tour in the United States and Canada* (London, 1824), 1: 304–5.

"Mother, Thou Are Avenged." From Mayne Reid, *The Death Shot* (Beadle's Dime Novel Library, New York, n.d.), p. 57. (From the Special Collections of the University of California at Los Angeles Library.)

When frontiersmen hoped for boy babies rather than girl babies because "a younker will be fit to turn a dollar one way or another by the time ten years is gone,"[19] he had succumbed to dollar grabbing to an almost fatal degree.

Why? Lord Bryce touched on the answer to that question when he noted that "all the passionate eagerness, all the strenuous efforts of the Westerner are directed toward the material development of the land."[20] Well they might be, for "development of the land" was the road to wealth and a better life. Unused land was a symbol of savagery, and must be converted at once into cultivated fields. Nothing of God's creation was sacred to the pioneer. "He loves the rustling forest," a character in German fiction observed, "—when he can use its limbs for boards and posts—he revels in murmuring brooks—when they flow fast enough to turn a mill, otherwise not."[21] Not beauty but utility was the frontiersmen's standard of excellence. Travelers asking directions were sent through villages and farmlands rather than virgin forests where "there was nothing to be seen but woods and mountains";[22] upstate New Yorkers early in the century, weary of pointing out the road to Niagara Falls, grumbled that "none but Englishmen were such fools as to go so far to see a heap of water tumbling down a rock."[23] Not an eyebrow was raised when a promoter proposed using Niagara's power by building a mill on Goat Island, even though one of Nature's grandest spectacles would be ruined; better that than to "let such a privilege of water lie idle."[24]

There was common sense in such proposals, given the pioneers' prejudices, for land brought into production guaranteed not only an abundant life but a haven against want in later years and security for one's children and for their children, for generations to come. Hence, every frontiersman's ambition was to secure as many acres as possible, knowing that their value would skyrocket with the thickening of population. This meant slovenly cultivation, for each had more acreage than he could care for properly. "Instead of five acres well managed," wrote a visitor, "they must have twenty acres badly managed."[25] No matter. Those twenty

[19] Frances Trollope, *The Life and Adventure of Jonathan Jefferson Whitlaw; or, Scenes on the Mississippi* (London, 1836), 1: 26.
[20] Bryce, *American Commonwealth*, 2: 895.
[21] Friedrich Gerstäcker, *Gold! Ein californisches Lebensbild aus dem Jahr 1849* (Leipzig, 1858), 1: 262.
[22] Hodgson, *Letters from North America*, 1: 398.
[23] E. Howitt, *Selections from Letters Written during a Tour through the United States, in the Summer and Autumn of 1819* (Nottingham, 1820), p. 116.
[24] Frederick Marryat, *A Diary in America* (London, 1839), 1: 209; Trollope, *Domestic Manners of the Americans*, p. 373.
[25] William Faux, *Memorable Days in America: Being a Journal of a Tour to the United States* (London, 1823), p. 177.

acres represented more wealth, and promised greater future security, than five acres. That was what counted.

They also assured a higher rung on the social ladder, for wealth in land was the measure of each man's status in society. The richer the individual as measured in productive acres, the higher his rank in the community's elite. This was to be expected in a land where there was no other basis for judgment. "Having no aristocracy, no honours, no distinctions to look forward to," wrote a British observer, "wealth has become the substitute, and, with very few exceptions, every man is great in proportion to his riches."[26] Given this incentive, the desire to accumulate wealth—and talk about wealth—was understandable. Tocqueville believed that the urge was greater than in any other country; a traveler added that "the poor struggle to be rich, the rich even richer."[27]

This, then, was the basis of frontier materialism. When the pioneer dedicated himself to the pursuit of the Almighty Dollar, even at the sacrifice of comfort and pleasure, he was seeking both security and status. And, most important, the plentiful lands of the West brought these goals within his reach as in no other portion of the world. The incentive was there, and the end achievable. So the image-makers reasoned, and they were not far from right.

Frontier Wastefulness

Moreover, this process must be hurried, no matter what the result. Land was useless—and unprofitable—until brought into production. Every natural obstacle was an enemy to be destroyed, no matter how ruthless the means. "Forests were there to be felled," wrote a European sadly, "or if that process is too slow and laborious, to be set ablaze; mountains are made to be honeycombed by his drills and sluices; rocks and hills exist only to be blasted or to be spirited away by the powerful jet nozzle of his hydraulic tube."[28] All must go: trees, streams, prairies, hills that hid precious metals, birds, and animals. To Europeans, long accustomed to parceling and hoarding Nature's dwindling resources, the wanton destruction of natural wealth along the frontiers was shocking. "He lives only to destroy," one wrote of the frontiersman early in the century; a hundred years later another deplored the "wanton savagery, the unthink-

[26] Marryat, A Diary in America, 1: 22–23. This view was also expressed in James Flint, Letters from America (Edinburgh, 1822), p. 170; Edward S. Abdy, Journal of a Residence and Tour in the United States of North America from April 1833, to October 1834 (London, 1835), 1: 70–71; Birkbeck, Notes on a Journey in America, p. 69; and Trollope, Domestic Manners of the Americans, 2: 136–37.

[27] Alexis de Tocqueville, Democracy in America (Cambridge, 1863), 1: 53.

[28] William A. Baillie-Grohman, Camps in the Rockies (New York, 1882), p. 21.

able ruthlessness of the way they destroyed what can never be re-placed."[29]

Along the forested frontiers the tree was the pioneer's principal enemy. "He seems," declared a French visitor, "to have declared war on the whole species."[30] Timeless forest giants were attacked with maniacal hatred; they were felled, burned, rooted up, slashed down, lopped off, and chopped up, all with "unrelenting fury." Those that were not at-tacked personally were set ablaze, leaving the countryside ugly with blackened skeletons.[31] All were fair game: trees needed for shade, wind-breaks, shelter, firewood, lumber, even maple sugar. Clearing "in the American style" meant a bare landscape, stripped of vegetation. The fron-tiersman's ideal was a flat plain, denuded of all growth save a profitable crop. "When a patch of ground is completely naked," a traveler reported, "he tells you that it looks handsome."[32]

Soils were ravaged as recklessly as forests. Fields were planted year after year to the same crop until their mineral salts were depleted with no thought of manuring; animal dung was thrown into streams or allowed to accumulate unused. Planting was determined by the workability and profit of the crop, not its usefulness in preserving or restoring the soil's fer-tility. This made sense to the pioneer farmer. In the Old World where land was scarce and labor abundant conservation was necessary; in the New World where land was plentiful and labor expensive the soil's riches could be squandered. "In the one country," explained one image-maker, "the farmer aims to assist, and in the other to rob nature."[33] In frontier America higher profits were assured by planting the most profitable crop until the soil was exhausted, then moving on, clearing fresh land, and starting over again. The war on Nature would continue so long as virgin fields lay to the westward.

The habits bred into the pioneers as they ravaged the frontier's patrimony encouraged wastefulness in all things. Why skimp when one lived amidst abundance? Europeans were shocked to see a fortune in food thrown away after every meal at a frontier inn, half-finished cigars tossed

[29] Talleyrand, quoted in Henry T. Tuckerman, *America and Her Commentators* (New York, 1864), pp. 114–15; Charles Boissevain (1882), quoted in J. W. Schulte-Nordholt, "This Is the Place: Dutchmen Look at America," *Delta: A Review of Arts, Life and Thought in the Netherlands* 16 (Winter 1973–74): 39.
[30] Edouard de Montulé, *Travels in America, 1816–1817* (Bloomington, 1950), p. 170.
[31] Basil Hall, *Travels in North America, in the Years 1827 and 1828* (Edinburgh, 1829), p. 46.
[32] Frances Wright, *Views of Society and Manners in America* (London, 1821), p. 197. Similar opinions are in Thomas Ashe, *Travels in America, Performed in 1806, for the Purpose of Exploring the Rivers Allegheny, Monongahela, Ohio, and Mississippi* (London, 1808), 2: 238–39; Charles Lyell, *Travels in North America* (London, 1845), 1: 20–21; James S. Buckingham, *The Eastern and Western States of America* (London, 1842), 2: 294; and Camille Ferri-Pisani, *Lettres aux les Etats-Unis d'Amérique* (Paris, 1862), p. 208.
[33] Patrick Shirreff, *A Tour through North America* (Edinburgh, 1835), p. 341.

aside, apples and peaches left rotting in orchards, enough wheat and corn unharvested to feed a whole parish, fields so carelessly cultivated that they yielded only a fraction of their potential.[34] Americans suffered no such qualms. They knew that so long as cheap lands lay westward, theirs would be a land of plenty. Such was the image transmitted across the Atlantic by travelers and guidebook writers.

The Restless Temper

Waste and mobility went hand in hand, for exhausted soils compelled a constant shift westward to virgin fields. What began as a necessity among the pioneers soon became a habit—and a passion. The true frontiersman was incessantly, determinably, perpetually on the move, sure that richer lands, greener pastures, more precious metals, lay beyond the horizon. "Like the sons of Ishmael," a traveler wrote, ". . . they are in a constant state of migration, tarrying awhile here and there, clearing land for others to enjoy—building houses for other to inhabit, and in a manner, may be considered the wandering Arabs of America."[35] Image-makers vied in coining phrases worthy of this extraordinary compulsion: a "migratory people," they called them, living in a constant "state of transition," so driven by a "restless temper" that "after they have passed through every part of the land of promise, they will, for the sake of one more change, re-turn to the seaboard again."[36] "If Hell lay to the West," another added, "they would cross Heaven to reach it."[37]

The wandering instinct was most noticed among the backwoodsmen and the squatters on the outer edge of the frontier. Among them periodic moving seemed almost a psychological necessity; let a neighbor settle within a few miles, let the sound of an axe disturb the morning stillness, and they were ready to sell their "improvements," and push more deeply into the wilderness. During the first half of the century they formed numerous processions as they trudged over the wilderness trails, their scant belongings in ramshackle wagons or on their backs, driving a cow or a few pigs before them, and always with the gleam of hope in their eyes.[38]

[34] John Knight, *Important Extracts from Original and Recent Letters Written by Englishmen in the United States of America to Their Friends in England* (Manchester, 1818), 2: 36.
[35] Francis Wyse, *America: Realities and Resources* (London, 1846), 2: 355–56.
[36] Estwick Evans, *A Pedestrious Tour, of Four Thousand Miles, through the Western States and Territories* (Concord, 1819), 39. Similar comments by Hungarian travelers are in Anna Katona, "Hungarian Travelogues on the Pre–Civil War U.S.," *Hungarian Studies in English* 5 (1971): 70.
[37] Baillie-Grohman, *Camps in the Rockies*, p. 330. Other expressions of the same sort are quoted in J. E. Alexander, *Transatlantic Sketches, Comprising Visits to the Most Interesting Scenes in North and South America and the West Indies* (London, 1833), 2: 114–15, and Tyrone Power, *Impressions of America during the Years 1833, 1834, and 1835* (London, 1836), 1: 332–33.
[38] Friedrich Gerstäcker, *The Wanderings and Fortunes of Some German Emigrants* (New York, 1848), pp. 193–94; Oliver, *Eight Months in Illinois*, p. 189.

"We could scarcely look before or behind without seeing some of them," a visitor reported. "The Canterbury pilgrims were not so diversified nor as interesting as these."[39]

Such was their compulsion that many left half-settled communities or bypassed good land in the hope of still better prospects ahead. Travelers reported seeing abandoned farms among still-uncleared fields; they told also of being offered excellent farms by starry-eyed owners who had heard that in the next state the soil was "four feet deep, and so fat that it greased your fingers."[40] There was no holding back these perennial movers, those with a passion for turning new soils and destined forever to serve in the van of the great westward-moving army of frontiersmen. They were, as a French observer noted, a new breed of men "who cannot settle upon the soil that they have cleared," but were forced by instinct to "push forward, inclined perpetually towards the distant points of the American population."[41]

A breed, moreover, unique to the American Wests and as different from their European ancestors as day from night. They fascinated the image-makers, who never tired of describing their urge for loneliness and their eagerness to escape the society of their fellows. Europeans accustomed to crowded villages were enthralled by the ever-repeated tales of the travelers: of the backwoodsman who complained, "I can't stand it no longer; one can't go out into the woods but he hears the sound of the axe and the crash of trees";[42] of the armies of pioneers urged onward by a "universal disposition" to be on the way; of men and women who felt themselves "charged with a special providential mission" to serve in the vanguard in the conquest of Nature.[43] To those of such a bent "every day was moving day."[44] "Heaven itself," one wrote of them, "would lose its attraction if they only knew of some place farther west."[45]

Backwoodsmen of this ilk tarried so briefly in any one place that they contributed little to the battle against Nature. Each halting place was, as Tocqueville noted, only "a temporary submission to necessity." A half-cleared field large enough to be classed as an "improvement," a crazy-quilt lean-to or a log cabin designed to keep out so little of the weather that it could be abandoned without regret, a tumbled-down log fence—these

[39] Flint, *Letters from America*, pp. 48–49.

[40] Charles F. Hoffman, *A Winter in the West*, (New York, 1835), 1: 183–84.

[41] François-A. Michaux, *Travels to the Westward of the Allegheny Mountains, in the States of Ohio, Kentucky, and Tennessee, in the Year 1802* (London, 1805), p. 192.

[42] Oliver, *Eight Months in Illinois*, p. 190.

[43] Francis J. Grund, *The Americans, in Their Moral, Social, and Political Relations* (Boston, 1837), p. 206.

[44] Knut Hamsun, *Fra det Moderne Amerikas Aandsliv* (Copenhagen, 1889), p. 2.

[45] Unonius, *A Pioneer in Northwest America*, 1: 225.

were the only scars left on the countryside.[46] Why labor on a farm or home when leaving was only a matter of time? "The American plan," immigrants were told, "is rather to go to new land than to improve and foster the old"; the American genius was for "clearing and bringing in, while that of the Englishman is for cultivating and enriching."[47] These were ways of life a world apart.

A frontier way of life, too, that bred no such attachment to home and fireside as Europeans knew. A home was important only for the price it would fetch, and could be forsaken without a qualm once that was high enough. "The American," a French novelist explained, "is not, like the rustics, attached from father to son to the soil which has been the cradle of the family."[48] Frontier youths had none of the memories, none of the affections, that made moving a heart-rending agony for European children; they had lived in a dozen different homes by the time they were ready to fly the nest, and scarcely remembered any of them. So they were as ready to adopt nomadic ways as their fathers had been—and to infect their own children with movingitis.[49] "He knows no devotion to the soil," a German novelist wrote; "to him the earth is merchandise just like anything else and if someone offers him a good price for it today, tomorrow he packs up what is left to him and sets out to seek a new home."[50] The image-makers were constantly shocked at the indifference with which the frontiersmen left their friends and relatives, and predicted that future Americans would lack the emotional stability that went with security and permanence.

They were fearful, too, that constant moving about would disrupt the family relationships that were the cement of normal societies. Families were large on the frontier, and as each child came of age he set forth on his

[46] Shirreff, *A Tour through North America*, p. 263; Adlard Welby, *A Visit to North America and the English Settlements in Illinois* (London, 1821), pp. 82–83; William N. Blane, *An Excursion through the United States and Canada, during the Years 1822–23* (London, 1824), p. 170; Clyde Thogmartin, "Prosper Jacotot: A French Worker Looks at Kansas in 1876–1877," *Kansas Historical Quarterly* 41 (Spring 1975): 18.
[47] William and Robert Chambers, *The Emigrant's Manual: British America and the United States* (Edinburgh, 1851), p. 12.
[48] Gustave Aimard, *The Prairie Flower: A Tale of the Indian Border* (London, 1878). Among many travelers who expressed this view were: Hall, *Travels In North America*, 1: 147; Charles A. Murray, *Travels in North America during the Years 1834, 1835, and 1836* (London, 1839), pp. 148–49; and François-Marie Perrin Du Lac, *Travels through the Two Louisianas and among the Savage Nations of the Missouri* (London, 1807), p. 37.
[49] Gustave Aimard, *The Gold Finders: A Romance of California* (New York, n.d.), p. 97; Morris Birkbeck, *Letters from Illinois* (London, 1818), p. 21; Shirreff, *A Tour through North America*, pp. 262–63.
[50] Quoted in Bjorne Landa, "The American Scene in Gerstäcker's Fiction" (Ph.D. diss., University of Minnesota, 1952), p. 161. Similar comments are in Simon A. O'Ferrall, *A Ramble of Six Thousand Miles through the United States of America* (London, 1832), p. 167, and Charles G. B. Daubney, *Journal of a Tour through the United States and Canada, Made during the Years 1837–38* (Oxford, 1843), p. 189.

own—scattering "as naturally and with as little emotion, as young birds desert forever their native nests as soon as they have fledged."[51] Once the ties were broken they were seldom restored, for distances were long and means of communication few in the Wests; departing children simply vanished over the western horizon, to be heard from rarely if at all. One elderly lady on the Indiana frontier confessed that she had forgotten how many offspring she had: "I have them scattered in every direction, and have not heard of some of them for a long time."[52] How could civilization survive if the nuclear family on which it rested was shattered so completely?

As the image-makers debated that question, they asked themselves another: why this compulsive flying about on the frontier? They agreed that two irresistible desires were responsible. One, favored by the novelists, was the lure of adventure, for to the west lay a land of danger and excitement unrivaled in the East.[53] The other, and more important, was the hope of gain. Every pioneer was a speculator at heart, gambling that the next move would bring riches beyond his dreams: better soils, greener pastures, more valuable veins of gold. "Their spirit of speculation," an Italian traveler wrote, "would carry them to the infernal regions, if another Sybil led the way with a golden bough."[54]

What the image-makers understood, and many Americans did not, was that not gain alone but the excitement of the quest for gain was the impelling force behind frontier migration. This was as irresistible as the next turn of a card, the next spin of a roulette wheel, for a compulsive gambler. "Emigration was at first necessary to them," Tocqueville wrote, "and it soon became a sort of game of chance, which they pursue for the emotions it excites, as much as for the gain it produces."[55] When a French commentator spoke of the pioneer mover as "blown along with every wind of speculation,"[56] he was writing not of hard-headed businessmen who calculated their risks prudently, but of chance takers nurtured by hope rather than reason. An American frontiersman explained the difference between his countrymen and Europeans accurately: "Our enjoyment consists more in the striving after this gain, in anticipation, and in the very act of acquiring; theirs is possession and quiet fruition."[57]

[51] Michel Chevalier, *Society, Manners and Politics in the United States* (Boston, 1839), p. 415.
[52] Charles Barinetti, *A Voyage to Mexico and Havanna: Including Some General Observations on the United States* (New York, 1841), p. 30. For similar comments see Shirreff, *A Tour through North America*, p. 428, and Julian U. Niemcewicz, *Podróże po Ameryce 1797–1807* (Wrocław, 1959), pp. 220–21.
[53] Gabriel Ferry, *Les Squatters* (Paris, 1858), p. 39; Charles W. Webber, *The Gold Mines of the Gila: A Sequel to Old Hicks the Guide* (New York, 1849), p. 1.
[54] J. C. Beltrami, *Pilgrimage in Europe and America* (London, 1828), 2: 161–62.
[55] Tocqueville, *Democracy in America*, 1: 376–77.
[56] Chevalier, *Society, Manners and Politics in America*, pp. 223–24.
[57] D. Griffiths, Jr., *Two Years' Residence in the New Settlements of Ohio* (London, 1835), p. 54.

Only this realization would explain the reckless, often irrational, behavior of pioneer speculators. They were impelled not by sound reason but by passionate hope. Let a rumor spread of better lands ahead, or of a promising new gold discovery, and half the community was ready to leave at once, even though their community was still half-settled and their operation highly profitable. Better to sell to later-comers and press on; this was the road to riches, not the patient cultivation of the land. "I want to make some money now," one frontiersman explained, "and I am not going to waste my time planting for those who come fifty years hence."[58]

This was common sense, for experience showed that virtually every move returned some profit. So long as the westward tide was flowing, buyers were available, and partially cleared land sold at a higher price than virgin land. This price differential might range from a dollar or two to fifteen or more dollars an acre, and was as certain as death or taxes. Make a few improvements, clear a bit of timber or turn a few acres of prairie sod, sell out to a later-comer, and move westward to begin the process anew—that was the way of life along the outer frontiers. Some profit was assured, and always the dream of a spectacular gain kept hope alive. "It is because of this," a Polish traveler wrote, "that the population of the United States is so widely dispersed."[59]

What dreams these tales of a constantly moving frontier—and of the fortunes to be made by the movers—must have inspired in European peasants tilling their tiny farms that their fathers and grandfathers had tilled— and that would be tilled by their sons and grandsons. In America lay a new world where profit awaited the enterprising as well as the industrious, and where vast fortunes were within the grasp of the fortunate. The image-makers said little of the impossibly hard work of pioneering (although they did warn that special skills were necessary and they did caution immigrants to avoid the outer edges of the frontier). Instead they preached of a land of hope where any European with the slightest trace of a gambler's blood in his veins might reap a king's ransom if he were lucky. Here was a magnet that the adventuresome found hard to resist.

Optimism and the Spirit of Progress

Because rainbow chasing was an occupational necessity among frontiersmen, they were incurably optimistic, hopelessly committed to the belief that tomorrow would surely be better than today. Pessimism and fear for the future were outlawed among them. Their thought, no less than their

[58] *American Settler*, 10 September 1881.
[59] Julian U. Niemcewicz, *Under Their Vine and Fig Trees: Travels through America in 1797–1799, 1805* (Elizabeth, N.J., 1965), p. 242.

way of life, was geared to the inevitability of progress; land values were sure to rise, the most reckless speculation certain to shower wealth on the speculator, the tiniest hamlet destined to become a bustling metropolis. This was logical in a land where expansion was the order of the day and sure to continue for generations to come. So the image-makers preached, and so Europeans believed. They pictured the pioneers as clad in rose-tinted glasses, forever pursuing illusive hopes as they moved westward. Frontiersmen, one grammatically minded traveler noted, always used the present indicative rather than the future subjunctive when they spoke, for what "might be" was as certain to them as "what was."[60]

Such optimism meant that the pioneers, as Lord Bryce noted, "seemed to live in the future rather than in the present."[61] This was a psychological necessity, for there was little in the present for them to enjoy: a landscape littered with the debris of clearing, back-breaking labor, an uncomfortable log dwelling, the aching loneliness of isolation from their neighbors. But better days were ahead; on those better days their hopes were focused. "The frontiersman," one visitor observed, "lives on hope and expectation."[62] His was an almost childlike faith that the joys of the future were worth the sacrifices of the present. They were as certain as the succession of the equinoxes in a land where expansion and progress were destined to rule for the forseeable future.

Given this faith, the pioneers saw not only themselves but their country as it would be, not as it was. "Other nations," a traveler noted, "boast of what they are or have been, but the true citizen of the United States exalts his head in the skies in contemplating what the grandeur of his country is going to be."[63] The image-makers noted that both the Old World and the New gloried in what each had the most of; Europe the past, the United States the future. Americans looked ahead because they had too little to look back on, particularly in the emerging societies along the frontiers. There they "guessed" and "calculated" and "presumed"—as a visitor to Texas recorded—that the future "will be a glorious one, when the brilliant *past* of the old world shall be the only treasure to which *it* can lay claim."[64] There was no place for doubt in frontier thought. In the

---

[60] Birkbeck, *Notes on a Journey to America*, pp. 40–41.
[61] Bryce, *American Commonwealth*, 2: 847.
[62] *American Settler*, 6 September 1884. Similar statements are in George W. Featherstonhaugh, *Excursion through the Slave States* (New York, 1844), pp. 61–62; Harriet Martineau, *Society in America* (New York, 1837), 2: 165; and Murray, *Travels in North America*, 2: 221.
[63] Quoted in John G. Brooks, *As Others See Us: A Study of Progress in the United States* (New York, 1908), p. 62.
[64] Matilda J. F. Houstoun, *Hesperos; or, Travels in the West* (London, 1850), 1: 116–17. Similar comments are in Thomas Nichols, *Forty Years of American Life, 1820–1861* (New York, 1937), p. 46, and Paul Bourget, *Outre Mer, Impressions of America* (New York, 1895), p. 261.

Der Kommandant kam zur rechten Zeit. Seine Pistolen streckten zwei der Sioux zu Boden und den Dritten schmetterte er mit dem Kolben seiner Büchse nieder.

Front cover of Wilhelm Frey, *In Indianerhänden* (Mülheim, n.d.).
(From the collections of the Yale University Library.)

Wests everyone spoke "of the past with triumph, the present with delight, and the future with growing and confident anticipation."[65]

This same exuberant spirit sustained the frontiersmen as they labored to build their dream castles in the western wilderness. So long as they lived in the future the dismal tasks of frontiering became adventures, not drudgery. They were hurrying the coming of tomorrow with incredible speed. What had been a dank forest one day was a clearing the next, a self-sustaining farm a day later, and a wealthy estate the day after that.[66] People in the smallest towns talked gleefully of the thousands of newcomers who would crowd their streets and built schools and courthouses and jails to accommodate them—certain that they would be there. "The Englishman," a traveler noted, "builds according to his means—the American according to his expectations." If his "means" were sufficient for a two-storied house, "he will raise it to four stories on speculation."[67] Why not? The westerner was a gambler, and so long as expansion went on the cards were stacked in his favor.

Nowhere was this spirit better illustrated than among town planters. Every site was destined to become another London or New York, and in a remarkably short time; towns grew so rapidly that promoters had no time to think of fancy street names, settling instead on "A Street," "B Street," or "1st Street."[68] Europeans might complain that a "city" being shown them was still buried beneath a tangled forest, that Third Avenue, "in the fashionable district," was only a path through a bog, and the "town center" a mass of impenetrable underbrush. They might be incredulous when shown a "city" consisting of a lone shanty on the prairie, or amused when they heard the promoter of such a metropolis asked if "anyone was talking of building a second house in that city,"[69] but this was only because they did not understand the frontier temperament. "Out here," reported a traveler on a newly built western railroad, "nobody talks of the present. In all the towns that have sprung up along the railroad, people talk only of what is to come."[70]

Even temporary setbacks could not quench the go-ahead enthusiasm of the westerners. A San Francisco hotel proprietor whose costly new building had just gone up in smoke was seen consulting a builder about an even larger replacement while the flames still licked about the old; the fire was a

---

[65] Quoted in Charlotte Erickson, *Invisible Immigrants: The Adaptation of English and Scottish Immigrants in Nineteenth Century America* (London, 1972), p. 117.
[66] Gustave Aimard, *The Missouri Outlaws* (London, n.d.), p. 40.
[67] Marryat, *Diary in America*, 2: 214–15.
[68] Louis L. Simonin, *The Rocky Mountain West in 1867* (Lincoln, Nebr., 1966), p. 63.
[69] Laurence Oliphant, *Minnesota and the Far West* (Edinburgh, 1855), pp. 150–51; Foster B. Zincke, *Last Winter in the United States: Being Table Talk Collected during a Tour through the Late Southern Confederation, the Far West, the Rocky Mountains,* (London, 1868), p. 209.
[70] Nicolaus Mohr, *Excursion Through America* (Chicago, 1973), p. 128.

blessing, not a disaster, in his eyes.[71] A traveler reported a conversation between two merchants whose establishments had been consumed in the same fire:

"Flat?" one asked.
"Flat as a damned pancake."
"It's a great country."
"It's nothing shorter."

And they separated to arrange rebuilding their stores.[72] There was no dampening such enthusiasm. The frontiersman was an optimist because he knew that progress was as certain as the succession of day and night.

The Work Ethic

The frontiersman was also wise enough to see that his dreams of the future could only come true if he and his neighbors did their part. This meant hard work. Squatters on the cutting edge of the frontier might be seduced into indolence by Nature's abundance, but once the pioneer farmers and merchants appeared on the scene leisure was outlawed. Too much must be done to win the battle against the wilderness for society to tolerate laziness. All must pitch in, all must hurry—hurry—hurry to achieve to-morrow today. The image-makers noted that westerners drove themselves at a furious pace night and day—"nothing stops them in their go-ahead career."[73] Each wanted to perform in a day what a European would accomplish in a week; "ten years in America are like a century in Spain."[74] Travelers estimated the longitude by the time required to consume meals—the farther they went west, the faster food was gulped down and work resumed.[75] Even plaster dried faster on the frontier, laundry needed to be hung out a shorter time, and ink required less blotting.[76]

The locomotive pace of western life was easily explained: every man there was a speculator driven onward by the spirit of enterprise. He must make his improvements, clear his fields, open his store, build his gristmill, in time to profit from the flood of newcomers sure to appear.[77] His was no distant goal, no illusive pot of gold. The end of his rainbow was in sight, and he must be prepared to capitalize on immediate opportunity. Progress

71 Gerstäcker, *Gold! Ein californisches Lebensbild*, 1: 190–91.
72 Frank Marryat, *Mountains and Molehills* (London, 1855), pp. 22–23.
73 M. G. Houstoun, *Texas and the Gulf of Mexico* (London, 1844), 1: 262. Similar statements are in Martineau, *Society in America*, 1: 355; Marryat, *A Diary in America*, 1: 18.
74 Francis Lieber, ed., *Letters to a Gentleman in Germany* (Philadelphia, 1834), p. 287.
75 Hodgson, *Letters from North America*, 1: 153; Hall, *Travels in North America*, 1: 138.
76 Quoted in Terry Coleman, *Passage to America, A History of Emigrants from Great Britain and Ireland to America in the Mid-Nineteenth Century* (London, 1972), p. 47.
77 Featherstonhaugh, *A Canoe Voyage up the Minnay Sotor*, 2:221.

was so certain, future prospects so bright, that the laziest laggard was infected with the will to succeed.

What originated as individual enterprise was transformed into community spirit. Those who shirked their duties were sinners against society as well as against themselves. "Labor," wrote Tocqueville, "is held by the whole community to be an honorable necessity of man's condition."[78] There was no shirking or delegating this responsibility; prospective immigrants were warned that once they reached the frontier they would be expected to labor from dawn to dusk, whatever their wealth or social position. The leisure pace of work in older countries would not be tolerated. An American watching British laborers dawdling through their tasks with frequent pauses for talk or tea was guilty only of caricature when he remarked: "Why, we would have had the house built up and burnt down before you have finished the foundation."[79]

This was the penalty that all must pay for life in a land where opportunity was limitless and the governmental system geared to encourage individual enterprise. Every man was his own master, free to use Nature's resources to the limit of his skills and energy. To the success-motivated pioneer that very opportunity was a rigid taskmaster; the image-makers saw the hope of success, not the Puritan ethic, as responsible for the work compulsion in the Wests. "Nothing is impossible to the American nation," an Hungarian marveled as he watched this beehive activity.[80] He was right, but the penalty was a heavy one when measured in terms of hard labor.

For in such a society the leisure deemed essential to comfort and culture by upper-class Europeans was taboo. Inherited wealth or position were no guarantors of admission to the upper ranks of frontier society; those who had not earned their own right to social respect were scorned by the elite. Each must win his place in the hierarchy by incessant work. "Idlers are out of element here," newcomers were warned, "and the being who is technically called a man of rank in Europe, is despised in America."[81] Those who lived well without working might be known as "gentlemen" in the Old World, but were branded as "loafers" in the New. "America," wrote a visitor," is the only country in the world where one is ashamed of having nothing to do."[82] Even travel for pleasure was frowned upon, as many a European found when he was forced to endure a barrage

[78] Tocqueville, *Democracy in America*, 2: 162. A similar passage is in Chevalier, *Society, Manners and Politics in the United States*, pp. 283–84.
[79] *American Settler*, 17 December 1881.
[80] Ágoston Haraszthy, *Utazás Északamerikában* (Pest, 1844), 1: 3–4.
[81] John Melish, *Travels through the United States of America, in the Years 1806 & 1807, and 1809, 1810, & 1811* (London, 1818), p. 628.
[82] Quoted in Arthur M. Schlesinger, "What Then Is the American This New Man?" *American Historical Review 48* (January 1943): 232.

of questions on *why* he was traveling if not for business. One inquisitor, having failed to satisfy his curiosity, turned to the traveler's wife with: "Well, Ma'am, I wonder now if your husband, who's got nothing to do but to *spend* his money, is as happy as we Americans, who are busy *making* ours. I doubt he isn't."[83] Nonworkers were traitors to the spirit of enterprise that motivated westerners.

Frontier Ingenuity

The image-makers were wise enough to recognize that hard labor was no more desired by frontiersmen than by Europeans. They labored hard and long simply because so many tasks must be accomplished to hurry their profit making; if those tasks could be bypassed without slowing the drive for wealth, society would benefit no less than the individual. Hence invention and innovation were the order of the day. The frontier environment vastly stimulated creativity, so long as the creations could be used for practical purposes; the typical frontiersman was a would-be inventor, seeking constantly for new machines, new processes, new ways to increase productivity and lessen the demands on labor. In the Wests the "old ways" would suffice only until "new ways" were developed.

Innovation was at a premium there as it was not in settled areas. Travelers recognized this truth, and suggested many reasons why. One was sparse population; people were so thinly spread that the division of labor normal in the Old World was impossible. In Europe crafts were passed from father to son, with the resulting products exchanged for others produced by different specialists. Along the frontier each family must care for its own needs. The father must build his own home, fashion his own tools, clear his own fields, create his own implements, even make his own shoes; the wife must spin wool, weave cloth, make clothes, manufacture soap and candles, prepare maple sugar, minister to the sick, and midwife the delivery of calves—and her own children. Robinson Crusoe, Mrs. Trollope believed, was no more self-sufficient than a frontiersman.[84] Routine tasks, accomplished in a routine way, were outlawed by the pioneer's way of life.

This jack-of-all-trades existence stimulated innovation, partly by breaking the cake of custom, partly by challenging every westerner to ease his own burdens by perfecting labor-saving tools and techniques, and partly by encouraging inventors to rise to a proven demand. The inventors, understandably, produced the most spectacular results; isolated farmers had neither the skill nor the means to create original implements.

---

[83] Houstoun, *Hesperos*, 1: 149.
[84] Trollope, *Domestic Manners of the Americans*, p. 49.

Even in the eighteenth-century inventors, inspired by frontier demand, catalogued a whole list of labor-saving devices: a machine for sowing grain mechanically, another to dig the ditches needed in swamp drainage, a third to improve on the sickle in harvesting crops, still another to pile logs for burning, yet another to provide movable storage for harvested grain.[85] During the next hundred years this list was multiplied a thousand fold. The profit incentive for inventors who could perfect improved machinery that would allow labor-starved frontier areas to increase their productivity was a powerful stimulant to invention.

The image-makers, however, were even more intrigued by the innovative genius that they found among the pioneers—and that they believed lacking in Europeans. Travelers never tired of cataloging examples: a raft improvised of logs and harness to cross a swollen stream, gadgets to ease the task of plowing and harvesting, a clothes-washing machine devised by a frontier housewife, equipment for placer mining, a church designed to serve for grain storage when needed, dozens more.[86] If we may believe one visitor who had listened overlong to western tall-tale tellers, these included a shelf with a trapdoor suspended beneath the perches of a chicken house to allow the newly laid eggs to drop into a net below. This invention ended in tragedy for the hens, who, turning to admire the results of their industry and finding no egg there, kept on laying. When the housewife returned the next day she found eighteen eggs in her trap, and in the nest only a beak, two claws, and a handful of feathers.[87] "There is nothing an inventive American believes he cannot accomplish," wrote an admiring recent arrival, "even if he has no previous experience."[88]

To drive home their point, European observers frequently contrasted frontier innovation with the stubborn insistence of emigrants on using time-tested Old World techniques. Swedes and Norwegians were chided for clinging to old-fashioned axes they had brought with them rather than adopting the well-balanced blades that had been adapted to frontier needs—and were twice as efficient in clearing. Germans and Englishmen were ridiculed for using servants to clear their lands in European style because they disliked the littered fields left by Americans—and usually ended in bankruptcy. Pioneers had learned that their sloppy techniques might offend the eye but were essential in a frontier settlement where

[85] These inventions are described in Gilbert Chinard, "Eighteenth Century Theories on America as a Human Habitat," *Proceedings of the American Philosophical Society* 91 (1947): 50–51.
[86] James Caird, *Prairie Farming in America* (New York 1859), pp. 56–57; Baillie-Grohman, *Camps in the Rockies*, pp. 21–22; William A. Bell, *New Tracks in North America* (London, 1869), 2: 193–97; Wiśniowski, *Ameryka 100 Years Ago*, pp. 32–33.
[87] Quoted in Theodore C. Blegen, ed., *The Land of Their Choice: The Immigrants Write Home* (Minneapolis, 1955), pp. 314–15.
[88] Unonius, *A Pioneer in Northwest America*, 1:216–17.

labor was harder to obtain than land.[89] Success in the Wests depended on adaptation, not tradition.

The image-makers who learned this lesson had only praise for the ingenuity of the frontiersmen. The spirit of enterprise among them, travelers believed, "is not surpassed, not even equalled, by any nation in the world."[90] The "sackful of expedients" that each carried as he went about his tasks, their complete lack of reverence for "old landmarks and time-hallowed institutions," meant that they had perfected "a creative genius of the highest order."[91] They might be jacks of all trades and masters of none, but they were far superior to Europeans in their realistic adaptability to the needs of their unique occupations. Unshackled by tradition, ill-supplied with labor, distant from suppliers, and above all inspired by the hope of heady profits, the frontiersmen were pictured to Europeans as masters of ingenuity and the most inventive people in the world.

Frontier Puffing

They were also possessed of another trait that the image-makers found not only annoying but downright deplorable. This was their incessant boasting—"puffing" in the language of the day—as they regaled all who would listen with the glories of their communities, their nation, and themselves. In their eyes the United States was "the most enlightened nation of the world," and American institutions "a perfect example of human wisdom."[92] The American people were "*more* learned, *more* powerful, and altogether *more* extraordinary than any other people in the world."[93] Their recently completed Erie Canal was "the wonder of the world, the glory of the age, . . . and equal to the Pyramids of Egypt, or the Wall of China."[94] When one traveler heard a frontier landlord summon his guests to dinner by shouting, "Gentlemen, we are a great people,"[95] we can understand why another would predict that within a few years frontiersmen would be boasting that the United States was "not only the most powerful and the most learned, but the oldest nation in the world."[96]

[89]   Martineau, *Society in America*, 1: 338.
[90]   Friedrich Gerstäcker, quoted in Weber, *America in Imaginative German Literature*, p. 156.
[91]   Michel Chevalier, *Lettres sur l'Amérique du Nord* (Paris, 1836), 2: 122–23; Avraham Yarmolinsky, *Picturesque United States of America, 1811, 1812, 1813: Being a Memoir on Paul Svinin* (New York, 1930), p. 7; Baillie-Grohman, *Camps in the Rockies*, pp. 20–21.
[92]   John Bristed, *The Resources of the United States of America* (New York, 1818), pp. 460–61; Constantin F. Volney, *A View of the Soil and Climate of the United States of America* (Philadelphia, 1804), p. xvi; P. I. Poletica, *A Sketch of the Internal Condition of the United States . . . by a Russian* (Baltimore, 1826), p. 41.
[93]   Houstoun, *Hesperos*, 2: 24–25.
[94]   Isaac Candler, *A Summary View of America* (London, 1824), pp. 122–23.
[95]   Charles Lyell, *A Second Visit to the United States of America* (New York, 1849), 2: 160.
[96]   Hodgson, *Letters From North America*, 2: 31.

Newly arrived immigrants were warned to respond to every question about their views of the countryside with "marvelous," "beautiful," or "magnificent."[97] If they did not, they might open the floodgates of such a spread-eagle boaster as the one who proclaimed:

America has more and longer rivers than any country in the world. They are muddier, deeper, flow faster, rise faster, and cause more destruction. She has more lakes, and they are deeper, larger, and clearer than those of any other country. The locomotives are larger, run faster, and kill more people than in any other country. The steamboats are loaded heavier, are longer and wider, blow up their boilers more often, and send their passengers higher in the air. The captains curse better than those of other nationalities. The American men are taller and heavier and can fight better and longer. The ladies are richer, more beautiful, better dressed, use more money, break more hearts, wear larger rings and shorter skirts. They can dance longer and better than the ladies of any other land. The children yell louder, grow faster, and become twenty years old more quickly than the other children of any land on earth. It is a marvelous land.[98]

Even caricature could not disguise the fact that the pioneers were deplorably boastful and unabashedly patriotic; "my feelings for my country," one admitted, "are not a passion, they are a fanaticism."[99]

With glorification of the United States went a down-the-nose disdain for European nations and people. Westerners outspokenly believed that Europe consisted of "a heap of medieval feudal states . . . which have not enough vitality to rise from the abyss of misery and corruption into which they have fallen as the result of centuries of ignorance and despotism."[100] The European people were worthy of only contempt and pity; travelers were greeted with such expressions as: "They're a horrid tyrannical set o' fellers in Britain, ain't they?" or, "I wonder you are not sick of kings, chancellors, and archbishops."[101] "They think every Englishman is a slave," one complained.[102] Europe was lost to despotism and decadence; soon the mantle of world leadership would pass to the United States. "In a short time," one traveler was told, "England would only be known as having been the mother of America."[103]

[97] Aurél Kecskeméthy, *Éjszak-Amerika 1876-ban* (Budapest, 1877), p. 157.
[98] Franklin D. Scott, quotes this passage from *Folketidende,* 8 July 1874, in his article "Søren Jaabaek, Americanizer in Norway," *Norwegian-American Studies and Records* 17 (1952): 105.
[99] Paul Duplessis, *Les Mormons* (Paris, 1859), 6: 119–200.
[100] Ole Munch Raeder, *American in the Forties: The Letters of Ole Munch Raeder* (Minneapolis, 1929), pp. 83–84.
[101] John Regan, *The Emigrant's Guide to the Western States of America* (Edinburgh, 1852), p. 132; Trollope, *Domestic Manners of the Americans,* pp. 160–61.
[102] Weld, *Travels through the States of North America,* 1: 125.
[103] Marryat, *A Diary in America,* 2: 89.

The image-makers learned to hide their embarrassment when they listened to ignorant frontiersmen lambaste their native lands, but they were less able to conceal their alarm when westerners proclaimed the warlike intentions of the United States. Time and again they were told that within three generations the nation would be strong enough to conquer all of the Americas and begin the conquest of Europe; Mexico would come first, then Latin America and Canada, and finally the Old World itself—"it can *swaller* Mexico, gouge out both eyes of Britain, and whip all creation."[104] An irresistible urge to dominate the world drove the pioneers onward; they were, a French novelist believed, "perpetually gazing at the distant horizon—those men in whose ear a secret voice constantly murmurs, as to the Jew of legend, 'Onward, Onward!' "[105] That urge, Europeans were told, could be satisfied only when the frontiersmen had won for their country all the civilized world.

How account for this flaming of a warlike nationalism along the frontiers? The image-makers pondered this question often, and emerged with two sensible answers. The pioneers, they saw, had had no time to develop local attachments, and hence focused their loyalties on the nation. "This Patriotism," a Norwegian visitor observed, "is more concentrated and therefore stronger than it would be if people bestowed their affection upon some particular state or community."[106] Coupled with this attachment was the spirit of conquest that had been inflamed by the winning of the continent. If the frontiersmen could conquer the vastness of the American West they could conquer the world. The very success of their enterprise stirred imperialistic dreams and patriotic ardor. They were a favored people, confident of their own destiny—and eager to hurry its coming.

They were also convinced of the perfection of their democratic institutions, particularly in the Wests where the spirit of self-rule flamed most strongly. The frontier saw itself as the cradle of democracy, and was desperately eager to defend its infant offspring against any criticism. The pioneer, as one image-maker put it, felt personally responsible for defending not only the honor of his country but his country's institutions.[107] His was an awesome responsibility, for in his mind the world's future depended on his success. If he succeeded, the shining light of democracy would lead mankind into a better future; if he failed Europe's despotism would again prevail. Given the inner doubts inevitable when burdened with such a task, the frontiersman's reliance on boasting to bolster his own self-assurance was understandable. So Europeans reasoned as they des-

---

[104] Houstoun, *Hesperos*, 2: 54. A similar opinion is in the novel, William Black, *Green Pastures and Piccadilly*, (London, 1878), p. 369.
[105] Aimard, *The Gold Finders*, p. 97. Aimard repeated these warnings in many of his books.
[106] Raeder, *America in the Forties*, p. 148.
[107] Chevalier, *Society, Manners and Politics in the United States*, p. 435.

perately sought to understand a trait that they could not help deplore.

And deplore they did. "Nothing," Tocqueville wrote, "is more embarrassing in the ordinary intercourse of life than this irritating patriotism of the Americans."[108] Newcomers branded the pioneer "an intolerant fellow-citizen";[109] even the most tolerant found his constant self-praise downright annoying and "not properly modified by reflection."[110] Only a few German liberals refused to be bothered, largely because they hoped that their fatherland would soon boast the unity and strength that the "puffers" ascribed to the United States.[111]

Unpleasant and ununderstandable as the typical pioneer was to the image-makers—overworked, undercultured, inexplicably addicted to a wandering life, dedicated to the pursuit of the Almighty Dollar—they found his boasting the least attractive of his many unattractive traits. Recognizing that his chest-thumping self-confidence stemmed partly from a lack of confidence in himself, they saw him as a potentially dangerous threat to the peace of the world. Goaded on by the urge to justify his own pretensions, he might well involve the United States in imperialistic conquest and bloody wars. The conquest of the continent would be followed, Europe believed, by the attempted conquest of other lands. Once again the image-makers were not too far astray, as the imperialism of the late nineteenth century proved.

[108] Tocqueville, *Democracy in America*, 1: 311–12.
[109] H. Arnold Barton, ed., *Letters from the Promised Land: Swedes in America, 1840–1914* (Minneapolis, 1975), p. 25.
[110] Candler, *A Summary View of America*, p. 476.
[111] Gerstäcker, *Gold! Ein californisches Lebensbild*, 3: 118–19.

X

Land of Opportunity

THE FRONTIER described by novelists and hostile travelers—a land of savage beasts, bloodthirsty Indians, and unmannered pioneers—was hardly appealing to European peasants accustomed to the security and companionship of a compact social order. Yet during the nineteenth century thousands upon thousands of those peasants left the comforts and safety of the Old World to risk their lives and property in the New. Why? How account for an exodus that seemed to fly in the face of all reason and common sense?

To answer that question is to explore the complexity of human motivation and the variety of forces—expelling and attracting—operating at that time. But the answer also reveals the operation of another group of image-makers who were obviously more successful than the first. These were the optimists—travelers, guidebook authors, writers of "America Letters," even some novelists—who saw the American West as a land of milk and honey where all ate meat three times a day, owned their own farms, and were assured prosperity and security for themselves and their heirs. These golden-voiced Pied Pipers labored so effectively that millions of Europe's underprivileged were willing to brave the dangers and discomforts of pioneer life to better their lot and that of their children.

Their message was not new; since the dawn-days of settlement promoters had tried to lure Europeans to the New World with promises of

"Fat Mutton and Liberty of Conscience."[1] Their propaganda was only mildly successful until the close of the Napoleonic Wars when conditions in Europe stirred a new interest in migration. Overcrowding was the principal concern. Population had increased steadily there since the middle of the seventeenth century as it responded to an expanding food supply made possible by potato growing, medical discoveries that lengthened the life span, and a long period of peace. "Potatoes, vaccine, and peace" exerted an impossible pressure on the nonexpandable supply of land. By mid-century, when a devastating potato rot upset the delicate balance, thousands of small farmers were trying to scratch a living from submarginal lands that had been pressed into use to meet demands. With the spread of the potato famine, malnutrition became an international plague. Publicists who wrote mournfully of "the miseries of a collapsing society," were signaling that the time was ripe for the greatest mass exodus in history.[2] Here was a made-to-order opportunity for promoters to direct that migration to the American West.

The Garden of the World

Their appeal was built on long-standing precedent, for earlier image-makers of the late eighteenth and early nineteenth centuries had made much of frontier opportunity. Their message was directed not to the dispossessed, but to European intellectuals who were dreaming of brave new worlds during the Age of Romanticism. To these head-in-the-clouds idealists the Old World was on a toboggan slide toward decadence. There the heaped-up dust of the past clogged the path into the future; there the weight of centuries leadened the pace of change and stifled enterprise in government or business. Europe was old and dying. Youth lay beyond the Atlantic where tradition did not clamp progress, and where the future was aborning—"a sheet of white paper . . . where everything has to be begun; everything is new."[3] Bishop Berkeley could write that:

> Westward the course of empire takes its way;
> The first four acts already past,

---

[1]   Quoted in Carl Bridenbaugh, *Spirit of '76* (New York, 1975), p. 23. Excellent discussions of this early propaganda are in two works by Howard Mumford Jones, "The Colonial Impulse: An Analysis of the 'Promotion' Literature of Colonization," *Proceedings of the American Philosophical Society* 90 (1946): 121–61, and *O Strange New World: American Culture: The Formative Years* (New York, 1964), pp. 40–43.
[2]   The situation in Denmark is admirably described in Kristian Hvidt, *Flight to America* (New York, 1974), pp. 8–20, and in Norway and Sweden in Theodore Saloutos, "Immigrant Contributions to American Agriculture," *Agricultural History* 50 (January 1976): 53–55.
[3]   Quoted in Oscar Handlin, ed., *This Was America* (Cambridge, 1949), p. 322.

A fifth shall close the drama with the day;
Time's noblest offspring is the last.[4]

The New World was destined as a "new, enlarged and improved version of the Old."[5] There the future lay.

Within the New World the heartland of progress was the West. That was the land of beginning; eastern America was already showing the signs of decay that had debauched Europe's civilization. Along the frontiers all was vibrance and youthful exuberance; there a virgin culture was shaping, beckoning Europeans who were "tortured by fate and hounded by their fellow men."[6] Novelists built their plots on the contrast between the "simple and sincere" manners of frontier folk and those in Europe where men had "substituted duplicity for candour, and cunning for wisdom."[7] For Europeans eager to improve themselves or their lot in this world the American West was truly the land of opportunity.

There, the image-makers preached, they could be transformed into yeoman farmers. This was the ultimate in perfectionism, for to European idealists in the early nineteenth century, still swayed by Romanticism, the small farmer was the happiest of all men, stirring masculine envy and setting female hearts pitter-patter. Only he was worthy of life in the flower-decked Eden that lay to the West. There reincarnated Adams could recapture those Arcadian days of old; there they could repose on flowered bowers as they listened to "the sweet singers of the forest" that warbled "their tender notes in unison with love and nature";[8] there the tuneful shepherd could "compose sweet sonnets to his mistress."[9] When a British traveler could salute a backwoods Kentuckian with: "Happy man! . . . who, ignorant of the deceits of artifice attendant on a state of civilization, unpracticed in the vices and dissipations of degraded humanity . . . how much I envy you"[10]—when such a speech could be inspired by a semi-illiterate squatter whose manners were abominable and whose talents were limited to frontiering, the image-makers had succumbed so completely to the agrarian myth that they had lost touch with the humbler Europeans who were to people the American Wests.

Yet so persuasive was the myth that its rhetoric, if not its appeal, per-

[4] Bishop George Berkeley, *The Works of George Berkeley, D. D.*, ed. Alexander Frazer (Oxford, 1901), 4: 36.
[5] Károly Nendtvich (1858), quoted in Anna Katona, "Hungarian Travelogues on the Pre–Civil War U.S.," *Hungarian Studies in English* 5 (1971): 61.
[6] Friedrich A. Strubberg, *Bis in die Wildnis* (Breslau, 1858), p. 231.
[7] Gilbert Imlay, *The Emigrants* (Dublin, 1794), pp. 179, 291.
[8] Gilbert Imlay, *A Topographical Description of the Western Territory of North America* (London, 1792), pp. 39–40.
[9] Imlay, *The Emigrants*, p. 159.
[10] Francis Baily, *Journal of a Tour in the Unsettled Parts of North America in 1796 and 1797* (London, 1856), p. 173.

sisted well into the nineteenth century. The Mississippi Valley, with its lush farmlands, naturally suggested the "Garden of the World" to propagandists—an Eden that rivaled Adam's garden in beauty and productivity, and would shower its bountiful fruits on all mankind. When a bard could extol the virtues of Texas with:

> Know'st thou the land where the lemon-trees bloom—
> Where the gold orange glows mid' the deep thicket's gloom,
> Where a wind, ever soft, from the blue heaven blows,
> And the groves are of laurel, and myrtle and rose,[11]

the spirit of romanticism was still very much alive. Yet the appeal of commercialism was such that even such a message was muted. The West was not only the "Garden of America," but "a garden of cereals for the support of millions."[12]

The lofty prose of the romanticists had little impact on Europe's masses, but the image of pastoral America as a haven from dying Europe continued to play a role among intellectuals through much of the century. What impractical dreams they dreamed! A group of Polish idealists, planning a utopian colony in California, were typical in their fantasies: "What joy! To bleach linen at the brook like the maidens of Homer's Iliad! To recite poems, or to listen to the mockingbird. And listening to our songs would be charming Indian maidens, our neighbors, making wreaths of luxuriant wild flowers for us."[13] Here was idealism carried to absurdity. Yet it mirrored the enduring vision of the West as a land of rebirth, of rejuvenation, for the hopes of Europeans. Johann Goethe caught that spirit in his famous lines:

> America, you have it better
> Than our continent, the older:
> No castles in decay, no halls that moulder;
> No memories of use to fetter,
> No needless idle strife
> To cramp the innermost
> In times astir with life.
> Go use the present and fare well.[14]

The United States was, and would be, a land of opportunity, even of a sort impracticable and outworn.

[11] William Kennedy, *Texas: The Rise, Progress, and Prospects of the Republic of Texas* (London, 1841), 1:1.
[12] Mayne Reid, *The Scalp Hunters; or, Romantic Adventures in Northern Mexico* (London, 1851), 3:237.
[13] Helen Modjeska, *Memories and Impressions* (New York, 1910), pp. 250–51.
[14] I am indebted to the late Ulrich Carrington for this sensitive translation of Goethe's well-known poem.

From Karl May, *Het Testament van den Inca* (Amsterdam, c. 1904),
a Dutch translation. (Copy in my possession.)

The American Urge

The hundreds of thousands of peasants and tradesmen who succumbed to the siren call of frontier America had probably never speculated on Europe's decay or heard of the Mississippi Valley as the "Garden of the World." They were practical folk, seeking not a fairyland where impossible dreams would come true, but tillable fields, a market for their goods, and a chance to better their status in society. They learned of this haven not from poets and philosophers but from friendly travelers, guidebooks, immigration newspapers, agents of immigration companies and steamship lines, advertising by land-grant railroads and land speculators, propagandists for western states and territories, and the "America Letters" written by successful emigrants to their friends and relatives in their homelands. What they learned might be confusing—one reader remarked wryly that he had learned that a "great many different states were the best in the Union"[15]—but one basic fact was perfectly clear: that the American West was a land of opportunity where a farm of one's own was within the reach of the most humble and where a man of small means was assured a competence.

That point was backed by indisputable evidence, and by a chorus of agreement. Every book, every newspaper, every glib agent, made perfectly clear that the American frontier was a Land of Canaan, a haven where the most extravagant hopes could be translated into reality, a Midas-like treasury of Nature's riches. The fate of each peasant who reached there would be that of the family shown on the gaudy posters displayed in every village: life first in a tidy log cabin, then "Ten Years Later" in an ornate frame house where elegant ladies and well-dressed gentlemen sported on the spacious lawn and a nearby barn overflowed with the fruits of their labor. Norwegians told each other (exaggerating a bit with each telling) of "Cleng Peerson's Dream": of how Cleng saw himself standing on a hilltop in Illinois with a paradise of luxuriant growth spread before him, and thanked God for leading him to the promised land.[16] To reach that land of plenty was the "collective utopian dream" of half the peasantry of Europe.[17]

And what a spine-tickling dream that was, even though cast in an image so vast that Europeans were scarcely able to comprehend. Those who could were hopelessly captivated. A Slovenian lad testified that when

[15] Edward Money, *The Truth about America* (London, 1868), p. 43.
[16] Theodore B. Blegen, "Cleng Peerson and Norwegian Immigration," *Mississippi Valley Historical Review* 7 (March 1921): 319–20. A large body of evidence on this point is in Merle Curti and Kendall Birr, "The Immigrant and the American Image in Europe, 1860–1914," *Mississippi Valley Historical Review* 37 (September 1950): 215–16.
[17] René Dubos, "The Despairing Optimist," *American Scholar* 43 (Autumn 1974): 544–45.

he heard a returned emigrant, handsomely clad and shamelessly exhibiting a heavy gold watch, talk of *ranches* larger than the entire province of Carniola where a man must ride a whole day to reach the borders of his property, he felt that he could never rest content again in cramped Europe.[18] And the wealth that such estates would produce! Wealth beyond the hopes of any peasant. One who had migrated from his Macedonian village sent back a draft for forty Napoleons—far more money than anyone there ever hoped to possess.[19] Who could resist the "America Fever" when a friend had been that fortunate? The tragic heroine in Ole Rölvaag's *Giants in the Earth* described the reaction of a town where this occurred, the people "drifting about in a sort of delirium, like sea-birds at mating time; then they flew toward the sunset, in small flocks and large—always toward Sunset Land."[20]

Migration became a compulsion as the image-makers did their task, and one too strong to be resisted. No one was too old or too young to escape; gray-bearded patriarchs dreamed of beginning life anew amidst America's riches and small boys cheered their parents with: "When I grow up, I shall go to America and send you a sackful of money."[21] Why not? All things were possible in that land of opportunity. Realists might caution against pitching hopes too high, but who would listen? Friedrich Gerstäcker sensed the impact of the "America Urge" when he wrote in one of his novels: " 'To America!' With those words they leave behind their old lives, their works, their creations, leave the ties of blood and friendship, leave the hopes that excite them, the cares that depress them. 'To America!' "[22] That was the cry of half of Europe, and the image-makers helped shape their dreams.

The Lure of Pioneering

For the American West promised the poorest peasant his ultimate hope: a farm of his own. This was within the reach of the most humble; those without capital could preempt a site and let the land pay for itself within the four years allowed by the government, or after 1862, claim 160 acres (a veritable estate by European standards) under the Homestead

[18] Louis Adamic, *Laughing in the Jungle* (New York, 1932), pp. 5–6.
[19] Stoyen Christowe, *This Is My Country*, (New York, 1927), pp. 7–10.
[20] Ole Rölvaag, *Giants in the Earth: A Saga of the Prairie* (New York, 1927), p. 220. Other examples are in David M. Emmons, *Garden in the Grasslands: Boomer Literature of the Central Great Plains* (Lincoln, Nebr., 1971), pp. 101–2.
[21] Berthold Auerbach, *Der Viereckige oder die amerikanische Kiste* (1852) quoted in Paul C. Weber, *America in Imaginative German Literature in the First Half of the Nineteenth Century* (New York, 1926), p. 221.
[22] Friedrich Gerstäcker, *Nach Amerika* (1855), quoted in Alfred Kolb, "Friedrich Gerstäcker and the American Frontier" (Ph.D. diss., Syracuse University, 1966), p. 136.

Act.[23] The more honest image-makers took pains to point out that conflicting titles and cheating jobbers lay in wait for the unwary, and that the first settlers on a raw frontier might have to defend their rights with a gun, but they usually made light of such dangers. "What is such a price for such a diamond," one asked.[24] For the industrious and the lucky, a farm—and a fortune—were assured.

Add to this the thrill of pioneering and the "America Urge" was well-nigh irresistible. Guidebook authors particularly recognized this, and larded their pages of statistics with the adventures of newly arrived Germans or Hollanders or Hungarians as they went about the business of acquiring their first farms. Each was pictured as poring over guidebooks or talking with frontiersmen first, weighing the merits of this alluvial plain or that fertile valley so temptingly described, then setting out for the site to make a final judgment. The land selected, he hurried to the nearest land office to file his claim; there no greedy tax collectors or petty officials waited to demand a fee; the government was eager to parcel out its lands to the worthy and only a small down payment was required.[25] He must, however, make a vital decision: should he use his funds to buy as much as possible for speculative resale as American frontiersmen did, or should he purchase only the acreage that he could till? Tempting though speculation might be, most image-makers advised buying a workable farm of forty acres.[26] And why not? That was an estate that a wealthy landlord in Europe might envy.

Then came that supreme moment when he realized that he owned a whole farm! A farm of his own! How impossible that had seemed in the

---

[23] The ease of obtaining land was stressed in virtually every book about America, including such diverse works as A. R. Fulton, "An Invitation to Immigrants," *The Palimpset* 18 (July 1937): 236, and Friedrich Gerstäcker, *Mississippi-Bilder: Licht-und Schattenseiten Transatlantischen Lebens* (Jena, 1847–48), p. 506.

[24] Ágoston Haraszthy, *Utazás Északamerikában* (Pest, 1844), 1: 121. Similar advice is in: William Savage, *Observations on Emigration to the United States of America* (London, 1819), p. 24; Gunnar J. Malmin, ed., "The Disillusionment of an Immigrant: Sjur Jørgensen Haaeim's 'Information on Conditions in North America,'" *Norwegian-American Historical Association Studies and Records* 3 (1928): 7–8; Kalikst Wolski, *American Impressions* (Cheshire, Conn., 1968), pp. 48–49; and *Cassell's Emigrants' Handbook: Being a Guide to the Various Fields of Emigration in All Parts of the Globe* (London, 1852), p. 24. Friedrich Gerstäcker's novels, particularly his *Nach Amerika*, devoted pages to warnings against land jobbers. These are discussed in Nelson Van de Luyster, "Gerstäcker's Novels about Emigrants to America," *German-American Review* 20 (June–July 1954): 23.

[25] Moritz Beyer, *Das Auswanderungsbuch oder Rührer und Ratgeber bei der Auswanderung nach Nordamerika und Texas* (Leipzig, 1846), pp. 144–45, 164, 169–70. For comparable opinions see Axel Bruun, *Breve fra Amerika* (Oslo, 1870), p. 25; M. Wilson Gray, *Self-Paying Colonization in North America* (Dublin, 1848), p. 20; and *Wiley and Putnam's Emigrant Guide* (London, 1845), pp. 82–83.

[26] Among the many guidebooks warning against taking up too much land were: William Darby, *The Emigrant's Guide to the Western and Southwestern States and Territories* (New York, 1818), pp. 297–98; and Henry Duhring, *Remarks on the United States of America with Regard to the Actual State of Europe* (London, 1833), p. 173.

crowded Old World. Now the land was his forever, for no emperor or king or duke or count or bishop shared in his freehold. His forever, to use as he wished. If anyone did try to take it from him he had the right to put a bullet through the intruder's head or call in the neighbors for a lynching bee. He and his children and his children's children were guaranteed freedom from want and care forever and forever. No need to fear old age now; the twilight years of his life would fade away "as serenely as a prairie sunset."[27] He had earned the good Lord's favor by obeying the Eleventh Commandment of all frontiersmen: "Go forth and possess good land."[28]

There were still payments to be completed, but that posed no problem. Two or three good crops within the four-year period allowed by the government would meet that obligation, with enough left over to support the family. Farm implements, seed, draft animals, tools, and livestock would be needed, but those cost little; estimates for all expenses, including land, in the Mississippi Valley at mid-century ranged from $277.50 to $345, although one realistic guidebook author warned that as much as $1,115 might be necessary.[29] Food was no problem; enough potatoes could be planted in the spring to last the family through the winter, while game was plentiful ("in the whole United States hunting and fishing is absolutely free"), and the wild hogs that roamed the countryside belonged to anyone who would bother to slaughter them.[30]

For those with absolutely no financial resources jobs were easy to find along the labor-hungry frontiers, as farm workers for men and kitchen helpers for women. Wages of a dollar a day were usual, allowing a thrifty young man who could live on two dollars weekly, to save the five dollars each week needed to buy four acres of government land.[31] Or he might choose to work for a farmer who would pay off in land, usually at the rate of fifty acres a year, plus keep and a small wage.[32] Young women could do almost as well, earning enough as servants in a year to buy their husbands a farm. Many a story was told of penniless newcomers who worked for six months to buy fifty acres of land, added a cabin and livestock, and within

[27] Henryk Sienkiewicz, *Portrait of America: Letters of Henryk Sienkiewicz* (New York, 1959), p. 38. Similar glowing accounts are in George M. Stephenson, "When America was the Land of Canaan," *Minnesota History* 10 (September 1929): 241–42.

[28] John Regan, *The Emigrant's Guide to the Western States of America* (Edinburgh, 1852), p. 203.

[29] *Emigration: Who Should Go; How to Get There; and What to Take* (London, 1843), p. 9; Gray, *Self-Paying Colonization in North America*, p. 27; Ralph Gregory, ed., "Count Baudissin on Missouri Towns," *Missouri Historical Society Bulletin* 27 (January 1971): 113.

[30] William G. Bek, ed., "Gottfried Duden's Report," *Missouri Historical Review* 12 (January 1919): 170–71.

[31] Michel Chevalier, *Society, Manners and Politics in the United States: Being a Series of Letters on North America* (Boston 1839), p. 343; Vere Foster, *Work and Wages* (London 1855), p. 14.

[32] Alan Conway, ed., *The Welsh in America: Letters from the Immigrants* (Minneapolis, 1961), p. 84; *Advice to Immigrants who Intend to Settle in the United States of America* (Bristol, 1832), p. 18; *America*, 1 January 1883.

four years sold out for $500 or more, then used their profits to buy four times as much land farther to the west.[33] "There is no country in the world," wrote a Scottish traveler, "where a farmer can commence operations with so small an outlay of money."[34]

The first farm was only the beginning. Following the pioneers was a wave of later-comers that would continue to flow so long as land in the West remained cheaper than in the East. As they bid for farms they drove prices higher and higher; land that had been cleared only a few years before was normally worth from eight to ten times its original price. This, said the image-makers, allowed an ambitious pioneer to sell out, move westward, and purchase a new farm double the size of the old one, with a tidy profit to boot. Only a few such moves were needed to build a fortune. On this point evidence was abundant; "America Letters" by the score told of farms worth between fifty and one hundred thousand dollars that had begun with a one hundred-dollar investment.[35] So commonplace was belief in this miracle that a French novelist was taken seriously when he described a character who planned to invest $125 in a single-acre farm, plant corn that would produce a whole ear from a single kernel, use the proceeds from that acre to buy ten more, and within a few years become a millionaire.[36] Why not? All things were possible in that land of promise.

This was the message repeated time after time in guidebooks, immigration newspapers, and "America Letters," varying in language but never in theme, as successful emigrants described their successes:

"Here a young man can soon become a well-to-do farmer if he works hard."

"Any man here that will work and save his earnings, and make use of his brains will grow rich."

"The ease of making a living here and the increasing prosperity of the farmers, year by year and day by day, exceeds anything we anticipated."

"One crop is enough to pay for the land and the labor and a good year's wage for the man at the end."

"A farm hand, starting without a cent, can in three or four years possess himself of his own homestead of thirty or forty acres, his own free for all time."

[33] F. A. Evans, *The Emigrant's Directory* (London, 1833), p. 78; Theodore C. Blegen, ed., *The Land of Their Choice: The Immigrants Write Home* (Minneapolis, 1955), pp. 23–24.
[34] Patrick Shirreff, *A Tour through North America: Together with a Comprehensive View of the Canadas and United States* (Edinburgh, 1835), p. 446.
[35] *American Settler*, 1 January 1872, 17 July 1880, 28 January 1888; George M. Stephenson, ed., "Typical America Letters," *Yearbook of the Swedish Historical Society of America* 7 (1921–22): 91; Lyder L. Unstad, "Norwegian Migration to Texas: An Historical Resume with Four 'America Letters,'" *Southwestern Historical Quarterly* 43 (October 1939): 193.
[36] Gabriel Ferry, *Les Squatters* (Paris, 1858), p. 15.

Land of Opportunity

"A man can make more money here in three months . . . than he can in England in twelve months." ·

"I can see no reason why, with ordinary good luck, blessed with patience and perseverance, you should not prosper equal to your utmost expectations."[37]

These were not the views of profit-seeking promoters; this was the testimony of friends and neighbors, never to be questioned. The London *Times* was only half facetious when it noted that if one believed the claims of successful emigrants there was more money to be made honestly in the West than by stealing in the East.[38]

Best of all, these assured profits could never be drained away by tax collectors, or squandered by wastrel children. Taxes were unknown in frontier communities, the image-makers assured their readers; oft-repeated was the assurance of recently arrived emigrants that "all we grow is our own; we have no tax, nor poor rates."[39] Children, while no less plentiful than in Europe, were an asset rather than a liability. Even as youngsters they could be used for small tasks, and as they grew older assume more and more of the farm duties. Nor were they a drain on their parents when they matured, for all had the experience and means to become pioneer farmers themselves on cheap land farther to the west. When an emigrant wrote that "a numerous family is the most profitable kind of cattle we can raise," he was voicing an appeal that many an over-burdened family head in the old country found irresistible.[40] "Mr. Malthus," another wrote, "would not be understood here."[41]

The rewards of pioneering were abundant and certain, but they were not for all Europeans. On this most image-makers agreed, although they differed on one point. Most advised new arrivals to avoid the cutting edge of the frontier, pointing out that only experienced pioneers possessed the stamina and skills required in the initial conquest of the wilderness. "By no means go to the *backwoods* or *new* settlements, for which Americans are perfectly well qualified, but for which Englishmen are totally unquali-

[37] Blegen, ed., *Land of Their Choice*, p. 38; Arnold Schrier, *Ireland and the American Emigration, 1850–1900* (Minneapolis, 1958), p. 25; H. Arnold Barton, ed., *Letters from the Promised Land: Swedes in America, 1840–1914* (Minneapolis, 1975), p. 30; Conway, ed., *The Welsh in America*, p. 111; *American Settler*, 9 April 1881; *America and England Contrasted, in a Series of Letters from Settlers in the United States and Canada* (London, 1832), p. 320; John B. Newhall, *The British Emigrants' Hand Book and Guide to the New States of America* (London, 1844), pp. 62–63.
[38] *Times* (London), 9 January 1883.
[39] *American and England Contrasted*, p. 31. A number of similar remarks by travelers are in Jane L. Mesick, *The English Traveller in America, 1785–1835* (New York, 1922), pp. 26–27.
[40] D. Griffiths, Jr., *Two Years' Residence in the New Settlements of Ohio* (London, 1835), p. 44.
[41] William T. Harris, *Remarks Made during a Tour through the United States of America, in the Years 1817, 1818, and 1819* (Liverpool, 1819), p. 91.

fied," one guidebook warned.[42] Those who held the opposite view answered with one indisputable fact: unsettled lands were cheaper, and the chances for spectacular profits on the outer fringes greater than for those who served as "fillers in." This was worth any risk. A timid immigrant who warned a friend on his way to the outer settlements that "hardship, hunger, want in every way is before you," was answered: "Yes—and a fortune."[43]

That fortune was not for all, wherever they settled. Even the most eloquent propagandists were careful to point out that only the sober and industrious could share in the West's cornucopia of riches, and to warn those unwilling to labor, or unable to accept the frontier's strict moral code, to stay at home. There was no place for the drone in the beehive of frontier activity. Cruelly hard work was the lot of all who would succeed, for "by the sweat of thy brow shalt thou eat bread," was a firmly enforced commandment along the frontiers. The first-comers bore the brunt of these labors, but even those who came later were expected to work from dawn to dusk. Those unwilling to share would be driven out or "hated out" of the community. "For the lazy, good-for-nothing, dissolute and scandalous," they were told, "this land is of as little value as their Fatherland."[44]

This warning was drummed home over and over again. The aged who were beyond the years of active labor,[45] idealists expecting to spend their days in contemplation rather than physical labor (one Hungarian intellectual seeking a job was turned away at farm after farm when the owner found his hands uncalloused),[46] and idle dreamers who "supposed that roast pigeons fly about, crying 'come eat me,' " were doomed to failure.[47] Repeated endlessly by guidebooks and emigration newspapers and "America Letters" was the same refrain: "In America one gets nothing

[42] William Cobbett, *The Emigrant's Guide, in Ten Letters Addressed to the Tax-Payers of England* (London, 1829), p. 124. This same advice was repeated in dozens of books, ranging from such fictional accounts as Gerstäcker, *Mississippi-Bilder*, p. 507, to serious discussions of emigration such as Gray, *Self-Paying Colonization in North America*, p. 16.

[43] *American Settler*, 2 September 1872. Similar views are in *Tegg's Handbook for Emigrants; Containing Useful Information and Practical Directions* (London, 1839), pp. 12–13; Julian U. Niemcewicz, *Podróże po Ameryce 1797–1807* (Wrocław, 1959), p. 41; and Imre Somogyvári, *Amerikai levelek* (Budapest, 1883), pp. 20–25.

[44] Conway, ed., *The Welsh in America*, p. 273.

[45] *The Pacific Northwest* (New York, 1882), p. 78; Fredrika Bremer, *America of the Fifties: Letters of Fredrika Bremer* (New York, 1924), p. 208; Barton, ed., *Letters from the Promised Land*, p. 195.

[46] Sándor Lukácsy, ed., *László Arvay: Hányódásom Amerikában* (Budapest, 1953), pp. 127–28.

[47] Friedrich Gerstäcker, *The Wanderings and Fortunes of Some German Emigrants* (New York, 1848), p. 103. A comparable statement is in Newhall, *The British Emigrants' Hand Book*, pp. 74–75.

Land of Opportunity

without work"; "Work!—work!—work!—must be the order of the day for all who emigrate"; "America is not the place for young men who have not made up their minds to work"; "Everybody must work here with his own hands"; "Nobody in Norway knows what it means to work oneself bone-tired."[48] This was the word from on high. Europeans were left with no doubts that labor was essential to success in the American West.

They were also left with no doubt that labor along the frontiers brought its just rewards as it did not in Europe. Let a man work hard, let him be prepared to live modestly and sacrifice a few comforts, and he would be assured a degree of prosperity unknown in the "labour-stocked quarters of the globe."[49] This was the basic difference between the New World and the Old; in one dawn-to-dusk toil meant affluence, in the other sustenance. As a new arrival from Wales put it, "You need to work as hard here as in any part of the world, but elsewhere it is to pay taxes, whereas here it buys a farm."[50] The European peasant groaned through his daily tasks for he realized that others would reap the profits; the frontiersmen was cheerfully happy in his work for he knew that he was "in a fair way of realizing a happy independence."[51] This was the basic difference, and an important one. For the industrious the American West was truly a land of promise.

The Rewards of Labor

Prosperity was assured the hard-working, the image-makers insisted, because agricultural prospects on the frontier were boundless. America's virgin soils had only to be stirred to pour forth their fruits in unbelievable abundance. The Mississippi Valley particularly inspired guidebook authors and land promoters to rapturous prose, with those touting each territory outdoing their rivals in extravagant claims: Ohio's soils were "truly astounding"; those of Illinois "inexhaustively productive" with vegetable mould fifty to sixty feet deep; in Minnesota the "fat black mull" would never lose its richness; in Iowa "from five to twenty feet of rich black earth," stretched for miles "as flat as a board without a single stone near it"; in Missouri a "thick bed of black leaf-mould," not only filled every valley but extended over hills and mountains; in Nebraska hundreds of

[48] Theodore C. Blegen, ed., *Ole Rynning's True Account of America* (Minneapolis, 1926), p. 93; Regan, *The Emigrant's Guide to the Western States*, p. vi; Emmons, *Garden in the Grasslands*, pp. 33–34.
[49] Alice Mann, *The Emigrant's Complete Guide to the United States of America* (Leeds, 1850), pp. iv–v.
[50] Conway, ed., *The Welsh in America*, p. 273.
[51] Ibid., p. 70.

[*231*]

thousands of acres could be tilled "with no stones or stumps to hinder the cultivator's plow"; in Texas a "black, waxy soil" rich in vegetable mould covered the surface to a depth of twenty feet with "nothing like a hillock or stone," to bother the plowman.[52] Cultivating soils such as these was child's play, a "light and happy work" to be compared to that of children making mud pies.[53] And, best of all, millions and millions of acres awaited the plow—enough to provide every peasant in Europe with a farm.[54]

Such lands required almost no care. After the first plowing the pioneer needed only throw seed into the furrow, and the Good Lord did the rest; the second and successive plantings were even easier, for then the earth had only to be lightly scratched to produce abundant crops. Once placed under cultivation the fields could be ignored, for the soils were so rich and deep that they needed no manuring for at least a century. A traveler in Illinois talked with a farmer who was about to burn down his barn because it was too full of manure to admit his animals; the land was no better for fertilizing, he said, so "what's the use on't."[55] Some even maintained that the soil grew richer with each planting, with the crops multiplying in size correspondingly.[56]

The yields from such soils were predictably gargantuan—as the image-makers described them. Every unused space was blanketed with natural grasses standing four to six feet tall, offering free pasturage.[57] Wheat, barley, and rye normally grew to a height of ten or twelve feet and produced fifty bushels to the acre (in contrast with the fifteen or eighteen in Europe), with some yields of a hundred bushels reported.[58] Corn, the

[52] Charles Sealsfield, *The Americans As They Are: Described in a Tour through the Valley of the Mississippi* (London, 1828), p. 11; Roy W. Swanson, "Some Swedish Emigrant Guide Books of the Second Half of the Nineteenth Century," *Swedish Historical Society of America Yearbook* 40 (1926): 109; Fredrika Bremer, *The Homes of the New World: Impressions of America* (New York, 1853), 1: 143; Conway, ed., *The Welsh in America*, p. 111; Alice H. Finckh, "Gottfried Duden Views Missouri, 1824–1827," *Missouri Historical Review* 43 (October 1949): 335; Barton, ed., *Letters from the Promised Land*, p. 187; Charles Sealsfield, *Frontier Life; or, Scenes and Adventures in the South West* (New York, 1855), p. 78; *American Settler*, 1 August 1873. Virtually every issue of the *American Settler*, an immigration newspaper published in London between 1872 and 1892, contained lengthy informative articles on agricultural prospects in the western states, all so favorable that they were probably prepared by emigration and land promoters.
[53] E. A. Curley, *Nebraska, Its Advantages, Resources and Drawbacks* (London, 1875), pp. 219–20.
[54] William and Robert Chambers, *The Emigrant's Manual: British America and the United States* (Edinburgh, 1851), p. 105, contains a typical statement.
[55] Regan, *The Emigrant's Guide to the Western States*, p. 52.
[56] Blegen, ed., *The Land of Their Choice*, p. 356.
[57] Unstad, "Norwegian Migration to Texas," pp. 184–85; George M. Stephenson, ed., "Documents Relating to Peter Cassel and the Settlement of New Sweden," *Swedish-American Historical Bulletin* 2 (February 1929): 22–28, 55–62.
[58] *American Settler*, 1 November 1872.

staple crops of the frontier, sent up twenty-foot stalks "as thick as little trees," with each stalk having from fifteen to twenty ears of a thousand kernels each.[59] Two or more crops a year were usual, for the long growing season and the rich soils hurried ripening.[60]

Stories of each abundance inspired a whole libraryful of tall tales that were eagerly reprinted by travelers—and perhaps not entirely unbelieved: land so waxy-rich that settlers made candles by dipping wicks in mud puddles; fields that yielded one hundred acres of corn when cultivated, seventy-five when not, and fifty when not even planted; soils so fertile that a crowbar stuck in the ground produced a crop of nails by morning; a Texan whose sheep starved to death because they were so fat that they could not move to the next pasture.[61] Clearly anything was possible in that wonderland of Nature.

Bountiful crops meant abundant food. To Old World peasants existing on a little fish, potatoes, and bread "as black as the earth and as hard as stones" (as one of them remembered)[62] the accounts of the image-makers were mouth-watering assurance that a land of plenty waited beyond the seas. There wild game was plentiful, for no laws and no snooping officials restrained hunters; a few hours of shooting would yield "a fat buck and a young bear, . . . several wild geese, and a turkey or two," or if one was lucky as many as a full dozen bears and several dozens of deer."[63] Add these to the cereals and pork and fruits produced on every frontier farm and the humblest newcomer could live better than lords and ladies in Europe.

Not a farmer but whose table groaned under a variety of foods. Meat, so seldom available to the Old World peasant, was part of the daily diet; the phrase "we eat meat three times a day" was repeated in "America Letter" after "America Letter" that crossed the Atlantic. And with meat, all manner of delicacies unfamiliar to Europe's poor: "We have good bread and wheat flour and as much beef and pork as we desire at each meal"; "We have all the butter, eggs and milk we need"; "We have wheat bread and meat every day, sugar syrup at every meal, and eggs as well as many

[59] *American Settler*, 7 August 1880; *Sequel to the Counsel for Emigrants* (Aberdeen, 1834), p. 22; Ferdinand Ernst, *Bemerkungen auf einer Reise durch das Innere der Vereinigten Staaten von Nord-Amerika im Jahre 1819* (Hildesheim, 1820), p. 93; Blegen, ed., *Ole Rynning's True Account of America*, pp. 79–80.
[60] Hans A. Foss, *Tobias: A Story of the Northwest* (Minneapolis, 1899), p. 23.
[61] James K. Paulding, *The Lion of the West: Retitled the Kentuckian, or a Trip to New York* (Stanford, 1954), p. 62; *American Settler*, 12 March 1881.
[62] Franklin D. Scott, "The Causes and Consequences of Emigration in Sweden," *The Chronicle: A Quarterly Publication of the American-Swedish Historical Foundation* 2 (Spring 1955): 28.
[63] Charles W. Webber, *Tales of the Southern Border* (Philadelphia, 1853), p. 295; Charles Sealsfield, *The Squatter Chief; or, The First American in Texas* (New York, 1844), p. 277.

other things as often as desired"; "Our daily food consists of rye and wheat bread, bacon, butter, eggs, molasses, sugar, coffee and beer."[64] Norwegians reveled in unaccustomed luxuries—strawberries, raspberries, blackberries—and a delicious new dish "which is called *pai.*"[65] "The hired labourers," a traveler reported, ". . . are provided with better fare than falls to the lot of thousands of the 'genteel' classes in England."[66]

The lavishly spread tables of frontier inns were a favorite theme of travelers, novelists, and balladists. Old World gourmets might raise eyebrows at a breakfast table groaning under "pigsfeet pickled in pepper and vinegar, corncakes drowned in molasses, custards, a roast turkey, venisons, hams, eggs, with an immense quantity of fruits preserved in sugar or vinegar, persimmons, the delicious Louisiana cherry, prunes and wild grapes," but those with less sensitive palates could only envy.[67] Nor could half-starved Europeans weep over the plight of one pioneer who twice filled his plate with chicken, turkey, venison, yams, meat, fish, and potatoes, then ordered a bowl of soup because "soup trickles down . . . where roast beef and ham try to enter in vain."[68]

Here was abundance worth celebrating, as the ballad makers recognized. They responded with a will:

> In America the hogs eat their fill of raisins and dates
> that everywhere grow wild, and when they are thirsty
> they drink from ditches flowing with wine.[69]

Or they sang:

> Over there, tea and coffee and clotted cream fairly
> drown the settlers; pork and wheat are one's daily
> bread, and everyone lolls in the lap of fortune.[70]

Or they tempted the young with:

> Candy for bread comes wherever one goes,
> And in chocolate muffins you wade;

[64] Stephenson, ed., "Typical America Letters," pp. 78, 82; Blegen, ed., *The Land of Their Choice,* p. 268.
[65] Blegen, ed., *The Land of Their Choice,* pp. 269–70. A similar letter of 1830 records that "they have on the table puddings, pyes, and fruits of all kinds that was in season, and preserves, pickles, vegetables, meats, and everything that a persons could wish." G. Poulett Scrope, *Extracts of Letters from Poor Persons Who Emigrated Last Year to Canada and the United States* (London, 1832), p. 104.
[66] William Chambers, *Things As They Are in America* (London, 1854), pp. 342–43. Similar sentiments are in *America and England Contrasted,* p. 38; Cobbett, *The Emigrant's Guide,* p. 67; *Counsel for Emigrants, and Interesting Information from Numerous Sources, with Original Letters* (Aberdeen, 1834), p. 129; and Ernst, *Bemerkungen auf einer Reise,* 106.
[67] Sealsfield, *The Squatter Chief,* p. 308.
[68] Charles Sealsfield, quoted in *America Glorious and Chaotic Land: Charles Sealsfield Discovers Young United States,* ed. E. L. Jordan (Englewood Cliffs, N. J., 1969), p. 45.
[69] Stephenson, ed., "Documents Relating to Peter Cassel," p. 182. The same ballad, in somewhat different form, is in Barton, ed., *Letters from the Promised Land,* pp. 33–34.
[70] Theodore C. Blegen, ed., *Norwegian Emigrant Songs and Ballads* (Minneapolis, 1936), p. 69.

> With sugar pebbles it hails and snows
> And rains with lemonade.[71]

In that land of plenty (as one Swedish balladist wrote) "chickens fly in on
the table with knife and fork in their thighs," begging to be eaten.[72] This
did not seem improbable amidst such abundance.

Europeans who failed to take advantage of such a golden opportunity
were to be pitied, not scorned. Why, the image-makers asked, should the
ambitious remain in decaying Europe where a family ate less in a year
than was thrown to the dogs in a week by frontier housewives?[73] Why,
with hundreds of thousands of fertile acres lying idle, should Europe's im-
poverished despair of the future for themselves and their children?[74]
Asked a ballad maker:

> Why should men strive and faint with pain and cold,
> For want of purer air and stronger food;
> When o'er the seas lie plain, and hill, and wood,
> Nigh tenantless: Where, if the heart be bold,
> The leagues of land bear fruit an hundred fold.[75]

Sighed an immigrant who had succeeded in the New World: "It often
weighs on my heart that I am to enjoy all the good things alone."[76] Thousands of those left behind were convinced by the image-makers that they
should ease their heartache by joining him in the good fortune.

Frontier Success—and Failure

One question must have haunted would-be emigrants as they read these
rose-tinted accounts of frontier abundance: could they be believed? Was
the West really the land of milk and honey promised by the novelists and
guidebook authors and land salesmen? The credibility of the least responsible promoters was justifiably questioned; the greater the exaggeration
the less effective the propaganda. Instead the image-makers who proved
most influential were those who promised the least, and who had themselves been tested by the frontiering experience. Their testimony, balanced against the dire warnings of the few who failed, offered a reasonably
fair picture of the prospects and perils of the American West.

[71] Christian Winther, *The Flight to America, Rewritten from the Danish by Piet Hein Gyldendal* (Denmark, 1978), unpaged. This delightful ballad, first published in Denmark in 1830, tells of a little boy who was determined to run away from home but changed his mind when his mother called him to dinner. I am indebted to Professor Vagn Wåhlin of the Historical Institute, Aarhus University, for a copy.

[72] Robert L. Wright, ed., *Swedish Emigrant Ballads* (Lincoln, Nebr., 1965), p. 39.

[73] Gottfried Duden, *Bericht einer Reise nach dem westlichen Staaten Nord-Amerikas und eines mehrjährigen Aufenthalts am Missouri (1824–1827)* (Elberfeld, 1829), pp. 233–34.

[74] Regan, *The Emigrants Guide to the Western States*, p. 46.

[75] *American Settler*, 1 February 1872.

[76] Quoted in Weber, *America in Imaginative German Literature*, pp. 219–20.

The theme of these moderates was a sensible one: the American frontier did not guarantee a future of affluence and security but the chances for both were higher there than in overcrowded Europe. A manifesto signed in 1845 by eighty newly arrived Norwegians put the case fairly: "We have no expectation of gaining riches; but we live under a liberal government in a fruitful land . . . where each of us is at liberty to earn his living practically as he chooses."[77] Vast fortunes might be the lot of the fortunate few, they were saying, but for the many the assurance of daily bread must suffice—an assurance that Europe could not provide. A successful emigrant summed up the matter when he told his former neighbors: "I am where neither affluence nor poverty is known, where every man may produce by his own industry, everything in the world to make him comfortable."[78] The West, in other words, was a Land of Opportunity, not a Land of Abundance. This was the true message of the image-makers who could be trusted.

That message was amply documented by the testimony of emigrants who had settled along the frontiers—and succeeded. Now and then a particularly successful—or boastful—individual could not help bragging of the fortune he had accumulated: a four-thousand-acre farm that had quadrupled in value in four years; a Texas estate so productive that its owner would soon be able to do nothing but sit in the shade and drink wine made from his own nectarines; a rancher with such large herds that he thought he owned fifteen thousand horses but was not sure.[79] Most made no such pretentions. Instead they listed their modest successes in simple prose: "I have a capital farm of one hundred acres cleared and under crops"; "Our farm is worth 5 or 6 thousand dollars"; "We sold our farm last winter for $880"; "We have five horses, seventeen cattle, thirteen sheep, and twenty-four hogs"; "I own a nice dwelling house with stables attached, four horses, eight milk cows, ten head of cattle, nine head of young cattle, and six pigs"; "We have got one black cow and one heifer. I have built a cowshed and we have got six cart loads of hay."[80] Unspectacular

[77] Quoted in Blegen, ed., *The Land of Their Choice*, pp. 194–95.
[78] Quoted in Charlotte Erickson, "Agrarian Myths of English Immigrants," in *In the Trek of the Immigrants*, ed. Oscar F. Ander (Rock Island, 1964), pp. 74–75. Similar views are in Mann, *The Emigrant's Complete Guide*, p. 68; Theodore C. Blegen, ed., "Norwegians in the West in 1844: A Contemporary Account," *Norwegian-American Historical Association Studies and Records* 1 (1926): 118; and Sienkiewicz, *Portrait of America*, pp. 105–6.
[79] Schrier, *Ireland and the American Emigration*, pp. 38–39; Mark E. Nackman, *A Nation within a Nation: The Rise of Texas Nationalism* (Port Washington, N.Y., 1975), János Xantus, *Utazás Kalifornia déli részeiben* (Pest, 1860), p. 11.
[80] The quotations are from the following sources: Chambers, *Things As They Are in America*, pp. 129–30; Charlotte Erickson, *Invisible Immigrants: The Adaptation of English and Scottish Immigrants in Nineteenth Century America* (London, 1972), p. 188; George M. Stephenson, "The Background of the Beginnings of Swedish Immigration, 1850–1875," *American Historical Review* 31 (July 1926), pp. 719–20; *American Settler*, 7 May 1881; and Hvidt, *Flight to America*, pp. 184–85.

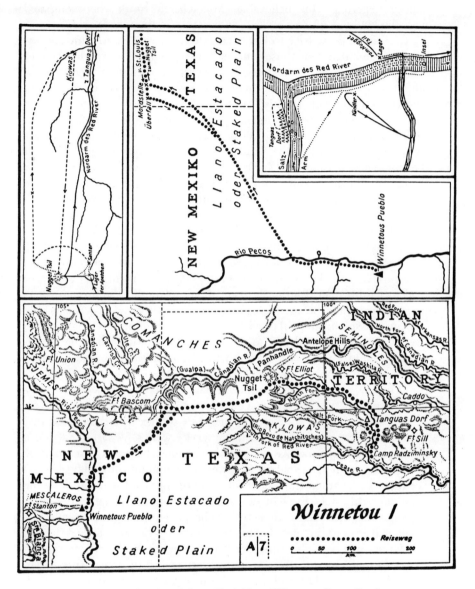

Map reproduced from Karl May, *Winnetou: Erster Band*
(Bamberg, West Germany, 1951). Rear endpaper.

triumphs, perhaps, but believable. And what fortunes when compared with the holdings of even well-to-do peasants in the Old World.

Even more persuasive to Europeans debating a move to America was the calm confidence of those who had just stepped aboard the frontier escalator. New arrivals, just about to purchase their first farms, never doubted that success awaited them; this was the sure fate of those bold enough to try. Wrote a British lad to his father: "I look forward, with a confident mind and well-founded hope, to the time, as not far distant, *when I shall be a freeholder.* . . . What others have done why may not I accomplish?"[81] And why not? Self-confidence underlay the whole spirit of the frontier. Over and over again the "America Letters" radiated faith in the future: "I can, myself, if I have luck and health, have, in two or three years as good a farm and house as any common farmer near Syke-House"; "If I have my life and health for a little while I shall be a burden to no one";[82] This seemed reasonable. As a balladist proclaimed, "Uncle Sam is rich enough to give us all a farm,"[83] and with land the future was secure.

For those with an itch for greater riches, a spirit of daring-do, and a little capital, speculation in town sites and village lots offered a quicker road to wealth than frontier farming. Town planting, the image-makers pointed out, could be anyone's business; all that was needed was a little land, permission from local officials, a hired surveyor or two to lay out the streets, and enough audacity to set up shop. This meant bribing a merchant to build a store, a blacksmith to take up residence, and a householder or two to build ramshackle cabins, and the business of selling lots could begin.[84] Profits could be spectacular. Europeans learned that thirty years after the land on which Chicago was located was purchased for $500, a single lot sold for $10,000; of the ex-soldier who discovered that bounty lands awarded him for military service were now part of a western city and valued at $300,000; of frontier villages where lots that could be brought for five dollars sold for five times that amount thirty days later.[85] For those with capital and a taste for adventuring, land speculating in the West offered as much excitement—and danger—as hunting grizzly bears.

Success stories such as these were believable to Europeans because the image-makers—or the most honest among them—did not conceal the fact that failure was possible in frontier America. They made no secret of the fact that emigrants must be constantly alert against dishonest speculators and land-sharpers. Oft-told were tales of newcomers who arrived with

[81] Cobbett, *The Emigrant's Guide,* 47.
[82] *America and England Contrasted,* 34–35; Conway, ed., *The Welsh in America,* 56.
[83] *The Welsh in America,* p. 112.
[84] Gregory, ed., "Count Baudissin on Missouri Towns," p. 115.
[85] Wolski, *American Impressions,* pp. 64–65; Chambers, *Things As They Are in America,* pp. 143–44; *American Settler,* 1 January 1885.

high hopes, fell into the hands of a glib-tongued scoundrel who sold them barren land far from transportation, were cheated of the rest of the capital by loan sharks, and were reduced to performing menial tasks for others.[86] "I started to build castles in the air when I left the Kløfta Station," one such account began, then went on to describe how he had lost his property and wandered from job to job until all hope was gone.[87] Such stark tragedies were repeated all too often along the frontiers.

Yet not as often as the image-makers suggested, many Europeans believed, for antiimmigration propagandists were suspected of being hirelings of wealthy landlords and factory owners alarmed by the diminishing supply of labor. There was some basis for these suspicions. By the closing years of the century the lessening supply of workers was driving wages upward in Germany and the Scandinavian countries, sending a wave of apprehension among employers. Their concern, and the vast influence that they and their wealth exerted, stirred a counterdrive that offset much of the favorable propaganda that had glorified the land of promise.

This took many forms, all stressing the theme of frontier failure. Novelists played a leading role. Their books, popular especially in Germany, were many, with those of Theodor Griesinger (*Emigrantengeschichten*), Graf Adelbert von Baudissin (*Peter Tutt*), and Friedrich Gerstäcker (*Deutsche Auswanderer*) most prominent. All played a common tune: trusting emigrants lured to the frontier by lying propagandists, duped of their savings by dishonest land agents, broken by the hardships of pioneering, and ending as pitiful failures lamenting the fact that they had ever left the Fatherland.[88] Playwrights, too, capitalized on the them: Henrik Wergeland's *The Mountain Hut* cast the villain as a silver-tongued sharper who lured young men to disaster by promising them that in America "silver and gold will jingle in every man's purse."[89]

Antiemigration propaganda played a particularly prominent role in Norway where the exodus of young men stirred upper-class resentment to the boiling point. Typical was a bitter novel by Hans A. Foss, *Hvide Slaver*, published in 1893 as agrarian discontent was sweeping the American West. Foss's grim tale told of a band of Norwegians making their way across the "grassy, endless, plains," scorched by the sun and drenched by torrential rains, to an out-of-the-way settlement where they had been

[86] Theodore C. Blegen, ed., *Peter Testman's Account of His Experiences in North America* (Northfield, 1927), pp. 48–49; Malmin, "The Disillusionment of an Immigrant," pp. 3–8; Conway, ed., *The Welsh in America*, p. 130.

[87] Nebraska letter in the possession of Professor Ingrid Semmingsen.

[88] These works are examined in Preston A. Barba, "Emigration to America Reflected in German Fiction," *German-American Annals* 16 (November–December 1914): 216–21. Gerstäcker's tragic story has been published in translation as *The Wanderings and Fortunes of Some German Immigrants* (New York, 1848).

[89] The plot is summarized in Blegen, ed., *Norwegian Emigrant Songs and Ballads*, pp. 75–98.

bilked into buying land. They found a run-down community of ram-shackle cabins, crowded with saloons and overrun by moneylenders who lay in wait to rob them of their holdings. "One saw," Foss wrote, "how the farmers lounged about the saloons in a delirium, while the wheat ripened on the stalks and dropped into the field—while hay rotted in stock on the hay-racks, while the plow lay rusted and unused by the field's edge—while the mortgage bonds stung and sucked the farmer's necks like Spanish flies, and wives and children sat waiting and weeping through nights and days."[90] Gross exaggeration, of course, but strong medicine was necessary to offset the image-makers who for a century had pictured the American West as a land of milk and honey.

Hans Foss's bitter judgment was a product not only of the anti-emigration sentiment inspired by landlords struggling to retain cheap labor, but of changed conditions in the western United States. The prolonged agricultural depression that underlay Grangerism and Populism was indeed changing the West from a land of opportunity to a land of despair. By the 1890s too, word was spreading in Europe that good lands in the public domain were nearing exhaustion as the frontier era drew to a close.[91] America was still a land of opportunity for Europe's dispossessed, but the magnets that attracted them in the years ahead were to be mills and factories, not virgin fields. Frontier opportunity, and the image-makers who had trumpeted its prospects, had played their role and were to vanish into history.

[90]   Hans A. Foss, *Hvide Slaver: En Social-politisk Skildring* (Oslo, 1893), pp. 150, 156–157. An excellent case study of the antiimmigration movement in one nation is Franklin D. Scott, "Sweden's Constructive Opposition to Emigration," *Journal of Modern History* 37 (September 1965): 307–35.
[91]   *American Settler*, 5 May 1888, 18 July 1891.

XI

Land of Equality

IF ANY PHRASE appeared more often in "America Letters" than "We eat meat three times a day," it was "Here we tip our hats to no one." For the West of the image-makers' creation was not only a Land of Opportunity but a Land of Equality, where every man saw himself as good as his neighbor, where each was free to think as he pleased, and where the humblest peasant was as powerful in political decision making as the most elegant gentleman. In all the United States, but especially along the frontiers, equality, liberty, and democracy were enshrined, not as distant goals, but as the accepted rules of society.

This was a startling—and appealing—concept to Europeans, accustomed to life in a land where authority was concentrated in the landed class. There all with property to exchange for labor—whether landlords or factory owners or shop keepers—expected unquestioning obedience from their employees, and with obedience went subservience. This relationship could be maintained only by a strict separation of classes; employers and employees lived on different social levels, with any mingling frowned upon. Any bridging of this gap was unthinkable.

Nor was it possible for a peasant farmer or worker to move upward into the employer class, for the tradition of an immobile social order was too firmly established to be questioned. One was born to a trade and status, and there one remained. A cottager or a clockmaker or a miller knew that he would be a cottager or a clockmaker or a miller all his life, just as his father before him and his children after him. He knew also that he had been assigned a position in society as "wealthy," "of modest circumstances," "low paid," or one of the "worthy poor." This was as much his fate as to be tall or short, fat or thin, light or dark.

Even the most outspoken social reformers accepted these divisions as irrevocable, and never dared suggest that the "worthy poor" be moved up a notch to become the "low paid." This was as unthinkable as it was impossible. When a Danish critic wrote of the deprived classes he was seeking to aid that "they have their needs, and we have our duties," he gave not the slightest thought to the possibility that "they" could become "we." Instead reformers sought to alleviate the sorry plight of the poor by assuring them a larger slice of the pie, not by allowing them to move upward to a better post suited to their talents.[1] They, and the entire populace, accepted as an immutable law of nature the division of society into rigidly defined classes that determined a man's status from birth to death. "A confederacy of the few to reduce the many to subjugation," one critic complained, with some justification.[2]

To a growing army of liberals, and to a good many of the common folk, this stagnant social system was increasingly irksome. Their hopes for a better world had been stirred by the French Revolution and the uprisings of mid-century, only to be dashed in a resurgent wave of conservatism. Now they saw the working classes trapped in an immutable class system, condemned forever to "the old dog-trot way of their forefathers."[3] To those who harbored such discontent, the news of a land beyond the seas where men were judged by their worth rather than their lineage, and where no traditional restraints bound a person to his trade or class, came as a wind of hope. In such a land,

> Where a man is a man if he's willing to toil
> And the humblest may gather the fruits of the soil,

ambition and merit could be properly rewarded.[4] To reach that land became the dream of half Europe's people. More than sixty percent of those

---

[1]   Most of these concepts are borrowed from Daniel Levine, "Conservatism and Tradition in Danish Social Welfare Legislation, 1890–1933," *Comparative Studies in Society and History* 20 (January 1978): 64–67. Additional insights are in Halvdan Koht, *The American Spirit in Europe: A Survey of Transatlantic Influences* (Philadelphia, 1949), pp. 72–74.

[2]   Morris Birkbeck, *Notes on a Journey in America* (London, 1818), p. 114.

[3]   Francis Baily, *Journal of a Tour in the Unsettled Parts of North America in 1796 and 1797* (London, 1856), p. 308.

[4]   Samuel Gompers, *Seventy Years of Life and Labor* (New York, 1925), 1: 19. Gompers testifies that his own desire to migrate was stirred by this song.

asked why they were leaving Holland between 1831 and 1856 answered that they wanted "to improve their social status, their means of livelihood and their fortune."[5]

The Basis of Frontier Equality

Why this difference between Europe and the United States? The image-makers agreed on one sensible answer: in America, they said, and particularly in the American Wests, a man's status was determined by his wealth, not by his heredity. Those with the skill and the energy to accumulate material riches could rise to the very peak of the social order, whatever their background. "Wealth," a visitor wrote, "is the only mark of rank, the only thing that in itself serves to erect a wall or boundary between the lower and the so-called upper classes."[6] In a forming society all were judged not by their lineage but by the rewards (as measured in dollars) that they had earned through service to the community. "What can you do?" not "Who are you, who was your father?" was the question asked of a newcomer to a frontier settlement.[7] When one frontiersman was asked about his ancestors, he replied: "We don't vally those things in this country. It's what's above ground not what's under, that we think on."[8] The lowly born were just as likely to succeed as the scions of the most distinguished families.

Nor would a man's success stir jealousy and envy as it would in Europe, for the more he succeeded in bettering himself, the more he bettered those about him. This was bound to be the case when society was in its infancy and all were striving to increase their wealth and living standards. New arrivals found that "the spirit here is to rejoice in the good fortune of others as well as one's own," and that the wealthiest labored to elevate, rather than depress, those about them.[9] All would benefit as the level of wealth in the community escalated and attracted more settlers and more business. Here was an incentive for self-advancement unknown in older nations.

The image-makers also discovered that frontier conditions doomed the rigid craft system that barred individual progress in the Old World. With a multitude of tasks to be performed, all who could perform them were

[5]   Bertus Wabeke, *Dutch Emigration to North America, 1624–1860* (New York, 1944), pp. 93–94.
[6]   Gustaf Unonius, *A Pioneer in Northwest America, 1841–1858: The Memoirs of Gustaf Unonius* (Minneapolis, 1950–51), 1: 228–29.
[7]   Joseph Hatton, *Today in America* (London, 1881), 2: 38–39.
[8]   Alexander Mackay, *The Western World* (Philadelphia, 1849), 2: 29.
[9]   George M. Stephenson, ed., "Typical America Letters," *Yearbook of the Swedish Historical Society of America* 7 (1921–22): 60–61. Similar sentiments are quoted in Andrew J. Torrielli, *Italian Opinion on America, As Revealed by Italian Travelers, 1850–1900* (Cambridge, 1941), pp. 93–94, and Daniel Blowe, *A Geographical, Historical, Commercial, and Agricultural View of the United States of America* (London, 1820), pp. 72–73.

welcomed, whatever their past occupations. Travelers reported meeting young men who had served successively as teachers, lawyers, preachers, and farmers, or had been peddlers, schoolteachers, tavern keepers, and doctors.[10] Moving from job to job was a sign of enterprise, not shiftlessness, in a land where countless jobs needed doing. "It is a great advantage of this land," said a character in a German novel, "that each may earn his living the way he wants, and doesn't need to be ashamed of it."[11] He might have added that this fluid system awarded individual enterprise and encouraged the ambitious to contribute evermore to society's advance.

These incentives, the image-makers saw, stemmed partly from the opportunities for economic self-advancement made possible by the abundance of untapped natural resources, partly from an open-ended class system that allowed economic success to assure social success. They never tired of stressing the ease with which fortunes could be acquired along the frontiers. So long as land was cheap and labor scarce, anyone willing to work was assured of a well-paid job leading eventually to land ownership. That land was sure to escalate in price as population thickened, allowing more land to be purchased with a corresponding increase in profits. These were his alone; "he has," a visitor reported, "no dread of their being wrested from him by the idle drones who infest other countries."[12] Instead, he could pile riches on riches, for by this time he had been infected with the American craving for the Almighty Dollar, and was doomed never to know contentment. "His idea of equality is to be inferior to none," a French observer noted.[13] This meant constant striving, but it meant also a handsome fortune.

Those who preached this doctrine could parade countless Horatio-Algerish success stories before their readers: the penniless peasant who now basked in luxury; the common laborer who now had his own carriage and "was honored as a person of eminence"; the serving girl who had married the village banker; the blacksmith's helper who had become a successful doctor.[14] Irish lads hearing such tales, could sing joyously:

[10] Charles Barinetti, *A Voyage to Mexico and Havanna; Including Some General Observations on the United States* (New York, 1841), p. 36.
[11] Extracts from the works of Friedrich Gerstäcker that make this point are printed in Bjorne Landa, "The American Scene in Gerstäcker's Fiction" (Ph.D. diss., University of Minnesota, 1952), pp. 145–146.
[12] James Flint, *Letters from America* (Edinburgh, 1822), p. 177.
[13] Michel Chevalier, *Society, Manners and Politics in the United States: Being a Series of Letters on North America* (Boston, 1839), p. 277.
[14] Frederick Gustorf, "Frontier Perils As Told by an Early Illinois Visistor," *Journal of the Illinois State Historical Society* 55 (Summer, 1962): 144; William A. Bell, *New Tracks in North America* (London, 1869), 2: 13; John (János) Xantus, *Letters From North America* (Detroit, 1975), p. 179; William A. Baillie-Grohman, *Camps in the Rockies* (New York, 1882), pp. 348–49.

For it's when we get there, O it's there we'll have plenty
In that bright land of freedom far over the sea.[15]

Every dream of riches would come true in the shining land across the Atlantic.

And with riches something even more important: a chance to be treated as an equal by their betters, a chance to "rise in the world, and to associate with higher company."[16] For on the frontier the social order was fluid, not frozen as in the older countries of the world. In Europe, every station in society was occupied and every place full; in the United States "a man may *create* stations and *make* places."[17] A place among the elite waited the most humble. "Here," a traveler noted, "a gentleman can be made from the coarsest stuff in half a lifetime."[18] A less sympathetic visitor made the same point when he sniffed that "people nowadays use coats of arms who wore coats without arms a few years back."[19]

This was more or less true for all the United States, but the image-makers made clear that social status was most easily elevated amidst frontier abundance. "The farther one goes toward the West," one wrote, ". . . the greater the feeling of equality and democracy."[20] This was inevitable as long as status was determined by wealth rather than lineage, for on the frontiers wealth was more easily attained than in settled societies. There, as one traveler noted, "the ease with which property is acquired by the industrious produces an equality unknown in the Old Countries."[21] In the Wests, too, the social order was in its infancy, with no established elites and no hereditary distinctions. Nothing blocked the road to the top for the ambitious. "Here it is that true republican equality exists," a visitor wrote from a frontier village, "and here only can it exist."[22]

Most important of all, the division of labor essential in established societies was lacking in the thinly settled Wests, and with it the association

[15] Robert L. Wright, ed., *Irish Emigrant Ballads and Songs* (Bowling Green, 1975), p. 118.
[16] *Counsel for Emigrants, and Interesting Information from Numerous Sources, with Original Letters* (Aberdeen, 1834), p. 128.
[17] Calvin Colton, *Manual for Emigrants to America* (London, 1832), pp. 61–62.
[18] Mackay, *The Western World*, 2: 68.
[19] Emily Faithfull, *Three Visits to America* (New York, 1884), p. 136.
[20] Ference Pulszky, *Életem és korom* (Budapest, 1880–82), p. 114. A similar passage is in Charles A. Murray, *Travels in North America during the Years 1834, 1835, and 1836* (London, 1839), 1: 218–19.
[21] Elias P. Fordham, *Personal Narrative of Travels in Virginia, Maryland, Pennsylvania, Ohio, Indiana and Kentucky; and of a Residence in the Illinois Territory, 1817–1818* (Cleveland, 1906), pp. 124–25.
[22] Murray, *Travels in North America*, 2: 85–86. Similar views are in François, marquis de Barbé de Marbois, *Histoire de la Louisiane et de la cession de cette colonie par la France* (Paris, 1829), pp. 48–49; Gilbert Imlay, *A Topographical Description of the Western Territory of North America* (London, 1792), p. 197, and many other travel accounts.

of status with craft. In Europe each occupation was rigidly linked to a spot in the class structure; the lawyer enjoyed a higher place in society than the miller, the cottager than the laborer. In frontier communities where all must labor together to elevate the living standard, every occupation was essential—and respected. The farm worker was as needed as the merchant, the shopkeeper as the distiller, the farmer as the lawyer. "It is immaterial what one does," a Swedish visitor wrote, "so long as he is respected and does his work efficiently."[23] Social distinctions were blurred when menial posts were as important to the community—and paid almost as well—as the professions.

In such a society those who labored hardest to improve themselves, and thus improve the community, were most respected and awarded the highest posts in the social hierarchy, whatever their lineage. "It is a feature of American democracy," an Hungarian observed, "that work is valued, and that birth is not."[24] All were not equal, for some succeeded while others did not, but all were potentially equal. Those who arrived in the West with a distinguished ancestry or a modest fortune had no better chance for social or political success than those who came in rags. An American visiting in England, learning that a rich father intended to give his son £2,000 to buy his way into a western settlement, asked to be allowed to dispose of the sum in the boy's best interest, then burned the money. The son would better succeed by proving himself, he told the irate father, than by any display of wealth.[25] The American West was a land where "the poor were worth as much as the rich," where "the vote of the common man carries as much authority and influence" as that of the wealthy, and where democracy existed "not only as an institution and theory but also in man's relations with one another."[26] So the image-makers insisted, and their message stirred the hope of many an European.

Frontier Equality

Given these attitudes, and given the fact that frontier opportunity promised eventual equality to all, the class distinctions normal in older societies were bound to weaken in the American Wests. In a land where the poorest laborer might reap a fortune with a happy speculation, or the poverty-stricken prospector become a millionaire with a turn of a shovel, traditional boundaries between the classes were outmoded. "Equality of position," as Tocqueville called it, created a unique situation on the frontier

[23] Franklin D. Scott, ed., *Baron Klinkowstrom's America, 1818–1820* (Evanston, 1952), p. 132.
[24] A. S. Glenn, *Amerkai levelek* (Budapest, 1914), p. 4.
[25] Baillie-Grohman, *Camps in the Rockies*, pp. 322–23.
[26] Quotations in Wabeke, *Dutch Emigration to North America*, p. 93.

and accounted for the aggressive egalitarianism that the image-makers discovered there.

Certainly frontier communities gave abundant evidence that class distinctions had disappeared. To observers no one was rich and no one was poor—"a happy state of mediocrity," one called it.[27] Poverty in the European sense was unknown; there were "no beggars, no paupers, no whining crew to whet a false conceit upon."[28] Every farmer owned the house he lived in, the fields that he tilled, and the tools that he used; every hired laborer expected to be a landowner and acted the part. All dressed alike, whether master or servant. Europeans complained that they could not determine a man's position by the clothes he wore and were frequently embarrassed when they shook hands with waiters under the impression they were landlords. Servant girls flaunted finery that their mistresses might have envied in Norway or Germany; "I can dress as well as any lady in Sedlescomb," one boasted in a letter home.[29] To class-conscious Europeans this was an unforgiveable sin, for it underlined the disagreeable fact that all on the frontiers, whatever their status, thought of themselves as equal.

This was a reality that no image-maker could ignore. "There is nothing in America," one wrote, "that strikes a foreigner so much as the real republican equality existing in the Western states."[30] All noted that frontiersmen refused to recognize anyone as their superiors and insisted on being treated as equals—just as they treated others as equals. To them, as one visitor wrote, "all are equal; but not with a nominal equality, not equal on paper merely. There every man with a coat to his back is a gentleman, quite as good as his neighbor."[31] Phrases such as these, echoing throughout Europe, were convincing. When Germans arriving during the

[27] Isaac Weld, *Travels through the States of North America, and the Provinces of Upper and Lower Canada, during the Years 1795, 1796, and 1797* (London, 1807), 1: 232–33.
[28] John Regan, *The Emigrant's Guide to the Western States of America* (Edinburgh, 1852), p. 218.
[29] William Cobbett, *The Emigrant's Guide, in Ten Letters Addressed to the Tax-Payers of England* (London, 1829), p. 59. For other examples of this view see William Faux, *Memorable Days in America: Being a Journal of a Tour to the United States* (London, 1823), p. 224; Alexis de Tocqueville, *Democracy in America* (Cambridge, 1863), 1: 228–29; Matilda J. F. Houstoun, *Hesperos; or, Travels in the West* (London, 1850), 1: 97; Adam Hodgson, *Letters from North America, Written during a Tour in the United States and Canada* (London, 1824), 1: 184; and Chevalier, *Society, Manners and Politics in the United States*, p. 431.
[30] John Melish, *Travels through the United States of America, in the Years 1806, & 1807, and 1809, 1810, & 1811* (London, 1818), pp. 48–49.
[31] Michel Chevalier, "The Western Steamboats," *Western Monthly Magazine* 4 (1835): 414. The same remark, slightly rephrased, is in his *Society, Manners and Politics in the United States*, 219. Abundant evidence on this point is in such works as Paul Duplessis, *Le Batteur d'estrade* (Paris, 1862), 1: 12; Baillie-Grohman, *Camps in the Rockies*, p. 364; Gábor Fábián, "Travels by Steamer in the United States," *The Athenaeum* 2 (1838): 345; Harriet Martineau, *Society in America* (New York, 1837), 2: 168; and H. Arnold Barton, ed., *Letters from the Promised Land: Swedes in America, 1840–1914* (Minneapolis, 1975), pp. 27, 32.

1850s were questioned on their reasons for migrating, they universally answered that they had chosen the United States because there "every man was an equal."[32]

Equality was practiced as well as preached. Travelers watched with amazement as common laborers and teamsters joined a group of well-spoken gentlemen during a political discussion, as a troop of militiamen paused to debate whether they should follow an order shouted by their commanding officer, as a delegate to a state constitutional convention rebelled against references to "a jury of his peers," on the grounds that "we don't want *peers* in this country—we've not got a monarchy."[33] There would be no taking orders or bowing to upper-class snobs in that community of equals.

This applied even to master-servant relationships. Indeed, there were no "servants" or "waiters" in the West; those words implied a subserviency that had been outlawed. When a British visitor in a frontier inn called for a waiter he was rudely reminded: "You are not in England now! There are no waiters here."[34] All were "helps" or "helpers" or "hired hands," and all expected to be treated as equals. Most who took such posts were recently arrived from abroad, for few self-respecting Americans would demean themselves by accepting such positions. "American lads," a traveler noted, ". . . would feel degraded at brushing a coat or washing a tea cup or spoon, or acting in what they term a 'menial' capacity."[35]

Those who did, whether newcomers or less advantaged natives, refused to admit their servility. Just as there were no "servants" in the West, so were there no "masters." A stranger who asked a worker if his master was at home was likely to be told: "I have no master . . . I'm Mr. ——'s *help,*" or "that son of Belial ain't been born yet."[36] In that land of opportunity every man was his own master, whatever his status in society. As an Irish balladier put it:

> There we'll be happy where we are our own masters
> In that land of plenty and sweet liberty.[37]

Equality was as much a part of employer-employee relationships as it was of social intercourse.

[32] Livia Appel and Theodore Blegen, "Official Encouragement of Immigration to Minnesota during the Territorial Period," *Minnesota History* 5 (August 1923): 189.
[33] Frances Trollope, *Domestic Manners of the Americans* (London, 1832), p. 100; *California: Its Past History; Its Present Position; Its Future Prospects* (London, 1852), p. 165.
[34] E. Howitt, *Selections from Letters Written during a Tour through the United States, in the Summer and Autumn of 1819* (Nottingham, 1820), p. 227.
[35] Murray, *Travels in North America*, 1: 219–20. Similar comments are in Trollope, *Domestic Manners of the Americans*, p. 52; William T. Harris, *Remarks Made during a Tour through the United States of America, in the Years 1817, 1818, and 1819* (Liverpool, 1819), p. 8; and Frances Wright, *Views of Society and Manners in America* (London, 1821), p. 228.
[36] John J. Fox, "The Far West in the '80's," *Annals of Wyoming* 21 (January 1949): 38.
[37] Wright, ed., *Irish Emigrant Ballads and Songs*, p. 138.

"The Camp of the Delaware." From Friedrich Armand Strubberg, *Amerikanische und Jagd-und Reiseabenteuer aus meinem Leben in den westlichen Indianergebieten* (Stuttgart, 1858). (From the collections of Albert Hümmerich of Berlin.)

Servants and waiters made this clear, for they expected to be addressed as equals just as they demanded to be treated as equals. Travelers from more aristocratic lands soon learned that they could escape insult and injury only by requesting rather than commanding; "If you please, Sir," or "Would you be so kind, Madame," were necessary as a preliminary to any service, while any reprimand for slow or slovenly attention was considered an insult answerable with a torrent of abusive profanity.[38] This was as it should be in a land where the waiter knew that his vote counted just as much as that of his employer in electing the president, and was aware that he was performing a service essential to society.

Visitors also learned that they must perform many tasks that servants were expected to perform in Europe. Hostlers in frontier inns, offended by a bit of uppity behavior, might decide not to rub down, or even to feed, a horse of a traveler lest they violate the spirit of equality. Foreigners were expected to carry their own luggage, make their own beds, and polish their own boots. These were menial chores, and any order to carry them out was almost sure to be met with a curt "Do it yourself."[39] Call bells were unknown in frontier hostelries, for no self-respecting citizen would allow himself to be summoned in such an humiliating manner.[40]

Travelers cited endless examples of their sad lot when they forgot the West's egalitarian rules: the hostler ordered to waken a guest shouting "call yourself and be damned"; the traveler asking for a cup of coffee and being told "will you have it now or will you wait until you get it"; the British lady requesting a bowl of water to wash before retiring and being answered "you must be dirty, I expect, to want to wash this time o'night."[41] Stories were told of a guest who was pommeled by a waiter in a frontier inn when he complained of the food; of a landlord who pointed a pistol at the head of a dissatisfied customer and ordered him to "eat them fishballs"; of a railroad conductor who snatched a newspaper from a passenger's hands and settled himself comfortably to read; of a train crew that el-

[38] Xantus, *Letters from North America*, p. 59. Similar comments are in William Savage, *Observations on Emigration to the United States of America* (London, 1819), pp. 38–39; Paul Borget, *Outre-Mer: Impressions of America* (New York, 1895), p. 261; and Weld, *Travels through the States of North America*, 1: 29.

[39] Baillie-Grohman, *Camps in the Rockies*, p. 363. The same viewpoint is expressed in Weld, *Travels through the States of North America*, 1: 114–15; Richard Parkinson, *A Tour in America in 1798, 1799, and 1800* (London, 1805), 1: 30–31; Flint, *Letters from America*, p. 268; and Ferdinand Ernst, *Bemerkungen auf einer Reise durch das Innere der Vereinigten Staaten von Nord-Amerika im Jahre 1819* (Hildesheim, 1820), pp. 78–79.

[40] Basil Hall, *Travels in North America, in the Years 1827 and 1828* (Edinburgh, 1829), pp. 142–43; Patrick Shirreff, *A Tour through North America: Together with a Comprehensive View of the Canadas and United States* (Edinburgh, 1835), p. 287.

[41] Adlard Welby, *A Visit to North America and the English Settlements in Illinois, with a Winter Residence at Philadelphia* (London, 1821), p. 35; *American Settler*, 11 August 1883; Houstoun, *Hesperos*, 2: 7.

Land of Equality

bowed its way into the washroom, which they left cluttered with dirty towels.[42]

Two such episodes captured the spirit of frontier egalitarianism. An Hungarian traveler asked a servant to run an errand and was told that it was raining:

"That's exactly why I don't want to go myself. The umbrella is right there."
"You don't think I want to ruin my boots in this mud? You call a cab and I'll go."[43]

A generation later a titled Britisher on a camping trip asked his guide to fill the tub for his bath. The guide suggested that he bathe in the river instead, then flew into a rage, shouting: "You ain't quite the top-shelfer you think you is; you ain't even got a shower-bath for cooling your swelled head . . . but I'll make you a present of one, boss!" And pulling his revolver, he shot the tub full of holes.[44]

Just as shocking to visitors as such insolence was the easy familiarity with which hostlers and waiters and stagecoach drivers mingled with "gentlemen" on terms of perfect equality. Waiters commonly leaned over guests' chairs to listen to—or join in—the conversation; stewards often shed their coats when dinner was over to join the diners in a game of cards.[45] One traveler in Montana was horrified to see a waitress take a fan from a lady's hand and use it to cool herself. Servants sent to a neighbor's with messages made themselves at home while waiting a reply, sprawling in an easy chair, shedding their coats, and helping themselves to the host's cigars. A dirt-encrusted laborer came swaggering into an inn where President Andrew Jackson was dining, seated himself, dominated the conversation, and left with never a word of thanks or appreciation.[46] Any reprimand for such behavior was likely to be answered with: "After all, we're all equal, ar'n't we?"[47]

If servants in frontier inns demanded such familiarities, the hired hands and kitchen helpers in frontier families expected even more. All in-

---

[42] *American Settler*, 22 September 1883; Zsigmond Falk, *Budapestől San-Fransicóig: Amerikai uti jegyzetek* (Budapest, 1877), p. 94.
[43] János Xantus, *Xantus János levelei Északamerikából* (Pest, 1857), p. 33.
[44] William A. Baillie-Grohman, *Fifteen Years' Sport and Life in the Hunting Grounds of Western America and British Columbia* (London, 1900), p. 88.
[45] Shirreff, *A Tour through North America*, pp. 268–69; George W. Featherstonhaugh, *A Canoe Voyage up the Minnay Sotor* (London, 1847), 2: 178.
[46] Parkinson, *A Tour in America*, 1: 31–32; Baily, *Journal of a Tour in the Unsettled Parts of North America*, p. 199; Elias Regnault and Jules Labaume, *Suite des Etats-Unis depuis 1812 jusqu'à nos jours* (Paris, 1849), pp. 157–58.
[47] Houstoun, *Hesperos*, 2: 219.

sisted that they eat with the family, attend all social occasions, be driven
to church, and allowed to mingle with the guests as equals. A common
saying along the frontiers, the image-makers reported, was "If a man is
good enough to work for me, he is good enough to eat with me," and that
rule was rigidly enforced by employers and employees alike.[48] Serving
girls counted on the same privileges. Often told were tales of the newly
hired girl who found only two places set at the table and flounced from the
house with "I guess that's because you don't think I'm good enough to eat
with you"; of the servant who threw the supper dishes in the sink when
told that her employers wanted one meal by themselves; of the maid who
refused to allow her mistress to ring for her unless she could ring for the
mistress in turn whenever she desired "to have speech with her."[49] So universal was the belief in equality that manuals for immigrants warned girls
that they must expect to be treated as equals in the West, and that they
must act accordingly.[50]

This spirit was carried into the realm of address, for in the West all
men were "gentlemen" and all women "ladies" whatever their status in society. Europeans complained that they could never tell the servant from
his master when being introduced, for an illiterate hostler was likely to be
referred to as a "gentleman" and a slatternly chambermaid as a "lady"
while their master was merely "Mr. So-and-So."[51] These designations fascinated travelers who chronicled instance after instance: the landlord pag-
ing a coachman who had just delivered a passenger by shouting: "Where is
the gentleman who brought this man here?" The stage driver who asked a
German duke, "Are you the man going to Portland, because if you are I'm
the gentleman that's going to drive you there"; the witness in a court trial
who testified that "he and another gentleman were shoveling mud"; the
newspaper report of the "two gentlemen who were sentenced to six month
imprisonment for horse-stealing."[52] They also reported with unrestrained
delight hearing of "the lady over the way who takes in washing," or of
"that there lady, out in the gully, that is making drip candles," or of the

[48] D. Griffiths, Jr., *Two Years' Residence in the New Settlements of Ohio* (London, 1835), p. 80.
[49] Trollope, *Domestic Manners of the Americans*, pp. 54–55; Lady Duffus Hardy, *Through Cities and Prairie Lands: Sketches of an American Tour* (New York, 1881), p. 267; T. C. Grattan,
Civilized America (London, 1859), 1: 268.
[50] D. R. Thomason, *Hints to Emigrants or to Those Who May Contemplate Emigrating to the
United States of America* (Philadelphia, 1848), p. 26.
[51] Gustorf, "Frontier Perils," p. 149; Philip S. Robinson, *Sinners and Saints: A Tour Across
the States and Round Them, with Three Months among the Mormons* (London, 1883), p. 47; Houstoun, *Hesperos*, 1: 177–78; Flint, *Letters from America*, p. 144; Rebecca Burlend, *A True Picture
of Emigration; or, Fourteen Years in the Interior of North America* (London, 1848), pp. 19.
[52] Charles Lyell, *Travels in North America* (London, 1845), 1: 49; Jean-Jacques Ampère,
Promenade en Amérique: États-Unis, Cuba, Mexique (Paris, 1855), 1: 175; Simon A. O'Ferrall, *A
Ramble of Six Thousand Miles through the United States of America* (London, 1832), p. 308.

barkeeper and stage driver who when quarreling "seriously accused each other of being 'no gentleman.' "[53]

Shocking as this usage was to Europeans, it seemed logical to frontiersmen. In the American West the hired hand was the potential farmer, the serving girl the future wife of the town's leading citizen. Why be servile when servility was but the temporary lot of a soon-to-be gentleman? Image-makers commented that there was nothing peasantlike about frontier farmers, even of the most humble status. "The clumsy gait and bent body of our peasant is hardly ever seen," one commented; "everyone walks erect and easy."[54] The pioneer farmer never thought of himself as a peasant; why should he when he was sure of becoming a landlord within a few years? He had already adjusted emotionally and mentally to his new status, and acted the part.

Nowhere was the egalitarian spirit of the frontier better exhibited than in the crude log dwellings that served as inns throughout the West. There masters and servants, judges and teamsters, legislators and hog drivers, were seated about a common table, ate the same food, and conversed as equals. A "promiscuous assemblage," one traveler called it; " a most almighty beautiful democratic amalgam," an American answered.[55] These democratic arrangements also governed sleeping facilities, with two, three, or four persons assigned to a bed in order of their arrival, regardless of their wealth, status, or cleanliness.[56] Europeans who tried to protect their privacy by barricading the door to the sleeping quarters were assaulted by a "murmuré quelques god-dam" (as a French traveler put it), and driven from the inn.[57] Even Old Shatterhand had to bed with strangers when he wanted to "board cheap."[58] This was trying enough for the fastidious, but worse was the innkeeper's refusal to change the sheets. A visitor who complained was haughtily assured that "since *Gentlemen* are

[53] O'Ferrall, *Ramble of Six Thousand Miles*, p. 230; Trollope, *Domestic Manners of Americans*, p. 100.
[54] Welby, *A Visit to North America*, p. 73. Similar comments are in Charles J. Latrobe, *The Rambler in North America* (London, 1835), 2: 139; and Joel Palmer, *Journal of Travels over the Rocky Mountains, to the Mouth of the Columbia River, Made during the Years 1845 and 1846* (Cincinnati, 1847), pp. 152–53.
[55] Hodgson, *Letters from North America*, 1: 169; William Kelly, *A Stroll through the Diggings of California* (London, 1852), p. 47. Frontier inns are well described in Paton Yoder, *Taverns and Travelers: Inns of the Early Midwest* (Bloomington, 1969), pp. 135–51.
[56] Charles G. B. Daubney, *Journal of a Tour through the United States, and in Canada, Made during the Years 1837–38* (Oxford, 1843), p. 159; Flint, *Letters from America*, pp. 135–36; Baillie-Grohman, *Camps in the Rockies*, p. 65; J. E. Alexander, *Transatlantic Sketches, Comprising Visits to the Most Interesting Scenes in North and South America and the West Indies* (London, 1833), 2: 76; Edouard de Montulé, *Voyage en Amérique, en Italie, en Sicile, et en Egypt pendant les années 1816, 1817, et 1819* (Paris, 1821), 1: 221.
[57] Montulé, *Voyage en Amérique*, 1: 243.
[58] Karl May, *Old Sureband* (reprint ed., Vienna, 1953), 2: 6.

all alike, people do not see why they should not sleep in the same sheets."[59]

Such a dedicated belief in the principle of egalitarianism meant that any attempt at superiority by visiting easterners or Europeans would be met with insult and perhaps mayhem. The slightest display of ostentation, of nose-in-the-air snobbery was resented. A French visitor was refused admission to several homes until he discarded his fancy clothes and expensive luggage; a British traveler was welcomed only when he learned to pass off his servant as his son; another heard a boatman threaten to beat a passenger because he wore brass buttons.[60] A dandy, strolling down the street of a western town was likely to hear: "Hold on tha'r, stranger! When you go through this town go slow, so folks kin take you in," or, "Mister, how much do you ask for it?" "For what, sir." "Well, for the town; you look as if you owned it."[61] "In the West," a charitable Englishman observed, "the true gentleman is heartily liked, but the swell is heartily hated."[62]

The ultimate in bad taste was to treat a westerner as an inferior. A honeymooning couple lost their driver when they failed to invite him to dine with them; a visiting easterner who sent word for a tailor to come to his hotel to measure him for a suit was haughtily refused because such servility "wasn't republican"; a cowboy who threatened to shoot a visitor for refusing to drink with him was excused on the grounds that "snobbishness is not the proper thing in this country, and sensible men generally try, while in Rome, to do as Rome does."[63] Trivial incidents, perhaps, and certainly not typical of all frontier behavior, but they accurately mirrored an attitude that image-makers encountered everywhere in the West. "A west-country American," one wrote, "would rather die like a cock on a dung-hill, than be patronized."[64]

Given this robust frontier faith in equality, why did westerners address each other as "Colonel" or "Judge" or "Squire" or a bewildering variety of titles? This was a custom that puzzled, and delighted, the image-makers, and they never tired of reporting absurd examples. Perhaps one exaggerated slightly when he reported that he could not throw a stick in a frontier village without hitting five major generals; perhaps

[59]   Ferdinand Bayard, *Travels of a Frenchman in Maryland and Virginia* (Ann Arbor, 1950), p. 36.
[60]   François, duc de La Rochefoucault-Liancourt, *Travels through the United States of North America* (London, 1799), 1: 39–40; Daubney, *Journal of a Tour through the United States*, pp. 156–57; Alexander, *Transatlantic Sketches*, 2: 64.
[61]   Baillie-Grohman, *Camps in the Rockies*, p. 30.
[62]   Ibid., pp. 30–31.
[63]   Frederick Marryat, *A Diary in America* (London, 1839), 2: 156; Edward Marston, *Frank's Ranche, or, My Holiday in the Rockies* (Boston, 1886), p. 196.
[64]   O'Ferrall, *A Ramble of Six Thousand Miles*, pp. 111–12.

others stretched the truth when they told of a landlord who shouted "General" and was answered by thirty men; or of finding that four of his six mates in a stagecoach were addressed as "Colonel."[65] But there was no denying that a startling number of menial tasks along the frontier were performed by men with impressive titles; a general serving as a tavern keeper, a colonel as a hostler, a major as a bartender, a captain as a wagon driver, a brigadier general as a store clerk.[66] Europeans soon learned that most "squires" were former justices of the peace, "judges" lawyers who never graced a bench, and "generals" officers in the local militia. At one gathering an Italian visitor was introduced to a "president" (of a dancing society), a "senator" (a defeated candidate for the state legislature), a "general" (of a private drill brigade), and a "commodore" (the captain of a freight barge).[67] Why the practice of glorifying the undeserving in this undemocratic way?

The more astute image-makers found the answer in the tendency of frontiersmen to award those who were of greatest use to the community. These were titles that had been granted not by hereditary kings, but by the people as a whole, and they paid tribute to those who had earned the right to be respected. Egalitarianism was too deeply rooted to be violated by unearned designations, or by those that honored ancestral achievement rather than the achievements of the individual himself.

Frontier Liberty

Personal liberty was as treasured by the pioneers as faith in equality. Once more the image-makers recognized this as a national belief that intensified with each step westward; social pressures might dictate conformity in eastern cities, but in the thinly settled Wests no popular tribunals, no kings, no business magnates, no magistrates, hampered the freedom of the individual to do and think as he pleased. "Here no emperor and no king has the right to command us to do anything," boasted a fictional frontiersman in a German novel; "here," added a traveler, "no proud tyrant can lord it over him; he has no rent to pay, no game laws, or timber laws or fishing laws to dread."[68] All were gloriously free to exploit Nature's

[65] William F. Butler, *The Great Lone Land: A Narrative of Travel and Adventure in the North-West of America* (London, 1872), p. 50; Godfrey T. Vigne, *Six Months in America* (Philadelphia, 1833), 1: 170–71; Charles F. Hoffman, *A Winter in the West* (New York, 1835), p. 64.

[66] Murray, *Travels in North America*, 1: 120; Weld, *Travels through the States of North America*, 1: 236–38; Unonius, *A Pioneer in Northwest America*, 1: 205–6.

[67] Quoted in Torrielli, *Italian Opinion on America*, p. 94.

[68] Berthold Auerbach, quoted in Paul C. Weber, *America in Imaginative German Literature in the First Half of the Nineteenth Century* (New York, 1926), p. 220; Blowe, *A Geographical, Historical, Commercial, and Agricultural View of the United States*, p. 112. A similar comment is in Julian U. Niemcewicz, *Podróże po Ameryce 1797–1807* (Wroclaw, 1959), pp. 395–96. Writers unfamiliar with the West often committed ludicrous errors when they assumed that Euro-

riches without interference, and they prospered accordingly. Sang an Irish balladier:

> We have no queen, or lords to keep
> In this thriving happy land,
> Our money is not drawn from us,
> To make them fine and grand.[69]

Echoed a recent arrival from Sweden: "If I talk to a high official I do not need to stand with my hat in my hand and with shaking knees."[70] Where all were equal, all could command, and none need be subservient.

This was a startling realization to new arrivals, but even more startling was the discovery that they could abuse their betters and their government leaders without fear of punishment. A hero in a German novel spoke for many an immigrant when he proudly proclaimed: "We are not mere serfs, day labourers or tenants who reside in cellar or attic from which any day we might be sent to Botany Bay or the Conciergerie should we have a mind to kill a rabbit that sits in our way, or to call Johnny [President John Quincy Adams] a booby."[71] All were free men and all were either property holders or eventual property holders; why bow and scrape to anyone? "Those who have lived over there," complained a French aristocrat, "do not know how to obey anymore."[72]

The image-makers were well aware that this spirit of liberty sprang from the abundance of opportunity for individual self-advancement in frontier areas. Crèvecoeur recognized a fundamental truth when he spoke of a "security that arises from property, and the general hope which every man has of increasing it."[73] He knew, as most Europeans who visited the Wests learned, that cheap land, linked with the absence of established elites, insured a degree of individual freedom, and hence secession from society's dictates, impossible to achieve in compact social units. He realized, too, that the reins of government were stretched thin along the frontiers, and that sparsely settled communities required less authoritarian controls than the more densely populated seaboard states. "Liberty in its most useful adornment of youthful innocence," a German novelist saw, "does not dwell on our coasts."[74]

---

pean regulations applied in America. Thus a captain from Kentucky who reached Bent's Fort was required to hand over "government documents and character references," before he was allowed to enter. Wilhelm Frey, *In Indianerhänden* (Mülheim, n.d.), pp. 7–8.

[69] Wright, ed., *Irish Emigrant Ballads and Songs*, p. 259.

[70] Quoted in Florence E. Janson, *The Background of Swedish Immigration, 1840–1930* (Chicago, 1931), p. 294.

[71] Charles Sealsfield, *The Courtship of Ralph Doughby, Esquire* (New York, 1844), pp. 88–89.

[72] Duplessis, *Le Batteur d'estrade*, 5:47.

[73] His views on this subject are discussed in Henry Nash Smith, *Virgin Land: The American West as Symbol and Myth* (Cambridge, 1950), pp. 125–26.

[74] Ernst A. Willkomm, quoted in Weber, *America in Imaginative German Literature*, p. 215.

This the newcomers to the West realized, and they never tired of blessing the happy fate that had brought them to a land where they were free
to behave as they wished—where "freedom and equality are the rule in
civil and religious matters"; where they were as "cherished and defended
as life itself"; where "a free people are not chained down by any old class
or caste system."[75] A German, asked if he were glad he had settled in the
West, answered,
"Oh yes, very glad, a thousand times better here."
"You can have more comfort here?"
"Oh no, not so much . . .
"Why then, do you like it better here?"
"Because here I am free."[76]
When a promotional pamphlet promised that on the frontier "a person
begins to feel his full worth as a free man," it was for once not overly
trifling with the truth.[77]

Westerners, the image-makers noted, sometimes carried their right to
do as they pleased to annoying extremes. A traveler who reprimanded a
boatman for singing off key was profanely reminded that he was "in a land
of liberty, and had no right to interfere"; a minister who asked a prospective convert if he wanted to go to hell was rudely told that he was a free
citizen and would go where he chose; an English lady who protested
against building a hog-butchering plant in the fine neighborhood where
she lived was told that "that may do very well for your tyrannical country,
where a rich man's nose is more thought of than a poor man's mouth, but
hogs be profitable to produce here, and we be too free for such a law as
that."[78] Charles Dickens's Martin Chuzzlewit was righteously indignant
when he declared: "They've got such a passion for Liberty that they can't
help taking liberties with her."[79]

Travelers often complained that the children of frontiersmen were the
most unpleasant products of this spirit; they were allowed to come and go
as they pleased, interrupt adult conversations, contradict their elders, and
disobey orders with a flagrant disrespect for their parents. A few tolerant
Europeans recognized that independence was needed training for the not-
too-distant future when they would go forth to start their own careers, but

[75] "America Letters" quoted in Theodore C. Blegen, ed., *The Land of Their Choice: The Immigrants Write Home* (Minneapolis, 1955), pp. 6, 193–94, and 364.
[76] Frederick L. Olmsted, *A Journey through Texas; or, A Saddle-Trip on the Southwestern
Frontier* (New York, 1857), p. 282. The use of this theme is explored in Weber, *America in
Imaginative German Literature*, p. 79, and Augustus J. Prahl, "America in the Works of Gerstäcker," *Modern Language Quarterly* 4 (June 1943): 221.
[77] Nebraska Bureau of Immigration pamphlet, quoted in David M. Emmons, *Garden in the
Grasslands: Boomer Literature of the Central Great Plains* (Lincoln, Nebr., 1971), p. 111.
[78] Flint, *Letters from America*, p. 85; Howitt, *Selections from Letters Written during a Tour
through the United States*, p. 223; Trollope, *Domestic Manners of the Americans*, p. 105.
[79] Charles Dickens, *The Life and Adventures of Martin Chuzzlewit* (London, 1844), p. 346.

more found parental permissiveness one of the least attractive by-products of republicanism.[80] Frontier children were condemned as "stubborn and unmannerly creatures" who openly disobeyed their teachers, sauced their parents, and not only refused to recognize authority, but threatened bodily harm to those who imposed it.[81] One, reprimanded for stealing a piece of cake, was heard to answer: "Why, mother, aren't we in a free country now?"[82] Another, told by his father to fetch a piece of wood, shouted, "Go get it yourself, you old son of a b——h"; still another, scolded for his outrageous conduct, answered that he "was in a free country, where he could plunder, and do as he pleased."[83] A visitor to a frontier farm who heard a father order his son to come a dozen times only to have the boy answer, "I won't" and take to his heels, was amazed when the parent turned proudly and announced: "A sturdy republican, sir."[84] Given such conduct, a disgusted visitor could be excused when he wrote: "The word *liberty*, but which I call *licentiousness*, is a curse to this country."[85]

If parents fared badly from the overemphasis on liberty in western communities, the opposite can be said of the fate of women, for they were treated far better than in Europe or the East. The image-makers recognized two reasons for their good fortune: the newness of society and hence "fewer inherited ideas of what was 'suitable' for a woman to do,"[86] and their scarcity. Europeans were repeatedly reminded of the unbalanced ratio between men and women—five to one in the western states in the 1830s, twenty to one in the Far West a generation later—and just as repeatedly told of the veneration that ladies enjoyed as males competed for their company. Tales were told of prospectors who walked twenty miles just to gaze at a petticoat drying on a line; of crowds who gathered to watch a housewife hanging out her wash.[87] In Texas, one traveler learned, any sort of female was viewed as "a regular find; but a straight up-and-

[80] Typical were Shirreff, *A Tour through North America*, p. 51; Edward S. Abdy, *Journal of a Residence and Tour in the United States, of North America from April 1833, to October 1834* (London, 1835), pp. 70–73; Flint, *Letters from America*, pp. 170–71; Martineau, *Society in America*, 2: 271; and Montulé, *Voyage en Amérique*, 1: 277–78. The treatment of the subject in Norwegian novels is discussed in Dorothy B. Skårdal, *The Divided Heart: Scandinavian Immigrant Experience through Literary Sources* (Bloomington, 1974), pp. 246, 253–54.
[81] *Sequel to the Counsel for Emigrants* (Aberdeen, 1834), p. 27; Barinetti, *A Voyage to Mexico and Havanna*, p. xi.
[82] Quoted in George M. Stephenson, "When America Was the Land of Canaan," *Minnesota History* 10 (September 1929): 254–55.
[83] William French, *Some Recollections of a Western Ranchman, New Mexico, 1883–1889* (London, 1927), p. 109.
[84] Quoted in Richard L. Rapson, *Britons View America: Travel Commentary, 1860–1935* (Seattle, 1971), p. 99.
[85] Howitt, *Selections from Letters Written during a Tour through the United States*, pp. xii–xiii.
[86] *American Settler*, 12 December 1885.
[87] Hoffman, *A Winter in the West*, 2: 51–53; Bartolomèo Galletti, *Il giro del mondo colla Ristori* (Rome, 1876), p. 261.

down sort of critter—if she was ugly as a wild cat—was reckoned a perfect fortune."[88] The message of the image-makers was unmistakable: "Go West, young woman."

And particularly any woman seeking a husband. In the West, they made clear, any girl, whether old or young, rich or poor, beautiful or ugly, could find a mate before she could open her mouth to say yes. Women were so few that the men were not particular; girls who had "crossed the line," (as Norwegians dubbed those who had lost their virginity), girls poorly endowed by Nature, girls of any age between twelve and seventy, were eagerly courted. "I have," reported a rancher, "seen young girls of thirteen and hideous old girls of fifty snapped up as soon as they arrived in the country."[89] Travelers delighted in stories of the unmarried woman who was so showered with gifts that she soon owned every business in town; of another who was courted by so many of the leading citizens that she dared not choose lest she start a civil war; of a third who was returning from her husband's funeral when she was approached by one of the pallbearers with a proposal of marriage. "I'm sorry," she answered, twitching her black veil, "but you're late; the preacher just asked me."[90]

There was reason for such popularity, for women were recognized to be the advance agents of civilization, guaranteed by their mere presence to temper the roughness of an all-male society, at the same time elevating both the moral tone and real-estate prices. Let a lady arrive and pistols disappeared, knives were less frequently drawn, fewer oaths were heard, and the consumption of ardent spirits declined remarkably.[91] They were also recognized as valuable assets on a frontier farm, cooking and spinning and butter making and sewing and caring for the chickens—all at considerable less cost than a hired housekeeper. Wrote a recently arrived European from the Michigan Territory in 1835: "It is very likely that the next letter you receive from me will inform you that I am married, as I find it difficult to hire a woman to do my work in the house."[92]

[88] Charles Hooton, *St. Louis Isle, or Texiana* (London, 1847), pp. 149–150.
[89] Isabella Randall, *A Lady's Ranche Life in Montana* (London, 1887), p. 117. This theme is explored in such works as O. Drevdahl, *Fra Emigrationens Amerika* (Oslo, 1891), which has a whole chapter on "Female Work"; and Axel Bruun, *Breve fra Amerika* (Oslo, 1870), p. 47.
[90] Hooton, *St. Louis Isle*, p. 53; *Journey from New Orleans to California, 1849, and Other Excerpts from Chambers' Journal* (Edinburgh, 1857), p. 13; *American Settler*, 9 April 1887.
[91] Sealsfield, *Courtship of Ralph Doughby*, pp. 103–4; Felix P. Wierzbicki, *California As It Is, and As It May Be; or, A Guide to the Gold Region* (San Francisco, 1849), pp. 50–51; Henryk Sienkiewicz, *Western Septet: Seven Stories of the American West* (Cheshire, Conn., 1973), p. 108; W. Hepworth Dixon, *New America* (London, 1867), 1: 136.
[92] Quoted in Charlotte Erickson, *Invisible Immigrants: The Adaptation of English and Scottish Immigrants in Nineteenth Century America* (London, 1972), p. 119. Similar complaints by fictional characters are in Karl May, *Der Schatz im Silbersee* (reprint ed., Bamberg, 1973), p. 159; and Gustave Aimard, *The Border Rifles: A Tale of the Texan War* (Philadelphia, n.d.), p. 106.

Women might be useful in pioneering, but the image-makers made clear that they were never expected to do one thing accepted by all peasants' wives in Europe: work in the fields. This was revolutionary! Of course women were supposed to hoe corn, tend the kitchen garden, make hay, milk cows. But not in America. "They are not allowed to do any drudgery work," wrote a surprised guidebook author. "Their wood is chopped, their water drawn, their cows milked—by the men."[93] "To think," exploded a Norwegian hero, "that a grown man should sit down and pull at a cow's udder! A man as a milkmaid—as a barn boy!"[94] Unthinkable in the Old World, perhaps, but commonplace in the New. In the American West a woman's job was "to make a home and to make little Americans."[95] The men did all the rest.

This difference was reflected in the respect paid women in the United States, and particularly in the West. Aristocratic visitors could scarcely believe their eyes and ears as they saw females treated as equals, offered the choice seats on stagecoaches, ushered first into dining rooms, and listened to with courtesy and respect. This was madness. How else explain the man who gallantly offered a lady his seat on a stagecoach even though he would have to wait a week for the next, or the passenger who raised his umbrella on a coach roof to protect a young woman, thereby drenching the other passengers.[96] That was carrying a bad thing too far.

Just as ununderstandable was the frontier code that decreed that all women must be protected against danger, insult, and even crudities, particularly when traveling alone. "Every woman, even the youngest," a visitor to the mining West reported, ". . . is under the protection of all the men."[97] Let such a traveler be insulted or threatened and every man in the vicinity would rush to her aid, six-shooter in hand. A passenger on a Mississippi steamboat was chased from the table by the knife-wielding captain when he used an oath before a lady; a farmer about to shoot a gambler who had cheated him of his earnings pocketed his weapon when he saw that a woman was present.[98] Highwaymen in western thrillers always remembered their manners when females were about; when the stage to Hurricane Gulch was held up a young girl passenger was quickly assured, "we

[93] *Counsel for Immigrants*, pp. 127–28.
[94] Ole E. Rölvaag, quoted in Skårdal, *Divided Heart*, pp. 242–43.
[95] Charles V. C. de Varigny, *The Women of the United States* (New York, 1895), pp. 13–14.
[96] Xantus, *Letters from North America*, pp. 154–55; Ferdinand Roemer, *Texas: With Particular Reference to German Immigration and the Physical Appearance of the Country* (reprint ed., San Antonio, 1935), p. 107.
[97] Henryk Sienkiewicz, *Portrait of America: Letters of Henryk Sienkiewicz* (New York, 1959), p. 35.
[98] Ernest Duvergier de Hauranne, *A Frenchman in Lincoln's America* (Chicago, 1974); Xavier Eyma, *Scènes de moeurs et de voyage dans le nouveau monde* (Paris, 1862), pp. 53–56.

don't rob ladies; they're too scarce in this part of the Union."[99] Europeans might sniff at the "pertness of republican principles," revealed in the deference shown women in the frontiers, but European women saw the American West as a land where liberty and opportunity—and husbands—combined to create a modern Eden.

Frontier Democracy

Underlying and sustaining the egalitarianism and passionate belief in liberty that the image-makers identified with the American Wests was a democratic faith unparalleled in the world of that day. Because all men were equal and because all were free, all ruled, sharing equally in shaping the course of their communities and nation. And because all ruled, faith in the democratic processes was universal. Europeans found this acceptance to be uniquely American; no other nation, no matter what its political creed, could match the Americans' blind belief in their own institutions or the calm confidence with which they faced the future. When Crèvecoeur wrote, early in the nineteenth century, that "we are the most perfect society existing in the world," he spoke for all frontiersmen.[100] So did a character in a German novel a generation later when he avowed that other countries might imitate, but none could duplicate, the depth of democratic sentiment in the United States: "The Republican dress . . . is not made for them. Even John Bull, when he puts it on, looks so awkward that every reasonable man must pity him."[101] Americans had perfected a unique system of government that, in their eyes, surpassed in virtue all others.

In questing for an explanation of this deep-seated faith in democracy, the image-makers fastened on two probable causes: the economic equality bred of cheap lands and the recurring rebirth of society on each new frontier. The first was easily justified. "God Himself," wrote Tocqueville, "gave them the means of remaining equal and free, by placing them upon a boundless continent."[102] Cheap land created a society of property owners, none greatly different from his neighbors, and all freed of the jealousies and greed that stemmed from economic inequalities. Democracy would prevail so long as the public domain was available; when government lands were fully occupied, the United States would be "European-

[99] Edward S. Ellis, *Hurricane Gulch: A Tale of the Aosta and Bufferville Trail* (New York, 1892), p. 21. The coach driver later assured a lady passenger: "I've never met a road agent yet who was mean enough to rob a lady" (p. 109).
[100] Michel-Guillaume St. Jean de Crèvecoeur, *Letters from an American Farmer* (London, 1782), pp. 46–48.
[101] Sealsfield, *The Courtship of Ralph Doughby*, p. 77.
[102] Tocqueville, *Democracy in America*, 1: 373.

ized," with class warfare, crippling strikes, and finally a totalitarian government strong enough to suppress conflicts.[103]

Equally important in sustaining the democratic impulse was the recurring rebirth of political institutions as settlement advanced westward. Each new community was occupied by men and women from many places and a variety of backgrounds. None knew of the others' ancestry or social status or wealth; life was a blank sheet where each could record his own strengths and abilities. "The inhabitants are but of yesterday," Tocqueville wrote, "scarcely known to one another."[104] Hence there could be no deference paid inherited wealth or hereditary distinctions; all were starting afresh as equals. As all worked together to establish a government each new community served as a political laboratory where all were involved. Involvement bred interest, and interest bred enthusiasm for democratic practices. Each developing community became "a nursery of freedom. . . . a republic in embryo;"[105] each the scene of spirited contests as its citizens beat out a constitution and needed institutions. "Through these Herculean battles," a Polish commentator observed, "the talent for self-government, freedom, and decentralization is most powerfully developed."[106] With each, faith in democracy was deepened.

This was the message trumpeted across Europe by the image-makers. They were fascinated by the process of government making and described each example that they observed in detail: the new community lacking all government in its most primitive stage, the coming of disorderly elements to reap the advantages of a lack of law enforcement, the formation by respectable citizens of a band of "Regulators" to administer a rough brand of justice, the drafting of a primitive code of laws, the assembling of the first council or legislature in a log hut, the selection of the site of the territorial capital, the launching of a full-blown governmental system with the first elections.[107]

Each step involved the entire community, whether seasoned frontiersmen or newcomers from abroad, with all casting their ballots and none having more weight than his fellows. "The vote of the common man," Europeans were told, "carries just as much authority and influence as that of the rich and powerful men."[108] Recent immigrants filled their letters home with the excitement of their first elections, the thrill of casting a

[103] Scott, ed., *Baron Klinkowstrom's America*, p. 250; Attilio Brunialti, quoted in Torrielli, *Italian Opinion on America*, p. 81.
[104] Tocqueville, *Democracy in America*, 1: 64–65.
[105] Francis J. Grund, *The Americans, in Their Moral, Social, and Political Relations* (Boston, 1837), p. 211.
[106] Sienkiewicz, *Potrait of America*, pp. 137–38.
[107] Latrobe, *A Rambler in North America*, pp. 259–60; Napoléon-A. Murat, *A Moral and Political Sketch of the United States of North America* (London, 1833), pp. 58–59.
[108] Blegen, ed., *Land of Their Choice*, p. 22.

"Dangerous Moments." From Friedrich Armand Strubberg, *Amerikanische und Jagd-und Reiseabenteuer aus meinem Leben in den westlichen Indianergebieten* (Stuttgart, 1858). (From the collections of Albert Hümmerich of Berlin.)

ballot, the exultation as they realized that they were choosing the president of the United States. In America every man was a ruler. "A nation of sovereigns," an Irish newspaper proclaimed, and not without reason.[109]

Where all ruled, elected officials were seen as equals, not superiors, to be treated with a familiarity that shocked visitors from abroad. Legislators and governors and even the president lived and dressed as did the ordinary people, seated themselves among clerks and farmers at inns, talked with the common folk, and listened to gibes and criticism that would have led to the guillotine in many lands.[110] A shocked visitor heard a man in a small crowd that had gathered to greet President Grant in Laramie shout: "Which is Grant?" and be answered in a not-so-sotto voice: "I guess he's that red-faced coon in the plug-hat."[111] When a returning immigrant in a Czech village referred to Theodore Roosevelt as "Tedi" he was met with incredulous disbelief that mounted when he insisted that everyone called the President "Tedi."[112] There was no groveling before the mighty in the American West. Why should there be? An American character in a German novel answered that question when he proudly proclaimed: "I am a man. . . . No duke, no lord, no king, and no emperor is more than I."[113]

Westerners, the image-makers agreed, were not only boastfully democratic, but took their politics so seriously that they were the best-informed people of the world on electoral personages and apt in debate. When the acid-tongued Mrs. Trollope chided a frontiersman for wasting so much time reading about the candidates in one election she was sharply told: "How should free men spend their time but looking after their government, and watching that them fellers as we gives office to does their duty?"[114] With power went responsibility, and the image-makers agreed that the Americans bowed to no one in the exercise of that trust.

This dedication was not without its perils, for all were so involved, and all boasted such unshakable faith in this candidate or that, that every election led to an emotional explosion that shook the entire community. Travelers reported alarming examples: townspeople so badly divided that all social affairs were abandoned lest fistfights break out; discussions so heated that they ended lifelong friendships or turned relative against relative, strangers threatened by bullies unless they proclaimed their loyalty

---

[109] Quoted in Arnold Schrier, *Ireland and the American Emigration, 1850–1900* (Minneapolis, 1958), p. 19.
[110] O'Ferrall, *A Ramble of Six Thousand Miles*, pp. 179–80; Francis Hall, *Travels in Canada and the United States in 1816 and 1817* (London, 1818), p. 59; Trollope, *Domestic Manners of the Americans*, p. 119.
[111] Rose L. Price, *The Two Americas: An Account of Sport and Travel with Notes on Men and Manners in North and South America* (London, 1877), p. 309.
[112] Louis Adamic, *Laughing in the Jungle* (New York, 1932), p. 6.
[113] Ulrich S. Carrington, *The Making of an American: An Adaptation of Memorable Tales by Charles Sealsfield* (Dallas, 1974), p. 73.
[114] Trollope, *Domestic Manners of the Americans*, p. 102.

to a favorite candidate.[115] Mrs. Trollope deplored the fact that "election madness engrosses every conversation, irritates every temper, substitutes party spirit for personal esteem, and, in fact, vitiates the whole system of society."[116] She might have added that amidst the hoopla and excitement decisions were made that bore little relationship to the merits of the office-holders. One militia captain was chosen because he had, in the words of one of his supporters, invited the whole community to the local groggery "not to take a *little* of something to drink, but be J——s to drink as much as they had a mind to."[117]

Equally alarming to sympathetic image-makers was the tendency of democratic-minded Americans to accept the will of the majority, whether right or wrong. This faith in popular rule, they insisted, deadened cultural creativity, entrusted authority to the ignorant rather than the competent, and elevated the interests of the multitude above those of the community. Where the people ruled "as does the Deity in the Universe" (in Tocqueville's phrase), confusion in decision making and faulty decisions were bound to result.[118] So also was ill-treatment for minorities, for if by definition the majority was always right, the minority was always wrong. Travelers repeatedly told of the abuse of spokesmen for unpopular causes; one heard a group of passengers on a Mississippi steamboat plotting to throw an abolitionist overboard if he spoke for his cause.[119] The dissident voices essential in a true democracy were too much hushed in frontier society.

These warnings were little heeded, for to the vast majority of image-makers the American West remained throughout the nineteenth century a land of equality, liberty, and democracy, where the downtrodden could find not only a better life than aging Europe could provide, but a degree of self-respect unknown in the tradition-ridden Old World. The vision that they created was of a land of abundance where the newcomer would find (in the words of one guidebook author) "laws as pure as can be expected to be formed by man, . . . executed by a wise and judicious magistracy, chosen by the people."[120] Along the frontiers they would find an Eden for their minds and emotions as well as for their bodies.

[115] Flint, *Letters from America*, p. 172; Charles Sealsfield, *The Americans As They Are: Described in a Tour through the Valley of the Mississippi* (London, 1828), p. 9.
[116] Trollope, *Domestic Manners of the Americans*, p. 255.
[117] O'Ferrall, *A Ramble of Six Thousand Miles*, pp. 223–24.
[118] Tocqueville, *Democracy in America*, 1: 72.
[119] James Logan, *Notes of a Journey through Canada, the United States of America, and the West Indies* (Edinburgh, 1838), p. 78. Tocqueville devotes a whole chapter to "The Tyranny of the Majority," in his *Democracy in America*, 1: 337–40.
[120] Cobbett, *The Emigrant's Guide*, p. 91.

XII

Land of Savagery

DURING THE WANING YEARS of the nineteenth century, the European image of the American frontier underwent a gradual change. This was linked to the passing of the frontier era, and the dwindling supply of the cheap lands that had lured land-hungry peasants for almost three centuries. American opportunity still beckoned the dispossessed, but the lure now was not a farm of one's own, but a job in an eastern mill or factory, not economic independence and social equality, but a better living than that offered in overcrowded Europe. No longer could the image-makers picture the West as a haven for the ambitious, a land where industry was certain to be rewarded with affluence and a place among society's elite. Yet the taste of Europeans for frontier excitement must be satisfied. How?

The image-makers found the answer by elevating what in the past had been a minor theme to a major role in their imaginative creations. Where before they had pictured the West as a land of both opportunity and savagery, they would now picture it solely as a land where civilization had surrendered to barbarism, where justice was carried in holsters rather than in books, where robbery and mayhem were of daily occurrence, where personal revenge was substituted for the orderly working of the law, and where life was of uncertain but brief duration. This required no risk on their part. Throughout the nineteenth century the image of the frontier as a land of savagery had proven immensely popular, and was sure to lose none of its appeal now. By shifting their emphasis, they could make their books even more attractive to their sensation-seeking readers.

The precedent on which they could build had been firmly established many years before. Since the eighteenth century when horror tales of Indian captivities had thrilled sadistically inclined readers, novelists and hostile travelers had pictured the frontier as a Babylon of barbarism, an updated Sodom and Gomorrah where none but the foolhardy would venture and none but the strong could survive. They had also decided that such a state of lawlessness was inevitable in thinly settled territories, and would persist as long as frontier conditions persisted. Some of the image-makers had gone beyond to speculate on why this was the case, and to suggest any number of explanations.

Some of these had to do with the sparse population. Men living in thinly settled regions, they agreed, instinctively shed the habits of civilization and reverted to a primitive form of law enforcement in which the individual, not the social group, maintained order. In such areas, too, criminals could hide more readily, without gossipy neighbors to give them away. There they could prey on those who had reaped sudden fortunes without learning how to care for their wealth; prospectors and ranchers and farmers who had gleaned Nature's bounties to the full and lived in isolation were ready-made victims. Such a devil-sent opportunity was more than could be resisted by outlaws with a Falstaffian distaste for authority and a Faustian lust to improve themselves at the expense of their fellows. Where riches were so readily available by fair means or foul, too many would be tempted to adopt the foul.[1]

The passionate faith in liberty so strong on all frontiers—the "pestilent symptom of the gangrene of ultrademocracy" as a hostile critic put it—also encouraged lawbreaking. In Europe, where legality was seen as a vested handmaiden of civilization, the instinct was to obey traditional authority; along the frontiers, where every man thought of himself as a ruler rather than ruled, the law was viewed as an instrument of meddling despots. "Liberty here," wrote one image-maker, "means to do each as he pleases; to care for nothing and nobody, to cheat everybody."[2] Liberty to the frontiersman meant the right to battle with bowie knives, gun down enemies, and lynch suspected wrongdoers. Liberty meant a license to cheat and abuse in the name of private gain; one traveler was horrified when a steamboat captain refused to waste precious time by stopping to rescue a passenger who had fallen overboard, another when passengers

---

[1]   Franklin D. Scott, ed., *Baron Klinkowstrom's America, 1818–1820* (Evanston, 1952), p. 191; Charles V. C. de Varigny, *The Women of the United States* (New York, 1895), pp. 169–70.
[2]   William Faux, *Memorable Days in America: Being a Journal of a Tour to the United States* (London, 1823), p. 194.

collected funds to pay the captain's fine if he violated safety regulations to speed their journey.[3]

Lawlessness was also encouraged, the image-makers believed, by the migration process, for in the sifting that occurred, the timid and the law-abiding were left behind, the reckless and the rebellious were attracted. Among these were many out-and-out criminals fleeing punishment or lured by the ample opportunity for plunder—"Dünger" a German novelist called them—the dung that would fertilize a future civilization but stain the pages of the present.[4] One traveler reported a stagecoach journey with a forger from Norway, an escaped convict from the galleys of Naples, an outlaw from France, a rowdy from New Orleans, a deserter from Prussia, and a convict from Australia.[5] The image-makers singled out Texas as the ultimate haven for scoundrels—a sanctuary for every outlaw and every cutthroat fleeing justice in other lands. So many were concentrated there, they insisted, that the common greeting was "what war yer name afore yer moved to these parts?"[6] while the initials, G.T.T.—"Gone to Texas"—became an internationally used symbol for runaway criminals.[7] Safety and order could hardly be expected amidst such company.

Centers of Lawlessness: The Mississippi Valley

Long before Texas earned its dubious distinction, Europeans had fastened on other areas as centers of savagery, usually with some justification. The first to be glorified was the lower Mississippi Valley. That region's unenviable reputation centered about the boatmen who manned the scows, flatboats, barges, and keelboats that plied the waterways in the early nineteenth century. "Untutored savages" they were called—a crude, profane, drunken assemblage of bullies whose only distinction was the enormous strength required to propel their cumbersome craft against the river's current. This they were ready to use at the slightest excuse, usually in the form of hand-to-hand combat with fists or bowie knives.[8] Charles Dickens

---

3   James S. Buckingham, *The Eastern and Western States of America* (London, 1842), 2: 39; Frederick Marryat, *A Diary in America* (London, 1839), pp. 195–96.
4   Charles Sealsfield, quoted in William P. Dallman, *The Spirit of America As Interpreted in the Works of Charles Sealsfield* (St. Louis, 1935), pp. 107–8.
5   János Xantus, *Utazás Kalifornia déli részeiben* (Pest, 1860), pp. 8–9.
6   *America Settler*, 25 April 1874.
7   Thomas Hughes, ed., *G. T. T. Gone to Texas* (London, 1884), p. 5. The same views are expressed in Charles Hooton, *St. Louis Isle, or Texiana* (London, 1847), p. 15; Francis G. Sheridan, *Galveston Island; or, A Few Months off the Coast of Texas* (Austin, 1954), p. 95; Frederick Marryat, *Narrative of the Travels and Adventures of Monsieur Violet, in California, Sonora, and Western Texas* (London, 1843), 2: 44–45; and many other works.
8   Thomas Ashe, *Travels in America, Performed in 1806* (London, 1808), 2: 148–49; Gábor Fábián, "Travels by Steamer in the United States," *The Athenaeum* 2 (1838): 348–49.

created such a character: a brute of a man who carried a seven-shot revolver, a swordstick that he called his "tickler," and a great knife that he
labeled "The Ripper," because of its "usefulness as a means of ventilating
the stomach of an adversary in a close contest."⁹ Most lacked this dandy's
refinements in weaponry and were content to batter their opponents with
their fists or carve their torsos with butcher knives.

The depraved atmosphere that they created permeated all society;
even normally respectable merchants or gentlemanly lawyers carried
sword sticks and usually a revolver concealed about their persons. These
weapons were used regularly, usually in bloodlettings disguised as
"duels." Image-makers described these as daily affairs: the two riverboat
passengers who stepped outside the cabin to settle a quarrel and returned
after exchanging shots with one dying; the guest who took exception to
remarks made by the host at a dinner party, whipped out his knife, and
was only stopped from mayhem when the host unsheathed his weapon;
the session of the Arkansas legislature where the two law-makers staged a
knife duel on the floor with one killed; the Ohio legislature where battles
were so frequent that it was known as the "Bear Garden."¹⁰ Not even the
upper classes could escape the spirit of lawlessness that governed behavior
in the Mississippi Valley.

Their battles, however, were models of gentlemanly decorum when
compared to fights among the rivermen and common folk. In these no
Marquis of Queensbury rules spoiled the fun; opponents fought with their
hands, feet, knees, heads, and teeth—not to mention knives and revolvers—with the battle ending only when the loser had been battered
into unconsciousness or so seriously maimed that he had to surrender.
Their weaponry varied, although bowie knives were universally worn;
some wore lethally pointed spurs day and night to be ready for any
challenge. Most, however, preferred to rely on their own skills—"tearing,
kicking, scratching, biting, gouging"¹¹—to bring their enemies to submis-

⁹ Charles Dickens, *The Life and Adventures of Martin Chuzzlewit* (London, 1844), p. 390.
Comparable characters are described in John Bradbury, *Travels in the Interior of America, in
the Years 1809, 1810, and 1811* (Liverpool, 1817), p. 208; John Melish, *Travels through the
United States of America, in the Years & 1807, and 1809, 1810, & 1811* (London, 1818), 2: 94;
Henry B. Fearon, *Sketches of America* (London, 1818), p. 243; George W. Featherstonhaugh,
Excursion through the Slave States (New York, 1844), p. 100; Matilda J. F. Houstoun, *Hesperos;
or, Travels in the West* (London, 1850), 2: 62–63; and many other travel accounts.
¹⁰ Fredrika Bremer, *The Homes of the New World: Impressions of America* (New York, 1853), 2:
111; Charles G. B. Daubney, *Journal of a Tour through the United States, and in Canada, Made
during the Years 1837–38* (Oxford, 1843), p. 150; Buckingham, *Eastern and Western States of
America*, 2: 5, 13.
¹¹ Fortesque Cuming, *Sketches of a Tour to the Western Country* (Pittsburgh), 1810), p. 118.
Comparable descriptions are in William N. Blane, *An Excursion through the United States and
Canada, during the Years 1822–23* (London, 1824), p. 161; and Ferdinand M. Bayard, *Voyage
dans l'intérieur des Etats-Unis* (Paris, 1798), pp. 78–79.

sion. Nothing else was needed, for the battlers of the Mississippi Valley frontier brought hand-to-hand combat to new heights—or depths.

Their ultimate purpose in combat was to gouge out the eyes and bite off the ears and nose of their opponents. Some prepared for their careers from childhood, sharpening their teeth and toughening their thumbnails by smearing them with melted tallow daily until they became as hard as iron.[12] Thus equipped, they were ready to stage the contests that fascinated the image-makers. These were described in all their gory detail: the fighter whose nose had been bitten off and was being consoled by a friend who opened his hand to disclose an eyeball and said, "Don't pity me. Pity that fellow over there";[13] the winner who boasted that his opponent's right eye was "quite out of its socket and Joe was obliged to carry him home"; another who when reprimanded for gouging defended himself by saying, "But I did not take his eye quite out, only poked it halfway from its socket."[14] A visitor to a western jail reported three prisoners, one guilty of gouging, another of stabbing, and the third of biting off a nose.[15] So popular were such tales that one Hungarian short story (laid on a sugar plantation just outside of Buffalo) used as its theme the ultimate triumph of the hero, "Bird-eye," when he gouged out the eyes of the villain, then strangled him.[16] "One meets in this nation," wrote a British traveler, "few men who do not have one eye put out in this manner."[17]

This was utter nonsense, for there is no evidence that such affairs ever took place. Notably not a single image-maker described an eye gouging that he had actually witnessed; all repeated tales told them by frontiersmen as the gospel truth. That these yarn spinners were simply engaging in some fancy leg pulling at the expense of a gullible greenhorn seems probable. One visitor who heard a particularly gory account ("Lord J——s Alm——y!—as pretty a scrape as ever you *see'd*") and copied every word

[12] Louis Milfort, *Memoirs, or a Quick Glance at My Travels and My Sojourn in the Creek Nation* (reprint ed., Kennesaw, Ga., 1959), p. 117. Ashe, *Travels in America*, 1: 225–29, is the most complete—and imaginative—account of eye gouging by a traveler. Somewhat less detailed is Patrick Shirreff, *A Tour through North America: Together with a Comprehensive View of the Canadas and United States* (Edinburgh, 1835), p. 236.

[13] This story, told almost word for word, is in both Cuming, *Sketches of a Tour to the Western Country*, pp. 118–19, and Adlard Welby, *A Visit to North America and the English Settlements in Illinois* (London, 1821), p. 73, suggesting that the authors listened to the same tall-tale teller.

[14] Charles Sealsfield, *The Americans As They Are: Described in a Tour through the Valley of the Mississippi* (London, 1828), p. 26; Mark Beaufoy, *Tour through Parts of the United States and Canada by a British Subject* (London, 1828), p. 69. Similar accounts are in James Flint, *Letters from America* (Edinburgh, 1822), p. 114; Melish, *Travels through the United States of America*, pp. 398, 414–15; and Faux, *Memorable Days in America*, p. 231.

[15] J. E. Alexander, *Transatlantic Sketches, Comprising Visits to the Most Interesting Scenes in North and South America and the West Indies* (London, 1833), 2: 107.

[16] Tivadar Kompolthy, *In America: Stories and Sketches of American Life* (Veszprém, 1885), passim.

[17] Milfort, *Memoirs, or a Quick Glance at My Travels*, p. 116.

faithfully could not understand why listeners were convulsed with laughter during the whole telling. He did not recognize, as did a few of the less innocent image-makers, that he was the victim of a unique brand of frontier humor, and that the hearers were roaring at his own gullibility.[18] Unfortunately most Europeans who read of gouging and nose biting were as innocent as the authors, with never a thought that they were being "taken." Their image of the West as a land of savagery rested on a false base, but was nonetheless accepted.

Centers of Lawlessness: The Far West

Even the Mississippi Valley as seen by early image-makers was a land of peace and calm compared to the plains and deserts of the Far West as they were described by a later generation of European novelists and travelers in the years after the Civil War. On the first the principal offenders had been the scum of society—rivermen and desperados—who gouged and dirked each other as might be expected of such riffraff; on the second *everyone* was a lawbreaker, for there no law existed save that carried in holster and boot top. Beyond the Missouri each individual must defend himself and his property. He was the only law, and must be sheriff, judge, jury, and executioner whenever justice was done.

Fortunately American ingenuity had provided him with the needed weapons: the bowie knife and the Colt revolver. The bowie knife—or "Arkansas tooth-pick" as it was affectionately called—a lethal bit of cutlery developed by one James Bowie, was the one essential tool on the far western frontier, suitable to every task from cleaning fish and picking teeth to carving up an enemy. The Colt revolver—"Judge Colt" or the "Great Equalizer," as the frontiersmen described it—was even more necessary. Perfected by Samuel Colt during the 1840s and in general use during the postwar years, the six-shooter was as much a part of any westerner's attire as his pants or his shoes, and generally had to be used a dozen times a day by those who wanted to stay alive.

So the image-makers said. They insisted that there was nothing wrong in this, and that the revolver was a valuable asset to civilization in a land teeming with renegades and outlaws. "I tell you, Hugh," said a character in a British novel, "that without the revolver there would be no living out here. No siree. The six-shooter puts us all on a level, and each man has got to respect another. I don't say as their ain't a lot wiped out each year,

[18] Simon A. O'Ferrall, *A Ramble of Six Thousand Miles through the United States of America* (London, 1832), pp. 169–70. Among the few travelers who recognized this were William A. Baillie-Grohman, *Camps in the Rockies* (New York, 1882), pp. 24–25; Charles A. Murray, *Travels in North America during the Years 1834, 1835, and 1836* (London, 1839), 1: 214–15; and Shirreff, *A Tour through North America*, p. 236.

because there is; but I say that it is better so than it would be without it."[19]
Especially since on that frontier any questionable behavior, any threatening gesture, and insulting remark, had to be handled at once by the individual concerned. "It is one of the most imperative laws of Western society," Europeans were told, "that, if a man insults you in any way, you are
bound to then and there shoot him dead."[20] If you did not you would be
shot yourself. This might be a "remnant of barbarism," as one traveler
called it, but those were the rules.[21]

Hence, all in the West—men, women, and children—were always
armed to the teeth. Armament was a necessity for the lower elements, for
any personal "difficulty" was sure to end in drawn weapons and probably
a corpse or two. So did the society's elite; in Nevada judges, lawyers, and
witnesses routinely unbuckled their gun belts when they entered the
courtroom, and in California no sensible person would think of leaving
home without a five-shot revolver, a long knife, and "some kind of mace
with a short handle weighted on both and with lead balls."[22] One traveler,
about to enter a new territory and wondering whether to buy a gun, was
told: "Well, you mout not want one for a month, and you mout not want
one for three months; but if you ever did want one, you kin bet you'll
want it almi'ty sudden."[23] In the West of the image-makers, every person
was a walking arsenal, and every stranger a potential foe.

With all armed, shootings were daily events. Some were affairs of
honor, but hardly in the European tradition. The townspeople were informed of the time and place first by a village crier, then came the duel itself.[24] This was of a sort to satisfy the most blood-thirsty reader: the antagonists locked in a darkened room to fight with bowie knives until one
was killed; or linked with a thirty-inch chain and armed with ten-inch
daggers; or lowered into a canyon to battle to the death with butcher
knives—"He plunged the knife into my side. As soon as I found his arm
thus stretched out, I cut the muscles of his arm near the right shoulder.
Immediately the knife dropped. While he was stooping to pick up his
knife, I sent my blade into his body from the back. . . ."[25] Strong stuff,
this, and "savage, untamed men who, when their thirst for blood has been

[19] G. A. Henty, *Redskin and Cow-Boy: A Tale of the Western Plains* (London, 1891), p. 184.
[20] Foster B. Zincke, *Last Winter in the United States: Being Table Talk Collected during a Tour
through the Late Southern Confederation, the Far West, and Rocky Mountains* (London, 1868),
p. 218.
[21] Archibald Prentice, *A Tour in the United States* (London, 1848), pp. 59–60.
[22] Hooton, *St. Louis Isle*, p. 16; *America*, 4 July 1883; Paul Duplessis, *Le Batteur d'estrade*
(Paris, 1862), 2: 3.
[23] Baillie-Grohman, *Camps in the Rockies*, pp. 25–26.
[24] Duplessis, *Le Batteur d'estrade*, 2: 2.
[25] Robert M. Ballantyne, *The Golden Dream; or, Adventures in the Far West* (London, 1861),
p. 218; Friedrich A. Strubberg, *Bis in die Wildnis* (Breslau, 1858), 3: 205–6; *American Settler*,
20 October 1883.

aroused, are worse than wild aniamls."[26] Or so the image-makers told Europeans.

In their eyes, these "duels" were well-ordered affairs when compared with the carnage that was a daily part of western life. With all frontiersmen armed, most quick-tempered, and all governed by a code that decreed instant gunfire in the case of insult or challenge, survival was reserved for those quickest on the draw. "Every stranger," a French novelist told his readers, "is at first glance an enemy, and hence persons generally accost each other at a distance, with the barrel of the gun advanced and the finger on the trigger."[27] In such situations quickness on the draw made the difference between life and death. "He who has the gun in his hand first," Old Surehand explained, "has the advantage. . . . When he commands "Hands up" (*Hände hoch!*) and fails to receive instant obedience, he shoots without hesitation. Everyone knows that."[28] When Hugh, a well-brought-up British schoolboy, did not instantly gun down a stranger who had falsely accused him of stealing a horse, he was severely reprimanded by his companions. "You did wrong in not shooting," they told him. "The rule of the plains is, if one man calls another either a liar or a coward, that fellow has the right to shoot him down if he can get his gun out first. That's the rule, ain't it boys?" The boys allowed that that was the rule, as any reader of western sensationalism should know.[29]

Given this "code of the West," the landscape described by European novelists was virtually carpeted with corpses. Some based their plots on the unsavory characters who contributed to this slaughter; Friedrich Gerstäcker's *Die Flusspiraten des Mississippi* and *Die Regulatoren in Arkansas* told of outlaw bands secretly led by community leaders that roamed the West until hunted down by an outraged citizenry, and Gustave Aimard's *The Pirates of the Prairies* described the exploits of a villainous gang of robbers who operated from a hollow-tree hideaway to shoot down victims and scalp Indians for the fifty-dollar government bounty. In an often-reprinted story by Charles W. Webber, the hero, Jack Long, after being flogged by ruffians when he bested their leader in a shooting match, hunted down and killed the whole gang, one by one by shooting each in the exact center of the left eye.[30] Even Old Shatterhand was well versed in

---

[26]   Friedrich Gerstäcker, *The Young Gold-Digger; or, A Boy's Adventures in the Gold Regions* (London, 1860), p. 320. Another typical tale of such a fight is in Xantus, *Utazás Kalifornia déli részeiben*, pp. 5–6.
[27]   Gustave Aimard, *The Prairie Flower: A Tale of the Indian Border* (London, n.d.), p. 27.
[28]   Karl May, *Old Surehand* (reprint ed., Vienna, 1953), 2: 12–13.
[29]   Henty, *Redskin and Cow-Boy*, p. 160. Comparable statements are in Gustave Aimard, *The Red Track* (New York, 1884), p. 88; and "Duels," *For Ungdommen* 4 (Norway, 1871): 366.
[30]   Charles W. Webber, *Jack Long; or, Shot in the Eye: A True Story of Texas Border Life* (New York, 1846), pp. 4–30. The identical story is in Webber's *Tales of the Southern Border* (Philadelphia, 1853), pp. 9–44.

the etiquette of mayhem, although killing offended his Teutonic standards. "In a land where death and betrayal threaten from every side," he told a companion, "man is forced to look out for himself and to avoid anything that might threaten his well-being."[31] Anything such as death, Karl May implied.

Fiction writers might be suspected of stretching the truth, but first-hand reports from travelers in the Far West were less easily questioned. And they told the same tale. Their books were studded with eyewitness accounts of corpses and blazing guns: the town where four or five murders a night was commonplace; the guest at an inn who was shot to death because he helped himself to too much gravy; the Texan politician who fitted his supporters in chain mail and built a special hospital for those injured in preelection brawls.[32] One visitor took seriously the obvious tall tale of a man who died of heart failure in a Denver saloon and was propped up at a table by his friends who then fled lest they be accused of his death. The bartender discovered the corpse just as two strangers entered, and recognizing his peril, shouted: "I did it in self defense."[33] Commented a French traveler with masterful understatement: "Human life is very cheap among them"; added a Polish commentator: "It does not mean any more to shoot someone here than to box someone's ears in our country."[34]

Distortions such as these did enough disservice to the truth, but more was done by the only faintly concealed approval of the image-makers for the carnage they described. Their justification was logical enough: where there was no public law, private law must suffice. "How in thunder would you keep order if it weren't for the six shooter?" asked one character. "There would be no peace, and the men would be always quarreling and wrangling."[35] Over and over again writers insisted that the Colt revolver was the only law needed on the frontiers, and that personal revenge was the surest and best means of keeping order. "The six-shooter," said one hero, "is my license, certificate and deed."[36] This was as it must be when courts and normal law-enforcement machinery were lacking. Once they were strong enough to keep order the frontiersmen could discard their guns but (as one character put it) "That won't be for some time yet."[37]

[31] Karl May, *Old Surehand* (reprint ed., Vienna, 1953), 2: 12–13.
[32] Marryat, *Narrative of the Travels and Adventures of Monsieur Violet*, p. 55; Robert Watt, *Hinsides Atlanterhavet: Skildringer fra Amerika* (Copenhagen, 1874), p. 23; Kalikst Wolski, *American Impressions* (Cheshire, Conn., 1968), pp. 195–205.
[33] Henry W. Lucy, *East by West: A Journey in the Recess* (London, 1885), 1: 63–64.
[34] Paul Bourget, *Outre-Mer: Impressions of America* (New York, 1895), p. 256.
[35] Henty, *Redskin and Cow-Boy*, pp. 183–84.
[36] Charles W. Webber, *The Prairie Scout; or, Agatone, the Renegade* (New York, 1852), p. 42. Similar remarks are in Webber, *The Texan Virago* (Philadelphia, 1852), p. 4; and Gabriel Ferry, *The Wood Rangers* (London, 1860), 1: 233.
[37] Henty, *Redskin and Cow-Boy*, pp. 185–86.

Personal justice might symbolize a step backward for civilization, but there was much to be said for it.

Particularly when it was necessary to defend the property that was the principal reward for pioneering. On this point the image-makers mirrored the materialistic prejudices of the westerners; they saw a man's possessions as fully as important as his life, and to be protected at any cost. Robbery was the supreme crime in the West, for it could never be excused by need in a labor-hungry land where there was work for all. Karl May, who could invent a "law of the West" for any occasion, had one now: "According to the laws of the Wild West, thievery shall be punished by death"; so did his creation Winnetou the Apache, who warned that "he who forces his way into my *wigwam* without my permission must expect, according to the law of the West, an instant death."[38] Fatalists were inclined to believe that the invention of the Colt revolver had been arranged by a benevolent deity just in time to allow westerners to guard their holdings in a land beyond the pale of the law.[39]

Because the primary concern of every frontiersman was to guard his possessions, his most-feared enemies were those who threatened his property, not his life. Fur trappers were far more apprehensive of other fur trappers than of Indians; the Indians would only kill but the whites would steal, and he treated both accordingly: "The Indians he shoots down as coldly as he would kill a wolf, buffalo, or bear, but the trappers he stabs with a real fiendish joy, as if he had delivered society from a great criminal."[40] Land in the West was particularly treasured, and any threat to it was certain to be answered by a bullet through the head. Western custom allowed whites to shoot an Indian at any time, kill each other in self-defense, murder for revenge, and take the law into their own hands when their lives were threatened, but it reserved the worst punishment for those who tried to steal land. "For any treacherous assault on a man's property," a Polish traveler observed, "he punishes ruthlessly by a death all too cruel."[41]

This made sense, for the robber was a greater threat to the frontier society than the murderer. Like as not a man that was killed was a worthless drifter who would not be missed while his killer was a respectable citizen whose services were of value to the community. With artisans so few and

---

[38]   May, *Old Surehand*, p. 317. May makes almost identical remarks in his *Der Schatz im Silbersee* (reprint ed., Bamberg, 1973), p. 46; and *Winnetou II* (reprint ed., Vienna, 1951), p. 288.

[39]   Webber, *Tales of the Southern Border*, p. 242.

[40]   Charles Sealsfield, *The Courtship of George Howard, Esquire* (New York, 1843), pp. 42–43.

[41]   Henryk Sienkiewicz, *Listy z podróży: Koleja Dwóch Oceanów Szkice Amerykánskie* (Warsaw, 1899), 5: 64–65. Similar comments are in Gustaf Unonius, *Minnen från en sjuttonårig vistelse i nordvestra Amerika* (Uppsala, 1862), 1: 162; and Jacques-Pierre Brissot de Warville, *Nouveau voyage dans les Etats-Unis de l'Amérique septentrionale en 1788* (Paris, 1791), 2: 214.

"The Duel." From Theodor Dielitz, *Atlantis. Bilder aus
dem Wald-und Prairieleben Amerika's* (Berlin, 1862).
(From the collections of Albert Hümmerich of Berlin.)

jobs to be done so many, frontier society was inclined to wink an eye at murder in such cases. One condemned killer was cut down from the gallows in Texas when sturdy men were needed to fight its revolution; another was saved by a crowd because he was the only good gunsmith in the region.[42] But let a criminal infringe on any man's property and public opinion demanded immediate punishment. Not a murmur of criticism was heard when a landowner posted a sign announcing: "I may be miserably damned if I don't send a bullet into the heart of the first one who crosses my field without replacing the barriers."[43] He had the right to guard his property, even by killing.

Given this "code," a man's possessions in the West were safer than (in the phrase of one image-maker) "among the refined inhabitants of London and New York."[44] Even in Texas with its unenviable reputation for lawlessness and the smallest towns boasting a half-dozen homicides a night, doors were never locked and windows never latched. "Thieves!" said an amazed innkeeper when asked about his open doors. "Lord bless you man. Th' ain't no thieves about these parts. . . . No! No! Old Abe never yet fastened his door on anythin' that could lift a latch."[45] The West of the image-makers might be a land of personal justice, sudden death, and excessive bloodletting; it might not (as a character in a German novel put it) administer justice "in accord with Mr. Blackstone," but at least one thing was safe there.[46] And one thing only. So Europeans were taught to believe.

Frontier Law Enforcement

This was the case even when thickening population required some form of law enforcement more tuned to society's needs. Three forms were popular among the image-makers: lynch mobs, popular tribunals initiated and operated by the orderly elements of the community, and federal or territorial courts staffed by easterners with a minimum legal knowledge and a maximum political influence. Unlike modern critics who are inclined to condemn all lynchers and extralegal bodies as little better than mob rule, novelists and travelers saw little bad in people's courts, vigilantes, or regulator committees, and little good in the primitive courts that signaled the coming of orthodox judicial procedures.

[42]   Carl of Solms-Braunfels, *Texas, 1844–1845* (Houston, 1936), p. 57; Charles Sealsfield, *Das Kajütenbuch oder nationale Charakteristiken* (Zurich, 1841), 1: 222.
[43]   Xavier Eyma, *Scènes de moeurs et de voyage dans le nouveau monde* (Paris, 1862), p. 90.
[44]   *American Settler*, 5 January 1884. Similar comments were printed in this paper on 7 August 1880 and 13 August 1881.
[45]   John Regan, *The Emigrant's Guide to the Western States of America* (Edinburgh, 1852), p. 56.
[46]   Ulrich S. Carrington, ed., *The Making of an American: An Adaptation of Memorable Tales by Charles Sealsfield* (Dallas, 1974), p. 63.

Their distrust of the courts is easy to understand. Accustomed as they were to the stately formalities of the European legal system, with its wigged judges and gowned attorneys, the early circuit courts seemed little more than caricatures of the Old World's most respected institutions. The presiding judge, traveling from county seat to county seat, arrived with a motley following of lawyers, litigants, preachers, office seekers, and assorted hangers-on, creating a carnival atmosphere that offended those with respect for the hallowed traditionalism. Some courts, Europeans were told, violated all standards by meeting out of doors; Karl May pictured the "prairie courts of *Savannengerichte*" as holding their sessions "under the free heavens."[47] How could justice be administered under such conditions? Or in the drafty log cabins or converted saloons that served as courtrooms on most occasions?

The proceedings were as offensive as their settings. The judge was likely to ascend the bench clad in dirty work clothes, a battered felt hat, and a worn shirt, usually with a cigar in his mouth or a quid of tobacco in his cheek, and sometimes so pleasantly inebriated that he nodded through the entire trial. Lawyers and litigants lounged about the room, their feet propped higher than their heads, shoes removed to disclose toes peeking through holes in their socks, busying themselves by whittling on the arms of their chairs, chewing, and spitting indiscriminately. And the juries! "What a motley assemblage," sighed a French traveler. Unshaved hunters in tattered leather jackets, farmers in home-fashioned clothes of domestic stuff, merchants and tradesmen and millers garbed in the uniforms of their trades, all with hats on and pocketknife in hand and cheeks bulging with chewing tobacco.[48]

Traditional legal customs stood no chance in such a gathering, where neither justices nor attorneys were overly burdened with a knowledge of Kent or Blackstone. Instead judges based their decisions on what they called "common sense" rather than precedent, and vigorously defended their right to do so. "The court knows well enough whiat it's abayt," one was heard to say; "it ain't a'going to do no sich thing as read all them law books by no manner of means, and it's no use to carry on so, for the court decides all pynts against you."[49] When the farcical trial was over the whole court—judges and attorneys and litigants and jury—commonly adjourned to the nearest saloon to "liquor up" on tangle-foot red-eye, their differences forgotten.

As often as not, too, popular pressures prevented both a fair trial and the execution of the sentence. Juries were impossible to assemble and fair

---

[47] May, *Old Surehand*, 2: 212.
[48] Faux, *Memorable Days in America*, 175; Marryat, *A Diary in America*, 3: 197–98; Napoléon A. Murat, *America and the Americans* (New York, 1849), pp. 54–55.
[49] Featherstonhaugh, *Excursion through the Slave States*, p. 79.

verdicts impossible to reach when everyone knew that friends of the criminal would gun down anyone who judged him guilty. One judge, unable to recruit a jury to try three murderers and a horse thief, was forced to ask the criminals themselves to serve; they agreed and solemnly voted themselves not guilty. Another, about to pronounce sentence on a criminal, was kidnapped and held hostage until he changed his mind.[50] Even those found guilty were likely to be freed by their confederates before they could be punished; one convicted murderer was plied with food and drink by his friends until nightfall in the local lockup, then whisked away.[51] Justice was only a travesty in western courts such as these—as they were pictured by the image-makers.

Almost none of those image-makers recognized that those courts were admirably tuned to the democratic spirit of the frontier, and that the justice they dispensed was exactly that desired by the majority of the people. But a few did. They realized that when the people made the laws, elected the magistrates, and financed court proceedings, no gowned justices were needed to force obedience, as was the case in Europe. When one traveler remonstrated against the lack of dignity he was told: "Yes, that might be quite necessary in England, to overawe the parcel of ignorant creatures who have no share in making the laws; but with us a man's a man, whether he have a silk gown on him or not; and I guess he can decide as well without a wig as with one."[52] When the people were their own judge and jury, they could never complain against themselves.

Where even these primitive courts were lacking, as was always the case in the newest settlements, the people were willing to serve not only as judge and jury, but as executioner as well. In their eyes, horse thieves and rustlers deserved immediate punishment, and if legal justice was not available, extralegal substitutes must be devised. Two were most common: lynching and vigilante committees. Westerners saw these as essential along the frontiers, partly because the West was a harbor for an extraordinary assemblage of thieves, harlots, and desperados attracted by the quick wealth and lack of law enforcement, partly because the nearest established courts were usually hundreds of miles away. "In a society composed . . . of the very outcasts of the world," one visitor agreed, "it is well that even a

---

[50] William Ballantine, *The Old World and the New* (London, 1884), pp. 163–64; Featherstonhaugh, *Excursion through the Slave States*, p. 106; *Nieuwe Rotterdamse Courant*, 6 September 1876.
[51] George W. Featherstonhaugh, *A Canoe Voyage up the Minnay Sotor* (London, 1847), 2: 81–84.
[52] O'Ferrall, *A Ramble of Six Thousand Miles*, pp. 243–44. A novelist expressed similar views in Mayne Reid, *The Headless Horseman: A Strange Tale of Texas* (London, 1865), pp. 412–13, and a guidebook author in Regan, *The Emigrant's Guide to the Western States*, p. 109.

code of this sort should exist" if the community was "to pass from a primitive to a civilized state."[53]

Surprisingly this sentiment was almost universally favored by the image-makers. They saw lynch law and vigilantism not as brutal relics of a barbarous past but as essential to an orderly present and future. The least-approving viewed them as necessary evils, to be deplored, but still essential if life and property were to be protected. "We are not yet in a position here in our state," quoth a character in a German novel, "to bring criminals into a court and keep them in custody. Everything is yet too new here."[54] Better to hang a few than turn them loose on the community. Lynch law and vigilantism might be severe and cruel, they might offend the sense of order bred into Europeans, but they were better than no law at all. Even British Tories, suspicious as always of anything that smacked of popular rule, admitted that they were "perhaps necessary in the turbulent and chaotic state in which society was placed in those remote districts."[55]

Image-makers less restrained by antidemocratic prejudices saw lynching and vigilantism not as a temporary evil but as a positive good. Novelists particularly viewed extralegal justice as a divinely sanctioned institution, a "law of the prairies," based on the biblical injunction of an eye for an eye, a tooth for a tooth. "In the desert," the villainous Don Stefano was told by the masked riders who had kidnapped him, "where the laws of cities are powerless to punish the guilty, there is a terrible, summary, implacable legislature, to which, in the common welfare, every aggrieved person has a right to appeal." "And what is this law?" asked Don Stefano, his face a cadaverous hue. "Lynch law," came the terrible answer.[56] In the West, where the laws of man could not prevail, the law of the Almighty must, the law that decreed that "he who kills by the sword will perish by the sword."[57] "That law," a French novelist believed, "is as ancient as the world, it emanates from God Himself; it is the duty of all honest people to run down a wild beast when they meet him in their passage."[58] This was a divine edict, and this was the edict of the people. "Us free Americans," a character in a German novel announced, "don't care for lawyers and

[53] Richard G. A. Levinge, *Echoes from the Backwoods; or, Sketches of Transatlantic Life* (London, 1846), 2: 26–27; Sienkiewicz, *Listy z podróży*, 5: 64–65.
[54] Friedrich Gerstäcker represented this view. His ideas are discussed in Paul C. Weber, *America in Imaginative German Literature in the First Half of the Nineteenth Century* (New York, 1926), p. 154; and Augustus J. Prahl, "America in the Works of Gerstäcker," *Modern Language Quarterly* 4 (June 1943): 221.
[55] Francis Wyse, *America: Realities and Resources* (London, 1846), 1: 206–7.
[56] Gustave Aimard, *The Indian Scout; or, Life on the Frontier* (Philadelphia, n.d.), p. 174.
[57] Gabriel Ferry, *Le Coureur des bois* (reprint ed., Paris, 1932) 2: 23–24.
[58] Gustave Aimard, *The Trappers of Arkansas; or, The Loyal Heart* (London, 1864), pp. 165–66.

courts who dish out justice to those who pay them most. We make our own rules, and by jingo, you had better live up to them or else."[59]

"Or else," meant summary justice at the end of a hangman's rope. Readers of European Westerns soon learned that the cry, "lynch him," was a sure prelude to a gory hanging: highwaymen and road agents hunted down like wolves and strung to the nearest tree, a train robber hoisted to a railroad sign and his body peppered with revolver shots as it writhed in the air; a rustler "stretching rope" on the beams of a corral gate.[60] And woe unto anyone who tried to interfere. One British lad hurried to a lynching only to see the body of the victim swaying in the wind. "Surely you have been too hasty," he exclaimed, only to have a dozen guns leveled as he was profanely assured they would be fired at anyone who tried to cut the victim down.[61]

That legal-minded English youth was unusual, for chracters in most European novels were unabashedly sympathetic to Judge Lynch. One who missed the fun when he arrived just after a whole rogues' gallery of villains had been strung up consoled himself by remembering that "sometime later I had the good fortune to be able to join in lynching a couple of similar fellows."[62] There were no tears of compassion for the victims and no mourning over the disservice to the legal heritage among the image-makers. "Rough and ready, as well as harsh, though their proceedings were," a British novelist judged, "they accomplished the end in view most efficiently."[63] The end justified the means; property protection was more important than maintaining the sanctity of the law. "Such," said a hero, "is the stern, necessitarian logic of the frontier."[64]

If the image-makers confessed an ill-concealed admiration for lynch mobs, they were even less restrained in their praise of vigilante committees, or bands of regulators, that they described as ever-present in newer communities of the West. These, they pointed out, were not mobs; they were "peoples' courts" organized and supported by the better elements, based on public need, and willing to allow the accused a modicum of defense. They were, above all, necessary to protect the lives and property of honest citizens. "*Honest* men have nothing to fear from us," one band of

---

[59] Carrington, ed., *The Making of an American*, p. 172.
[60] *American Settler*, 14 March 1891.
[61] Robert M. Ballantyne, *Digging for Gold: Adventures in California* (London, n.d.), pp. 85–86. Similar scenes are described in Friedrich Gerstäcker, *Gold! Ein californisches Lebensbild aus dem Jahr 1849* (Leipzig, 1858), 3: 253–54; and Friedrich A. Strubberg, *An der Indianergrenze* (Hanover, 1859), pp. 142–45.
[62] Jens Tvedt, *Sihasapa-Indianerne: Norske Udvandreres Hendelser i Amerika* (Stavanger, 1887), pp. 29–31.
[63] Ballantyne, *Digging for Gold*, pp. 88–89.
[64] Charles W. Webber, *Old Hicks the Guide; or, Adventures in the Comanche Country in Search of a Gold Mine* (New York, 1848), p. 31.

vigilantes told the townspeople; "on the contrary, we afford them every protection we can give."[65] Wherever they operated "a purification takes place that is much to the advantage of society."[66] Once more, as so often along the frontiers, necessity was the mother of change.

The vigilantes were also made to order for the European taste for sensationalism and chivalry; their gallant sweeps across the plains and their ruthless pursuit of wrongdoers might have come straight out of medieval legend. But legend improved upon by the imagination of the novelists. Their stories followed a pattern: a gang of outlaws threatening the community, the citizenry increasingly concerned, the leader of the regulators summoning his righteous band with a blast on a conch shell and a shouted "To horse! To horse!" In a trice all were mounted and away "on their swift and hearty steeds, in the true spirit of the ancient chivalry."[67] The villain captured after a spirited chase, the vigilantes prepared for the trial, arranging a circle of buffalo skulls on the broad prairie for the jurors, and selecting some of their members as prosecutors and defenders, just as had the Holy Velm on the banks of the Rhine in the olden days.

Then the questioning, the display of documents, the closing arguments, and the verdict. "What penalty does the culprit deserve?" asked the judge. "Death," the jury echoed. Turning to the prisoner, the judge addressed him in a stern voice: "You, who came into the desert with criminal intention, have fallen beneath the stroke of Lynch Law; it is the law of God; eye for eye, tooth for tooth; it admits of only one punishment, that of retaliation; it is the primitive law of old times restored to humanity." Then the sentence: to be buried alive with the right arm free and a revolver within reach so that he could end his suffering when it became unendurable. "Is this sentence just?" asked the judge. "Yes," chanted the jurors. "Eye for eye, tooth for tooth."[68]

Not all criminals were dispatched in such romantic style; most were jerked into eternity at the end of a hangman's rope. The novelists who described their deaths made up for lack of glamour by piling gory detail on gory detail. Karl May's usual technique was to have them hanged with a sudden jerk: "A powerful pull ripped the body of Ik Senadas into the air. For a moment the feet of the frenzied man sought to touch the ground; then he swung about in the air, moving in convulsive, spasmodic jerks which gradually became weaker and weaker. Then the body began to elongate and the half-breed was dead."[69] Other novelists varied this for-

[65] Gerstäcker, *The Young Gold-Digger*, p. 280.
[66] Marryat, *A Diary in America*, 3: 241.
[67] Webber, *The Texan Virago*, p. 46.
[68] Aimard, *The Indian Scout*, pp. 195-96.
[69] Quoted in Richard Cracroft, "The American West of Karl May" (M.A. thesis, University of Utah, 1963), p. 48.

mula: several men weighing down the branch of a tree to which the victim
was hung, then leaping off to let the limb swing upward; stringing the
criminal up so gently that he still lived, then naming a jury of twelve to
riddle it with bullets—a method that was highly popular "for it is always
amusing to get an opportunity to fire some live shots, even into a dead
body"; hanging the victim by his arms and coating his body with honey,
then letting him swing until flies and birds consumed his flesh; placing
him on a skittish horse with a noose about his neck to wait for the moment
when the animal moved and he was jerked to his death.[70] The latter device
was a favorite means for disposing of horse thieves; "it gave the animal itself an opportunity to wreak vengeance for all the wrongs received."[71]

Other writers gloried in highly sadistic descriptions. Jack Harkaway
witnessed such an execution: "His face became as black as night, as the
blood surged up into his head, and there stopped. He uttered incoherent
cries, and then a dull gurgle was all that issued from his lips. His limbs,
however, struggled spasmodically. 'Let him down three feet or more with
a run, and bring him up short,' said the leader. This was done. Sol Pike
was lowered with a jerk till his feet came within a dozen inches of the
ground. The jerk broke his neck."[72] A Negro named Ring, who had trai-
torously aided the Narraganset Indians (!) when they attacked the Colorado Village of Sierra Lawana, met an even crueler fate: "When three
men lifted him to the gallows he twisted like a snake, like an earwig in a
spider's web, and tried to bite so that the trappers had to be careful, for to
be bitten by this raving Negro could have had serious consequences. He
foamed at the mouth, and the froth oozed out and down his chin in long
threads. 'Help-murder-fire! Cut the rope, it is strangling me—Oh! Doctor
have mercy—I'll serve———be———damned.' The rest of the curse was
so terrible that we prefer not to render it. Soon all was still with the exception of some strange shudders—a kind of rattle from the hanged man."[73]

These inhuman torture scenes did nothing to dim the enthusiasm of
the image-makers for vigilantism. The acid test was effectiveness, and
they agreed almost unanimously that if westerners were to be protected,
the law must be both swift and cruelly administered. Of its swiftness they
left no doubt. "Very quick justice in this country, Mr. Dalton," said a
character in one novel; "deuced quick! . . . and doubtless very pleasant for

[70]   Friedrich Gerstäcker, *Western Lands and Western Waters* (London, 1864), p. 52; Eilert
Storm, *Alene i Urskogen: Fortælling fra Amerika* (Oslo, 1899), p. 130; Gustave Aimard, *The
Trapper's Daughter; A Story of the Rocky Mountains* (London, 1877), p. 174.
[71]   Robert M. Bird, *Nick of the Woods: A Story of Kentucky* (London, 1837), 2: 168–69.
[72]   Bracebridge Hemying, *Jack Harkaway in America* (London, n.d.), p. 114.
[73]   Thomas Krag, *Fældejægeren eller Skovløberens forræderi: Fortælling fra Colorados vildnis*
(Oslo, 1890), pp. 41–43. Charles W. Webber, *The Gold Mines of the Gila: A Sequel to Old Hicks
the Guide* (New York, 1849), p. 151, has an equally gory scene in which he describes the
lynching of one man by another.

the chief personage; for all the torture of examination and waiting death are done away with."[74] It was also judged effective. "One can say whatever one likes about lynch law," a Norwegian traveler insisted, ". . . but one thing is certain: this law has many times proved to be as appropriate as just, and under the present conditions it is more effective than any other law in maintaining order and preventing crime."[75] Most criminals did not have to be hanged or even flogged; once a peoples' court began operating, they hightailed into the next county. "Judge Lynch," wrote a British commentator, "inspires more terror into the hearts of evil doers than any other judge in the country."[76]

If proof were needed, the image-makers had only to point to the rapid decline of crime in regions where the vigilantes operated. Even in the gold fields, where robbers and road agents outnumbered miners, a few executions were enough to end all problems. "Murderers and thieves were hanged . . . with such promptitude," a novelist reported, "that it struck terror into the hearts of evil-doers; and the consequence is, that we of this valley are now living in a perfect state of peace and security."[77] Lynch law was effective because it was founded "on the highest principles of morality . . . and is worthy of the jurisprudence of the highest civilization."[78] Properly administered as it was in the American West, it was "exactly the same as the ancient *lex talionis* of the Hebrews"; under it "the innocent were more likely to get a fair trial than in the higher civilization of England."[79] High praise, this, for an extralegal procedure that we know today to have sent many an innocent victim to his death, and undermined respect for statute law through the West.

European authors might praise Judge Lynch and his kangaroo courts, but their defense only sharpened the image of the frontier as a land of savagery among their readers. Vigilantes who gloried in jerking their victims into eternity, or who took sadistic delight into pumping bullets into a still-dangling corpse, were men of a different breed from law-respecting Europeans. Readers of Westerns might enjoy their plunge into such vicarious bloodbaths or thrill when the villainous One-Eyed Pete met his just fate at the hands of the regulators, but their impression of frontiersmen as barbarian seceders from civilization, ill-fitted for the companionship of cultured Europeans, was deepened.

[74] Gerstäcker, *Western Land and Western Waters*, p. 52.
[75] Unonius, *Minnen från en sjuttonårig vistelse*, 1: 117.
[76] Richard A. Preston, ed., *For Friends at Home: A Scottish Emigrant's Letters from Canada, California and the Cariboo, 1844–1864* (Montreal, 1974), pp. 150–51.
[77] Ballantyne, *The Golden Dream*, p. 108. For similar stories see Storm, *Alene i urskogen*, pp. 131–32; and A. O. Ansnes, *Amerikanske Streiftog: Oplevelser og Indtryk fra de Forenede Stater* (Kristiansund, 1889), p. 142.
[78] *American Settler*, 13 June 1874.
[79] Reid, *The Headless Horseman*, p. 448; Aimard, *The Trapper's Daughter*, p. 172.

Frontier Nativism

This gulf was widened when the image-makers piled incident on incident to demonstrate that the West disliked, mistreated, and sometimes abused all foreigners foolhardy enough to settle there. This prejudice was directed principally against non-Aryans—Latins, Negroes, Orientals, and Jews—but even British and German and Scandinavian immigrants were scorned as culturally inferior and as unwanted competitors for jobs. When a cultured German read of a westerner who described a steamboat explosion as "d——d lucky" because no one was killed—"only a parcel of those Dutch"—he began to suspect that he would find a more congenial welcome elsewhere.[80]

This impression was deepened as Europeans read of state after state in the West passing laws to limit landholdings and loans to foreigners, of the savage attacks of the Know-Nothings in mid-century, of the increasing western pressure on Congress to "save America for the Americans" by ending all immigration. They learned from novels and travelers of the mounting sentiment against aliens who "come over here in order to plunder our mines and rob us so that they can return home rich"; they learned too, that any German or Irishman was not only seen as dirty and unkempt but so cowardly that he would rather take a beating than fight back.[81] Life among such bigots would certainly be unpleasant and probably dangerous.

The ultimate in abuse, however, was reserved for non-Aryans. Negroes received more than their fair share. To most westerners they were an inferior people, subhuman, and so lazy and indolent that the country would benefit if they were shipped back to Africa. When Karl May's Old Surehand berated a frontiersman for calling a black a "Nigger," he was sharply told, "According to natural history they are counted among men . . . but my God, what men they are! A nigger is such a low form of life that he's not worth talking about."[82] Even the Indians were more tolerant of Negroes than the pioneers—if the image-makers are to be believed. When a Pawnee chief in one novel met his first black he first tried to rub the color from his face, then addressed him in stately prose: "Black-deer is a Sachem of his nation, his tongue is not forked, and the words his chest breathes are clear, for they come from his heart; Black-face will have his

---

[80] Murray, *Travels in North America*, 1: 200.
[81] *American Settler*, 15 August 1891; Gerstäcker, *Gold! Ein californisches Lebensbild*, 1: 43; Theodore C. Blegen, ed., *The Land of Their Choice: The Immigrants Write Home* (Minneapolis, 1955), p. 304. Some of the most strident criticism of newcomers was expressed by recent arrivals who had established themselves.
[82] May, *Old Surehand*, p. 128. Similar comparisons are in Heinrich Martels, *Briefe über westliche Teile der Vereinigten Staaten von Nordamerika* (Osnabruck, 1834), p. 65; and Paul Duplessis, *Les Mormons* (Paris, 1859), 4: 70–71.

place at the Council fire of the Pawnees, for from this moment he is the friend of a chief."[83] Let Americans hark to such noble words and be ashamed.

The Chinese fared less well than the Negroes in western esteem. They were seen as cunning and immoral, ready to turn against their best friends for a profit, and unpleasant competitors for jobs—"blacklegs, working for a quarter of the American wage."[84] Yet Europeans were told that even such undesirable immigrants hardly deserved the treatment they received from the frontiersmen. The image-makers were clearly shocked as they reported the heartless race wars that swept through the Chinese sections of western cities,[85] and clearly disturbed as they chronicled the racial slurs that were a part of the frontier speech: the insistence that the Chinese represented a new level of Darwinism that might be called "the survival of the meanest"; their condemnation as "soft, cowardly, unmasculine heathens," with voices that blended "the shriek of madmen with the spit of cats"; their abandonment of religion as they worshiped "horrible, misshapen idols." Chinese women were all prostitutes, Chinese men blackguards who would accept starvation wages to take jobs away from white men. There was no living with them; the choice was between "European civilization and Chinese barbarism."[86]

These were hardly flattering comments, but they were words of praise and affection when compared with those leveled against the Mexicans. Frontier invective reached new heights as the image-makers reported the array of adjectives summoned to the cause: "dark dogs," "yellow-skinned monsters," "yellow-bellied scum." "I don't call the Mexicans white," said a Texan in a Norwegian novel, "and neither does anyone else in these parts."[87] Even their flag symbolized cowardice, for the Mexican eagle emblazoned on it was "a dirty, cowardly creature that feeds upon carcasses, and will hardly attack a live rabbit."[88] They deserved the ill-treatment that was their lot in the Southwest, where they were flogged, murdered, and lynched for sport; one literary society there debated the topic: "Is it wicked to lynch Mexicans on Sunday?"[89]

Frontier hatred was mirrored in the numerous novels that were based on the Texan Rebellion and the Mexican War, both favorite themes among European authors. Texans, their authors argued, were perfectly

[83] Gustave Aimard, *The Border Rifles: A Tale of the Texan War* (Philadelphia, n.d.), p. 43.
[84] Alan Conway, ed., *The Welsh in America: Letters from the Immigrants* (Minneapolis, 1961), p. 278.
[85] *American Settler*, 30 May 1874; 23 November 1885; 13 March 1886.
[86] *American Settler*, 16 November 1889; *Nieuwe Rotterdamse Courant*, 6 April 1876.
[87] E. A. Hagerup, "The White Steed of the Prairies," *Børnenes Blad* 12 (Norway, 1872), no. 26.
[88] Webber, *The Gold Mines of the Gila*, p. 72.
[89] *American Settler*, 17 September 1881.

right in separating from Mexico, for who could endure being governed by "bigoted, idle and ignorant" peons who were "both morally and physically inferior to themselves." A war with such scum was no war at all, for two or three thousand Texans could deal with a whole army of the "pigmy, spindle-shanked" cowards, "none of them so big or half as strong as American boys of fifteen." A single Kentuckian with a riding whip could drive the whole lot into a whimpering retreat.[90] Even the Negro slaves who had escaped into Mexico were braver, and would take over the country when they became numerous enough.[91]

Mexican cowardice and incompetence could be laid squarely at the door of the idolatry that they paraded as religion. The image-makers, and the frontiersmen that they represented, made no secret of their scorn of Roman Catholicism. In their eyes the church debased the peons, robbed them of their sustenance, corrupted their morals, and condemned their souls to eternal damnation. Priests were heartless idolators who misled their parishioners with a gibberish of pretended Latin, bet on cockfights, and seduced young women in their flocks with Jesuitical skill. Even Karl May's Old Firehand, who was as loyal a Catholic as Karl May himself, judged them to be "either stupid or insane."[92]

Worst of all, the church encouraged the cruelty that was bred into every Mexican by his savage ancestry. The sabbath was consistently desecrated by church-sponsored carnivals where bulls were thrown to the ground by their tails, cocks pitted against each other, and mounted horsemen competed in snatching heads from chicks that had been buried in the ground. "It is doubtful," wrote an English novelist, "whether a thought of cruelty ever entered the mind of a New Mexican."[93] Women were as badly treated as animals; any girl who dared resist a priest's lecherous advances was stripped to the waist, tied to the back of a mule, and mercilessly beaten by ruffians chosen for their strength: "the strokes were deliberate and measured—they were counted! Each seemed to leave its separate wale upon the skin."[94]

Clearly the image-makers, whether British or German, Protestant or Catholic, had little love for the Mexicans and their religion, but even they were shocked by their harsh treatment at the hands of the American frontiersmen. Novelists liked nothing better than to detail incidents of the torture they endured, well spiced with American comments on the Mexican character; "the cowardly, half-starved, filthy Mexican," who was so dirty

[90] Charles Sealsfield, *Frontier Life; or, Scenes and Adventures in the South West* (New York, 1855), pp. 171, 173–74.
[91] Webber, *Tales of the Southern Border*, p. 49.
[92] Karl May, *Im Tal des Todes* (reprint ed., Vienna, 1951), p. 204.
[93] Mayne Reid, *The White Chief: A Legend of Northern Mexico* (London, 1855), 1: 95.
[94] Ibid., 3: 172.

"Hunting the Grizzly Bear." From Theodor Dielitz, *Atlantis. Bilder aus dem Wald-und Prairieleben Amerika's* (Berlin, 1862).
(From the collections of Albert Hümmerich of Berlin.)

that the lariat used to hang him had to be thrown away; the Texan who reprimanded a greenhorn for saving a "filthy hog of a Mexican," adding, "why I had much sooner have stamped his entrails out!"; the band of frontiersmen who set fire to a Mexican village to smoke out a villain and burned several hundred women and children to death, justifying their act with, "What were Mexican women and children born for but to afford them the amusement of seeing them roast"; the trappers who resented having to form a barricade of their dead horses, complaining that they "would much prefer sacrificing our Mexicans; unfortunately they were so skinny that they could not be as much help as the horses."[95]

Such were the impressions of frontier savagery planted in the minds of Europeans by the image-makers. By the end of the nineteenth century readers were being fed a constant diet of sensationalism by novelists and travelers who saw westerners as primitive throwbacks in the scale of civilization, heartlessly cruel, murdering themselves and their enemies, practicing lynch law, and bent on exterminating the Indians whose lands they coveted. The American West might beckon the dispossessed with its opportunities, but it was sure to repel any sensible soul who lacked the courage and the recklessness to risk his life among barbarians, red and white.

Yet this hostile picture stimulated, rather than diminished, European interest in the frontier. As the image of a land of savagery gained credence, so did its fascination to the farmers and shopkeepers of England and Norway and Germany. For generations they had been able to escape the monotony of life by vicarious journeys to that never-never land beyond the western horizon. As they read they daydreamed of riding pell-mell across the boundless plains, six-shooters blazing as another redskin bit the dust; they had heard in their imagination the piercing war cry of the Sioux and the thunder of the giant buffalo herds as they stampeded beneath the azure-blue skies. Those impressions were too firmly planted, and too enticing, to vanish with the closing frontier. The images of the West as a land of unbridled lawlessness, of battles to the death with bowie knives and Colt revolvers, of black-shirted desperados, of vigilantes and lynch law, were a part of Europe's folklore now, as treasured as they had been in the past. The Wild West was to live on into the twentieth century, to spice the dreams of Europeans and influence their attitude toward the United States down to the present.

[95] Webber, *Gold Mines of the Gila*, pp. 82, 164; Duplessis, *Le Batteur d'estrade*, 1: 28.

XIII

The European Reaction

NO SINGLE IMAGE of the American frontier monopolized the European mind during the nineteenth century. Instead each reader as he devoured the novels and travel accounts and guidebooks and "America Letters" that described conditions ·there formed his own impression, shaped partly by what he chose to read, partly by his own beliefs and prejudices. Some were convinced that the West was a forbidden horror-land, where dense forests or parched deserts tested human frailty, where savage Indians and bloodthirsty bandits lurked, where daily battles with bowie knives and six-shooters took their toll; and where unkempt squatters and tobacco-spitting pioneers mirrored the decay of civilization. Others gained the impression that the frontier was a golden Land of Promise, where untold riches waited the industrious and where the humblest peasant could be transformed into a respected gentleman. Which of these visions was true? Was the West a "Land of Promise," or a "Land of Savagery?"

We can never know what was in each European's mind as he groped for an answer. Certain books were immensely popular; Gottfried Duden's *Bericht einer Reise nach dem westlichen Staaten Nord-Amerikas* convinced thousands upon thousands of peasants that a move to the West assured riches and respectability, but Karl May's *Winnetou* taught even more that life there would be risky and probably brief. How did these readers react to these conflicting images? Did a cottager in Silesia decide to migrate when stirred by Duden's glowing prose, then read of Karl May's Old Shatterhand and change his mind? Probably not. Were the guidebooks and "America Letters" that promised wealth and prestige to those who migrated read solely by discontented farmers, and were stories of western brutality marketed only among urbanites seeking vicarious adventure? This also seems unlikely.

More probably the two images of the American West reacted on Europeans in a variety of combinations. A farm laborer might hear a mouthwatering "America Letter" read from his village pulpit on a Sabbath morning, then spend the afternoon with friends discussing the latest adventures of Pistol Pete as he mowed down a sizable segment of the West's population. Each reader would reconcile these two visions to his own satisfaction. Some chose to believe one rather than the other; others to accept both but discount the one that interfered with their personal ambitions. A Norwegian folk ballad described a young peasant as he debated which to believe:

I know the venture will cost me dear in the hardships and exposure to sun and storm, in fierce battles with scorpions and serpents and wild beasts, in deadly battles with drawn daggers. But that is better than to fight one's own people and get nothing for it.[1]

This was a conflict that must have been resolved by each of the millions of Europeans who grappled with the most important decision they would ever make: to migrate or stay at home.

Their problem was complicated by the fact that the image-makers confused the attractions of frontier life with those of life anywhere in the United States. Most realized that opportunity and equality were more readily attainable anywhere in America than in Europe, and that the new nation's much-touted liberty was as much a product of Revolutionary theory as of frontier plenty. Few, however, bothered to distinguish between the genesis of American democracy among the Founding Fathers and its enhancement in western practice.[2] This confusion further clouded the picture of the West as a haven for the discontented; would they find the freedom of their dreams there, or anywhere in the New World?

But dream they did as they read and listened, for the image-makers were irresistibly appealing. So popular were they that something about the United States and its borderlands were known to every European, no matter how remote. "The most illiterate peasant in the Balkans," wrote

---

[1]   Theodore C. Blegen, ed., *Norwegian Emigrant Songs and Ballads* (Minneapolis, 1936), p. 274.
[2]   This subject is excellently discussed in J. H. Elliott, *The Old World and the New, 1492–1650* (Cambridge, 1970), pp. 80–85, and Franklin D. Scott, "The Study of the Effects of Emigration," *Scandinavian Economic History Review* 8, no. 2 (1961): 166–67.

one, "who did not even know the name of his county-seat, knew America, about its free land and the absence of landlords."[3] The image-makers were the Pied Pipers who helped lure millions of emigrants to the land of promise beyond the seas, and in doing so forced the countries of the Old World to reshape their institutions and social philosophy.

Emigration and Its Impact

One obvious result of the barrage of propaganda laid down by travelers, guidebooks authors, and "America Letters" was tangible, measurable, and to Europe's elites thoroughly alarming. This was the exodus of millions of able-bodied young men and women who had been convinced that a better life awaited them in the Land of Promise beyond the seas. Their departure brought European policy makers face to face with a question of enormous complexity. Should the emigrant tide be allowed to flow unchecked, relieving the Old World of an excess of population that might eventually burden society? Landlords and factory owners had a ready answer: workers were needed at home, and should be kept there. But how? In their attempt to answer that question, publicists and legislators and reformers advanced a number of ideas that were destined to help reshape the social system, and ushered Europe into the twentieth century.

Underlying these changes was the realization that a definite connection existed between the better life promised emigrants by the image-makers and the rate of flow of the immigrant tide. This, in turn, was linked to conditions in Europe; the more alluring the promises the less attractive Europe appeared during periodic intervals of economic stagnation. A constant factor, however, was the fact that society in the Old World was less plastic than in the New, restricting the opportunity for land ownership and social escalation even in the best of times. The volume of emigration might fluctuate with changing conditions, but the flow never ceased, with a corresponding drain on the labor supply. This was the realization that forced European reformers to reexamine the whole structure of society there.

To do so meant to recognize that there was little opportunity for upward mobility in the prevailing social order. Throughout most of Europe a rural economy persisted during the nineteenth century, despite the inroads of the Industrial Revolution. Life centered in the local village, just as it had since the manorial era; there the peasant farmer sold his small surpluses and there he purchased the few essentials that he could afford. Class lines were firmly drawn, with an established gentry owning most of

[3]   Peter Drucker, quoted in Franklin D. Scott, "American Influence in Norway and Sweden," *Journal of Modern History* 18 (March 1946): 37.

the land, a rapidly growing peasant-proprietor class that was beginning to challenge the gentry's authority, and at the bottom level cotters who worked small rented plots and laborers who hired themselves out to the peasant-proprietors. All save the gentry lived not far above the subsistence level.

In such a tightly knit society there was no place for the sons and daughters of peasant-proprietors as they reached maturity. Crofts where they could become independent farmers were virtually nonavailable, forcing them from the arable valleys into forested lands or hilly country where patches of tillable soil could sometimes be found amidst rocky debris. Cultivation of these marginal fields was hazardous, for a single crop failure or a dip in the economy spelled disaster. Nor could they hope to rise on the social scale; only rarely did a laborer succeed in penetrating the cotter level, or a cotter become a peasant-proprietor. An emerging middle class of tradesmen and peasant-proprietors was slowly securing some political power and cultural recognition in northern Europe, but the upper ranks—those of the gentry, clergy, military, and nobility—were forever closed to the ambitious. This was particularly aggravating to younger sons of peasant-proprietors and industrialists who had risen one step on the ladder and were eager to climb higher. Their only hope was to emigrate.

To make matters worse, Europe's population was steadily expanding during the nineteenth century as a declining death rate, more abundant food supplies, and the long period of peace that followed the Napoleonic Wars stimulated growth. Thus in Sweden the population doubled from 2,347,000 in 1800 to 5,136,000 in 1900, while the amount of arable land remained almost constant. At the same time some half a million sons and daughters of crofters, cotters, and peasant-proprietors entered the labor market, and were unable to find work.[4] Only a few were absorbed by industry; all the rest formed a made-to-order market for the image-makers who preached the gospel of a land of plenty beyond the seas.

And a receptive audience they were. An American congressional commission found in 1891 that nine-tenths of those who had reached the United States during the past half-century came from rural districts where employment opportunities were few and where land was almost totally unavailable. The vast majority were attracted by the prospects of a farm of their own; higher wages, superior living conditions, shorter work hours, escape from military service, and greater personal liberty were also listed as inducements.[5] Add to this the thrill of adventuring—the dream of life on an open frontier where each could carve out his own destiny—and the

[4]   Franklin D. Scott, *Sweden, the Nation's History* (Minneapolis, 1977), pp. 334–39, has an excellent brief discussion of economic conditions in northern Europe.
[5]   This report is summarized in David M. Emmons, *Garden in the Grasslands: Boomer Literature of the Central Great Plains* (Lincoln, Nebr., 1971), pp. 99–100.

lure of western America becomes understandable. What British cottager, reading one of Mayne Reid's adventure tales amidst the chill and fog of a Midlands winter, could suppress a longing for a tent beside a crystal stream on the High Plains, its waters mirroring the azure skies above, its banks alive with myriad-colored birds and flowers, untrodden save by the moccasined feet of a passing red man. "I am going to compete with the freedom of the eagle flying above me," exulted a young Hungarian as he planned his move to the West.[6]

And so they came—by the thousands and tens of thousands and millions. By the 1830s 70,000 emigrants were leaving Europe each year; by the 1850s, 400,000. By this time the "America Fever" was reaching epidemic levels; shop windows throughout Europe blossomed with guidebooks; emigrant journals multiplied; "immigration Societies" sprang up in village after village to stir enthusiasm and offer advice. By this time, too, "returning emigrants" were beginning to appear, splendid in frock coats and top hats, talking grandly of their acres of land and herds of cattle, boasting that in America they tipped their hats to no one. Was that really Nils, the son of a *husmand*, a mere tenant farmer? As the fever spread so many cotters left Norway that their class almost disappeared; so many small farmers departed Ireland that the "America Wake"—with feasting and drinking and a procession to "convoy" the departing emigrant to the dock or railroad station—was almost a daily event in some districts.[7] For a time during the American Civil War the tide slowed, only to accelerate again during the 1870s and 1880s when some fourteen million Europeans reached the land of plenty, many of them attracted the promise of a free farm under the Homestead Act of 1862. So many Germans settled in Kansas during those years that the Indians who traded with them learned German rather than English as their second language.[8]

This mass exodus was sufficiently alarming to landowners and mercantilistic officials in Europe, but even more disturbing were statistics demonstrating that most were young farmers or laborers, drawn from the better-soil regions that produced much of the Old World's food supplies. The reason was obvious: all the productive lands in such areas were monopolized by the gentry and large proprietors; young laborers, unable to obtain farms of their own, had (as one of them put it) "only a choice between America and the poor house."[9] Each departure robbed the propri-

[6]   Tivadar Ács, ed., *New–Buda* (Budapest, 1941), p. 29.
[7]   Scott, "American Influences in Norway and Sweden," p. 42; Halvdan Koht, *The American Spirit in Europe: A Survey of Transatlantic Influence* (Philadelphia, 1949), pp. 69–71; Brynjolf J. Hovde, "Notes on the Effects of Emigration upon Scandinavia," *Journal of Modern History* 6 (September 1934): 271–72; Arnold Schrier, *Ireland and the American Emigration, 1850–1900* (Minneapolis, 1958), pp. 84–91.
[8]   Everett Dick, *The Sod-House Frontier* (New York, 1937), p. 168.
[9]   Kristian Hvidt, *Flight to America* (New York, 1974), pp. 127–29.

etor class of a needed farm worker and elevated the wages of those who remained behind. Here was cause for real alarm among Europe's most influential classes.

Their first reaction was to demand that emigration be halted by law. "This government," Sweden informed the United States in 1861, "are opposed to this emigration and will do all in their power to discourage and prevent the loss of their subjects."[10] This "discouragement" took a variety of forms, all persuasive rather than by decree, that ranged from laws forbidding immigration agents to glorify America's attractions to inducements to local publicists to emphasize the hardships and dangers of frontier life. These bore some fruit; by the 1880s the German and the Scandinavian press, with a few exceptions, was campaigning vigorously to keep workers at home. Some novelists fell into line; books such as Leopold Schefer's *Die Probefahrt nach Amerika* detailed the hardships of frontiering and described in shocked prose the sufferings of emigrants who had been led to disaster by land sharpers and corrupt loan sharks.[11] These efforts culminated at the close of the century in the formation of national societies to combat the "America Fever"—Sweden's "National Society against Immigration" was typical—all warning against the perils of emigration and urging Europeans to stay at home.

This was whistling in the wind, for so long as opportunity beckoned, so would the ambitious respond. If European governments were to check migration, they must improve conditions at home, not condemn conditions abroad. A Swedish commission learned this when it questioned a number of departing immigrants. Their reasons for leaving ranged from wanderlust to dissatisfaction with the static social order, but all stressed two points: the desire to have a farm of their own and their eagerness to escape the indignities suffered at the hands of a dominant ruling class.[12] Give us land, they were saying, and give us a democratic social system, and we will stay at home.

The Political Impact

These demands touched off a debate that lasted for nearly a century and that revealed the extent to which the image of the American West as a land of opportunity and equality influenced European thought. This revolved

[10] Robert L. Wright, ed., *Swedish Emigrant Ballads* (Lincoln, Nebr., 1965), p. 11.
[11] Paul C. Weber, *America in Imaginative German Literature in the First Half of the Nineteenth Century* (New York, 1926), pp. 206–9; Merle Curti and Kendall Birr, "The Immigrant and the American Image in Europe, 1860–1914," *Mississippi Valley Historical Review* 37 (September 1950): 227–28.
[12] Franklin D. Scott, "The Causes and Consequences of Emigration in Sweden," *The Chronicle, A Quarterly Publication of the American-Swedish Historical Foundation* 2 (Spring 1955): 4–8.

around the relationship between cheap land and democratic institutions. Conservatives and liberals alike agreed that the American workingman was better off than the workingman in Europe. They disagreed on why. Liberals credited American democracy; give our workers and farmers the chance to shape their own destinies, they said, and they will enjoy the same prosperity that American workers enjoy. Nonsense, said the conservatives. Prosperity in the United States stems from the cheap land available along the frontiers, and hence is unattainable in Europe. There was, they insisted, a direct relationship between property and suffrage; in the United States nine out of ten citizens owned property and nine out of ten voted; in Europe one out of ten owned property and one out of ten voted. This was as it should be. Lacking a frontier, Europeans must resign themselves to autocratic rule.[13]

Conservatives based their argument on two premises: that widely dispersed land ownership created a responsible citizenry capable of self-rule, and that frontier opportunity operated as a "safety valve" by draining off malcontents who would otherwise disrupt orderly government. To entrust the reins to the common people of Europe, where no such safety valve functioned, would be to surrender control to irresponsible tenants with no stake in society, and to the perennially dissatisfied who might resort to revolutionary tactics. To prove their points, they must show that a "safety valve" did operate in the United States, and would continue to operate so long as a frontier remained.

This meant, in turn, that they must demonstrate that displaced workers in the East, dislodged by hard times, could become independent farmers in the West. Scholars today insist that they could not; the cost of moving and farm making, the lack of agrarian skills among factory-oriented workers, and the psychological barriers to adjustment to a rural society, all were insurmountable barriers to relocation. No such quibbling bothered the image-makers of the nineteenth century. They piled evidence on evidence to prove that the poorest eastern laborer could "squat" on western government land for a year or two while selling sufficient of his surplus to meet his preemption payments, or that he could earn enough as a farm laborer to purchase a farm within a few months.[14] Nor were special skills necessary. Travelers repeatedly met mechanics and tradesmen from the East bound to the frontier with every confidence of becoming farmers. "In such times," wrote a recent migrant during a depression era, "there are

[13]   G. D. Lillibridge, *Beacon of Freedom: The Impact of American Democracy upon Great Britain, 1830–1870* (Philadelphia, 1955), pp. 34–35.
[14]   Typical were John Bradbury, *Travels in the Interior of America, in the Years 1809, 1810, and 1811* (Liverpool, 1817), pp. 296–97; Edouard de Montulé, *Travels in America, 1816–1817* (Bloomington, Ind., 1950), p. 171; and Sidney Smith, *The Settler's New Home; or, The Emigrant's Location* (London, 1849), pp. 87–88.

a number of macanics moves back to the land where there is plenty for them to do and gives more room to the others."[15] There was no nonsense in these accounts about farm-making costs for psychological barriers. Wrote a French commentator: "The West stands open as a refuge for all who are unemployed."[16]

There was general agreement, too, that the operation of the "safety-valve" raised the wages of those who chose not to migrate, thus lessening the chance of explosive protest. "In Europe," a traveler recorded, "a coalition of workmen can only signify one of two things: raise our wages, or we shall die of hunger . . . which is an absurdity; or, raise our wages, if you do not we will take up arms, which is civil war. . . . In America such a coalition means, raise our wages or we will go West."[17] Cheap land transformed malcontents into respectable citizens. A British journalist was well aware of that fact when he wrote that "the inexhaustible fund of unoccupied land" along the frontiers "exempts the great body of the lower orders from what in other countries is the most usual and fruitful source of popular discontent and tumult, namely, the pressure of want."[18] But that cheap land was in frontier America, not in Europe.

These opinions gained political significance as Europe debated whether to bow to popular demand by broadening the franchise. Over and over again conservatives warned that democracy had operated, and could operate, only in the United States where boundless acres waited "to receive all the redundant population, and all the restless, adventurous and discontented spirits."[19] Once those cheap lands were occupied, democracy would fall. "The safety-valve is open," wrote a British editor in 1835; "the high pressure has not commenced on the engine. But wait until that huge receptacle of discontented multitudes is filled up."[20] Then the United States would have its Manchesters and Birminghams where thousands of out-of-work laborers threatened rebellion. "Then," an English publicist warned, "your institutions will be fairly brought to the test."[21] From Germany came the same ominous threat; the United States would

[15]   Quoted in Charlotte Erickson, *Invisible Immigrants: The Adaptation of English and Scottish Immigrants in Nineteenth Century America* (London, 1972), p. 168.
[16]   Michel Chevalier, *Society, Manners and Politics in the United States: Being a Series of Letters on North America* (Boston, 1839), pp. 143–44.
[17]   Ibid., p. 144. A similar expression is in Harriet Martineau, *Society in America* (New York, 1837), 1: 292–93.
[18]   *Quarterly Review*, 1832, quoted in Lillibridge, *Beacon of Freedom*, p. 93.
[19]   *Quarterly Review*, 1835, quoted in William M. Tuttle, Jr., "Forerunners of Frederick Jackson Turner: Nineteenth-Century British Conservatives and the Frontier Thesis," *Agricultural History* 41 (July 1967): 222–23.
[20]   *Blackwood's Edinburgh Magazine*, 1835, quoted in Tuttle, "Forerunners of Frederick Jackson Turner," pp. 219–20.
[21]   Thomas B. Macauley in G. O. Trevelyan, *The Life and Letters of Lord Macauley* (New York, 1909), p. 451.

resemble Europe, wrote the philosopher Friedrich Hegel, "only after the immeasurable space which that country presents to its inhabitants shall have been occupied, and the members of the political body shall have begun to press back on each other."[22] Let the Americans take heed. Their democracy was doomed to vanish with the frontier. This was the gospel of European conservatives as they battled to hold their bastions against proponents of self-rule.

Liberals were not quite ready to agree—they continued to insist that the common folk would prosper if they were allowed to govern themselves—but they were forced to recognize the relationship between land ownership and American democracy. If they accepted this as valid, they could have only one solution to Europe's problems: to redistribute land there so widely that a base could be provided for democratic institutions. Such a concept was too revolutionary to be accepted at mid-century, but it gained credence among radicals, particularly in England, where a little group labeling themselves "Charterists" began agitating in the 1840s for a "People's Charter" embodying universal suffrage. They were sufficiently alert to the American example to know that they could succeed only by creating a "safety valve" of unoccupied land; hence they urged the distribution of all great estates among the poor, at the same time forming a "Chartist Cooperative Land Company" to hurry the process by buying large holdings and parceling them out to small farmers.[23] This idealistic solution won few followers, but it did reveal the image of the frontier as a force for reform.

This image played a far more significant role as Europe debated broadening the franchise during the second half of the century. The public and parliamentary discussion over Britain's Reform Bill of 1867 brought the issues fairly into the open; should England open the ballot box to the underprivileged when it had no "safety valve" to drain off "the peccant political humours of the body politic?"[24] Now, however, a new dimension had been added with the well-publicized Homestead Act of 1862; now the American frontier offered not just cheap land but free land. Both liberals and conservatives saw this as an irresistible lure to emigrants, and hence a major element in their own social planning. Why make democratic concessions when the discontented were soon to leave England anyway. Now the American West was a safety valve not only for the American East but for all of Europe as well.

So argued the conservatives, and the liberals could only agree. Let the malcontents and surplus workers depart in peace. England—and

---

[22] W. Stull Holt, "Hegel, the Turner Hypothesis, and the Safety-Valve Theory," *Agricultural History* 22 (July 1948): 175–76.
[23] Lillibridge, *Beacon of Freedom*, pp. 67–71.
[24] Tuttle, "Forerunners of Frederick Jackson Turner," pp. 224–27.

Europe—with no effort on their part, had been blessed with what one publicist called the "cheapest and most effectual remedy for some of our most formidable national ills."[25] That needed vent had opened at exactly the right time to save Europe from threatened revolution. "Had the spirit been pent up," a London editor saw, "and the pressure of population on the means of existence not been relieved, what would have been the history of Europe?" Famine, rioting, rebellion, anarchy—instead of the peace it was now enjoying.[26] The image of the frontier as a land of plenty had traditionally lured enough emigrants to keep Europe on an even keel; now it had demonstrated its success as a "safety valve" at a crucial moment in history.

If conservatives took solace in the belief that frontier opportunity had lessened unrest in Europe, they found little to their liking in the democratic ambitions stirred by the image of the West as a land of equality that was widely publicized in the Old World. They realized, to their sorrow, that so long as the American West was seen as a land of democratic flowering, where all shared in governmental policy making, liberals would use the frontier example in urging democratic reform. Each travel account detailing the workings of a western democracy, each "America Letter" describing a village election in which the whole community participated, was a firebrand that threatened to ignite a holocaust among Europe's discontented. The "American Mirage" was a dangerous threat to the Old World's monarchical institutions, and would so remain so long as frontier democracy thrived.

Liberal image-makers saw to that by providing grist for the propaganda of the antimonarchists. Travelers and publicists who extolled America's democratic institutions—writers such as Alexis de Tocqueville, Michel Chevalier, Harriet Martineau, and Fredrika Bremer—were widely read by European reformers. Tocqueville played an especially important role; his persuasive volumes were overnight successes in France where they appeared in thirteen editions before 1850, and were translated into English, German, Italian, Spanish, Danish, Russian, Serbian, and Hungarian within a few years.[27] When their enthusiasms were bolstered by the testimony of countless "America Letters," a sizable propaganda machine was set in motion, certain to influence the thought of Europe's common people.

Its role can never be exactly appraised, but Europeans sensed its impact. Peasants who read or heard of that golden land where all were rich

---

[25]   *London Observer*, quoted in Oscar O. Winther, "Promoting the American West in England, 1865–1900," *Journal of Economic History* 16 (December 1956): 506.
[26]   *American Settler*, 22 October 1892.
[27]   Koht, *American Spirit in Europe*, p. 35.

"Kidnapping." From Theodor Dielitz, *Atlantis. Bilder aus
dem Wald-und Prairieleben Amerika's* (Berlin, 1862).
(From the collections of Albert Hümmerich of Berlin.)

and all were equal would never be the same again; their horizons had been broadened and their ambitions whetted, for they knew from the image-makers that they could escape poverty and subservience by migrating to America. No longer was their fate sealed; they could live in hope, not despair. That these beliefs played a role, no matter how minor, in the liberal uprisings of mid-century seems probable. That they continued to inspire democratic reform over the next decade seems equally likely. When Friederich Gerstäcker returned to his homeland from the American West he not only filled his novels with praise for frontier democracy but became a power in a German society urging reforms, the Coburger Verein.[28] Not many were privileged to play his dual role, but many an image-maker was inspired by the institutions that had influenced Gerstäcker, and influenced his readers in turn.

There seems little question that their principal impact was on the reformers who were agitating for a broader franchise leading eventually to manhood suffrage. Their activities were centered in England and northern Europe where autocratic authority was less firmly entrenched than in the South and East, and there they enjoyed some success. England's liberals nudged the nation into notable reforms in the acts of 1832 and 1867; Sweden's began urging manhood suffrage as early as 1868, although not until 1891 was their progress incorporated in a party platform (the Venstre [Liberty] party), and not until 1898 was it enacted into law.[29] This orderly reform, and comparable movements in other nearby countries, owed a debt to the frontier example that was intangible, but none the less real.

So did the crusade for women's rights. This was inevitable, for the enviable lot of the frontier housewife was repeatedly described in "America Letters" and travel accounts, and was sure to stir a few feminist leaders in Europe to protest their own lowly lot. Their leader was Fredrika Bremer whose years on the Minnesota frontier convinced her that the status of women in her native Sweden was woefully outmoded. Her widely publicized campaign yielded few results—the belief that women were physically and intellectually inferior to men was too widely accepted to be dislodged at once—but her efforts did open some minor political offices to women, enlarged their educational opportunities, and won them the right to teach in schools. Gradually the movement spread, until in 1888 an International Council of Women was feasible, its purpose to coordinate reform efforts throughout Europe.[30] Change had begun, and was to con-

[28] George H. R. O'Donnell, "Gerstäcker in America, 1837–1843," *Publications of the Modern Language Association of America* 42 (December 1927): 1042.
[29] Franklin D. Scott, "Søren Jaabaek, Americanizer in Norway," *Norwegian-American Studies and Records* 17 (1952): 95.
[30] Koht, *American Spirit in Europe*, pp. 52–55.

tinue under its own momentum until the equality of women was recognized in most of western Europe.

The role of the image-makers was less dramatic in eastern Europe where semifeudal institutions, despotic governments, and a controlled press stifled reformers. There the torch was carried by a small band of intellectuals who pinned their hope on the American example. In Hungary they eagerly read the works of Sándor Farkas and Ágoston M. Haraszthy, both based on travels in the United States in the 1820s and 1830s, and both but faintly disguised pleas for republicanism. Their impact was measurable; a second edition of Haraszthy's *Utazás Északamerikában* was banned by the Vienna government, while both authors were quoted by reformers in the parliamentary debates that followed the 1848 revolutions.[31] Later travelers drove home the point again in the 1860s and 1870s when Ferenc Pulszky and Béla Széchenyi and their contemporaries used their travel accounts to propagandize for democratic change, pointing out the "unmatched self-restraint" that had brought orderly reform in the United States in contract with the violence needed to combat Europe's autocratic rulers.[32] Here was a message for tyrants to hear and ponder.

The same message was popularized in Poland, where intellectuals seized on Polish travelers in America as guides into the better world of their hopes. "What are we compared to Americans," one regretted, "but an old man full of bad habits compared to a well brought-up youth whose heart has not had time to be tainted by bad example."[33] Such a gloomy appraisal had no happy ending, for Poland was too firmly controlled by tzarist tyrants to accept republican principles or even to allow the American example to be publicized there. Generations must pass before the "People King," as Poles labeled American voters, could find a counterpart in eastern Europe.

Viewing the Old World as a whole, there seems little doubt that frontier liberty and opportunity as magnified by image-makers contributed to the stirrings of protest that eventually liberalized political processes. There seems little doubt, too, that their role was but small indeed; internal conditions and the inexorable course of history underlay democratic reform, not the American example. Yet that example did exist, and was widely publicized in Europe. Conservatives, at least, saw it as a dangerous menace to their ambitions; one who defined his purpose in life as

[31] Anna Katona, "Hungarian Travelogues on the Pre–Civil War U.S.," *Hungarian Studies in English* 5 (1971): 56–58.
[32] István Gal, "Széchenyi and the U.S.A.," *Hungarian Studies in English* 5 (1971): 117.
[33] Jerzy Jedlicki, "Images of America," *Polish Perspectives* 18 (November 1975): 31–32. These views are well represented in Jakub Gordon, *Podróż do Nowego Orleanu* (Leipzig, 1867), pp. 168–69.

undermining "the influence of the universal suffrage and republican government of the United States," was testifying to the influence of the image-makers on European thought.[34]

The Social Impact

Even more alarming to Europe's conservatives than the impact of America's political liberalism on their constituents was the social equality that the image-makers described with such enthusiasm. The "Great Pox of Liberty," they called it,[35] a virus that if allowed to spread would prove fatal to the aristocratic structure that sustained society in the Old World. The oft-repeated tales of the travelers who reported examples of ill-bred commoners pretending equality with gentlemen, the accounts in "America Letters" of peasants mingling as equals with the elites of their villages, the returned emigrants who refused to bow and scrape before their betters, all demonstrated that frontier America's example must never be imitated. Returning emigrants were especially dangerous to the status quo. "They walk through the streets as if they were our equals," complained one Italian landlord; "they make bad blood," added a Swedish pastor. "Servants are already beginning to speak up, saying that nobody can stay here and keep on slaving till one spits blood."[36]

A Norwegian novel captured the magic of the moment when one returnee was telling his old friends that he was equal to anyone in the village just as the greatest man there, a colonel, arrived. All tipped their hats but the American:

Then something singular happened. The Colonel stopped, looked across at the stranger, and went right up to him in the sight of everybody! The others all stepped back, leaving a clear space around the two men.

"You've just come from America, haven't you?" the Colonel asked (mercy on us! He was talking to Scraggy Olina's son as politely as if he had been at least a captain!).

"That's right," said Erik; he had raised his hat slightly when the Colonel addressed him, but had put it on again at once, and now he stood there looking quite as tall and composed as the other. The bystanders heard the Colonel say: "It would interest me to hear a little about the conditions over there. If you can spare the time, you might look in one day at my place."

"Certainly I will," answered Erik Foss, in the tone of one doing a service to an equal.

---

[34] Quoted in Lillibridge, *Beacon of Freedom*, p. xiv.
[35] Richard Parkinson, *A Tour in America in 1798, 1799, and 1800* (London, 1805), 1: 19.
[36] Edward A. Steiner, *The Immigrant Tide: Its Ebb and Flow* (New York, 1909), p. 167; H. Arnold Barton, ed., *Letters from the Promised Land: Swedes in America, 1840–1914* (Minneapolis, 1975), pp. 72–73.

Then the Colonel passed on into the church, but the others forgot to follow as long as Erik Foss remained standing there.[37]

Was this how one acted in America, they were asking themselves? To be treated as an equal by the Colonel was worth battling wild beasts and deadly reptiles and red Indians. In the West a man learned to be a man, and could hold his head high.

Thoughts such as these were tinder that would soon feed the flames of a social revolution that would rock Europe, but before they could spread, conditions there must worsen economically for small farmers. That they did was partly due to developments on the American frontier. The millions of pioneers—natives and immigrants—who cleared farms there were soon producing surplus cereals and meat that flooded European markets, underselling homegrown produce in the local exchanges. This had a dual effect on the European economy; on the one hand it drove marginal farmers from their lands and thus fed the emigrant stream, on the other it forced those in the better-soil regions to diversify their production by concentrating on crops that were less competitive with imports.

Both of these trends profoundly affected the economic, and hence the social structure. For centuries the landowning classes had controlled the food supply of Europe, and had used that control to shape society to their own tastes and the tastes of their aristocratic friends. This they could do as long as no competitors threatened their monopoly. Now their "corner" had been broken; western American foods, cheaply imported on steam packet ships, could be peddled at prices competitive with those grown on their own estates. The way was open for a complete restructuring of society, for tenant and peasant farmers, newly aware of their economic importance, could demand a larger degree of social importance.

Men and women in this position were sure to listen when they heard of a land beyond the seas where all were treated as equals and all governed themselves. To them the "American System" was an ideal to be sought, even if one remained at home. "Its influence," wrote a British publicist in 1881, "is to spread a discontent among those who remain, for they seek to account for the difference; and wonder if by changes in the social structure a change as beneficial to the masses might not be wrought on this side, too."[38] The progression was inevitable; from emigration to economic change to social change. Let one step in the process be obstructed, and violence might be substituted for orderly evolution. Or so most Europeans believed. They saw that some reform was necessary to forestall revolution.

[37] Johan Bojer, *The Emigrants* (1925), quoted in Dorthy B. Skårdal, *The Divided Heart: Scandinavian Immigrant Experience through Literary Sources* (Bloomington, 1974), pp. 125–26.
[38] *American Settler*, 12 March 1881.

Yet change of any sort was difficult, for European custom was so firmly rooted in tradition that any deviation was suspect, even among reformers. Their pleas for laws that would better the lot of the people stressed past precedent, not future good: "This proposal is nothing new," or, "This law is built on existing foundations." Liberals were as emphatic as conservatives in insisting that every step must be based on accustomed practices.[39] This being the case, unusual pressures were essential to any change. These existed largely in countries that had lost most heavily to emigration, and hence required the greatest readjustment; in those where reformers had easiest access to the advanced ideas of reformers in the United States; and in those capable of producing effective leaders at the right moment. Those conditions were best met in Scandinavia, England, and Germany.[40]

In these nations particularly, and to a lesser degree in the rest of Europe, the American example inspired drastic alterations in agricultural practices. Frontiering had encouraged Americans to experiment with mechanization to offset the perennial labor shortage; now these techniques must be copied if European farmers were to compete with imports. Returning immigrants made this clear by their open scorn of the archaic methods of the Old World. "They don't know nothing about machine work," one would say. "Look at 'em—there they'd keep six men for a week to mow twelve acres, but I'd just take one of our mowing machines and do it all in one day."[41] Only adopting these modernizations would, as a London editor put it, "allow the British farmer to compete with the prairie."[42] This was a lesson well learned, if Europe's agriculture was to survive.

That learning came slowly, for tradition was deeply rooted. The newfangled McCormick reaper was introduced into England in 1851 with but slight success, Gradually, however, the few who purchased convinced others by their mounting profits, until by the end of the century so many American farm implements were in use that a critic moaned that England's firms had become "Implement· Agents rather than Implement Makers."[43] Elsewhere the story was much the same. A Norwegian commission spoke for much of northern Europe when it reported the rural dis-

[39] An excellent discussion of this attitude is in Daniel Levine, "Conservatism and Tradition in Danish Social Welfare Legislation, 1890–1933," *Comparative Studies in Society and History* 20 (January 1978): 61–62.
[40] Scott, "Study of the Effects of Emigration," pp. 162–63, 167–68.
[41] Charles L. Brace, *The Norse Folk* (1857), quoted in Ingrid Semmingsen, "Emigration and the Image of America in Europe," in *Immigration and American History: Essays in Honor of Theodore C. Blegen*, ed. Henry S. Commager (Minneapolis, 1961), pp. 42–43.
[42] *American Settler*, 12 January 1889.
[43] Andrew C. Jewell, "The Impact of America on English Agriculture," *Agricultural History* 50 (January 1976): 127–31.

tricts unrecognizable after a generation of change. "The returned Americans put their stamp upon it all," the commission wrote. ". . . . The farmers were not so burdened with debt as before; people live better, eat better, clothe themselves better—thus the population improves itself. All those who come from America . . . bring home with them much practical experience and understanding which redounds to the advantage of the whole region."[44] This was gross exaggeration, of course; the European economy had simply stabilized at a higher level after its initial adjustment to competition with American agriculture. Yet Europeans believed that the American image and the American example had been primarily responsible for their better lot in life.

They were less sanguine when reformers made frontier democracy the model for the new social order that they hoped to build in western Europe. The reformers made no secret of their ambitions. "Make our dear old Sweden as much like America as possible"—"Strive to copy the legal principles of the New World"—these were the slogans used to introduce each legislative measure aimed at reconstructing society along more democratic lines.[45] The Americans were hailed as "the tutors of the Old World,"[46] a phrase that liberals used with delight, conservatives with scorn. They saw the social reforms as sprinkling the seeds of revolution, certain to rack the established system as violently as American democratic principles were racking the political system. Every image-maker who praised frontier equality and liberty found himself hailed—or condemned—as a pamphleteer in the cause of reform.

Crusaders for change had one unanswerable argument that won the support of a sizable portion of the upper classes: unless they were heeded, they insisted, continued emigration would weaken the Old World's economy by depleting its labor supply. This could be checked only by making Europe so attractive that young men and women would be content to stay at home. The American example made clear what was needed: a widened franchise, weakened class barriers, proper assurances of respect by the elite, and a certain opportunity for self-improvement and upward escalation socially. "Let us," urged a Swedish reformer, ". . . create more and more opportunity for the humble to acquire their own property, . . . show the laborer respect and consideration, and remove unnecessry restrictions on religious freedom—in short, let us 'move America over to Sweden.' "[47] These were bold words for that day, but they were tuned to reality. Europe's masses had learned that a better life was possible, and

[44] Quoted in Hovde, "Notes on the Effects of Emigration upon Scandinavia," pp. 277–78.
[45] Scott, *Sweden*, p. 403; Scott, "Søren Jaabaek, Americanizer in Norway," p. 100.
[46] A. T. Boyesen, *Udvandrerens Veileder og Raadgiver* (Oslo, 1869) unpaged.
[47] Ernst Beckman, a member of the Riksdag and founder of the Liberal party, quoted in Hovde, "Notes on the Effects of Emigration upon Scandinavia," pp. 257–58.

they wanted their share. "This people," wrote a pamphleteer in 1870, "which has for so many years been satisfied with its meagre lot, has begun to reason with itself and has found that things could be better than they are."[48] Such observations were music to the ears of reformers. They had, as one put it, "used emigration as a vehicle for social legislation," and were ready to reap the harvest.[49]

But how? What social legislation would heighten Europe's attraction to the discontented who were considering emigrating? How duplicate young America's frontier opportunity in Old Europe? These were questions that must be answered before the tide of emigration could be slowed.

One answer, clearly, was to create artificial frontiers by making cheap land available. As early as the 1840s a liberal Norwegian editor urged interest-free government loans to allow the sons of cotters and small proprietors to purchase farms on undeveloped land,[50] but not until the Homestead Act sent tremors of alarm through Europe's upper classes did this campaign move into high gear. Their fears seemed justified. Throughout the Old World economists were warning that millions of the ablest young men would be lured to frontier America by the free lands, depeopling Europe of its best workers, and adding ever more producers to those in America whose exports were already depressing European agriculture. Emigration could be checked only by assuring European peasants farms of their own, and with them, the opportunity for self-advancement offered by frontier opportunity.

Each of the northern European countries tried to solve this problem in its own way. In Germany reformers urged that artificial frontiers be created by dividing the great Prussian estates among small operators, but the powerful Junker landholders would have none of that. Liberals were forced to settle for "colonization laws," modeled after the exemption provisions in the Homestead Act, that freed family homes from fianancial threats. In Denmark the so-called Husmand Movement was more successful; there the parliament in 1899 authorized the government to acquire and sell large estates to the *Husmand*, or small farmers. Implementing this law proved difficult, for the landholding classes were all-powerful, but from that time on the liberal Social Democratic party insisted that adequate land was the God-given right of all farmers. Its repeated measures, often called "Homestead Acts" in imitation of America, failed to carry, but they did testify to the effectiveness of the frontier example.[51]

[48] Franklin D. Scott, "Sweden's Constructive Opposition to Emigration," *Journal of Modern History* 37 (September 1965): 310.
[49] Franklin D. Scott, *Emigration and Immigration* (Washington, 1966), p. 57.
[50] Quoted in Hovde, "Notes on the Effects of Emigration upon Scandinavia," p. 273.
[51] Folke Dovring, "European Reactions to the Homestead Act," *Journal of Economic History* 22 (December 1962): 471.

Norway and Sweden also responded to the challenge by opening new frontier settlements along their northern borderlands, clearing forests for occupation, and urging the settlement of unoccupied areas in Lapland—the "Great Plains of the Northland" as it was frequently called. Sweden also sought to check emigration by a series of bold measures that provided state aid to home buyers, the government financing of low-interest loans, a primitive form of old-age insurance, a state mortgage bank, guaranteed religious freedom, and universal suffrage, all adopted in the late nineteenth and early twentieth centuries. Their purpose, the government acknowledged, was "to strengthen the economic position of the less-well-off, counteract emigration, and promote cultivation of the land."[52] Here was the response of the Old World to the challenge of the New.

No sensible person would argue that the social changes that swept Europe at century's end were solely, or even primarily, a product of the frontier image. The European social order by that time had evolved to a point where educational reform, the improving economy, the demographic changes accompanying industrialization, and a dozen other forces had transfered a modicum of power to the masses and provided them with an incentive to improve themselves. Yet it cannot be denied that the attractions of a land where opportunity and equality awaited all stimulated a mass exodus that sent western Europe into an era of soul-searching. Nor can it be questioned that this self-analysis set in motion an era of social engineering that helped break the mold of tradition that had slowed change for generations. Men and women in Warsaw and Stockholm and Berlin and London had been convinced by the image-makers that the status quo was not sacred, and they had only to stir themselves to secure the opportunities for self-advancement that the frontier was providing for their cousins who had migrated.

A British editor in the 1890s wrote a fitting epitaph to the travelers and novelists and guidebook authors and promoters who for a century had idealized the American West as a land of opportunity and equality:

By the settlement of America mankind secured a new order of civilization, fresh fields and green pastures; something novel to work out unhampered by the old ways on the other side of the Atlantic. This . . . gave scope and freedom to the brain which is a distinctive mark of the American character. The reaction on the Old World has been beneficial, and is likely to be far more so in the future than in the past. There are new forms of government as well as new ways of living, a less trammeled field for liberty; indeed liberty could never have thrived if it had not been cast into the boundless prairies to grow and thrive unheeded, till the strength had become too great to attack. If the nations of America owe their birth and

---

[52] Scott, "Causes and Consequences of Emigration in Sweden," p. 9.

being to Europe, Europe may owe the liberty it enjoys, and may in still greater scope enjoy, to America.[53]

The image-makers had played their role in a drama that had been acted on both sides of the Atlantic. They were ready to pass from the scene with the frontier they had glorified. But that frontier refused to die. It lived on through the twentieth century, not as a haven for the dispossessed, but as a legend to stir the blood of armchair voyagers and thrill seekers after vicarious adventure in Europe as well as America.

In this new garb the West as a land of opportunity was forgotten, and the West as a land of savagery perpetuated.

[53]   *American Settler*, 22 October 1892.

XIV

Epilogue:
The Persisting Image

AS ENGLAND'S LORD BRYCE watched America's frontier era draw to a close he asked a pertinent question: where in the future could mankind find "a land of freedom and adventure and mystery" to match the vanishing Wild West? Where could bold spirits discover "a field in which to relieve their energies when the Western world of adventure is no more?"[1] An age was ending, a chapter in the history of man's wanderings concluded. Americans and Europeans had to awaken to the fact that they could no longer flee civilization to quest for opportunity and excitement in virgin territories. No new world waited their conquest, no untapped resources waited their exploitation.

Lord Bryce's obituary was premature. The frontier refused to die; it was destined to live on, not as a land of rebirth for the dispossessed, but as a land of legend, perpetuated by image-makers on both sides of the Atlantic. In that wonderland of their creation, noble heroes and beetle-browed villains would continue to battle as they had before, unrestrained now by any restrictions of reality. Armchair adventurers in London and Berlin and Oslo could still thrill to the sound of blazing guns, still sweep boldly across the open plain on imagined steeds, still share the spine-tingling adventures that the real frontiersmen had known in the past. The image-

---

[1]   James Bryce, *The American Commonwealth* (New York, 1888), 2:930.

[*311*]

makers created a fantasy world suited to the tastes of the twentieth century, and more enduring than the true West of the past.

In the United States, where the pattern emerged that Europe was to follow, nostalgic enthusiasm for the West-that-was mounted steadily through the first half of the twentieth century—and beyond. It showed itself first in the vogue of dime-novel Westerns, then in two new cultural forms: cheap, pulp-paper "cowboy" magazines that cluttered the newsstands for a generation, and the so-called literary Westerns pioneered by Owen Wister and popularized by hundreds of writers from Zane Grey to Louis L'Amour. Western films followed, captivating millions with their appealing vistas of plains and deserts, and by their to-the-death battles between blonde cowboy demigods and dastardly redskins guilty of trying to defend their tribal lands against greedy interlopers. Television soon added a new dimension—and millions of new viewers—by glorifying the frontier as the favorite setting for its fast-paced adventure series.

Given this multiplication of media devoted to perpetuating the image of the West as a land of romance and adventure, there is little wonder that by mid-century a frontier craze was sweeping the nation. Western artists such as Charlie Russell and Frederic Remington skyrocketed to such popularity that prices for their paintings rivaled those of the Old Masters. Promoters sprinkled the land with fake "Dodge Cities" and "Frontier Villages" where the venturesome could "ride shotgun" on "genuine" stagecoaches, or "pan for real gold." Western museums lured crowds by displaying the quilt that had once covered Calamity Jane or the hardware worn by some paranoid sadist in a famed bank robbery. Western cities staged "Frontier Days" complete with hastily bearded merchants who stumbled about in high-heeled boots and "cowboy" shirts. Such was the passion for anything western that even such blatant commercialism paid off.

On a more elevated level, scholars, falling into step behind the historian Frederick Jackson Turner, who in 1893 advanced the thesis that the distinctive characteristics of the American past stemmed from the frontiering process, rewrote the history of the nation's economic progress, literary developments, and political evolution to pay proper respect to the influence of westering. Frontier buffs, many of them prominent lawyers and physicians and businessmen, began organizing "corrals" of "Westerners," each complete with a "sheriff" to preside over monthly meetings, a "keeper of the chips" to collect dues, and a "posse" or "trail bosses" to plan programs and arrange for an annual "rendezvous." The "Westerners" were so tuned to the times that within thirty years after the first "corral" was organized in Chicago in 1944, nearly a hundred met regularly in cities and towns throughout the United States.

Such enthusiasm, no less than the popularity of western artists and the success of western commercial ventures, was a clear indication that the frontier had not passed from the minds and hearts of the American people, even though the last arable lands of the continent had been occupied. Why its enduring impact? Why the persistence of an image that was usually false, but nonetheless appealing? Did the continuing vogue rest solely on the bloodletting and violence usually associated with frontier themes? Or were there more subtle appeals associated with the pioneering process that reveal traits in the American character that persist long after the "closing" of the frontier?

Students of American thought have isolated three reasons for the persistence—and exaggeration—of the frontier myth in the twentieth-century United States: a strong back-to-Nature urge among a sizable portion of the people, a rebellion against conventionalism, and a longing for individualistic expression and opportunity in an industrial society increasingly restrained by governmental controls. Advocates of each have created in their own imaginations an image of a frontier that they believe to have existed, and that admirably satisfies their longings. That those frontiers never did exist is not important; they are nonetheless real to their creators and wondrously suited to the psychological needs of today.

This is true of the back-to-Nature cultists, even though their beliefs are directly opposite of those of the true pioneers. Throughout the nineteenth century the frontiersmen in particular, but all Americans in general, saw Nature as the enemy of progress; the wilderness must be subdued to make way for man's triumphant conquest of the continent. By century's end this belief was being questioned by a growing group of conservationists who saw the impending passing of the frontier as a threat to basic American values. National forests and national parks and wilderness areas must be set aside, they insisted, not only to protect natural vacation lands from urban sprawl and corporate greed, but to assure future generations the spiritual, physical, and emotional rejuvenation that contacts with unspoiled Nature made possible. Such contacts had endowed the Founding Fathers with the wisdom and spirituality needed to establish the Republic; now continuing contacts were essential if that Republic was to survive. Nature was seen by members of the wilderness cult much as it had been by Thomas Jefferson and Crèvecoeur—as a balm for mankind's ills and a counterweight against the evils of civilization.

Just as appealing as this "Walden Impulse" with its glorification of Nature's curative powers was a second virtue of the frontier past: its role as an escape hatch for men and women stifled by the rules and pressures of an urban industrial society. To millions of modern Americans the frontier seemed in retrospect a land of liberty, a land of freedom from convention, where the shackles of the modern world could be discarded and men and women could behave as they pleased. Scholars called this mythical land

the "Injun Territory" in tribute to Huck Finn's determination to escape
Aunt Polly's soap and sermons by running off to the Indian Territory.[2]
That such a frontier never did exist made no difference; in their nostalgic
longings rebellious Americans endowed it with a reality that helped them
survive a society that they found distasteful.

Never-say-die individualists similarly found escape into the frontier
past a satisfying psychological experience. The West that they created in
their imagination was totally without societal or governmental controls;
there each individual could carve out his own destiny free of any interference by federal bureaucrats or meddling state officials. There a man could
make his own way and his own fortune, and devil take the hindmost. No
such frontier actually existed, of course; the profit-hungry farmers and
hard-headed business men who took over every pioneer community as
soon as it demonstrated its potential for survival wanted peace and order
and a regulated economy, just as did their eastern counterparts, and this
meant laws and regulations. What had been, however, was unimportant.
Rugged individualists of the twentieth century could bask in the belief
that frontier America was better suited to their talents than modern
America, and wish nostalgic wishes as they returned in their imaginations
to that happier era.

All who glorified the pioneering past shared one thing in common: an
urge to escape the pressures and conventions of modern society. That they
fastened upon the frontier as their ideal, rather than some other time and
place that would meet their psychological needs, was a result of a revised
image of pioneer days devised by twentieth-century writers. The formula
that gave the West its vast appeal was applied by Owen Wister in his influential novel, *The Virginian*, published in 1902. Its hero was a bigger-
than-life cowboy whose badge of courage was his six-gun and whose
moral code was the book's binding thread. This code decreed that he must
face the villain in a shoot-out, even though all of civilization's conventions
(symbolized by his sweetheart who swears never to speak to him again if
he does) demand that he refrain from violence. In the end when she sees
her lover in danger she accepts reality and the rustler-villain meets the fate
of all evildoers. Thus the individual's rebellion against society's restraints
is approved.[3] This was the plot that was to be repeated in thousands of
Westerns over the next years, with each repetition strengthening the
image of the West as a land of personal vengeance, bloodshed, and freedom.

[2]   René Dubos, "The Despairing Optimist," *American Scholar* 43 (Autumn 1974); 548. The
rise of this spirit is admirably described in Roderick Nash, *Wilderness and the American Mind*
(New Haven, 1967).
[3]   John G. Cawelti, "God's Country, Las Vegas, and the Gunfighter: Differing Visions of
the West," *Western American Literature* 9 (Winter 1975): 276–81, is excellent on these points.

"The Camp." From Theodor Dielitz, *Atlantis. Bilder aus dem Wald-und Prairieleben Amerika's* (Berlin, 1862). (From the collections of Albert Hümmerich of Berlin.)

The Virginian also established the characters who were to flit across their pages. The heroine was always a Minerva reincarnate, dispensing comfort and Victorian prudery, the hero an Olympian statue, slightly animated, and blending the virtues of Hercules and Thor with a dash of Errol Flynn added for glamour. All were cowboys, strong, tall, sinewy, faces weather-beaten by life in the open, eyes squinted against the sun, legs bowed from days in the saddle. All were identically clad in colorfully embroidered shirts, tight-fitting trousers protected by leather chaps, and high-heeled boots, a handkerchief looped about the neck, a broad-brimmed Stetson worn over longish blond hair, two six-shooters slung low about the waist, and a lariat hung from the saddle of the trusty horse who was his constant companion. His uniform symbolized his bravery and his elevation above ordinary folk; his roles, whether in books or on screen, stamped him as an individualist who would take the law into his own hands if necessary to assure the triumph of Good over Evil—but only when necessary. If the cowboy raised a bit of hell occasionally by shooting up a saloon or hazing an innocent tenderfoot, the loneliness of the Long Drive excused a slight bending of the rules; even the Norse gods had vis-ited the earth now and then for a bit of pleasure. His very weaknesses humanized him, and assured his place in the pantheon of American folk heroes. And certainly his virtues guaranteed that his role as a cultural image was secure; the cowboy personified in looks and conduct the strength, freedom, and individualism that was the American ideal in the postfrontier world.[4]

One question remained: would the cowboy prove as popular among Europeans as among Americans? To catapult him into the hero role would be to discard a venerable tradition, for during the nineteenth century woodsmen and plainsmen had held the spotlight, each in his own way symbolizing the degenerative impact of Nature on civilized man. Now Nature was the friend of man, and the cowboy its supreme product. Not that there was any nonsense among the European image-makers about glo-rification of the hero through his contacts with Nature; that was a sen-timent that proved unexportable. Instead their cowboys could be real men, hard-riding gunslingers who made no apology for slaughtering vil-lains, and who had been brutalized, not purified, by life in the West. They were unrestrained by either civilization or savagery.

This was a transformation that elevated western stories to new heights of popularity in Europe. Since the early days of the frontier readers there had shivered vicarious shivers as they thrilled to tales of bloodshed and vi-

---

[4]   Marshall W. Fishwick, "The Cowboy: America's Contribution to the World's Mythology," *Western Folklore* 11 (April 1952): 81–82; David B. Davis, "Ten Gallon Hero," *American Quarterly* 6 (Summer 1954): 111–25.

olence; now they could enjoy sensationalism without any twinges of conscience. French intellectuals, jaded by a life-style that elevated sophistication above more basic values, testified to their excitement when the first western films were shown in Paris playhouses; as they listened to the rhythm of galloping hooves and the chatter of six-shooters they experienced a new sense of manhood.[5] Here was tonic for tired blood, dreams for the bored, a whole new world of adventure for the red-blooded. The image of the frontier as a land of savagery was one that they understood, especially when it was no longer contrasted with the image of the West as a land of opportunity. Its appeal was to prove phenomenal.

The Role of Western Fiction

European readers showed their tastes first by gobbling up American imports, the wilder and more sensational the better. Books by the most lurid writers were favored; some such as Edward S. Ellis were relics of the dime-novel days with such titles as *Snake-Eyed Sol and the Roundup; or, Geronimo's Last Raid;* others, such as Zane Grey were newcomers to the scene but won overnight popularity. Grey was first discovered by Europeans during the 1920s when his novels catapulted to the best-seller lists in Norway, Spain, and Central Europe; in Spain alone forty-nine of his titles were published in translation between 1928 and the close of the 1950s, some of them in edition after edition. By the early 1960s *The Spirit of the Border* was in its sixth printing, the *Heritage of the Desert* in its ninth, and *Nevada* in its eleventh.[6]

Native geniuses soon rose to challenge these imports. In France the leading tub-thumper for frontier violence was George Fronval, who in the fifty years before his death in 1975 was the author of no less than six hundred books, most of them about the American West, and fifty-four of them about Buffalo Bill Cody under such unlikely titles as the *Prisoner of the Ku Klux Klan, The Cavern of the Mammoths,* and the *Horseman of the Moon.* Fronval made no apologies for the bloodletting that was his stock-in-trade. "The Frenchman," he wrote ". . . wants the guns and the Indians and the shoot 'em up and the scalps."[7] He gave the Frenchman what they wanted, and in hefty doses.

Spaniards discovered the West during the late 1920s and during the Great Depression, but not until the 1950s did the industry there move into high gear. And industry it was. Not many participated; a relatively

[5] Philippe Soupault, *The American Influence in France* (Seattle, 1930), pp. 12–13.
[6] Finn Arnesen, "Why Norwegians Love Westerns," *The Roundup* 24 (October 1976): 1–3; Charles F. Olstad, "The 'Wild West' in Spain," *Arizona and the West* (Autumn 1964): 191–92.
[7] Jeffrey Robinson, "Le Cowboy," *Westways* 66 (April 1974): 40–41; Roberta Cheney, "He Brought France Thrills of the West," *The Roundup* 23 (April 1975): 12–13.

few authors managed to meet the considerable demand by writing from ten to sixty books each year (one set a record of sorts in 1958 with ninety-four titles), all of them 120 pages long, all luridly illustrated with strewn corpses and blazing guns, and all luring readers with such titles as *The Killer Wears Another Face*, *The Gallows Can Wait*, and *Two Men Too Many in Tucson*. Their heroes were inevitably men of action rather than words, their heroines beautiful, desirable, and incapable of any emotion more complex than anger and incipient desire. Their plots were such models of simplicity that the reader need not strain his memory by trying to recall what had happened a page before. Long chases across the plains and fast-draw confrontations between hero and villain were all that readers demanded; these were bloody affairs with guns barking, jaws splintering, and as the bullets found their marks, "red flowers" appearing on the bad man's shirt or a "third nostril" opening on his face.[8] The West that Spaniards pictured was no place for the timid.

In northern Europe where the tradition of interest in the frontier was strong, fictionalized Westerns continued to find a ready market. Norway's Kjell Hallbing, writing under the pseudonym of Louis Masterson and with a larger-than-life hero named Morgan Kane, was one of Scandinavia's best-read authors, as well he might be. In the seventy-odd novels in which he appeared, Morgan Kane served as a scout for Custer on the Little Big Horn, helped clean up Butch Cassidy's Wild Bunch, and dug some Black Hills gold even though he was suffering from prostate trouble at the time and had to spend much of the book fighting off a gang of homosexuals who wanted to "utilize" him.[9]

Germans began the twentieth century with a built-in taste for Westerns that was partly satisfied by the ever-popular novels of their own Karl May. May's books lost none of their appeal after his death in 1912; instead their sales steadily increased in the pre-Hitler and Hitler eras when his nationalistic effusions, his passionate love of the Fatherland, his thinly veiled dislike of Jews and foreigners, and his Messianic-inflated egotism vastly appealed to his imperialistic-minded countrymen.[10] Nor did the fall of Hitlerism end his popularity; over the next decades his books continued to circulate nearly a million copies each year, some in the familiar green-and-gold standard edition, some in the inexpensive *Volksausgabe*, and some in the prestigious offerings of a leading book club.[11] That the first American

[8] Olstad, "The 'Wild West' in Spain," pp. 191–201.
[9] Information supplied by Dr. Stig Thornsohn, Aarhus University, Denmark.
[10] H. J. Stammel and Friedrich Gassman, "The Literary Evolution of the 'Wild West' in Germany," *Los Angeles Westerners Brand Book No. 12* (Los Angeles, 1966), p. 169.
[11] D. L. Ashliman, "The American West in Nineteenth Century German Literature" (Ph.D. diss., Rutgers University, 1969), p. 228.

edition, and the first English translation of May's *Winnetou*, was published in 1977 suggests that his star is still on the rise.[12]

His continuing popularity brought a host of imitators into the field, particularly during the 1940s when German interest in the American frontier underwent a remarkable rejuvenation. At first a flood of cheap paperbacks sought to meet the demand, most of them modeled on the five-pfennig dreadfuls that circulated during the dime-novel era and all of them uncluttered by sufficient characterization or plot to test the competence of the semiliterate. Yet they proved so unbelievably popular that the fly-by-night publishers who inflicted them on the public became instant millionaires; six of these fortunates, some operating out of abandoned warehouses, by 1960 were circulating some ninety-one million copies yearly. Most were written by a handful of professional writers who used such pseudonyms as Johnny Baxter and Red Buster to create the illusion that they were cowboys. The best among them were paid between three and five hundred marks a title, and could write a book every five days.[13]

There was more bloodshed than literary grace in these potboilers, as critics and readers who wanted a somewhat more elevated fare were quick to point out. Their criticism helped convince the 25,000 lending libraries to bring pressure on legitimate publishers for books about the American West that would be less offensive to their subscribers. Publishers responded with enthusiasm; by 1964 the libraries were circulating 626,000 Westerns to their members, each of which was borrowed by an estimated 150 persons over a five-year period—a sizable portion of West Germany's population.[14] Westerns were almost as popular in England where the largest paperback publisher, Transworld Publishers, estimated in 1975 that it had sold more than three million yearly over the past five years.[15]

Not only books but western-style pulp magazines appealed to Europeans. In Norway *Wild West Magasinet* appeared in the 1930s, to be followed by *Cowboy* and *Western* in the 1950s. *Wild West* and *Cowboy* failed to survive, but *Western* prospered to the degree that it could attract even American authors with sizable cash prizes.[16] Even comic books fell into line, particularly in France where comic cowboys addressed each other in fluent French as they massacred villains who threatened the world's gold

[12] Karl May, *Winnetou; A Novel* (New York, 1977), translated by Michael Shaw. The volume contains translations of the first two volumes of the original German publication.
[13] D. L. Ashliman, "The American West in Twentieth Century Germany," *Journal of Popular Culture* 2 (Summer 1968): 84–85.
[14] Stammel and Gassman, "The Literary Evolution of the 'Wild West' in Germany," pp. 171–74.
[15] Report of Andrew Hirschhorn, English research assistant, to author, April 1975.
[16] Arnesen, "Why Norwegians Love Westerns," pp. 2–3; circular distributed to members of the Western Writers of America, June 1974.

supply. One, *Lucky Luke*, caricatured frontier mythology with his impossible skills; in one episode a band of soldiers defending a Mojave desert outpost became so entranced by the odor of leek soup emerging from the kitchen that they "Ohed" and "Ahed" and lip-smacked while the Apaches sneaked over the walls.[17] French cowboys might elevate gastronomic thrills over safety, but their appeal to readers was undiminished.

Celluloid Westerns

The fictionalized image of the frontier as a land of savagery and personal justice was sharpened by the flood of motion pictures that inundated Europe during the twentieth century, some imported from the United States, more produced at home. Here was a medium ideally suited to spread the message. The vastness of the western landscape was uniquely appealing to Europeans living in cramped valleys and crowded cities; producers made sure that films designed for their cinema palaces were made in Texas or New Mexico or Arizona where the distant horizons and boundless sky added to their lure. "All the room in the world for beauty and harmony and contrast," one French critic noted with approval.[18] Western films also offered escape from the increasingly routinized life-patterns of Europe's industrial-urban society; young men could forget the humdrum of countinghouse or farm by spending a few hours of an evening in a distant land where excitement was guaranteed, and where honesty, simplicity, and virtue were properly rewarded.

Best of all, western films were adjusted to the needs of unsophisticated audiences; their plots were so elementary that they could be followed by the uneducated and untraveled, and so obvious that the language barrier scarcely lessened their appeal. Films spoke through action rather than words, with the plots so standardized that no more than an idiot intelligence was needed to comprehend. Audiences, as one Swedish critic wrote, developed a "ritualistic passivity similar to that which one finds in a congregation at divine service," as they responded to the "same bewitching strength of incantation: the magic of repetition."[19] This combination of appeals catapulted the western film into the front rank as an image-maker during the twentieth century.

The test was in its overwhelming popularity. From the day when the

[17] John B. Jackson, "Ich bin ein Cowboy aus Texas," *Southwest Review* 38 (Spring 1953): 159–60; *Tegneserier: En ekspansions historie* (Kongerslev, Denmark, 1974), pp. 129–73. This whole chapter deals with western comic books.
[18] This quotation, and much of the material that follows, is taken from the useful work by George N. Fenin and William K. Everson, *The Western: From Silents to the Seventies* (New York, 1973). Another excellent survey of the subject is Jean-Louis Rieupeyrout, *Le Western ou le cinéma américain* (Paris, 1953), republished in translation as *Die Western* (Bremen, 1963).
[19] Harry Schein, "The Olympian Cowboy," *American Scholar* 24 (Summer 1955): 311.

first American imports featured William S. Hart—"Rio Jeem" the French
called him—as a hell-for-leather hero, Europeans of all nations have
flocked to cinema houses in numbers far surpassing those frequenting
book shops. Starting in 1910 they began producing their own Westerns,
crude imitations at first, then in versions more suited to their audiences.
For a time Denmark's Great Western Film Company led the way, but its
products were soon challenged by British and German filmmakers. Germany even developed a star with greater appeal than Bill Hart; films featuring Hans Albers, complete with Mexican villains named Don Josè or
Don Diego who shouted "Caramba" at the slightest excuse, and climaxed
by a dramatic chase across the plains after the heroine in a runaway
buggy, proved amazingly popular for a generation. By the time of World
War I, the western film was firmly planted in European culture.

Its golden age was still to come, for Europe's taste for vicarious adventuring on the silver screen did not reach its pinnacle until after World War
II. Two innovations by European filmmakers helped popularize their
products. One was to stress brutality, even to a degree that American
standards would not allow. Imports from the United States were relabeled
to enhance their appeal: *Clementine* became *The Fist Fight on the Prairie*, and
in France *La Poursuite infernale*; *The Panhandle* was renamed *The Avengers of
Texas*; and *Oh Susannah* appeared as *Apache Battle on Black Mountain*.[20]
These alterations symbolized the trend in European-made films; all were
increasingly forthright, realistic, brutal, and openly favorable to sadistic
scenes. Just as important to their image-making role was their changing
view of the Indian. Before World War II all red men had been pictured as
bloodthirsty savages bent on murder and rapine, fit prey for the bullets of
the hero. This stereotype was challenged in the early 1950s with the popularity of a French film, *La Flèche brisée*, which pictured the Indians as
reasonably humane, driven to bloodshed only by white avarice. From that
time on most European Westerns saw the Indians as helpless pawns of
American expansionists, seeking peace themselves, but robbed of their
lands by ruthless frontiersmen.[21]

The masters of this medium were the Italian filmmakers who dominated production during the 1960s, with those of France and Germany
not far behind. They catapulted to fame on the popularity of two motion
pictures produced in the mid-1960s: *Per en pugno di dòllari* (*For a Fistful of
Dollars*), and *Minnesota Clay*, both sadistically violent, realistically filmed,
and spiced with a degree of sex that Hollywood would not allow. Their
success, and that of such imitators as *La Battaglia di Fort Apache* and *Una
Pistòla per Ringo*, accounted for the fact that no less than 130 "Spaghetti

20   Ashliman, "The American West in Twentieth Century Germany," p. 88.
21   Fenin and Everson, *The Western*, pp. 18–19.

Westerns" (in the language of the trade) were released in 1964 and 1965, with a diminishing number following over the next five years.[22]

The vogue of "Spaghetti Westerns" was short-lived, but they set a pattern that has persisted among European filmmakers. The Grade-B pictures that have appealed to audiences in local cinema theaters ever since have almost universally pictured the Indian as the innocent victim of American expansion, and the frontier as a land steeped in violence and bloodshed. Theater marquees in France and Germany and Scandinavia have regularly glowed with lights urging audiences to see *Das Kriegsbeil* (*The War Hatchet*), or *Por qualche dòllari in più* (*For a Few Dollars More*), or some comparable production picturing American frontiersmen as ruthless predators of Indian rights and rebels against all legal restraints. Such has been the stress on violence that reformers, alarmed by the influence of such themes on Europe's youth, have regularly met to discuss the harm done by the glamorous adventures of "Hopalong Cassidy" and "Buffalo Bill," and to debate "Ist Billy Jenkins eine Gefahr für die Jugend?"[23] Films have helped convince generations of Europeans that the American West was, and is, a land of savagery.

So has the television screen for still later generations. Westerns—most of them imports from the United States—immediately captured a sizable portion of the audience; a serial called "Wanted—Dead or Alive" ranked among the most widely viewed programs in France during the late 1960s, while in Germany in 1972 viewers had their choice between "Colt 45," "High Chaparral," "Fargo Kid," "Tombstone Territory," "Pistols and Petticoats," ("Pistolen und Petticoats"), and a half-dozen more.[24] "High Chaparral" won top rating among Swedish viewers in 1977, while "Bonanza" was a perennial favorite throughout Europe for a decade, and "Gunsmoke" was syndicated in nineteen countries and seen by an estimated one-fourth of the world's population.[25] Observers at President Richard M. Nixon's reception for party Russian leader Leonid Brezhnev at San Clemente in 1973 noted that the one person the Soviet statesman embraced with bear-hug enthusiasm was Chuck Connors, the hero of a television series called "The Rifleman."[26]

The impact of this Niagara of silver-screen Westerns on the European image of the American West defies appraisal. Perhaps viewers were able to

[22]   Ibid., pp. 344–50; William K. Everson, *A Pictorial History of the Western Film* (New York, 1969), p. 234.
[23]   C. P. Westermeier, "Clio's Maverick—the Cowboy," *Denver Westerner's Monthly Roundup* 22 (October 1966): 11–13.
[24]   Kent L. Steckmesser, "Paris and the Wild West," *Southwest Review* 54 (Spring 1969): 168–69; Thomas Freeman, "The Cowboy and the Astronaut—The American Image in German Periodical Advertisements," *Journal of Popular Culture* 6 (Summer 1972): 103.
[25]   Barbara Francis, "Gunsmoke," *Emmy* 1 (Winter 1979): 33.
[26]   *Los Angeles Times*, 29 November 1973.

sift truth from fancy, and to recognize that the real frontier bore scant relationship to the legendary frontier. Perhaps the better-informed knew that Jesse James was little like the reincarnated Robin Hood that bore his name in western films, that Wyatt Earp was in real life an inferior lawman and a probable horse thief, and that Billy the Kid was a sniffling delinquent rather than a white knight incarnate.[27] Perhaps—but probably not. More likely the orderly West of fact became in the minds of Europeans the disorderly West of legend, a land where the law was defied, corpses littered the countryside, and the Indian was the innocent victim of frontier brutality.

This is not to say that knowledge of the real West was denied literate readers. A recent Hungarian anthology called *Vadnyugat* ("Wild West"), featuring short stories by such reputable writers as Owen Wister, Bret Harte, and Vardis Fisher, proved so popular that fifty thousand copies were sold—one for every five hundred inhabitants—while in Germany publishers recognized a large enough market among serious readers to justify a lavishly illustrated encyclopedia of the American West, *Der Cowboy: Legende und Wirklichkeit von A–Z*, edited by the well-informed H. J. Stammel. Even the germinal essay by Frederick Jackson Turner was made available to French readers in 1963, as "La Frontière dans l'histoire des Etats-Unis."[28] In England a well-read pictorial history of the frontier could honestly warn that "there has been nothing romantic about the 'real' American West except the scenery, despite every effort of film and television companies, and generations of authors, to prove otherwise."[29]

Notably, however, the best-informed European authors have reverted to type when writing of the West for their own countrymen, even while deploring the exaggeration. One of Britain's finest historians of the frontier, Joseph Rosa, chose to study Wild Bill Hickok and other outlaws rather than the true heralds of advancing civilization; even though he expertly deglamorized his characters his choice of subjects suggests their appeal to his readers. Similarly, Denmark's premier student of the West, Dr. Stig Thornsohn, chose as the subject of his first major book Buffalo Bill Cody, enshrining him in a handsomely illustrated volume featuring posters advertising his European appearances.[30]

Even the few schoolbooks that touch on the American West have stressed the image of a land of violence. In a Scottish Schools Council His-

[27] Joseph W. Snell, "The Wild and Wooly West of the Popular Writer," *Nebraska History* 48 (Summer 1967): 142.

[28] H. J. Stammel, ed., *Der Cowboy: Legende und Wirklichkeit von A–Z* (Gütersloh, W. Germany, 1972); Frederick J. Turner, *La Frontière dans l'histoire des Etats-Unis* (Paris, 1963).

[29] Robin May and G. A. Embleton, *The American West* (London, 1973), introduction.

[30] Joseph G. Rosa, *They Called Him Wild Bill: The Life and Adventure of James Butler Hickok* (Norman, 1964); Joseph G. Rosa, *The Gunfighter: Man or Myth* (Norman, 1969); Stig Thornsohn, *Buffalo Bill's Wild West* (Denmark, 1978).

tory Project, the two topics chosen for special discussion as typical of all
the frontier's history were "Plains Indians," and "Cowboys and Cattle-
men," with Custer's Last Stand emphasized in the first and the Johnson
County War in the second.[31] A Netherlands study pamphlet, *Het Wilde
Western: Feit or Fantasie*, widely used in schools, sought to set the record
straight by picturing cowboys not as barbarians but as "boys who never
complain but who say 'Go to Hell' if you ask them to plow a piece of
land," and as sober young men devoted to playing auction pitch and
dominoes rather than dancing. But it also told its young readers that cowboys circumvented the rules against carrying revolvers by leasing them for
ninety-nine years and that, in the words of one of them, "our lives are in
constant danger and we solve differences with our pistol or knife."[32] The
legend of the American West as a land of savagery was too deeply implanted to be challenged, even by responsible historians and schoolbooks.

So also was the belief that the frontiersmen were heartless extermi-
nators of the Indians. One might expect a Soviet encyclopedia to use such
a weighted word as *zakhvat* ("seizure") in characterizing the government's
policy toward Indian lands, and to conclude that "the entire history of em-
battled America is one of unheard-of violence and treachery, of mass destruction of the native peoples and their enslavement,"[33] but one might
hope that less politically oriented Europeans would express milder judgments. Instead such respected authors as B. Traven in West Germany and
Friedrich von Gagern in Austria, in widely read volumes such as *Der tote
Mann* and *Der Marterpfahl*, made the Indian their collective hero as they
pictured his futile struggle to maintain his moral and legal rights against
ruthless whites.[34] Europeans, whether addicts of books or the silver
screen, have been indoctrinated in the belief that the American colossus
was a land-hungry predator willing to rob and murder in its expansion
westward, and that the frontier was hopelessly sunk in savagery.

Frontier Cultism

The enthusiasm for the American West—real or legendary—generated by
a century of image-making found its most revealing expression in the
frontier worshipers who appeared in Europe during the 1960s and 1970s.
They emerged in all segments of society, and in virtually all nations. In
Denmark and Austria and Yugoslavia children played "Cowboys and In-

[31] "The American West, 1840–95," *Schools Council History* (Edinburgh, 1977), pp. 13–16.
[32] *Het Wilde Westen; Feit or Fantasie* (n.p., n.d.), p. 4.
[33] Quoted in Wilbur R. Jacobs and Edmund E. Mason, "History and Propaganda: Soviet
Image of the American Past," *Mid-America* 46 (April 1964), 84.
[34] Ashliman, "American West in Twentieth Century Germany," pp. 86–87; "The American West in Nineteenth Century German Literature," pp. 242–43.

dians" or walked "Indian File" through the cobbled streets, their make-
shift costumes contrasting strongly with the half-timbered houses; one
German confessed that she had immersed herself so deeply in these fantasies that forever afterward she dreamed that she was a Delaware tribes-
man, stalking silently through the virgin forest.[35] Children carried that
dreamworld into their play; in French shops during the 1970s frontier
soldiers and *panoplies indiennes* outnumbered model tanks and helicopters
by a ratio of three to two. One Dutch youngster, told that certain ruins
had been made by men fighting, asked "Cowboys?" The frontier was as
real to her as to the group of Swiss soldiers heard singing "Ich bin ein
Cowboy aus Texas."[36] Or to Scottish youths; a Glasgow health officer
complained that they were becoming round shouldered and hollow
chested from imitating the slouching stride of cowboys.[37]

The disease was particularly virulent in Germany where love of the
American West had been consistently nurtured since the days of Balduin
Möllhausen and Friedrich Gerstäcker. Karl May experienced a dramatic
revival during the 1960s and 1970s, with "Karl May Dolls" and "Karl May
Cards" and "Karl May Camping Equipment" advertised everywhere. Karl
May films vied for customers at cinema palaces, most of them made in
Yugoslavia with blue-eyed German actors as plainsmen and Indians. Each
summer a "Karl May Festival" attracted more than a hundred thousand
enthusiasts to Bad Segeberg to don Indian headdresses or fur caps, cheer
dramatizations of his novels, and escape for a few days into that never-
never land that the author made so real to them. His faithful worshipers
can never forgive the Soviet Union for dividing Germany, to a considerable degree because West Germans could no longer visit "Villa Shatterhand," at May's family home at Radebeul near Dresden, to admire his
lifesize statue, gape at his *Henrystutzen* and other weapons, or shudder
before the framed human scalp that he claimed to have "lifted." Not that
Karl May was ignored by the East Germans; his relics were still displayed
at Radebeul, not in his honor (for he was condemned as an "imperialistic
adventurer"), but to glorify the Indians slaughtered by Old Shatterhand
during their "struggle for freedom against imperialism." Winnetou might
not have approved of this distortion, but he would be delighted to know
that when children in East Germany played "Cowboys and Indians," the
majority wanted to be Indians.[38]

---

35 Ashliman, "American West in Twentieth Century Germany," pp. 86–87.
36 Jackson, "Ich bin ein Cowboy aus Texas," pp. 160–61.
37 Westermeier, "Clio's Maverick—the Cowboy," p. 13.
38 Klaus Mann, "Karl May, Hitler's Literary Mentor," *Kenyon Review* 2 (Autumn 1940):
232; Joseph Wechberg, "Winnetou of der Wild West," *Saturday Review* 45 (20 October 1962):
60–61; *Los Angeles Times*, 17 June 1973 and 3 December 1973; *Christian Science Monitor*, 10
September 1975.

Nor did Germany—West or East—monopolize the frontier craze. Western buffs in Paris could sip red-eye whiskey at "Jacky's Far Western Saloon," gape at scantily clad girls at the "Crazy Horse Bar," and dine at "Le Western" restaurant while they gazed through artificial windows at sun-drenched cactus and were served by red-shirted waiters who offered them such dishes as "Peg-leg Shorty's Chili con Carne," or "Son-of-a-Bitch Stew," the latter delicately translated as "la bourguignonne du Texas."[39] In Copenhagen aficionados could find a similar haven in the "Longhorn Steakhouse," where "Billy the Kid kunne have vaeret gaest hos os."[40]

Throughout Europe the particular could garb themselves in true Western style, buying at "The Western House," near the Arc de Triomphe or from the thriving chain stores in West Germany that offered everything from imitation Colt revolvers to cowboy shirts and Mexican saddles. True Westerners, according to the proprietor of one, refused to watch "Bonanza" or "The Rifleman" on television unless properly clothed.[41] Levis, worn cowboy style, were so popular during the 1970s that an international ring operating out of Switzerland made a fortune selling fake outfits bearing the forged label of the Levi Strauss Company at fifteen dollars each rather than the eighty dollars asked for the real article.[42] Even in Russia, where billboards branded the cowboy a capitalistic exploiter of helpless Indians, jeans were in such demand that youths gladly surrendered a month's pay for a pair and double that for authentic Levis.[43] Such was the fad that a Soviet humor magazine, *Yunost*, pictured the queues that formed to buy jeans as so long that buyers bought the eighteen-volume *Great Soviet Encyclopedia* to read while they waited.[44]

Advertisers leaped upon the bandwagon. Malboro cigarettes jumped to first in sales with their pictures of handsome cowboys roping steers or saddling their horses as they lighted another coffin nail. Germans were persuaded to buy a deodorant called "Lasso" by a western-clad beauty pointing two cans as though they were pistols, and told that "Rodeo After Shave" was "für Männer die's heiss mögen: Heisse Räder, Heisse Eisen, Heisse Musik, Hot Dogs" ("for men who like it hot: hot wheels, hot iron, hot music, hot dogs"). Jim Beam whiskey launched a major campaign of "Pictures from the Wild West," reminding buyers that Daniel Boone, Friedrich Gerstäcker, and Karl May had been there, and that the pioneers were "upright men, real fellows with coarse exteriors, but with hearts in

[39] *Los Angeles Times*, 6 November 1977.
[40] *Ekstrabladet* (Copenhagen), 9 January 1976.
[41] Ashliman, "American West in Twentieth Century Germany," p. 89; Steckmesser, "Paris and the Wild West," pp. 172–73.
[42] *Los Angeles Times*, 19 August 1977.
[43] *Los Angeles Times* 20 November 1973; 17 September 1975.
[44] "Inexpensive Jeans," *Yunost* 1 (January 1975): 1–2. Copy provided by Professor N. N. Bolkhovitinov.

French cultists stage a mock Wild West raid. (Photograph by Ch. Perrin, Mulhouse, France.)

the right place."[45] The West was as secure in the affection of Europeans in the twentieth century as in the nineteenth.

It remained for the western clubs and societies that sprang up over much of Europe in the 1960s and 1970s to reveal the frontier *geist* in its most violent form. For the serious-minded, genuinely interested in western history, "corrals" of the Westerners offered a convenient haven. This society began spreading beyond the United States in the 1950s, with such branches as the "Deutsche-Westerners Gesellschaft" and the "Deutsche-Amerikanische Westerners Vereinigung" leading the way. By the close of the 1970s Westerners were operating at Berlin, Cologne, Frankfurt, Memmingen, and Munich in West Germany; Gothenburg in Sweden; Porsgrunn and Oslo in Norway (with the "sheriff" of the latter the famed Kjell Hallbing whose Westerns had made his hero, Morgan Kane, a household word through Scandinavia); Paris; and in Denmark at Aarhus. In England an "English Westerners Society" (there was no nonesense about "corrals" and "sheriffs" in that bastion of traditionalism) boasted some two hundred members. Most met regularly to refight the Battle of the Little Big Horn, practice the quick draw or western dances, and recapture for an evening the thrill of pioneering. All sought to keep alive the spirit of the Old West in remote corners of the world.[46]

Most Westerners were serious students of the frontier (as testified by such corral publications as *Tagebuch von Lewis and Clarke* or *Indianische Skizzen*) but the many "Wild West Clubs," and "Wild West Encampments" that sprang up in France and Germany played a more glamorous role. Their purpose was to allow Europeans to experience frontier life in all its romance and discomforts—and a popular purpose it was. In France members of such clubs as "Le Cercle Peau-Rouge Huntka" (Huntka Redskin Circle) gathered regularly at "Camp Indien" near Paris to spend weekends in authentic tepees, dress as Comanches or Sioux, practice tomahawk throwing, and pretend to enjoy French imitations of Indian food.[47] Far to the east the "Trois Tribus Indiennes Campent sur les Bords du Rhin" lured several hundred enthusiasts to an annual gathering near Strasbourg to practice native dances, tan leather for costumes, and powwow in solemn councils.[48]

Nor was the cowboy forgotten in these western clubs. Dozens of worshipers at the shrine of Buffalo Bill Cody held regular meetings of the "Club Hippique du Lasso" or the "Arizona Boys" to strut about in Stetsons and chaps, practice the quick draw with their six-shooters, and gal-

45 Freeman, "The Cowboy and the Astronaut," pp. 90–91.
46 Corrals are listed in a publication of Westerners International, *The Buckskin Bulletin* 11 (Winter 1977): 3–6.
47 Steckmesser, "Paris and the Wild West," p. 172.
48 *Dernières Nouvelles de Strasbourg*, 7 June 1978. Copy provided by Mme Anne B. Schmitt.

lop about the countryside in pursuit of imaginary redskins.[49] Most drew no such occupational lines; Indians and cowboys cooperated in building campsites and staging regular three-day meetings. At a typical gathering at the "Dakota Trading Post," near Frankfurt, where a frontier fort and an Indian village were painfully constructed side by side, mock Indians dressed in breechcloths and eagle feathers mingled with spurred cowboys as they staged war games or met in solemn council. "We are German romantics," one explained. "Our own German history is too narrow, and so we go elsewhere—to the American West—for our hobby." In all some 120 of these clubs were scattered through West Germany in the 1970s, some with as many as 3,500 members.[50]

The elite of this group, members of sixty-three clubs grouped in the "Western Clubs Federation," held themselves aloof from those who only wanted to "play at being cowboys." Their purpose was to construct a western center as their club headquarters on the fringes of all German cities, each bearing a name such as *Prairiefreund* ("Friends of the Prairie"), or *Nu-Kla-Kai-At* (Siouan for "Home of Peace"), and each an authentic duplicate of a real frontier community. Days and months of research went into the designing of each building, fashioning each relic, creating costumes of leather tanned in the Indian manner, and practicing with guns exactly like those used in the real West. Some carried their perfectionism to the degree that they refused to watch such imported television shows as "Gunsmoke" and "The Virginian," because of their inaccuracies; no real Westerner they scoffed, ever said *Sie ritten da'lang* ("they went thataway") or *Streck die Hände zum Himmel* ("reach for the sky"). "We like to think of ourselves as historians dressed up as cowboys and Indians," one explained. So they were—even carrying realism to the uncomfortable extreme of using saddles for pillows during their camp-outs and banning Indian impersonators from the club saloon.[51]

Such extremists were not typical, but they only exaggerated the lure of the Wild West to millions of Europeans who immersed themselves in western novels, watched western films, and thrilled as synthetic Bat Mastersons and Wyatt Earps mowed down their weekly quota of villains on television screens throughout the Continent. "Why," asked a Swiss publisher in 1959, "does every twelve year old boy know at least as much about the Sioux Indians as about the native inhabitants of his own country?"[52] His question was a tribute to the image-makers who for two centuries had glamorized the frontier as a land of savagery where the law was

[49] Westermeier, "Clio's Maverick—the Cowboy," p. 10.
[50] *Los Angeles Times*, 16 October 1970.
[51] *Los Angeles Times*, 9 December 1973; *Time*, 18 June 1979, p. 51.
[52] Quoted in D. L. Ashliman, "The American Indian in German Travel Narratives and Literature," *Journal of Popular Culture* 10 (Spring 1977): 1.

enforced with knives and revolvers and where Europeans of all ages and nationalities could find the vicarious thrills that modern life denied them.

The Image in Modern Perspective

This image came home to roost for the American people after World War I. Until that time a dual image had persisted: one of the United States as a land of promise where the unfortunate could begin life anew, the other as a land of savagery where the "code of the west" allowed indiscriminate killing, where Judge Lynch administered his own brand of justice, and where Indians were slaughtered to clear them from lands legally theirs. Neither of these images stirred serious resentment among Europeans. Employers and landlords might deplore the exodus of sturdy peasants and laborers needed at home, but their protests were drowned in the chorus of approval from the masses who dreamed of escape to the bountiful lands of the West.

Nor did the image of the frontier as a land of savagery, bent on overwhelming the Indian peoples in its ruthless expansion westward, arouse serious protest among nineteenth-century Europeans. During the 1880s and 1890s Europe's major powers viewed imperialistic expansion as both inevitable and desirable, a natural by-product of the industrialization that required raw materials and markets. To those with such views, American expansion westward was a model to be imitated, not a crime to be deplored. In that age of geopolitics the future lay with nations that could grow as the United States had grown; vastness—what the French called *grandeur*—was essential to survival. Expansion into colonies meant not only profitable trade but power, self-confidence, the respect of one's neighbors. If a few thousand natives were killed or enslaved, as were the American Indians, what matter? The extermination of inferior peoples was justified if civilization and industry were to bring their proper rewards to the civilized and the industrious.

So long as the imperialistic urge dominated European thought, the image of the frontiersmen as heartless aggressors bore no stigma, but with the Spanish-American War at century's end a harsher evaluation began to surface. The United States emerged from that brief conflict with imperialistic ambitions of its own, pouring the energy that had carried its boundaries to the Pacific into a vast colony-grabbing program in the Caribbean and Far East. Faced with this new rivalry, European peoples reacted with predictable alarm; clearly the momentum of expansion would continue until the American colossus dominated the world. Instead of a friendly rival, the United States was a feared competitor, subject to criticism and retaliation.

The result was to sharpen the image of the Americans as heartless aggressors, trampling on the rights of minorities in the West Indies, the Philippines, Hawaii, and Asia as they had on the Indians. Now no vision of the West as a Land of Promise blurred that image. With the gates against immigration closed as they were during the 1920s, only the negative picture of a Land of Savagery persisted. Europeans who accepted this verdict were ready to believe that the frontiers shown them in film and sensational television serials were the real frontier, and that lawlessness and brutality reigned there.

That this was the image generally accepted in twentieth-century Europe seems probable. Englishmen have testified that the books they read and the films they saw as boys left them with the unshakable belief that only in a few cities—New York, Chicago, and San Francisco—was life safe from Indian attacks.[53] Europeans during World War II were surprised that American soliders did not walk bow-legged, shoot from the hip, hunt down the enemy in posses, and string their victims to the nearest tree.[54] Behind the Iron Curtain two young Soviets who stole guns from a museum so they could "act like frontiersmen" inspired an official edict against the "narcotic ideological propaganda of the West."[55] In Israel an army psychologist expressed delight that his company's soldiers did not use the weapons they brought home with them on leave; "there is," he explained, "no shooting like in the Wild West."[56]

Europe's prejudices were admirably illustrated by a minor incident that occurred in West Germany. An American Indian serving in the occupation force became a local hero when his lawyer pleaded that he had kidnapped a German couple for ransom only because his free-roving instincts rebelled against life in an army barracks in a strange land. Newspapers took up his cause in sentimental editorials, committees were formed to negotiate for his release, thousands of letters deluged the judge assigned to his trial, and even the couple he had kidnapped urged that he not be punished. This was no instant sentimentality; lifelong readers of Karl May were responding to the pleas of another Winnetou caught in the shackles of modern civilization.[57] Germans could provide a lesson in brotherhood and humanity to those barbarian frontiersmen who had virtually exterminated the poor red men in their ruthless expansion.

To say that their attitude—and the widespread image of the frontier as a land of savagery—seriously altered the views of Europeans concerning the United States as a whole is to draw a mountain of conclusions from a

53 Alistair Cooke, *Alistair Cooke's America* (New York, 1974), pp. 8–9.
54 Fishwick, "The Cowboy," pp. 77–78.
55 Westermeier, "Clio's Maverick—the Cowboy," p. 12.
56 *Los Angeles Times*, 19 February 1975.
57 Ernst A. Stadler, "Karl May: The Wild West under the German Umlaut," *Missouri Historical Society Bulletin* 21 (July 1965): 295.

molehill of evidence. That the image of America as a land of equality and a champion of democracy has eroded alarmingly since World War II cannot be questioned. The reasons for this erosion are less obvious. Peoples of the Third World and some Europeans insist that their faith in the United States crumbled when its intervention in Vietnam and its meddling in Southeast Asia revealed its imperialistic ambitions. They maintain, too, that the nation's willingness to support any dictatorial government that promised to maintain the status quo revealed that it was out of step with the spirit of progress on which its greatness was built.

That these opinions are right or wrong is unimportant. What is vital is that an alarming number of people see the nation as a ruthless predator, a foe of minorities, and an enemy of progress. Their views are more often based on the propaganda of Communist countries than on reality, but those views are nonetheless firmly planted—to the detriment of world harmony. And, tragically, those views are rooted in the long-held belief that frontier America—and to a lesser degree the United States as a whole—was a land where might ruled over right, where brutality was the way of life, and where an Indian minority was heartlessly wiped out by white aggressors. If these views helped shape the attitude of Europeans today, as the evidence seems to indicate, the image-makers played a larger role in history than they anticipated, and must be recognized if we are to understand the world we live in.

BIBLIOGRAPHICAL
NOTES

THIS BIBLIOGRAPHY makes no attempt to list the hundreds of European novels, travel accounts, guidebooks, and contemporary materials used in preparing this book; instead the first footnote citation to each item in each chapter contains complete bibliographical information, with a condensed title used thereafter. What it does attempt is to collect and evaluate the sizable number of books and articles that have been written *about* those novels and travel accounts and guidebooks and contemporary materials through which Europeans learned of the American frontier. Hence it does not follow the chapter pattern in the book itself; instead the arrangement is topical, save with materials used in the first and last chapters dealing with the periods before and after the nineteenth century.

THE IMAGE IN BROAD PERSPECTIVE

No single study of the European image of the American frontier has been attempted, but several books and articles deal with the image of the United States as a whole, or with the European view of individual sections or eras. Durand Echeverria, *Mirage in the West: A History of the French Image of American Society to 1815* (Princeton, 1957), is invaluable both for its expert analysis of the period and for its exploration of the whole concept of imagery. The story is continued in another able volume: René

Rémond, *Les Etats-Unis devant l'opinion française, 1815–1852* (2 vols., Paris, 1962). For the subsequent period Merle Curti and Kendall Birr, "The Immigrant and the American Image in Europe, 1860–1914" *Mississippi Valley Historical Review* 37 (September 1950): 203–30, is an excellent survey; so also is Jerzy Jedlicki, "Images of America," *Polish Perspectives* 18 (November 1975): 26–38, which deals brilliantly with the changing Polish image of the Indian and the American character. J. Martin Evans, *America: The View from Europe* (San Francisco, 1976), deals largely with the American image in recent European literature, although one section surveys the utopian and antiutopian visions from Columbian days to Martin Chuzzlewit. Paul M. Wheeler, *America through British Eyes: A Study of the Attitude of the Edinburgh Review toward the United States from 1802 to 1861* (Rock Hill, S.C., 1935), is too limited in scope to be of any use for my purposes; so also is Ronald A. Wells, "Migration and the Image of America in England: A Study of the *Times* in the Nineteenth Century," *Indiana Social Studies Quarterly* 28 (Autumn 1975). Wilbur R. Jacobs and Edmund E. Mason, "History and Propaganda: Soviet Image of the American Past," *Mid-America* 46 (April 1964): 75–91, deals with the recent image in Soviet writing.

A few studies of regional attitudes add slightly to the overall picture. Robert A. Burchell, "The Loss of a Reputation; or, The Image of California in Britain before 1875," *California Historical Quarterly* 53 (Summer 1974): 115–30, shows that the vision of the state as a center of Gold Rush lawlessness slowed immigration for two decades. Particularly valuable for its comments on imagery is Brian W. Blouet and Merlin P. Lawson, eds., *Images of the Great Plains: The Role of Human Nature in Settlement* (Lincoln, Nebr., 1975). Ralph Rusk, *The Literature of the Middle Western Frontier* (2 vols., New York, 1925), contains a number of excerpts from European writers on the Middle West. Both D. W. Brogan, *The American Character* (New York, 1944), and R. W. B. Lewis, *The American Adam* (Chicago, 1955), contain stimulating suggestions.

EARLY IMAGES OF THE NEW WORLD

Scholarship exploring the early European image of America and its frontier is extensive. Any study of the subject should begin with two stimulating works by Howard M. Jones, *O Strange New World: American Culture: The Formative Years* (New York, 1964), and "The Colonial Impulse: An Analysis of the 'Promotion' Literature of Colonization," *Proceedings of the American Philosophical Society* 90 (1946): 121–61; both devote a great deal of space to the picture of the New World created by explorers and would-be colonists during the Age of Discovery. Essential also are four lectures by the Mexican student, Edmundo O'Gorman, *The Invention of America*

(Bloomington, Ind., 1961), which shows how cartographers and philosophers of the post-Columbus era invented an America that bore little relation to reality. Equally valuable is J. H. Elliott, *The Old World and the New, 1492–1650* (Cambridge, 1970), a series of lectures dealing with the impact of the discoveries on Old World thought and economics. Carl Sauer, *Sixteenth Century America As Seen by Europeans* (Berkeley, 1971), describes the explorers, but says little of their views of the new land. Fredi Chiappelli, *First Images of America: The Impact of the New World on the Old* (2 vols., Berkeley, 1976), contains stimulating essays originally delivered at a conference on the subject.

The concept of America as a land of peace and plenty which bulked large in the seventeenth century is explored in Loren Baritz, "The Idea of the West," *American Historical Review* 66 (April 1961): 618–40, which traces the idea from ancient times, and Geoffrey Atkinson, *The Extraordinary Voyage in French Literature before 1700* (New York, 1920), which finds evidence of its origin in French writing. A helpful catalogue of an exhibit illustrating this theme is Hugh Honour, *The New Golden Land: European Images of America from the Discoveries to the Present Time (New York, 1976)*. How the New World's impact influenced Europe in the eighteenth century is the subject of two works by Michael Kraus, "America and the Utopian Ideal in the Eighteenth Century," *Mississippi Valley Historical Review* 22 (March 1936): 487–504, and *The Atlantic Civilization: Eighteenth Century Origins* (Ithaca, 1949).

The conflicting images of eighteenth-century America are the theme of Lois Whitney, *Primitivism and the Idea of Progress in English Popular Literature of the Eighteenth Century* (Baltimore, 1934). A brilliant work by Antonello Gerbi, *The Dispute of the New World: The History of a Polemic, 1750–1900* (Pittsburgh, 1973), originally published in Milan in 1955, explores the emerging view of America as a land of decay. Gilbert Chinard, "Eighteenth Century Theories of America As a Human Habitat," *Proceedings of the American Philosophical Society* 91 (1947), adds important details. Equally essential to an understanding of this period is Richard Slotkin, *Regeneration through Violence: The Mythology of the American Frontier, 1600–1800* (Middletown, Conn., 1973), a highly sophisticated interpretation of the frontier myth from its origins in Europe to its emergence in the character of Daniel Boone.

Changing European attitudes toward Nature, and the effect of these changes on the vision of America, are the theme of such diverse studies as Marjorie H. Nicolson, *Mountain Gloom and Mountain Glory: The Development of the Aesthetics of the Infinite* (Ithaca, 1959), which illustrates the transition by tracing the changing attitude toward mountains, and Samuel H. Monk, *The Sublime: A Study of Critical Theories in XVIII Century England* (New York, 1935), a study of the aesthetic standards that shaped the attitude of explorers toward the American wilds. The manner in which these views were reflected in garden design are described in general terms in Derek Clifford, *A History of Garden Design* (London, 1957), and more specifically in Henry V. S. Ogden and Margaret S. Ogden, *English Taste in Landscape in the Seventeenth Century* (Ann Arbor, 1955), and John D. Hunt, *The Figure in the Landscape: Poetry, Painting, and Gardening during the Eighteenth Century* (Baltimore, 1977). A pioneering article by Douglas Cole and Margaret Tippett, "Pleasing Diversity and Sublime Desolation: The 18th-Century British Perception of the Northwest Coast," *Pacific Northwest Quarterly* 65 (January 1974): 1–7, demonstrates the effect of changing concepts of Nature on the manner in which British explorers saw the American wilderness.

Shifting attitudes toward Nature influenced Europe's vacillating image of the Indian. An encyclopedic study of this subject that summarizes virtually every contemporary publication for the period is H. C. Porter, *The Inconstant Savage. England and the North American Indian, 1500–1660* (London, 1979). Several excellent monographic studies also explores aspects of the topic. Outstanding among these is Robert F. Berkhofer, Jr., *The White Man's Indian: Images of the American Indian from Columbus to the Present* (New York, 1978), which is concerned largely with the American image but touches on the European. Roy H. Pearce, *The Savages of America: A Study of the Indian and the Idea of Civilization* (Baltimore, 1953), similarly emphasizes American attitudes but touches on European thought. The subject is ideally summarized in the opening chapters of Bernard W. Sheehan, *Seeds of Extinction: Jeffersonian Philanthropy and the American Indian* (Chapel Hill, 1973). Elémire Zolla, *The Writer and the Shaman: A Morphology of the American Indian* (New York, 1973), also deals largely with American impressions, as does Gary B. Nash, "The Image of the Indian in the Southern Colonial Mind," *William and Mary Quarterly* 29 (April 1972): 197–230. Ronald L. Meet, *Social Science and the Ignoble Savage* (Cambridge, 1976), traces the history of the concept of emerging stages of civilization, and hence deals with the views of José de Acosta and other European image-makers.

Studies of the manner in which Europeans saw the Indian at various times from classical days onward shed much light on the early image of America. An excellent pioneering essay is Sidney Lee, "The American Indian in Elizabethan England," in Frederick S. Boas, ed., *Elizabethan and Other Essays by Sidney Lee* (Oxford, 1929), pp. 263–301. Arthur O. Lovejoy and George Boas, *Primitivism and Related Ideas in Antiquity* (Baltimore, 1935), traces the Noble Savage far back in European thought, while Edward Dudley and M. E. Novak, eds., *The Wild Man Within: An Image in Western Thought from the Renaissance to Romanticism* (Pittsburgh, 1972), collects a number of essays showing the evolution of the "Wild Man" concept. A useful essay tracing the concept of primitive man from classical times to Elizabethan England is Margaret T. Hodgen, "Montaigne and Shakespeare Again," *Huntington Library Quarterly* 16 (November 1952): 23–42. On a closely related subject, the origins of the Indians, two standard works are Don C. Allen, *The Legend of Noah: Renaissance Rationalism in Art, Science and Letters* (Urbana, Illinois, 1949), and Lee E. Huddleston, *Origins of the American Indians: European Concepts, 1492–1729* (Austin, Tex., 1967). A definitive biography of the leading exponent of the Noble Savage, now being prepared, is George D. Painter, *Chateaubriand: A Biography*, vol. 1: *The Longed-for Tempests* (New York, 1979).

Two important works on the emergence of the Noble Savage in European mythology are Benjamin Bissell, *The American Indian in English Literature of the Eighteenth Century* (New Haven, 1925), which is more notable for its generous quotations from authors than for its interpretations, and Hoxie N. Fairchild, *The Noble Savage: A Study in Romantic Naturalism* (New York, 1928). The "Captivity Narratives" that helped erode the Noble Savage tradition are collected in Wilcomb E. Washburn, ed., *North American Indian Captivities* (111 vols., New York, 1977), which contains facsimile reproductions of 311 titles. The introductory volume by Dr. Washburn is the best discussion of the subject. A factual account of Indian visits to Europe from the seventeenth century through the nineteenth is Carolyn T. Foreman, *Indians Abroad, 1493–1938* (Norman, Okla., 1943).

NOVELISTS AS IMAGE-MAKERS

THE AMERICAN BACKGROUND. American books about the West were frequently reprinted abroad and greatly influenced the writing of European Westerns. No systematic study of their impact has been made, but the subject is touched upon in such articles as Carl Wittke, "The American Theme in Continental European Literature," *Mississippi Valley Historical Review* 28 (June 1941): 3–26; and Clarence L. F. Gohdes, "The Reception of Some Nineteenth Century American Authors in Europe," in Margaret Denny and W. H. Gilman, eds., *The American Writer and the European Tradition* (Minneapolis, 1950), pp. 106–20. Jules Zanger, "The Frontiersman in Popular Fiction, 1820–1860," in John McDermott, ed., *The Frontier Re-examined* (Urbana, Ill., 1967), pp. 141–53, traces the evolution of the hero in western American literature as he influenced writing in Europe. Also useful in this context is Alexander Cowie, *The Rise of the American Novel* (New York, 1948), which describes American novels that were popular in Europe. The influence of American writing in specific European countries is the theme of Clarence Gohdes, *American Literature in Nineteenth Century England* (New York, 1944); Robert Magidoff, "American Literature in Russia," *Saturday Review of Literature* 29 (2 November

1946): 9–11; and John D. L. Ferguson, *American Literature in Spain* (New York, 1917).

The literature on the relationship between American and German writing is extensive. It includes such works as Clement Vollmer, *The American Novel in Germany, 1871–1913* (Philadelphia, 1918); Eugene F. Timpe, "The Reception of American Literature in Germany, 1862–1872," *University of North Carolina Studies in Comparative Literature* 25 (1964): 1–95; and Lawrence M. Price, *The Reception of United States Literature in Germany* (Chapel Hill, N.C., 1966), which contains extensive bibliographies. Morton Nirenberg, *The Reception of American Literature in German Periodicals, 1820–1850* (Heidelberg, 1970), summarizes reviews of American books in 150 magazines. Particularly useful are Paul C. Weber, *America in Imaginative German Literature in the First Half of the Nineteenth Century* (New York, 1926), which deals with minor as well as major writers, and Harvey W. Hewett-Thayer, *American Literature As Viewed in Germany, 1818–1861* (Chapel Hill, N.C., 1958), which reprints German reviews of American books. One chapter on "The American Frontier Novel" in Lawrence M. Price, "English Literature in Germany," *University of California Publications in Modern Philology* 37 (1953): 1–548, also contains essential material.

The definitive work on the dime novels, many of which were reprinted abroad, is Albert Johannsen, *The House of Beadle and Adams and Its Dime and Nickel Novels* (3 vols., Norman, Okla., 1950).

The impact of individual American writers has been extensively studied. Most attention has properly been paid to James Fenimore Cooper whose *Leatherstocking Tales* had so much to do with launching the vogue of European Westerns. Willard Thorp, "Cooper beyond America," *New York History* 35 (October 1954), pp. 522–39, expertly summarized the subject, while Marcel Clavel, *Fenimore Cooper and His Critics: American, British, and French Criticism of the Novelist's Early Work* (Aix-en-Provence, 1938), reprints many reviews. Specific studies of Cooper's impact on individual countries include: Paul Haertl, "Cooper in Germany," *American-German Review* 3 (June 1937): 18–20; Preston A. Barba, "Cooper in Germany," *Indiana University Studies* 21 (1914): 52–104; Karlheinz Rossbacher, *Lederstrumpf in Deutschland* (Munich, 1972); Regis Messac, "Fenimore Cooper et son influence en France," *Publications of the Modern Language Association* 43 (December 1928): 1191–201; Eric Partridge, "Fenimore Cooper's Influence on the French Romantics," *Modern Language Review* 20 (April 1925): 174–78; and Emilio Goggio, "Cooper's 'Bravo' in Italy," *Romantic Review* 20 (July–September 1929); 220–30.

The impact of other American writers who exploited western themes has also been touched upon. Robert Montgomery Bird whose *Nick of the Woods; or, The Jibbenainosay: A Tale of Kentucky* (2 vols., Philadelphia, 1837) greatly influenced European writing, has been the subject of a biography by his wife, Mayer M. Bird, *Life of Robert Montgomery Bird* (Philadelphia, 1945), while his works have been appraised in Clement E. Faust, *The Life and Dramatic Works of Robert Montgomery Bird* (New York, 1919); and Curtis Dahl, *Robert Montgomery Bird* (New York, 1963). The impact of other American authors who used western themes is surveyed in such works as: Walter A. Reichart, "The Early Reception of Washington Irving's Works in Germany," *Anglos* 74 (1956): 345–63; Walter A. Reichart, *Washington Irving and Germany* (Ann Arbor, 1957); Eugene F. Timpe, "Bret Harte's German Public," *Jahrbuch für Amerikastudien* 10 (1965): 215–20; and Edgar H. Hemminghaus, "Mark Twain in Germany," *Columbia University Germanic Studies*, n.s., 9 (1939): 1–170.

THE WESTERN NOVEL IN GERMANY. By far the most important work on German Westerns is D. L. Ashliman, "The American West in Nineteenth Century German Literature" (Ph.D. diss., Rutgers University, 1969). He has summarized his findings in "The Novel of Western Adventure in Nineteenth Century Germany," *Western American Literature* 3 (Summer 1968): 133–45. Useful also are such briefer works as George R. Brooks, "The American Frontier in German Fiction," in John F. McDermott, ed., *The Frontier Re-examined* (Urbana, Illinois, 1967), pp. 155–67; and H. J. Stammel and Friedrich Gassman, "The Literary Evolution of the 'Wild West' in Germany," *Los Angeles Westerners Brand Book No. 12* (Los Angeles, 1966), pp. 166–75. An older article, Lida von Krockow, "American Characters in German Literature," *Atlantic Monthly* 68 (December 1891): 824–38, shows how authors of German Westerns converted their heroes into Germans. Two works by Preston A. Barba deal with aspects of the subject: "The American Indian in German Fiction," *German American Annals* 15 (May–August 1913): 143–74; and "Emigration to America Reflected in German Fiction," *German American Annals* 16 (November–December 1914): 193–227. Ronald A. Fullerton, "Creating a Mass Market in Germany: The Story of the 'Colporteur Novel,' 1870–1890," *Journal of Social History* 10 (March 1977): 265–83, explains the revolution in reading tastes that helped popularize western stories.

Individual German authors of books about the West have also been extensively studied. A bibliography of Charles Sealsfield's many publications is Otto Heller and Theodore H. Leon, *Charles Sealsfield: Bibliography of His Writings* (St. Louis, 1939). The most useful study of Sealsfield's writings is Bernard A. Uhlendorf, *Charles Sealsfield: Ethnic Elements and National Problems in His Works* (Chicago, 1922), which reprints passages from his books dealing with Indians and the frontier. William P. Dallman, *The Spirit of America As Interpreted in the Works of Charles Sealsfield* (St. Louis, 1935), analyzes his works to appraise his views on liberty, equality, materialism, and other topics. Extracts from his novels and stories, printed in translation, are in E. L. Jordan, *America Glorious and Chaotic Land* (Englewood Cliffs, N.J., 1969), and Ulrich S. Carrington, *The Making of An American: An Adaptation of Memorable Tales by Charles Sealsfield* (Dallas, 1974). The latter especially catches the spirit of Sealsfield's writings. A complete edition of his works, edited by Karl J. R. Arndt, *Charles Sealsfield, Sämtliche Schriften* (New York), is currently being published.

Friedrich Gerstäcker has also been extensively studied. Most useful of the works about him are two doctoral dissertations: Bjorne Landa, "The American Scene in Gerstäcker's Fiction" (University of Minnesota, 1952), which summarizes scenes from many of his novels; and Alfred Kolb, "Friedrich Gerstäcker and the American Frontier" (Syracuse University, 1966), a study of the mythical element in his writings. Also essential is Augustus J. Prahl, "America in the Works of Gerstäcker," *Modern Language Quarterly* 4 (June 1943): 213–24, which stresses his views on backwoodsmen. Of use also is Nelson Van de Luyster, "Gerstäcker's Novels about Emigrants to America," *American-German Review* 20 (June–July 1954): 22–23, 36. His American experiences are the theme of George H. R. O'Donnell, "Gerstäcker in America, 1837–1843," *Publications of the Modern Language Association of America* 42 (December 1927): 1036–43; Clarence Evans, "Friedrich Gerstäcker, Social Chronicler of the Arkansas Frontier," *Arkansas Historical Quarterly* 6 (Winter 1947): 440–49; and Harrison R. Steeves, "The First of the Westerns," *Southwest Review* 52 (Winter 1968): 74–84. The latter argues that he once joined a group of vigilantes and based his stories on his adventures with them. A number of extracts from his writings are in Clarence Evans and Liselotte Albrecht, "Friedrich Gerstaecker in Arkansas: Selections from His *Streif-und Jagdzeuge durch die Vereinigten Staaten Nordamerikas*," *Arkansas Historical Quarterly* 5 (Spring 1946): 39–57.

A helpful biography of Balduin Möllhausen, laudatory in tone, is Preston A. Barba, "Balduin Möllhausen, the German Cooper," *Americana-Germanica Monograph Series* 17 (1914): 1–144. David H. Miller, "A Prussian on the Plains: Balduin Möllhausen's Impressions," *Great Plains Journal* 12 (Spring 1973): 175–93, deals with his American experiences. Another writer is expertly studied in Theodor Graewert, *Otto Ruppius und der Amerikaroman im 19. Jahrhundert* (Jena, 1935); a briefer survey of Ruppius's writings is Frederick F. Schrader, "Otto Ruppius, a Career in America," *American-German Review* 9 (February 1943): 28–33. Preston A. Barba, "Friedrich Armand Strubberg," *German American Annals* 14 (September–December 1912): 175–225, and 15 (May–August 1913): 115–42, is a detailed study with many summaries of Strubberg's books.

The importance of Karl May as a social commentator, if not as a literary stylist, has inspired a respectable body of writing. By far the most useful work in English is an unpublished master's thesis by Richard H. Cracroft, "The American West of Karl May" (University of Utah, 1963). The author has summarized his findings in "The American West of Karl May," *American Quarterly* 19 (Summer 1967): 249–58. A number of works in German on May include: Karl H. Dworczak, *Karl May, Das Leben Old Shatterhand* (Salzburg, 1950); Viktor Bohm, *Karl May und das Geheimnis seines Erfolgs* (Vienna, 1962); and Hans Wollschlager, "Karl May," in *Selbstzeugnisse und Bilddokumenten* (Reinbeck, West Germany, 1965). May's autobiography has been published as Roland Schmid, ed., *Ich. Karl May's Leben und Werk* (Bamberg, 1959), while a laudatory account of his one visit to the United States by his widow is Klara May, *Mit Karl May durch Amerika* (Radebeul bie Dresden, 1931). "Karl der Deutsche," *Der Spiegel* 16 (12 September 1962): 54–74, is a brief but well-researched study.

May's works have also been appraised in several articles in English. A pioneer survey, too brief to be of value, is Helen A. Read, "Karl May, Germany's Fenimore Cooper," *American-German Review* 2 (June 1936): 4–7. Klaus Mann, "Karl May, Hitler's Literary Mentor," *Kenyon Review* 2 (Autumn 1940): 391–400, reprinted as "Cowboy Mentor of the Führer," *Living Age* 352 (November 1940), attempts to show that May's views on race and authority helped pave the way for Nazism. Lighter in tone is Joseph Wechsberg, "Winnetou of der Wild West," *Saturday Review* 45 (20 October 1962): 52–53, 60–61, reprinted with useful notes by Richard H. Cracroft as "Winnetou of der Wild West," *American West* 1 (Summer 1964): 32–39. An excellent article that reproduces many extracts from May's works is Ernst A. Stadler, "Karl May: The Wild West under the German Umlaut," *Missouri Historical Society Bulletin* 21 (July 1965): 295–307; less useful is a popular account of his life, Ralph S. Walker, "The Wonderful West of Karl May," *American West* 10 (November 1973): 28–33.

May's works have been translated into twenty languages, but until recently, not into English. Two publishers, one in England and the other in the United States, are attempting to remedy this defect. Two volumes of May's short stories have appeared in England, both translated by Fred Gardner, *Captain Bill: Including the Talking Leather and 'One-Eyed' Joe Burkers* (London, 1971), and *Captain Cayman* (London, 1971). In the United States the Seabury Press has announced a series, "The Collected Works of Karl May," edited by Erwin J. Hawberle and translated by Michael Shaw. To date this includes two of May's books on the Middle East and the first two volumes of his Winnetou series compressed into one: *Winnetou* (New York, 1977). A simplified version of this book, in German and intended as reading in German courses, is Stanley L. Sharp and Alfred P. Donhauser, eds., *Winnetou* (Englewood Cliffs, N.J., 1969).

THE WESTERN NOVEL IN ENGLAND, FRANCE, AND SCANDINAVIA. An excellent survey of the frontier theme in better British novels is in the doctoral dissertation of Larry McDonald, "Reflections of the American West in Victorian Fiction" (Arizona State University, in progress); Mr. McDonald has allowed me free use of his materials to my great benefit. Useful also is Robert B. Heilman, "The New World in Dicken's Writings," *Trollopian* 1 (September 1946): 25–43, (March 1947): 11–26; The author has combed Dickens's works to identify all passages dealing with the United States, many of them with the West. Of the several works on British authors, the most useful has been Joan D. Steele, "The Image of America in the Novels of Mayne Reid: A Study of a Romantic Expatriate" (Ph.D. diss., University of California at Los Angeles, 1970), subsequently published as *Captain Mayne Reid* (New York, 1978). Reid is also the subject of Dudley Gordon, "The First 'Western' Author," *New Mexico Magazine* 25 (July 1957): 25–28, 66, a sketchy portrait; and Roy W. Mayer, "The Western American Fiction of Mayne Reid," *Western American Literature* 3 (Summer 1968): 115–32. Another important British author has been studied by Eric Quayle, *Ballantyne the Brave: A Victorian Writer and His Family* (London, 1967), a biography, and *R. M. Ballantyne: A Bibliography of First Editions* (London, 1968).

Works dealing with French authors include George D. Painter, *Chateaubriand: A Biography*, vol. 1: *The Longed-for Tempests* (New York, 1979), and an older work, Emma K. Armstrong, "Chateaubriand's America: Arrival and First Impressions," *Modern Language Association of America Publications* 22 (June 1907): 345–70. A more sensational author's works are explored in Virgil L. Jones, "Gustave Aimard," *Southwest Review* 15 (Summer 1930): 452–68.

Norwegian, Swedish and Danish fiction reflecting the immigrant experience is admirably described in Dorothy B. Skårdal, *The Divided Heart: Scandinavian Immigrant Experience through Literary Sources* (Bloomington, Ind., 1974). Ray A. Billington, ed., "The Wild West in Norway, 1877," *Western Historical Quarterly* 7 (July 1976): 271–78, reproduces portions of a Norwegian drama, "The Frontiersman's Daughter."

TRAVELERS AS IMAGE-MAKERS

Two older books, Henry Tuckerman, *America and Her Commentators* (New York, 1864), reprinted in 1961, and John G. Brooks, *As Others See Us: A Study of Progress in the United States* (New York, 1908), explore the attitude of visitors to the United States. Useful also is Dorothy A. Dondore, *The Prairie and the Making of Middle America* (Cedar Rapids, Iowa, 1926), which summarizes the findings of hundreds of travelers. Marc Pachter and

Frances Wein, eds., *Abroad in America: Visitors to the New Nation,*
1776–1914 (Reading, Mass., 1976), contains twenty-nine essays by
various authors on European travelers in America. The many distortions
and inaccuracies in works of eighteenth-century travelers are examined in
Percy G. Adams, *Travelers and Travel Liars, 1660–1800* (Berkeley, 1962).
Robert Lemelin, *Pathway to the National Character: 1830–1861* (Port Washington, N.Y., 1974), seeks clues to the national character in the works of
travelers, while Oscar Handlin, ed., *This Was America* (Cambridge, 1949),
reproduces extracts from books by visitors from Europe. European views
of the western army are summarized in Francis P. Prucha, "The United
States Army As Viewed by British Travelers, 1825–1860," *Military Affairs* 17 (Fall 1953): 113–24.

Specific western regions have often been described by Europeans.
Byron Y. Fleck, "The West As Viewed by Foreign Travelers, 1783–1840"
(Ph.D. diss., University of Iowa, 1950), is useful for the region between
the Appalachians and the Mississippi River during its frontier stage. The
impressions of three Germans who visited Missouri are recorded in: William G. Bek, ed., "Nicholas Hesse, German Visitor to Missouri,
1835–1837," *Missouri Historical Review* 41 (October 1946): 19–44, and 42
(April 1947): 241–48; Alice H. Finckh, "Gottfried Duden Views Missouri, 1824–1827," *Missouri Historical Review* 43 (July 1949): 334–42, and
44 (October 1950): 21–30; and Ralph Gregory, "Count Baudissin on Missouri Towns," *Missouri Historical Society Bulletin* 27 (January 1971):
111–24. Eugene L. Schwaab, ed., *Travels in the Old South: Selected from Periodicals of the Times* (2 vols., Lexington, Ky., 1973), deals largely with
American rather than European travelers; brief but helpful is Lawrence S.
Thompson, "German Travelers in the South from the Colonial Period
through 1865," *South Atlantic Bulletin* 37 (May 1972). Two articles on travelers in Texas are valuable: Mary Lee Spence, "British Impressions of
Texas and the Texans," *Southwestern Historical Quarterly* 70 (October
1966): 163–83, dealing largely with the 1840s; and Marilyn M. Sibley,
Travelers in Texas, 1761–1860 (Austin, 1967), which distills information
from hundreds of sources.

A number of monographic studies and collected series appraise visitors
in terms of the country of their origin. The brilliant introduction to Allan
Nevins, ed., *American Social History As Recorded by British Travellers* (New
York, 1923) relates the impressions of visitors from England to their politi-
cal prejudices. Three other books provide useful information on British
travelers: Jane L. Mesick, *The English Traveller in America, 1785–1835*
(New York, 1922); Max Berger, *The British Traveller in America, 1836–1860*
(New York, 1943); and Richard L. Rapson, *Britons View America: Travel
Commentary, 1860–1935* (Seattle, 1971). Particularly important is the

thoughtful book by Robert G. Athearn, *Westward the Briton* (New York, 1953), which reports the views of British travelers in the Far West between 1865 and the end of the century.

A remarkably complete listing of French travelers in the United States is Frank Moneghan, *French Travellers in the United States, 1765–1932* (New York, 1961). The contributions of visitors from other nations are surveyed in such works as: Andrew J. Torrielli, *Italian Opinion on America, As Revealed by Italian Travelers, 1850–1900* (Cambridge, 1941); Andrew F. Rolle, *The Immigrant Upraised* (Norman, Okla. 1968); Giuseppe Massara, *Viaggiatori Italiani in America, 1860–1970* (Rome, 1976); J. W. Schulte-Nordholt, "This Is the Place: Dutchmen Look at America," *Delta: A Review of Arts, Life and Thought in the Netherlands* 16 (Winter 1973–74): 32–52; and Anna Katona, "Hungarian Travelogues on the Pre–Civil War U.S.," *Hungarian Studies in English* 5 (1971): 51–94. Elizabeth Mészáros of Budapest was kind enough to allow me to use her manuscript on "America's Image in Hungary, 1776–1840," which promises to be an important contribution. The reaction of a Scandinavian commentator to her American experience is described in Signe A. Rooth, *Seeress of the Northland: Fredrika Bremer's American Journey, 1849–1851* (Philadelphia, 1955).

Travelers' views on various aspects of frontier life have been summarized by several scholars. Particularly useful is Gary C. Stein, "Federal Indian Policy As Seen by British Travelers in America, 1783–1860" (Ph.D. diss., University of New Mexico, 1975), a thorough analysis by a competent scholar. The author has compressed some of his findings in two articles: "Indian Removal As Seen by European Travelers in America," *Chronicles of Oklahoma* 51 (Winter 1973–74): 399–410, and "A Fearful Drunkenness: The Liquor Trade to the Western Indians as Seen by European Travelers in America, 1800–1860," *Red River Valley Historical Review* 1 (Summer 1974) 109–21. J. Ralph Randolph, *British Travelers among the Southern Indians, 1660–1763* (Norman, Okla., 1973), summarizes the views of early visitors; more limited in scope and too brief to be of value is A. E. Sheldon, "Accounts of the Pawnees by Early French Travelers," *Nebraska History* 10 (July–September 1927): 193–94. The opposite can be said of D. L. Ashliman, "The American Indian in German Travel Narratives and Literature," *Journal of Popular Culture* 10 (Spring 1977): 833–39, an excellent article. Professor Ashliman has also produced two valuable works on the Mormon frontiering experience: "Mormonism and the Germans: An Annotated Bibliography, 1848–1966," *Brigham Young University Studies* 8 (Autumn 1967), and "The Image of Utah and the Mormons in Nineteenth Century Germany," *Utah Historical Quarterly* 35 (Summer 1967): 209–27.

Bibliographical Notes

THE FRONTIER IMAGE AND IMMIGRATION

Many of the histories of immigration contains information on both the expelling and attracting forces underlying the great migration of the nineteenth century, including reference to the frontier and its image. Among those most helpful are two pioneering books by Marcus L. Hansen, *The Atlantic Migration, 1607–1860* (Cambridge, 1940), and *The Immigrant in American History* (Cambridge, 1940). Philip A. M. Taylor, *The Distant Magnet: European Emigration to the U.S.A.* (New York, 1971), is an excellent modern treatment. A searching investigation into emigrants' letters to determine why they left their homelands is in Charlotte Erickson, "Agrarian Myths of English Immigrants," in Oscar F. Ander, ed., *In the Trek of the Immigrants* (Rock Island, Ill., 1964), pp. 59–80.

Much information on the appeal of the West to emigrants is in studies of specific nationalities. Dutch immigration is studied in Bertus Wabeke, *Dutch Emigration to North America, 1624–1860* (New York, 1944), and Henry S. Lucas, *Netherlanders in America: Dutch Immigration to the United States and Canada, 1789–1950* (Ann Arbor, Mich., 1955). Particularly useful among the several books on Irish immigration and its causes is Arnold Schrier, *Ireland and the American Emigration, 1850–1900* (Minneapolis, 1958). Carl Wittke, *The Irish in America* (Baton Rouge, La., 1956), is concerned with the Irish experience in the United States, while William F. Adams, *Ireland and Irish Emigration to the New World from 1815 to the Famine* (New Haven, 1932), deals with conditions within Ireland.

The standard work on Norwegian immigration is Theodore C. Blegen, *Norwegian Migration to the United States* (2 vols., Northfield, Minn., 1931–40). Kenneth Bjork, *West of the Great Divide: Norwegian Migration to the Pacific Coast, 1847–1893* (Northfield, Minn., 1958), is concerned largely with the immigrants after they reached the West. Two studies of the conditions in Sweden that sparked emigration are George M. Stephenson, "The Background of the Beginnings of Swedish Immigration, 1850–1875," *American Historical Review* 31 (July 1926): 708–23, and Florence E. Janson, *The Background of Swedish Immigration, 1840–1930* (Chicago, 1931). Theodore C. Blegen, "Cleng Peerson and Norwegian Immigration," *Mississippi Valley Historical Review* 7 (March 1921): 303–21, tells the story of a leading promoter and his American career. An analysis of the social conditions that encouraged 300,000 Danes to migrate is in Kristian Hvidt, *Flight to America* (New York, 1974). Particularly important in understanding the West as a land of promise are Theodore C. Blegen, ed., *Norwegian Emigrant Songs and Ballads* (Minneapolis, 1936), and Robert L. Wright, ed., *Swedish Emigrant Ballads* (Lincoln, Nebr., 1965). Professor Wright has edited another essential book: *Irish Emigrant Ballads and Songs* (Bowling Green, Ohio, 1975).

The forces that led to the migration of one religious sect are examined in Philip A. M. Taylor, "Why Did British Mormons Emigrate?" *Utah Historical Quarterly* 22 (July 1954): 249–70; William Mulder, "Image of Zion: Mormonism As an American Influence in Scandinavia," *Mississippi Valley Historical Review* 43 (June 1956): 18–38; and William Mulder, *Homeward to Zion: The Mormon Migration from Scandinavia* (Minneapolis, 1957).

The importance of "America Letters" in stimulating and directing the migratory stream has been recognized by numerous students of immigration. A number have been collected: Theodore C. Blegen, ed., *The Land of Their Choice: The Immigrants Write Home* (Minneapolis, 1955); Alan Conway, ed., *The Welsh in America: Letters from the Immigrants* (Minneapolis, 1961); and H. Arnold Barton, ed., *Letters from the Promised Land: Swedes in America, 1840–1914* (Minneapolis, 1975). Charlotte Erickson, *Invisible Immigrants: The Adaptation of English and Scottish Immigrants in Nineteenth Century America* (London, 1972), is based largely on "America Letters," and reproduces many of them. Two earlier volumes also collected letters of their period: Nikolaj Slavinskij, *Letters on America and Russian Immigrants* (St. Petersburg, 1873), and Anthony Brummelkamp, *Stemmer uit Noord-Amerika, met begeleidend woord* (Amsterdam, 1847).

Briefer collections of "America Letters" published largely in journals also shed light on the image of the West as a land of promise. Two articles emphasize their importance: George M. Stephenson, "When America Was the Land of Canaan," *Minnesota History* 10 (September 1929): 237–60, and Frank C. Nelson, "The Norwegian-American Image of America," *Illinois Quarterly* 36 (April 1974): 5–27. Short collections are printed in George M. Stephenson, ed., "Typical America Letters," *Yearbook of the Swedish Historical Society of America* 7 (1921–22): 52–98; Lyder L. Unstad, "Norwegian Migration to Texas: An Historical Resume with Four 'America Letters,' " *Southwestern Historical Quarterly* 43 (October 1939): 176–95; and C. Terence Pihlblad, "Swedish Immigrant Letters in Dallas County, 1873–1908," *Missouri Historical Review* 48 (July 1954): 352–64. Letters from the California gold fields are in Richard A. Preston, ed., *For Friends at Home: A Scottish Emigrant's Letters from Canada, California and the Cariboo, 1844–1864* (Montreal, 1974).

THE IMAGE IN PROMOTIONAL WRITING

Guidebooks played a prominent role in picturing the American West as a land of opportunity. A number of the best guides published in England have been made available on two microfilm rolls as Charlotte Erickson, ed., *Emigrant Guides and Pamphlets*. An excellent bibliography of Swedish guidebooks is Oscar F. Ander, *The Cultural Heritage of the Swedish Immigrant: Selected References* (Rock Island, Ill., 1956). Their contents are analyzed in two useful articles: Roy W. Swanson, "Some Swedish Emigrant Guide Books of the Second Half of the Nineteenth Century," *Swedish Historical Society of America Yearbook* 11 (1926): 105–15, and Martha Ångström, "Swedish Emigrant Guidebooks of the Early 1850s," *American Swedish Historical Foundation Year-Book* (Philadelphia, 1947), pp. 22–48. Extracts from guidebooks popular in Norway are reprinted in Theodore C. Blegen, ed., *Peter Testman's Account of His Experiences in North America* (Northfield, Minn., 1927), Theodore C. Blegen, ed., *Ole Rynning's True Account of America* (Minneapolis, 1926), and Theodore C. Blegen, "Norwegians in the West in 1844: A Contemporary Account," *Norwegian-American Historical Association Studies and Records* 1 (1926): 110–25. The last is a chapter in translation from John R. Reiersen, *Pathfinder for Norwegian Emigrants to the United North American States and Texas* (1844). A German book that helped lure hundreds of peasants to Missouri is described in two articles by William G. Bek: "Gottfried Duden's 'Report,'" *Missouri Historical Review* 12 (October 1917) and 13 (April 1919): 251–58, and "The Followers of Duden," *Missouri Historical Review* 14 (October 1919): 29–73, and 19 (January 1925): 338–52. Particularly useful is Louis E. Brister, "The Image of Arkansas in the Early German Emigrant Guidebooks: Notes on Immigration," *Arkansas Historical Quarterly* 36 (Winter 1977): 338–45.

States and territories in the West established agencies to lure immigrants by propagandizing in Europe. A pioneer study of their efforts is Theodore C. Blegen, "The Competition of the Northwestern States for Immigrants," *Wisconsin Magazine of History* 3 (September 1919): 3–39, dealing largely with Wisconsin's activities. Maurice G. Baxter, "Encouragement of Immigration to the Middle West during the Era of the Civil War," *Indiana Magazine of History* 46 (March 1950): 25–38, stresses the efforts of Indiana, while David M. Emmons, *Garden in the Grassland: Boomer Literature of the Central Great Plains* (Lincoln, Nebr., 1971), centers on Nebraska and its neighboring areas. Halvdan Koht, "When America Called for Immigrants," *Norwegian-American Studies and Records* 14 (1944): 159–83, describes the efforts of the United States to convert its consuls into immigration agents.

The organizations established in western states to encourage immigration are the subject of numerous studies: Marcus L. Hansen, "Official Encouragement of Immigration to Iowa," *Iowa Journal of History and Politics* 19 (April 1921): 159–95; A. R. Fulton, "An Invitation to Immigrants," *The Palimpsest* 18 (July 1937): 226–42, which reproduces an Iowa promotional pamphlet; Livia Appel and Theodore C. Blegen, "Official Encouragement of Immigration to Minnesota during the Territorial Period," *Minnesota History* 5 (August 1923): 167–203; Theodore C. Blegen, "Minnesota's Campaign for Immigrants," *Swedish Historical Society of America Yearbook* 11 (1926): 3–83; Lars Ljungmark, *For Sale—Minnesota: Organized Promotion of Scandinavian Immigration, 1866–1873* (Chicago, 1971); Herbert S. Schell, "Official Immigration Activities of Dakota Territory," *North Dakota Historical Quarterly* 7 (October 1932): 5–24; Warren A. Henke, "Imagery, Immigration, and the Myth of North Dakota 1890–1933," *North Dakota History* 38 (Fall 1971): 413–19; J. A. Russell, *The Germanic Influence in the Making of Michigan* (Detroit, 1927), which, despite its title is concerned with promotional activities; Arthur J. Brown, "The Promotion of Emigration to Washington, 1854–1909," *Pacific Northwest Quarterly* 36 (January 1945): 3–17; and Herbert H. Lang, "The New Mexico Bureau of Immigration, 1880–1912," *New Mexico Historical Review* 51 (July 1976): 193–214.

The efforts of individuals and land companies to lure new settlers from abroad, and the propaganda they employed, is described in such works as: Wilbur S. Shepperson, *The Promotion of British Emigration by Agents for American Lands* (Reno, Nev., 1954), a sketchy book; Oscar O. Winther, "Promotion of the American West in England, 1865–1900," *Journal of Economic History* 16 (December 1956): 506–13; Oscar O. Winther, "English Migration to the American West, 1865–1900," *Huntington Library Quarterly* 27 (February 1964): 159–73; and Ronald A. Wells, "Migration and the Image of Nebraska in England," *Nebraska History* 54 (Fall 1973): 475–87.

Two pioneering articles on the methods used by railroads to attract settlers to their land grants are James B. Hedges, "The Colonization Work of the Northern Pacific Railroad," *Mississippi Valley Historical Review* 13 (December 1926): 311–42, and "Promotion of Immigration to the Pacific Northwest by the Railroads," *Mississippi Valley Historical Review* 15 (September 1928): 183–203. Harold F. Peterson, "Early Minnesota Railroads and the Quest for Settlers," *Minnesota History* 13 (March 1932): 26–44, adds little to Hedges's findings. The European efforts of the first land-grant railroad are admirably described in Paul W. Gates, *The Illinois Central Railroad and Its Colonization Work* (Cambridge, 1934), and "The Campaign of the Illinois Central Railroad for Norwegian and Swedish Immigrants," *Norwegian-American Historical Association Studies and Records* 6 (1936): 66–88.

The pioneering work of Hedges and Gates has led numerous historians to investigate the colonizing activities of other western railroads. One of the most important results is Richard Overton, *Burlington West: A Colonization History of the Burlington Railroad* (Cambridge, 1941), an excellent book. This may be supplemented by Ian MacPherson, "Better Britons for Burlington: A Study of the Selective Approach of the Chicago, Burlington and Quincy in Great Britain 1871–1875," *Nebraska History* 50 (Winter 1969): 373–407, a detailed study of the operation of the Burlington's British agency. Less authoritative are Barry B. Combs, "The Union

Pacific Railroad and the Early Settlement of Nebraska, 1868–1880," *Nebraska History* 50 (Spring 1969): 1–26, and Edna M. Parker, "The Southern Pacific Railroad and the Settlement of Southern California," *Pacific Historical Review* 6 (June 1937), 103–19. One chapter in Glenn D. Bradley, *The Story of the Santa Fe* (Boston, 1920), touches on the road's colonizing activities, while the reminiscences of one of its overseas agents are in C. B. Schmidt, "Reminiscences of Foreign Immigration Work for Kansas," *Kansas State Historical Society Transactions* 9 (1905–6). James P. Shannon, *Catholic Colonization of the Western Frontier* (New Haven, 1957), shows how church and railroad agents worked together to stimulate immigration.

Among the most important promotional publications were the "colonization newspapers" and magazines that appeared in many European countries. Among the most important of those appearing in Great Britain were: *The American Press* (London, May–June, 1875); *The American Settler* (London, January 1872–November 1892); *America* (London, January–December 1883); and *Emigration: A Weekly Journal* (London, March 1891–June 1891). Microfilm copies of these journals have been presented to the Huntington Library by Mrs. Oscar O. Winther.

THE IMPACT OF THE IMAGE ON EUROPE

The reaction of the European governments and people to the image of the American West as a land of opportunity offers a fruitful field for study. A number of articles explore aspects of the impact, particularly on Scandinavian countries where immigration played a major role in social change. A useful early study is Brynjolf J. Hovde, "Notes on the Effects of Emigration upon Scandinavia," *Journal of Modern History* 6 (September 1934): 253–79, which investigates the economic reaction. Halvdan Koht, *The American Spirit in Europe: A Survey of Transatlantic Influences* (Philadelphia, 1949), pays little attention to the frontier but offers a stimulating survey of the effect of migration on thought and politics. Folke Dovring, "European Reactions to the Homestead Act," *Journal of Economic History* 22 (December 1962): 461–72, deals largely with the reaction in Scandinavia, which was less than might be expected. A successful attempt to examine the concepts of America held by commonplace folk is Ingrid Semmingsen, "Emigration and the Image of America in Europe," in Henry S. Commager, ed., *Immigration and American History: Essays in Honor of Theodore C. Blegen* (Minneapolis, 1961).

By far the best studies of the Scandinavian reaction to emigration on the political, social, and economic levels are the thoughtful articles by Franklin D. Scott: "American Influences in Norway and Sweden," *Journal of Modern History* 18 (March 1946): 37–44; "Søren Jaabaek, Americanizer in Norway," *Norwegian-American Studies and Records* 17 (1952): 84–107;

"The Causes and Consequences of Emigration in Sweden," *The Chronicle* 2 (Spring 1955): 2–11; "The Study of the Effects of Emigration," *Scandinavian Economic History Review* 8, no. 2: 161–74; and "Sweden's Constructive Opposition to Emigration," *Journal of Modern History* 37 (September 1965): 307–55. Professor Scott has summarized many of his findings in a pamphlet issued by the American Historical Association, *Emigration and Immigration* (2d ed., Washington, 1966). Another enlightening treatment of the subject is Daniel Levine, "Conservatism and Tradition in Danish Social Welfare Legislation, 1890–1933: A Comparative View," *Comparative Studies in Society and History* 20 (January 1978): 54–69, which examines the obstacles facing reformers who sought to follow the American example.

An excellent study of the frontier's impact on British politics is G. D. Lillibridge, *Beacon of Freedom: The Impact of American Democracy upon Great Britain, 1830–1870* (Philadelphia, 1955). William M. Tuttle, Jr., "Forerunners of Frederick Jackson Turner: Nineteenth-Century British Conservatives and the Frontier Thesis," *Agricultural History* 41 (July 1967): 219–227, examines the same subject less thoroughly. Richard H. Heindel, *The American Impact on Great Britain, 1898–1914* (Philadelphia, 1940), is useful but deals largely with the postfrontier period. The reluctance of Britons to adopt American agricultural techniques is examined in Andrew C. Jewell, "The Impact of America on English Agriculture," *Agricultural History* 50 (January 1976): 125–36. An overall appraisal of the impact of emigration on Germany is in Mack Walter, *Germany and the Emigration, 1816–1885* (Cambridge, 1964).

THE PERSISTING IMAGE

The emergence of the cowboy as a legendary figure altered the image of the West in both the United States and England. Europeans first became aware of his glamour when Buffalo Bill Cody's Wild West shows and their successors toured the Continent. The best account of their role is in Don Russell, *The Lives and Legends of Buffalo Bill* (Norman, Okla., 1960). The reaction of the British press to these performances is the theme of Clifford P. Westermeier, "Buffalo Bill's Cowboys Abroad," *Colorado Magazine* 52 (Fall 1975): 277–98, while episodes connected with the tour are described by the show's manager in Nate Salsbury, "The Origin of the Wild West Show; Wild West at Windsor; At the Vatican," *Colorado Magazine* 32 (July 1955): 204–14.

The Wild West craze in Europe that was touched off by Buffalo Bill Cody's tours was nurtured by the popularity of western fiction published in the United States but circulated abroad. An excellent bibliography of these works is Richard W. Etulain, ed., *Western American Literature: A Bib-*

liography of Interpretive Books and Articles (Vermillion, S.D., 1972). Professor Etulain studies the evolution of the western novel in two articles: "The Origin of the Western," *Journal of Popular Culture* 5 (Spring 1972): 799–805, and "The Historical Development of the Western," *Journal of Popular Culture* 7 (Winter 1973): 717–26. Westerns are viewed against their social background in Russell Nye, *The Embarrassed Muse: The Popular Arts in America* (New York, 1970).

The cultural contributions of western novels are examined in such stimulating books as James K. Folsom, *The American Western Novel* (New Haven, 1966), and John G. Cawelti, *The Six-Gun Mystique* (Bowling Green, Ohio, 1971). Cawelti delves into aspects of the subject in his "Prolegomena to the Western," *Western American Literature* 4 (Winter 1970): 259–71, and "God's Country, Las Vegas, and the Gunfighter: Differing Visions of the West," *Western American Literature* 9 (Winter 1975): 273–83. The changing nature of the Western is the theme of Paul A. Hutton, "From Little Big Horn to Little Big Man: The Changing Image of a Western Hero in Popular Culture," *Western Historical Quarterly* 7 (January 1976): 19–45. Merle Curti, "Dime Novels and the American Tradition," *Yale Review* 26 (Summer 1937): 761–78, expertly examines the social significance of this type of writing, while a useful study of the difference between American and English novels is James K. Folsom, "English Westerns," *Western American Literature* 2 (Spring 1967): 3–13.

The reasons for the cowboy's popularity as a folk hero are examined in such works as Marshall W. Fishwick, "The Cowboy: America's Contribution to the World's Mythology," *Western Folklore* 11 (April 1952): 77–92; and David B. Davis, "Ten Gallon Hero," *American Quarterly* 6 (Summer 1954): 111–25. Differences between the cowboy of fact and the cowboy of mythology are examined in Joe B. Frantz and Julian E. Choate, Jr., *The American Cowboy: The Myth and the Reality* (Norman, Okla., 1955), and Clifford P. Westermeier, *Trailing the Cowboy: His Life and Lore As Told by Frontier Journalists* (Caldwell, Idaho, 1955). Warren French, "The Cowboy in the Dime Novel," *Studies in English* 30 (1951): 219–34, traces the evolution of the type from outlaw to Galahad of the plains. The cowboy in European imagery is discussed in Clifford P. Westermeier, "Clio's Maverick—the Cowboy," *Denver Westerner's Monthly Roundup* 22 (October 1966): 3–16, while John B. Jackson, "Ich bin ein Cowboy aus Texas," *Southwest Review* 38 (Spring 1953): 158–63, is an amusing description of the difference between cowboys in European and American comic books. In Finn Arnesen, "Why Norwegians Love Westerns," *The Roundup* 24 (October 1976): 1–4, the editor of Norway's leading western magazine explains their popularity in his country.

The European Wild West craze has been magnified by western films. An excellent history with chapters on the European vogue is George N.

Fenin and William K. Everson, *The Western* (2d ed., New York, 1973). William K. Everson, *A Pictorial History of the Western Film* (New York, 1969), is also useful. A classic history of the western film in Europe is Jean-Louis Rieupeyrout, *La Grande Aventure du Western* (Paris, 1964). A leading Swedish film critic comments on the changing nature of Westerns in Harry Schein, "The Olympian Cowboy," *American Scholar* 24 (Summer 1955): 309–20, as does James K. Folsom, "Western Themes and Western Films," *Western American Literature* 2 (Fall 1967): 195–203.

The vogue of the Wild West in France is described in such popular journals as "The Cowboy Craze in France," *Newsweek* 52 (28 July 1958): 54; "Cowboys Abroad," *Time* 80 (3 August 1962): 51; and Charles J. Belden, "The Spirit of the Old West Lives On in Paris," *Horse Lover's Magazine* 27 (December 1961–January 1962): 30–31. A more searching appraisal is Kent L. Steckmesser, "Paris and the Wild West," *Southwest Review* 54 (Spring 1961): 178–84. The career of a leading French writer of Westerns is briefly explored in Jeffrey Robinson, "Le Cowboy," *Westways* 66 (April 1974): 40–41, 85, and Roberta Cheney, "He Brought France Thrills of the West," *The Roundup* 23 (April 1975): 12–13. The reaction of French intellectuals to the vogue of the West is examined in Philippe Soupault, *The American Influence in France* (Seattle, 1930).

The spread of the frontier cult in modern Germany is admirably explored in D. L. Ashliman, "The American West in Twentieth Century Germany," *Journal of Popular Culture* 2 (Summer 1968): 82–92. Thomas Freeman, "The Cowboy and the Astronaut—the American Image in German Periodical Advertisements," *Journal of Popular Culture* 6 (Summer 1972): 83–103, has much to say about the western theme in advertisements, while "Sie Ritten Da'lang, Podner," *Time* (18 June 1979), p. 51, describes the current western clubs there. Modern Spanish Westerns are vividly pictured in Charles F. Olstad, "The 'Wild West' in Spain," *Arizona and the West* 6 (Autumn 1964): 191–202.

A searching investigation of the concept of frontier vastness as it influenced European imperial ambitions in the late nineteenth century is in Raymond F. Betts, "Immense Dimensions: The Impact of the American West on Late Nineteenth Century European Thought about Expansion," *Western Historical Quarterly* 10 (April 1979): 149–66.

INDEX

Acosta, José de, on origins of American Indians, 9–10

Adair, James, on American Indians, 16

Adamites, as religious sect on frontier, 185

Addison, Joseph, views of on garden design, 15

Agriculture, *see* Farming

Ague, prevelance of on frontier, 89

Aimard, Gustave, as author of Westerns, 41–43; popularity of, 44; treatment of Indians by, 107; on treatment of women by Indians, 115; attitude of toward Indians, 133; on American Indian policy, 144; on western outlaws, 274

Albers, Hans, as hero in German Westerns, 321

Alexandre, Roman d', views of New World, 2

Alligators, on western deserts, 85, 103

America Letters, as image-makers, 69–72; attract immigrants, 219; success stories in, 228–29; testimony on effects of, 236–37; on social equality, 241; effect of on migration, 291–92, 300; effect of on democratic reform, 300–301; urge equality in Europe, 304

American character, comments on by Europeans, 195–196

"American Fever," spread of in Europe, 225; induces emigration, 295

"American Mirage," as threat to Europe, 300

"American Wake," as used in Ireland, 295

Anghiera, Pietro Martire d', comment of on Indians, 3

Animals, on forested frontier, 84; on Great Plains, 93–95; in western mountains, 96–97; on deserts, 102–3

"Apache Death," described, 123

Apache Indians, use of canoes by, 100; described, 110–12; origins of, 113; homes of, 113–14; religion of, 114; ceremonies of, 114–17; military tactics of, 115–17; treatment of prisoners by, 116; cruelty of, 118–23; wars of, 119–20; as cannibals, 124; scalping